Fifty Years of Bangladesh Parliament

Brill's Asian Law Series

VOLUME 14

The titles published in this series are listed at *brill.com/asla*

Fifty Years of Bangladesh Parliament

A Critical Evaluation

By

M. Jashim Ali Chowdhury

BRILL | NIJHOFF

LEIDEN | BOSTON

Library of Congress Cataloging-in-Publication Data

Names: Chowdhury, M. Jashim Ali, author.
Title: Fifty years of Bangladesh parliament : a critical evaluation / by M. Jashim Ali Chowdhury.
Description: Leiden ; Boston : Brill/Nijhoff, 2025. | Series: Brill's Asian law series ; volume 14 | Includes bibliographical references and index. | Summary: "The introductory chapter dealing with the Parliament's constitutional design, Chapter 1, is followed by an introduction to the organisation, powers, and processes of the Bangladesh Parliament, Chapter 2. The next three chapters examine the Parliament's horizontal relationship with the Executive, Chapter 3, and Judicial branches, Chapter 4, and its vertical relationship with its electorate, the People, Chapter 5.
Identifiers: LCCN 2024055881 | ISBN 9789004720824 (hardback) | ISBN 9789004720831 (ebook)
Subjects: LCSH: Bangladesh. Jātīẏa Saṃsada–History. | Bangladesh. Jātīẏa Saṃsada–Rules and practice. | Legislative bodies–Bangladesh. | Parliamentary practice–Bangladesh. | Legislation–Bangladesh. | Justice, Administration of–Bangladesh.
Classification: LCC KNG2183 .C46 2025 | DDC 342.5492–dc23/eng/20241121
LC record available at https://lccn.loc.gov/2024055881

Typeface for the Latin, Greek, and Cyrillic scripts: "Brill". See and download: brill.com/brill-typeface.

ISSN 2214-6547
ISBN 978-90-04-72082-4 (hardback)
ISBN 978-90-04-72083-1 (e-book)
DOI 10.1163/9789004720831

Contents

Foreword

A country's Parliament or national assembly is the cornerstone of its democracy. Its internal procedures and processes provide the guarantee of popular representation and executive accountability. Their range and level of complexity range from the rights of opposition parties to adequate parliamentary time for debate and scrutiny of ministers, to the interrelationship between legislative and judicial power, and the procedures for parliamentary committees to gain access to official information.

The essentials of successful representative government, as Harold Laski once wrote, are a body of citizens fundamentally at one on all the major objects of governmental activity, that no class or group of importance in the country is excluded from power, and widely diffused habits of toleration throughout the nation.

However today, the functioning of Parliaments in almost every democracy in the world is facing huge challenges to their authority. They are struggling under immense pressures amid widespread dissatisfaction of a social and economic nature, magnified by the revolutionary technologies in mass communication. Populist tendencies in government are threatening to undermine and by-pass Parliaments altogether. The Bangladesh Parliament is no exception.

In this new book Dr Chowdhury provides a brilliant analysis of how and why the practice and procedures of the Bangladeshi Parliament have evolved over the period since 1972. He characterises it as a Westminster model of parliamentary government, but one that has been strongly moulded by Bangladesh's indigenous political culture, problems, and pressures. He argues that the Bangladesh Parliament needs to address a "selective dictatorship" in terms of its domination by the executive, with undemocratic tendencies in the political parties and a culture of majoritarianism that on occasion has even threatened the parliamentary opposition's right to exist.

The book looks to the future, setting out a realistic programme of moderate and incremental reform designed to strengthen the Bangladesh Parliament and its central role in the political process of the country. He puts forward a programme of valuable procedural proposals for strengthening the role and independence of individual Members and rebuilding public trust in Parliament with new techniques for public participation.

I welcome this excellent publication as a valuable addition to the academic literature on the parliamentary and constitutional affairs of Bangladesh and the Asian sub-continent, as well as for the study of comparative government around the world.

Robert Blackburn, KC *(Hon)* LLD
Professor of Constitutional Law
King's College London
October 2024

Preface

This book is based on my Doctoral Thesis on the Parliament of Bangladesh (King's College London, 2022). It critically evaluates the constitutional position and contribution of the Bangladesh Parliament (*Jatiya Sangsad*) during the fifty-one years of its existence (1973–2024). The framers of Bangladesh's original Constitution (1972) purportedly adopted a Westminster parliamentary system. Later, the country underwent different types of constitutional experiments, such as a one-party presidential, several military-backed and several non-political caretaker governments; several phases of contentious bipartisanships, a sixteen-year-long one-party monopoly and lastly, another ongoing round of extra-constitutional government. Interestingly, the 1972 scheme of the parliamentary system has shown a remarkable level of perseverance throughout the vicious cycles of constitutional dismemberment and restoration. Bangladesh has elected twelve parliaments since 1973. While none of the first six parliaments could complete their full tenure, they started doing so since the seventh one (1996–2001). However, the twelfth parliament (January–August 2024) was again dissolved abruptly after violent student protests reignited the debate about its electoral legitimacy and institutional powers.

At the outset, the book questions the popular political claim that the Bangladesh Parliament is not by design a Westminster-type parliament. This book argues that while a "dilemma of design" was apparent in the Bangladeshi constitution framers' words and actions, the structural template they chose for the country's legislative and executive branch was abundantly "Westminster". So, it evaluates the parliament through a "Westminster" lens but points out how and why the institution behaves in (un)Westminster, rather say the "Eastminster", ways. This is done through a separation of powers and checks and balances inspired design analysis of the Parliament, bringing it face to face with the three other constitutional organs – the government, judiciary, and the people. Within that framework, the Bangladesh Parliament's position as both an accountability and accountable institution seems to be fragile. Its operational logic is determined by a "selective dictatorship" system in public powers, internally undemocratic political parties, and a crude version of majoritarian politics that refuses even to recognise the opposition's right to exist.

Bangladesh's competitively parochial political parties and their leaders have resisted, on successive occasions of revolutionary moments, a drastic realignment of the *existing political arrangements.* They will likely continue this in the future too. Therefore, the future of parliamentarism in Bangladesh seems to hinge on some moderate and incrementally bound reforms within the procedural realm of parliamentary activities that could enhance its voice and profile as an accountability institution. This book identifies three such potential areas of incremental reforms. First, the Parliament and its committees need to reinvigorate their public relations, participation, and trust-building activities. Continuous engagement with the citizens, civil society and other "fourth branch" organisations should build its independent public support base. Parliament's own public support base should gradually challenge the dynastic political parties' exclusive claim to democratic representation and pave the way for the Parliament's institutional assertiveness. Secondly, moderate procedural reforms such as renouncing by the Speakers of their party affiliations and the relaxation of the Constitution's anti-defection clause that chokes the backbench voices may increase the parliament's standing as an independent constitutional organ. Thirdly, the Supreme Court judges and the parliamentarians may engage in a strategic "democratic dialogue" and consolidate their respective positions as co-equal constitutional branches *vis-à-vis* the executive branch. Assuming that Bangladesh's political system survives the intermittent military or extra-constitutional interventions, such as the latest one on August 2024, these incremental steps should prepare grounds for more fundamental reforms once the current equilibrium of the political party system breaks apart and a realignment arrives.

I sincerely thank the two supervisors of my Ph.D. thesis, Professor Robert Blackburn KC (Kings' College London) and Andrew Kennon (former Clerk, the House of Commons, UK) for their unwavering support throughout. Professor Blackburn has honoured me by writing a generous foreword for this book. The two external examiners of my thesis, Professor Dr M Rafiqul Islam (Macquarie University, Australia) and Professor Dr Mohammad Shahabuddin (Birmingham University, UK) have fundamentally shaped this monograph at its post-award development phase. I remain endlessly thankful to both of them. During the writing processes, I have benefitted from conference presentations and panel feedback at the Centre for Comparative and Public Law at the University of Hong Kong (December 2017) and the Asian Law Centre at the University of Melbourne, Australia (December 2019). I thank Professor Tarunab Khaitan (University of Oxford) and Professor Yap Po Jen (University of Hong Kong) for facilitating my travel and presentations there. I am thankful to several other scholars, including Professor Rehan Abeyratne (Western Sydney University, Australia), Ridwanul Hoque (Charles Darwin University, Australia) and Harshan Kumarasingham (University of Edinburgh, UK) who have read and commented on various occasions on some parts of this book. I am also grateful to Professor Dr Nizam Ahmed (University of Chittagong, Bangladesh), Professor Dr ATM Obaidullah (University of Rajshahi, Bangladesh), Professor

Dr Tofail Ahmed (Vice-Chancellor, the Britannia University, Cumilla, Bangladesh) whom I interviewed on several occasions.

I deeply acknowledge the encouragement and support of Professor Matthias Vanhullebusch, the editor of Brill's Asian Law Series in the completion of this project. I wish to thank all at Brill, particularly Ingeborg van der Laan, the Associate Editor and the other team members at Brill for their constant support throughout.

I convey my heartfelt thanks to the Commonwealth Scholarship Commission at the UK Foreign and Commonwealth Office, who awarded me the Commonwealth Academic Staff Scholarship 2017–2021 for conducting my Ph.D. on this topic. I am particularly grateful to my teachers and former colleagues at the University of Chittagong, namely, Professor Dr Abdullah Al Faruque, Professor Nirmal Kumar Saha and Professor Dr Rakiba Nabi, for their support during the difficult phases of my Ph.D. life.

Lastly, but with the highest emphasis, I am in endless debt to my Mother, Father, Brothers, Sisters, in-laws, and all other extended family members in Bangladesh who stood by me in every circumstance of my life. I acknowledge the support and compassion of my wife Khadiza Sultana. I am endlessly thankful to her. The two kids, Chowdhury Mijab E Rahmat and Chowdhury Zafar As Sadik made all the differences in my life.

I hope the book will be well received by the academics, researchers, students and general audiences of comparative legislative and constitutional studies.

Kingston upon Hull
November 2024

Abbreviations

AD	Appellate Division (The Supreme Court of Bangladesh)
AL	Bangladesh *Awami League*
AV	Alternative Voting
BAC	Business Advisory Committee (Bangladesh)
BJS	*Bangladesh Jatya Sangsad* (The Bangladesh Parliament)
BNP	Bangladesh Nationalist Party
CEC	The Chief Election Commissioner (Bangladesh)
CRA	The Constitutional Reform Act 2005 (The UK)
EC	The Election Commission (Bangladesh)
ECHR	The European Convention on Human Rights 1950
FPTP	First-Past-The-Post
GoIA	The Government of Indian Act
HCD	High Court Division (The Supreme Court of Bangladesh)
HC	The House of Commons
HL	The House of Lords
HRA	The Human Rights Act 1998 (The UK)
JCHR	The Joint Committee on Human Rights (The UK)
JI	*Jamaat e Islami*, Bangladesh
JP	*Jatya Party*, Bangladesh
JSD	*Jatya Samajtantrik Dal*, Bangladesh
MP(s)	The Member(s) of Parliament
NAP	National Awami Party
NPCG	Non-Party Caretaker Government (Bangladesh)
PAC	Public Accounts Committee (Bangladesh)
PBC(s)	Public Bill Committee(s) (The UK)
PCO	The Provisional Constitution Order 1972 (Bangladesh)
PIL	Public Interest Litigation
PM	The Prime Minister
PMQT	The Prime Minister's Question Time
PR	Proportional Representation
PQT	The Parliamentary Question Time
RoP	The Rules of Procedure (Bangladesh Parliament)
SCB	The Supreme Court of Bangladesh
UK	The United Kingdom
UKSC	The Supreme Court of the UK
US	The United States

Table of Cases

A. K. M. Shafiuddin v Bangladesh (2012) 41 CLC (HCD).
Abdul Mannan Khan v Bangladesh 64 DLR (AD) (2012) 107.
Abdul Momen Chowdhury and others *v Bangladesh and* others *2005*, 34 CLC (HCD).
Abdus Samad Azad v Bangladesh (1992) 44 DLR 354.
Adv Zulhas Uddin Ahmed & Manzil Morshed v Bangladesh 15 MLR (HCD) 2010.
Advocate Asaduzzaman Siddiqui v Bangladesh (2016) 10 ALR (AD) 03.
Advocate Asaduzzaman Siddiqui v Bangladesh 10 ALR (AD) 03 (2017).
Advocate Asaduzzaman Siddiqui v Bangladesh 2012 CLC (HCD) 41.
Advocate Idrisur Rahman v Bangladesh 60 DLR (2008) (HCD) 714.
Ain O Shalish Kendra & Ors v Government of Bangladesh 4 MLR (HCD) 358.
AKM Shafiuddin v Bangladesh (2012) 41 CLC (HCD).
Anwar Hossain Chowdhury v Bangladesh (1989) BLD (Spl) 1.
Anwar Hossain Khan v Speaker of Bangladesh Sangsad Bhaban 47 DLR (HCD) (1995) 42.
Anwar Hossain Monju v Bangladesh 16 BLT (HCD) 86.
Ataur Rahman Khan v Md. Nasim 52 DLR 16 (Bangladesh).
Attorney-General's Reference (No 1 of 1988), [1989] 2 WLR 729 (The UK).
AXA General Insurance v HM Advocate [2011] UKSC 46.
Bangladesh & Justice Syed Dastagir Hossain v Idrisur Rahman 15 BLC (AD) 49.
Bangladesh Italian Marble Works Ltd v Bangladesh 2006 (Special) BLT 1 (HCD).
Bangladesh Legal Aid and Services Trust v Bangladesh 55 DLR (2003) HCD 363.
Barrister Ziaur Rahman Khan v Bangladesh 20 BLD (HCD) 120.
Black Clawson International Ltd v Papierwerke AG [1975] AC 591.
Bradlaugh v Gossett [1884] 12 QBD 271.
Chairman, National Board of Revenue v Advocate Julhas Uddin (2010) 15 MLR (AD) 457(Bangladesh).
Council of Civil Service Unions v Minister for the Civil Service [1984] UKHL 9.
Cyril Sikdar v Nazmul Huda 46 DLR 555 (Bangladesh).
Dr. M. A. Salam v Bangladesh 18 BLT (Spl) (2010) 1.
Dr. Mohiuddin Farooque (BELA) v Bangladesh 55 DLR (HCD) 69.
Dr. Mohiudin Farooquee v Bangladesh 55 DLR (2003) (HCD) 613.
Dr. Moohiuddin Faruque v Bangladesh and Ors 49 DLR 1997 (AD) 1.
Dr. Nurul Islam v Bangladesh 1 BLD (1981) (AD).
Escoigne Porperties Ltd v I.R.C [1958] AC 549.
Fazlur Rahman v Md Abdul Hamid and ors (2004) 56 DLR (HCD) 448.
Foreign and Commonwealth Office v Warsama & Anor [2020] EWCACiv 142.

Gina Miller v Brexit Secretary [2017] UKSC 5.
Idrisur Rahman v Bangladesh 60 DLR (HCD) 714.
Kazi Mamunur Rashid v Government of Bangladesh 28 BLD (2008) (HCD) 87.
Kazi Mukhlesur Rahman v Bangladesh 26 DLR (SC) 44.
Keshavananda Bharati v State of Kerala (1973) 4 SCC 225 (India).
Khandker Delwar Hossain v The Speaker 51 DLR 1 (1999) (Bangladesh).
Khandker Delwar Hossain v Bangladesh 62 DLR (AD) (2010) 298.
Khondhker Delwar Hossain v Bangladesh Italian Marble Works Ltd and Others (2010) 62 DLR (AD) 298.
Kielly v Carson (13 E.R. 225, May 23, 1842).
Kudrat-E-Elahi Panir and Others v Bangladesh 44 DLR (AD) 319.
M v Home Office [1994] 1 AC 377.
Major General A K M Shafiullah v Bangladesh W/P No 4313/2009.
Md. Abu Safa v Abdul Momen Chowdhury and others V ADC (2008) 64 (Bangladesh).
Mofizur Rahman v Bangladesh 34 DLR (AD) 321.
Moudud Ahmed v Anwar Hossain Khan, 60 DLR (2008) (AD) 108 (Bangladesh).
Muhibur Rahman Manik v Bangladesh & ors 23 BLD (HCD) 26.
National Board of Revenue v Abu Saeed Khan 18 BLC (AD) 116 (Bangladesh).
Pepper (HM *Inspector of Taxes*) *v Hart and related appeals* [1992] BTC 591.
Powell v McCormack, 395 US 486 (1969).
Prebble v Television New Zealand Ltd [1995]1 AC 321(New Zealand).
Professor Nurul Islam v Govt. of Bangladesh & others 52 DLR 413.
R (Jackson) v Attorney General [2005] UKHL 56.
R (Miller) v Secretary of State for Exiting the European Union [2017] UKSC 5.
R (Miller) v The Prime Minister and *Cherry v Advocate General for Scotland* [2019] UKSC 41.
R (Westminster City Council) v National Asylum Support Service [2002] UKHL 38.
R v Secretary of State for Foreign and Commonwealth Affairs, ex parte Bancoult (Nos 2) [2008] UKHL 61.
R v Secretary of State for the Home Department, ex parte Brind [1991] 1AC 696.
R v Chaytor [2010] UKSC 52.
Rafique Hossain v Speaker Bangladesh Parliament, 47 DLR 361 (1995).
Saifuzzaman v State and others 56 DLR (2004) HCD 324 (Bangladesh).
Saleem Ullah v Bangladesh (2005) 57 DLR (HCD) 171.
Secretary, Ministry of Finance v Masdar Hossain 52 DLR (AD) 82.
Secretary, Parliament Secretariat v Khandker Delwar Hossain, 19 BLD (AD) 276 (1999) (Bangladesh).
Shamima Sultana Seema v Bangladesh 57 DLR (2005) 201.
Sheikh Abdus Sabur v Returning Officer 41 DLR (AD) (1989) 30 (Bangladesh).

Siddique Ahmed v Bangladesh (2011) 33 BLD (HCD) 84.
Special Reference No 1 of 2009 15 BLC (AD) 1 (Bangladesh).
Special Reference No. 1 of 1995, 47 DLR (1995) (AD)111 (Bangladesh).
Stockdale v Hansard [1839] 9 Ad &El 1 96.
Union of India v Association for Democratic Reforms (2002) 3 SCR 294.
Vishaka and others v State of Rajasthan and others AIR 1997 SCC 3011 (India).
Warsama v Foreign and Commonwealth Office [2018] EWHC 1461 (QB).
Wilson v First County Trust (2) [2003] UKHL 40, [2004] 1 AC 816.

CHAPTER 1

The Dilemma of Design

1 The "Westminster" Template

At its independence in 1971, Bangladesh purportedly adopted a Westminster Parliamentary System.[1] For the newly independent country, the system was a matter of tradition too. Like most postcolonial states in the British commonwealth, Bangladesh inherited its political institutions from the British Parliament based in the Palace of Westminster.[2] The country's 1972 Constitution established a majority party government[3] collectively and individually responsible to the Parliament[4] and a symbolic presidency replicating the British Monarch.[5] The Chairman of the Constitution Drafting Committee, Dr Kamal Hossain,[6] and other influential members of the Constituent

1 Ridwanul Hoque, 'The Founding and Making of Bangladesh's Constitution' in Kevin YL Tan and Ridwanul Hoque (eds.) *Constitutional Foundings in South Asia* (London: Hart Publishing 2021) 91, 108; Rounaq Jahan and Inge Amundsen, *The Parliament of Bangladesh: Representation and Accountability*, CPD-CMI Working Paper 2 (Centre for Policy Dialogue and Chr. Michelsen Institute, Dhaka and Bergen, 2012) 7; Delwar Hossain, 'Dhaka Discourse, Bangladesh: Domestic Politics and External Actors' (*Institute of Peace and Conflict Studies Blog*, 17 February 2014); Nizam Ahmed, *The Parliament of Bangladesh* (Ashgate: Aldershot 2002, Routledge Reprint 2020) 33; Nizam Ahmed, '*Jatya Sangsad*: the Parliament of Bangladesh' (*Hansard Society*, 26 May 2016) <https://www.psa.ac.uk/sites/default/files/Parliament%20of%20Bangladesh.pdf> accessed 28 July 2024.

2 RAW Rhodes, John Wanna and Patrick Weller, *Comparing the Westminster* (Oxford 2011) 66.

3 The Constitution of the Peoples Republic of Bangladesh 1972, art 57.

4 ibid, arts. 57(2) and 58(2).

5 ibid, art. 48(3).

6 In response to Sri Suranjit Sen Gupta's speech (24 October 1971) regarding the Prime Minister's power and Cabinet dominance over the Parliament, Dr Kamal Hossain, Chair of the Constitution Drafting Committee made specific reference to the British Parliamentary System (30 October 1972). Dr Hossain argued, "We see the same system in the UK. I would now read some parts from the Constitutional and Parliamentary Studies Journal (September 1971). It is explained there how the British Parliamentary System is" (The quote is translated from Kawser Ahmed (ed), *Proceedings of Bangladesh Constituent Assembly: Debates relating to the Constitution Making Volume 1* (Bangla) (Dhaka: Pencil Publication 2021) 195, 371). Dr Hossain expressly referred to the British Parliamentary System several times during his defence of the Prime Minister's power to advise the President for dissolution of parliament (Kawser Ahmed, ibid, 373), the partisan whipping of the MPs (Ahmed, ibid, 372), civil service and bureaucratic machinery (Kawser Ahmed, ibid, 374).

 | DOI:10.1163/9789004720831_002

Assembly[7] identified Westminster as their most favoured constitutional design.

The Westminster system is built on a curious mix of written rules and unwritten conventions surrounding a "sovereign" legislature connected "inwardly and outwardly"[8] with other state organs. Inwardly, Parliament controls its formation, procedure, and committees. The parliamentary majority party or coalition selects the Head of the Government and their team of Ministers. The Speaker leads the Parliament, maintains the order of the House, and interprets and applies its rules and conventions authoritatively. Though elected MPs in party tickets, the British Speakers conventionally detach from their parties and remain impartial in conducting the legislature. Outwardly, the Westminster Parliament is sovereign over other State organs – the executive and judiciary. The Head of State (*i.e.,* the Monarch) stands above the government and performs mostly ceremonial roles. The Monarch formally appoints the government and the judges and summons the Parliament. Parliament holds the government and the civil service accountable through its legislative, budgetary, and scrutiny works. Government backbenchers and opposition parties question the government and debate its policies and legislative proposals. A government losing the confidence of Parliament must fall, though the emergence of cohesive political parties has compromised the Parliament's accountability powers to a certain extent.[9]

"Parliamentary Sovereignty"[10] immunises the statute laws from judicial review. However, the relationship between the Parliament and the judiciary is not one of absolute subordination and acquiescence. The judiciary has historically been engaged in a "collaborative enterprise" with the Parliament.[11] The common law principle of legality at least impliedly limits the sovereignty of Parliament. In the recent past, the UK's Constitutional Reform Act (CRA) 2005 and the Human Rights Act (HRA) 1998 drastically redefined the judiciary-parliament relationship. The CRA 2005 separated the judiciary from

7 Home Minister Syed Nazrul Islam's speech on 19 October 1972 (Kawser Ahmed (n 6), 103); Abdul Momin Talukder 's speech on 30 October 1972 (Kawser Ahmed, ibid, 351); Badrunnessa Ahmed's speech on 27 October 1972 (Kawser Ahmed, ibid, 296–297).

8 Alan Trench, 'Wales and the Westminster Model' (2010) 63(1) Parliamentary Affairs 117, 118.

9 Wolfgang C Müller, 'Political Parties in Parliamentary Democracies: Making Delegation and Accountability Work' (2000) 37 European Journal of Political Research 309; Rudy B Andeweg, 'Parties in Parliament: the Blurring of Opposition' in WC Müller and HM Narud (eds.), *Party Governance and Party Democracy* (Springer 2013) 99–114.

10 For a brief introduction to the concept see: Jeffrey Goldsworthy, *The Sovereignty of Parliament: History and Philosophy* (Oxford 1999) 9–21.

11 Philip A Joseph, 'Parliament, the Courts, and the Collaborative Enterprise' (2004) 15 King's College Law Journal 321, 333.

the House of Lords (HoL) and established a separate Supreme Court for the UK (UKSC). The HRA 1998 has placed the UKSC within a tripartite structure of human rights protection. Before a legislative proposal enters the Parliament, the government reviews its human rights compatibility. Then, a committee of the Parliament – Joint Committee on Human Rights (JCHR) and the House of Commons (HC) – reviews the draft. Once the law is passed, the UKSC might be called to review its human rights compatibility.[12] Some call, radically perhaps, this new institutional arrangement a replacement of the UK's parliamentary sovereignty system with that of the separation of powers.[13] A relatively sober argument is that the UK's age-old concepts of parliamentary sovereignty and fusion of powers are now giving way to a "divided sovereignty" system akin to the separation of powers.[14] The Westminster system is evolutionist. Therefore, it is not unusual that the system is in a constant shape-shifting mode.

2 The Dilemma

In Bangladesh, the drafters of the original Constitution, despite their overt Westminster-fondness, could not hide the indecisiveness and contradictions. Thanks to their education, training, social background, and upbringing, they had an inner preference for the continuing colonial "hegemon"[15] – the Palace of Westminster. However, they carried an exceedingly difficult burden of distancing themselves from their discredited colonial predecessor too. Cautious not being branded as colonial imitators, they would vehemently oppose that they were implanting any "foreign template"[16] and claim that their Constitution had

12 Janet L Hiebert, 'Interpreting a Bill of Rights: the Importance of Legislative Rights Review' (2005) 35 British Journal of Political Science 235, 245.

13 Vernon Bogdanor, *The New British Constitution* (Oxford: Hart Publishing 2009) 285.

14 Roger Masterman, *The Separation of Powers in the Contemporary Constitution, Judicial Competence and Independence in the United Kingdom* (Cambridge 2011) 245–253.

15 Valeriano Ramos, Jr, 'The Concepts of Ideology, Hegemony, and Organic Intellectuals in Gramsci's Marxism' (1982) 27 Theoretical Review (Tucson Marxist-Leninist Collective, Encyclopedia of Anti-Revisionism On-Line).

16 General debate in Bangladesh Constituent Assembly of 1972 suggests that several of the Assembly members, particularly the most vocal opposition member Sri Suranjit Sen Gupta, showed clear disapproval for the Constitution's insinuation to the Westminster or foreign systems. In his speech on the Assembly floor on 24 October 1972, Mr. Gupta criticized the Chairman of the Drafting Committee Dr Kamal Hossain saying: "Honourable Law Minister has visited London few days ago. Westminster is not far from there. So, I see some shadow of the British Constitution here." Mr. Gupta was highly critical of the Prime Minister's power to advise dissolution of the parliament as granted in the constitution. He continued: "I see no problem is importing experience from abroad. An expert came

its "national ownership".[17] So, while imitating the coloniser's structural template, they would brush it with glosses from a few other systems through "cross-imperial or cross-colonial borrowing".[18] As a result, the Bangladesh Parliament (*Bangladesh Jatya Sangsad*, BJS)'s internal organisation and relationship with the executive and judicial branches, political parties, and the people differed significantly from the Westminster Parliament. Some of those differences were incredibly significant.

First, unlike the UK Parliament, the BJS was designed as a unicameral legislature. Secondly, the Constitution placed exceptionally high restraints on the MPs' voting rights in parliament[19] and prioritised party discipline over government accountability.[20] Thirdly, the BJS was not sovereign in the same sense as the UK Parliament was. Bangladesh rather embraced constitutional supremacy.[21] The BJS's legislative power was kept subordinate to the Constitution, and the Supreme Court was given the power to adjudicate the constitutionality of statute laws.[22] Fourthly, in line with their political ideologies, the Constitution framers sought to realise a "socialist" democracy based on social equality and distributive justice. BJS was perceived as a mere facilitator of the socialist project.[23] Some called the resultant system a blend of the British, American, and Soviet traditions.[24] Others described it as a "half-hearted"[25] blend of the US-style separation of power and the Westminster-style fusion of power. Overall,

---

(referring to Robert Guthrie, a UK drafting expert, who was invited to check the linguistic aspects of the text). But where we want to establish a socialist system, an expert came from the imperial coloniser Britain, who oppressed and enchained this country for hundreds of years." (The quote is translated from Kawser Ahmed (n 6) 197).

17 Ridwanul Hoque (n 1), 115.

18 Julian Go, 'Modeling the State: Postcolonial Constitutions in Asia and Africa', Southeast Asian Studies (2002) 39(4) Southeast Asian Studies 558.

19 Constitution of Bangladesh (n 3), art 70.

20 During the Constituent Assembly debates, members like Suranjit Sen Gupta, Md Abdul Aziz Chowdhury and MA Quddus were highly critical of article 70 (Kawser Ahmed (n 6) Introduction, XXII).

21 Constitution (n 3), art 7.

22 ibid, art. 26, 44 and 102.

23 Leading member of the Assembly elaborating on the Socialism and constitutional socio-economic rights included the then Finance Minister Tajuddin Ahmed (Kawser Ahmed (n 6) 320–336), Syed Nazrul Islam (Kawser Ahmed (n 6) 107–109), and Abdul Momin Talukdar (Kawser Ahmed (n 6) 352–53).

24 Ridwanul Hoque, 'Constitutionalism and the Judiciary in Bangladesh' in Sunil Khilnani, Vikram Raghavan and Arun K. Thiruvengadam (eds.) *Comparative Constitutionalism in South Asia* (Oxford: Oxford University Press 2013) 303, 306.

25 Nizam Ahmed, 'In Search of Institutionalisation: Parliament in Bangladesh' (1998) 4(4) The Journal of Legislative Studies 34, 40.

the system laid down an omnipotent executive, a minimally powerful judiciary, and a subdued legislature.

2.1 *A Less-than-Ideal Orientation*

The relative unimportance of the legislature in Bangladesh's constitutional design had its historical and social anecdotes. In their distant memories, the framers of the Constitution had a less-than-ideal picture of the parliamentary system. In 1909, a pseudo-parliamentary system was introduced in British India.[26] It was the first-ever opening of electoral politics and democratic representation for the natives in the colony's legislative and executive councils.[27] The Government of India Act (GoIA) 1909 was later substituted by the Government of India Acts 1919 and 1935, respectively. The GoIAs would constitute the constitutional blueprints for independent India and Pakistan. While the colonial governments were modelled in a Westminster fashion, the legislative branch was not given such powers as the UK Parliament. For understandable reasons, the newly coined Indian legislature remained a mere deliberative forum. The executive branch, controlled by the British Viceroy, Governor-General, and other Governors, would continue to legislate, execute, and rule. Though the GoIAs gave the Indians a taste of political representation and deliberation in the central and provincial legislatures, the faulty start with a mere deliberative parliament would continue to hurt the legislatures in the postcolonial states, including Bangladesh.

2.2 *A Continuing "Hegemon"*

In the late 1940s, on the eve of decolonisation, the Westminster parliamentary system was either "implanted" or "transplanted"[28] across the British colonies. Most imitated the colonial model but looked into other established systems too. For example, Julian Go's study on the postcolonial constitutions in Asia and Africa[29] shows that all of the postcolonial constitutions were either based

---

26 The Government of India Act 1909, also known as the Morley-Minto Reform Act, was named after the then Secretary of State for India Lord Morley and the Viceroy of India Lord Minto.

27 By 1909, India's two major political parties were already formed (Indian Congress in 1885 and Muslim League in 1906). See: *Minto-Morley Reforms (1909)* <https://www.britannica.com/topic/Indian-Councils-Act-of-1909> accessed 17 November 2024.

28 RAW Rhodes and Patrick Weller, 'Westminster transplanted, and Westminster Implanted: Exploring Political Change' in Haig Patapan, John Wanna and Patrick Weller (eds.), *Westminster Legacies: Democracy and Responsible Government in Asia and the Pacific* (University of New South Wales Press 2005) 1, 2–3.

29 Julian Go (n 18).

on "intra-imperial isomorphism"[30] and "trans-imperial" or "cross-colonial" borrowing.[31]

Intra-imperial isomorphism – the imitation – was sometimes imposed by the colonisers.[32] For example, the Constitution of Malaysia was drafted by a committee appointed by the British Crown and chaired by the British jurist Lord Reid.[33] Sir Ivor Jennings played an instrumental role in drafting the Sri Lanka, Nepal, and Maldives constitutions. There, he would replicate the British Model "stubbornly" and even at the risk of "dismissing the (countries') political context".[34] In most other circumstances, the newly independent colonies' political elites would imitate their colonisers' constitutional ideals and templates.[35]

The imitative tendency in the post-independence state-building process may appear perplexing – considering the political elites' staunch resistance to the colonial ruler during the pre-independence era. However, we may find an answer to the puzzle in Antonio Gramsci's "social hegemon thesis".[36] Gramsci, an Italian Marxist philosopher, reframed the Marxian class struggle as a battle for social hegemony between the working class and the fascist, capitalist, and imperialist colonial regimes. Traditional Marxist philosophers have long talked about a "third face of power", or "invisible power" gained through the circulation and popularisation of ideas, values and beliefs that help reproduce and sustain capitalist dominance over the proletariats.[37] Marxists acknowledge

30 ibid 562.

31 ibid 560.

32 ibid 561.

33 Ibrahim Ahmad and MP Jain, 'The Constitution of Malaysia and the American Constitutional Influence' in Lawrence W Beer (ed), *Constitutional Systems in Late Twentieth Century Asia*, 507–570 (Seattle: University of Washington Press 1992) 507.

34 Mara Malagodi, 'Ivor Jennings's Constitutional Legacy beyond the Occidental-Oriental Divide' (2015) 42(1) Journal of Law and Society 102, 119, 122. However, it is also important to note that, when the situation demanded, Jennings did not hesitate to subvert the "British constitutional tenets" either. For example, his support for Pakistani Governor-Generals and Presidents' unconstrained and often unaccountable discretionary powers created a so-called "Pakistan model" of presidentialism and dislodged the hopes of democratic sustenance in Pakistan (Upendra Baxi, 'Postcolonial Legality' in H Schwarz and S Ray (eds.), *A Companion to Postcolonial Studies* 540–555 (Oxford: Blackwell Publishing 2005) 541). Similarly, Jennings supported extensive emergency powers in the Nepali constitution and was ready to sustain cabinet government only "as long as practicable" (Malagodi, 'Ivor Jennings's Constitutional Legacy', 115).

35 Swati Parashar and Michael Schulz, 'Colonial legacies, postcolonial 'selfhood' and the (un)doing of Africa' (2021) 42(5) Third World Quarterly 867.

36 Valeriano Ramos, Jr. (n 15).

37 Andrew Heywood, *Political Ideas and Concepts: an Introduction* (London: Macmillan 1994) 100.

that a capitalist system does not survive merely on the power of economic exploitation of the proletariat. The system also needs to self-sustain through some form of ideological indoctrination. Engels called this a situation of "false consciousness",[38] which keeps the working class from even noticing the existence of oppression. While a capitalist state may allow the proletariat to gain a limited extent of material consciousness (which Lenin called a mere "trade union consciousness"[39]), it induces them to accept the inevitability of the capitalist system as such.[40]

In his celebrated *Prison Notebooks*, Antonio Gramsci took Engel's idea of "false consciousness" much further. He argued that the ruling class's dominance is sustained not by its political brute force but rather by its "social hegemony"[41] that helps rationalise their ascendance to, and sustenance in, the top echelon of power. In this sense, the rulers' "power" is in their "social hegemony" that begets them a "manufactured consent" of the ruled.[42] He applied the thesis to Mussolini's fascist regime in Italy: Gramsci argued that a capitalist state thrives not only on the force of a "political society" (comprising the bureaucracies and the rulers) but also on the persuasion of a "civil society" (comprising the wider social, political and intellectual elites).[43] Gramsci's political society is a public sphere where trade unions and mass-based political parties may gain some symbolic concessions from the ruling elites through electoral or deliberative processes. However, the bourgeois hegemony continues to sustain its legitimacy through "manufactured consent" created at the civil society level.[44] Gramsci would advise that a class struggle of the Marxian proletariat must focus on reversing the burgeons' social hegemony and replace it with one of the proletariats. A revolution at the political level will fail to establish the hegemony of the socialist forces if it is not accompanied by a successful "counter-hegemonic" struggle against the dominant capitalist ideals and

---

38 Frederick Engels, 'Engels to Franz Mehring, London, July 14, 1893' in *Marx and Engels Correspondence* (International Publishers 1968).

39 Vladimir Ilyich Lenin, 'What is to be Done? Burning Questions of our Movement' (The Spontaneity of the Masses and the Consciousness of the Social-Democrats) <https://www.marxists.org/archive/lenin/works/1901/witbd/ch02.htm> accessed 28 July 2024.

40 Andrew Heywood (n 37) 85.

41 Thomas R Bates, 'Gramsci and the Theory of Hegemony,' (1975) 36(2) Journal of the History of Ideas 351, 351–52.111.

42 Antonio Gramsci, *Selections from the Prison Notebooks*; (New York: International Publishers 1971).

43 AM Brighenti, 'Antonio Gramsci's Theory of the Civil Society' in Moebius, S, Nungesser, F, Scherke, K (eds.) *Handbuch Kultursoziologie* (Wiesbaden: Springer Reference Sozialwissenschaften 2016) 1–7.

44 Heywood (n 37) 100–101.

beliefs at the societal level. Without this, a political change could, at best, be a "passive revolution"[45] that continues the oppressive power structure of the fallen system.

Gramsci's "passive revolution" and "counter-hegemonic struggle" gained popularity in the postcolonial studies.[46] His concepts travelled freely across the postcolonial world,[47] sometimes with over-generalisation and too much stretching.[48] On the intellectual front, he inspired prominent orientalists like Edward Said,[49] Stuart Hall[50] and Partha Chatterjee.[51] Among the Indian intellectuals, Partha Chatterjee popularised a genre of postcolonial literature called the "subaltern studies".[52] Subaltern theorists question the social and ideological hegemony of the intellectual and political elites in the post-colonies.[53] They argue that the political and constitutional design of the newly independent colonies was largely determined through a system of elite preferences rather than through a participatory and inclusive process.[54] The colonial master promoted those elites to the higher societal echelon. In India and Pakistan, for example, the British imperial regime transferred the sovereignty and powers to those they trusted – typically Anglicised local leaders like Nehru and Jinnah.[55] Partha Chatterjee argues that the "India" so produced was a continuation of

45 Gramsci (n 42).

46 David Scott, 'The Aftermaths of Sovereignty: Postcolonial Criticism and the Claims of Political Modernity' (1996) 48 Social Text 1.

47 Nazih Ayubi, *Over-stating the Arab State: Politics and Society in the Middle East* (London: I.B. Tauris 1996) 9.

48 Neelam Srivastava and Baidik Bhattacharya (eds.), *The Postcolonial Gramsci* (London: Routledge 2013); John Chalcraft and Yaseen Noorani (eds.), *Counter-Hegemony in the Colony and Postcolony* (London: Palgrave Macmillan 2007); Adam David Morton, *Unravelling Gramsci Hegemony and Passive Revolution in the Global Political Economy* (Pluto Press 2007); Adam David Morton, 'A Double Reading of Gramsci: Beyond the Logic of Contingency' (2005) 8(4) Critical Review of International Social and Political Philosophy 439.

49 Edward W. Said, *Orientalism* (Pantheon Books 1978).

50 Stuart Hall, *The West and the Rest: Discourse and Power* (Duke University Press 2018).

51 Partha Chatterjee, *The Nation and Its Fragments: Colonial and Postcolonial Histories* (Duke University Press 2018).

52 Bailey Betik, 'Postcolonial Studies@Emory: Subaltern Studies' (*The Scholars Blog*, Emory University. 2020).

53 Julian Go, The Subaltern Standpoint' chapter in *Postcolonial Thought and Social Theory* (Oxford: 2016).

54 Swati Chattopadhyay and Bhaskar Sarkar, 'Introduction: the subaltern and the popular' (2005) 8(4) Postcolonial Studies 357, 359.

55 Kevin YL Tan and Ridwanul Hoque, 'South Asian Constitutional Foundings: Beyond History' in Kevin YL Tan and Ridwanul Hoque (eds.), *Constitutional Founding's in South Asia*, 1–18 (Oxford: Hart Publishing, 2021) 9, 12–13.

imperial values and culture even though leaders like Nehru and Jinnah were highly critical of imperialist domination.[56]

Chatterjee examined how and to what extent the marginalised people participated in India's promised nationhood[57] and what democracy meant for them.[58] He argued that based on their religious, gender, ethnic, and racial identities, the "subaltern" social groups remained marginalised or even ignored in the postcolonial state-building process.[59] As Granville Austin wrote about the Indian Constitution-making process, the guiding hand of an "Oligarchy", including the likes of Nehru, Patel, Rajendra Prasad, and Maulana Azad, single-handedly steered the agenda and debates in the Indian Constituent Assembly. The Constitution that emerged at the end was "presented to the nation as the realisation of Nehru's aim."[60] Though an Indian Assembly drafted it, the elites were influenced by scholars like Harold Laski. They attended constitutional conferences in London, and critical decisions were allegedly made by the English policymakers.[61] The framers imported, unchanged, large parts of the GoIA 1935 and incorporated its arsenal of strong executive powers in the new Constitution. A lead drafter of the Indian Constitution, B R Ambedkar, was unapologetic about it:

> As to the accusation that the Draft Constitution has produced a good part of the provisions of the Government of India Act, 1935, I make no apologies. There is nothing to be ashamed of in borrowing.[62]

In that sense, the hegemony of the colonies' newly established political elites was the continuation of the hegemony of their colonial masters and their preferences and ideals. Therefore, the system devised at independence facilitated the continuation of colonial legacies. In a Gramscian sense, the

56 Sanjay Krishnan, "The Place of India in Postcolonial Studies: Chatterjee, Chakrabarty, Spivak" (2009) 40(2) New Literary History 265, 266.

57 William Wheeler, 'Partha Chatterjee' *Stanford Presidential Lectures in the Humanities and Arts* (Stanford University Library, 2007).

58 Partha Chatterjee, *The Politics of the Governed: Considerations on Political Society in Most of the World* (New York: Columbia University Press 2004).

59 Partha Chatterjee, *Nationalist Thought and the Colonial World: a Derivative Discourse?* (London: Zed, 1986).

60 Gyan Prakash, 'Anxious Constitution-Making' in Gyan Prakash, Michael Laffan and Nikhil Menon (eds.), *The Postcolonial Moment in South and Southeast Asia*, 141–162 (Bloomsbury Academic 2018) 147.

61 Sir Ivor Jennings, *The Commonwealth in Asia* (Oxford: Clarendon Press 1949) 57.

62 Indian Constituent Assembly Debate, Vol. VII (4 December 1948).

postcolonial political elites gained their people's "manufactured consent" to sustain and continue the colonial templates and philosophies of governance. Gramsci's counter-hegemonic struggle did not happen in the post-colonies. Decolonisation resulted in a mere change of political society without a change in the society. The postcolonial elites mobilised the people in the name of a "national" revolution but did not break from entrenched landed and upper-caste interests. The myth of revolution represented a "false independence"[63] that disguised the continuance of imperialist ideologies and systemic oppression. Ranajit Guha calls this a Gramscian "passive revolution" accomplished without an accompanying radical social revolution and a "dominance without hegemony".[64] So, the established governance framework required the infusion of coercion over persuasion.[65] The post-independence rulers essentially spoke in two voices – one of the sovereign people and the other of the administrator.[66] The sovereign voice was applied to achieve radical socialist transformation. On the other hand, the administrator's voice sought to regulate, restrict, and control the political opposition within some constitutionally set boundaries.[67] As BR Ambedkar put it:

> Democracy in India is only a top-dressing on Indian soil, which is essentially undemocratic. In its hierarchy-ridden society, India's constitutional morality cannot be left in the safe hands of democratic processes. It should rather be entrusted in the hands of the intellectual and political elites.[68]

In Bangladesh, the constitution-makers were also at natural ease with the Westminster model. Like their subcontinent forerunners, the prominent Bangladeshi constitution framers were educated in England and grew up politically within the Westminster system.[69]

63 Rotem Geva, '"False Truth": Disillusionment and Hope i the Decade after Independence' in Gyan Prakash, Michael Laffan and Nikhil Menon (eds.), *The Postcolonial Moment in South and Southeast Asia*, 11–29 (Bloomsbury Academic 2018) 17.

64 Ranajit Guha, *Dominance Without Hegemony: History and Power in Colonial India* (Cambridge, MA: Harvard University Press, 1998).

65 ibid.

66 Sandipto Dasgupta, "A Language Which Is Foreign to Us': Continuities and Anxieties in the Making of the Indian Constitution' (2014) 34(2) Comparative Studies of South Asia, Africa, and the Middle East 228.

67 Gyan Prakash (n 60) 157.

68 Indian Const. Assem. Debate (n 62).

69 Rainer Grote, 'Westminster Democracy in an Islamic Context: Pakistan, Bangladesh, Malaysia', in Rainer Grote and Tilmann J Röder (eds.) *Constitutionalism in Islamic*

2.3 *"Cross-imperial or Cross-colonial Borrowing"*

Another facet of the postcolonial state building is what Julian Go calls "intra-imperial or cross-colonial borrowing".[70] Go's study shows that at least half of the postcolonial constitutions had provisions that could not be traced to their former imperial ruler. In those cases, the postcolonial states turned to models circling across, rather than within, empires and regions. The borrowing also showed a potentially globalising trend.[71] The postcolonial moment had a flawed beginning in the immediate decades of the post-WWII era. The UN-inspired decolonisation process was not a straightforward case of power transfer or an inevitable succession from an imperial to a postimperial stage of history. The fragility of a global Cold War between capitalist and socialist blocks marked the international legal or political order. The nascent states of South and Southeast Asian nations had to make momentous decisions about their preferences. The Cold War was not a phenomenon that these nations could not simply ignore.[72]

To take the Indian example again, the constitution framers attempted to realise a socialist system through a strong executive government. In the process, the framers allegedly mixed the American and French approaches to public power.[73] The scope of political power was distinctive in the American and French revolutions. The Americans saw the political powers as the source of tyranny and tried to restrict it. They put social questions like slavery and native land claims out of their constitutional discourse, at least initially. In contrast, the French revolutionaries licensed political power to redress material deprivation and social inequality.[74] Uday Mehta suggests that Indian constitution makers saw their newly gained political power as a tool for achieving their promised full national unity, economic development, and social change. Under this discourse, freedom becomes a subsidiary of securing unity, social uplift, and international recognition. Accordingly, the Indian framers adopted a constitution establishing an all-powerful notion of politics and state power.[75]

Countries: Between Upheaval and Continuity (Oxford: Oxford University Press 2012) 447, 454.

70 Julian Go (n 18).

71 Julian Go (n 18) 580.

72 Odd Arne Westad, *The Global Cold War: Third World Interventions and the Makings of Our Times* (Cambridge: Cambridge University Press, 2007).

73 Uday Singh Mehta, 'Indian Constitutionalism: the Articulation of a Political Vision' in Dipesh Chakrabarty, Rochona Majumdar, and Andrew Sartori (eds.), *From the Postcolonial to Colonial: India and Pakistan in Transition,* 13–30 (Delhi: Oxford University Press, 2007).

74 Gyan Prakash (n 60) 156.

75 ibid.

As mentioned earlier, cross-colonial borrowing was apparent in the Bangladesh constitution too.[76] Bangladesh's basic equation of the executive-legislative relation was modelled in the Westminster way. However, the executive's accountability to the legislature, particularly the Parliament's power to unseat the government, was practically closed by inserting a strict anti-defection clause in the Constitution. Informed by the history of unstable governments in the erstwhile Pakistan era, the anti-defection law has essentially bent the Parliament to its knees. Next, the design of the judiciary, with a responsibility to enforce fundamental rights against the government and the Parliament, was inspired by the American constitutional system. However, the appointment and control of the judiciary were left almost exclusively in the hands of the government. Again, the presidential office was designed in the British Monarch's template. However, in opportune moments, the Bangladeshi presidents interfered in politics, controversially suspended the Constitution, imposed martial laws, declared emergencies, and tempered with election-time caretaker governments. All these resulted in a crude majoritarian and partisan executive dictatorship in Bangladesh.

3 Fitting a Misfit

State-building processes under the implanted or transplanted Westminster systems were an onerous task. The Constitution framers may have written down the imposed, imported, or borrowed colonial institutions and concepts in the Constitution. However, fitting those within the "very different social structures, religious texture and cultural values"[77] was even more challenging. Each country had their unique history, culture, and internal societal tensions. Therefore, their attempt to replicate the colonial system while adjusting it to their internal struggles with religion, rights, social inequality, national identity, etc.,[78] resulted in controversial and sometimes chaotic prototypes of the Westminster parliamentary system.

---

76 Muhammad Ekramul Haque, 'Constitutional borrowing and transplants', *The Daily Star* (Dhaka, 4 November 2022).

77 W Elliot Bulmer, *The Global Development of The Westminster Model, Chapter – Constituting Scotland: the Scottish National Movement and the Westminster Model* (Edinburgh University Press, 2016).

78 Ratna Ghosh, Ali A Abdi and M Ayaz Naseem, 'Identity in Colonial and Postcolonial Contexts: Select Discussions and Analyses' in AA Abdi and G Richardson (eds.), *Decolonizing Democratic Education: Trans-disciplinary Dialogues* 57–66 (Sense Publishers 2008).

While the white-settler colonies like Australia, Canada and New Zealand "transplanted" the system in cultural contexts largely similar to the UK, the non-white colonies in the East adapted and "implanted" it with various structural and cultural adaptations.[79] It was sometimes intertwined with un-Westminster concepts like federalism (Australia),[80] traditions (Papua New Guinea and Fiji),[81] etc. In some other cases, it got overshadowed and infused by hegemonic traits like military authoritarianism (Pakistan, Myanmar),[82] monarchic paternalism (Nepal and Bhutan),[83] developmental one-party monopoly (Singapore, Malaysia),[84] and illiberal, clientelist and dynastic party systems (India, Pakistan, Bangladesh)[85] etc.

The Westminster system and its bipartisan temperament got a particularly tough cultural challenge in the Southeast Asian block. Here, the "Asian Values" argument is frequently advanced as an alternative political philosophy[86] that emphasises the collectivist and duty (not rights)-prone social ideals and, therefore, shows strong presidential or one-party tendencies. It allegedly offers "ideological rationalisation" for authoritarianism and one-party dominance at the cost of constitutional opposition and civil society activism.[87] For example,

79 RAW Rhodes and Patrick Weller (n 28), 2–3.

80 Jean Holmes, 'The Australian Federalism System' (1984) 5(4) International Political Science Review /Revue internationale de science politique 397.

81 Matthew Louis Bishop, 'Slaying the 'Westmonster' in the Caribbean? Constitutional Reform in St Vincent and the Grenadines' (2011) 13(3) The British Journal of Politics and International Relations 420.

82 Samina Ahmed, 'The Westminster Model and Pakistan: a Continuing Mirage', in Haig Patapan, John Wanna and Patrick Weller (eds.), *Westminster Legacies: Democracy and Responsible Government in Asia -and the Pacific* (University of New South Wales Press 2005) 36–62.

83 Patrick Weller and Bishnu Sharma, 'Transplanting Westminster to Nepal: the stuff of dreams dashed', in Haig Patapan, John Wanna and Patrick Weller (eds.), *Westminster Legacies: Democracy and Responsible Government in Asia -and the Pacific* (University of New South Wales Press 2005) 63–80.

84 Thio Li-ann, 'The Right to Political Participation in Singapore: Tailor-Making a Westminster-modelled Constitution to Fit the Imperatives of Asian Democracy' (2002) 6 Singapore Journal of International & Comparative Law 181.

85 Haig Patapan and John Wanna, 'The Westminster legacy: Conclusion' in Haig Patapan, John Wanna and Patrick Weller (eds.), *Westminster Legacies: Democracy and Responsible Government in Asia and the Pacific* (University of New South Wales Press 2005) 248.

86 Takashi Inoguchi and Edward Newman, *"Asian Values" and Democracy in Asia* (First Shizuoka Asia-Pacific Forum: the Future of the Asia-Pacific Region, Hamamatsu, March 1997).

87 Garry Rodan, 'Westminster in Singapore: Now you see it, now you don't' in Haig Patapan, John Wanna and Patrick Weller (eds.), *Westminster Legacies: Democracy and Responsible Government in Asia and the Pacific* (University of New South Wales Press 2005) 124–125.

Malaysia and Singapore's electoral system has long been suitably doctored to legitimise the absolute dominance of one ethnic group (Malay)[88] or party (People's Action Party).[89] While Malaysia is called an "adapted" one, Singapore is described as a "Westminster transformed".[90]

The problem of cultural misfit was no less acute in the South Asian region. The Westminster systems in the Indian subcontinent are branded as systems "approaching the Westminster".[91] In India, for example, the constitution-making process was largely deliberative, though not ideally participatory. There was a consensus for a parliamentary form of government.[92] The new system's procedures and institutions proved resilient in the early post-independence period.[93] They succeeded in channelling, managing and reconciling political competition through a relatively free, fair and periodic election system and the successful subordination of the military to the civilian authorities.[94] However, the party system and religious pluralism remained very big stumbling blocks.[95] India endured a "structural authoritarianism" of the Indian Congress party during its initial decades.[96] In the later decades, the decay of institutions, increased fragmentation of the party system, centralisation and

88 Deborah A Johnson and Anthony Milner, 'Westminster Implanted: the Malaysian Experience' in Haig Patapan, John Wanna and Patrick Weller (eds.), *Westminster Legacies: Democracy and Responsible Government in Asia and the Pacific* (University of New South Wales Press 2005) 102.

89 Diane K Mauzy and RS Milne, *Singapore Politics Under the People's Action Party* (London: Routledge, 2002).

90 Thio Li-ann (n 84).

91 Saul Rose, 'The New Constitutions in South Asia' (1973) 63(252) *The Round Table 439, 440.*

92 Sudhir Kumar Suthar, 'Postcolonial and Post-Soviet Experiences of Constitution-making: Comparing India and Russia' (2014) 51(1–4) International Studies 56, 61–62.

93 Zillur R Khan, 'Bangladesh's Experiments with Parliamentary Democracy' (1997) 37(6) Asian Survey 575, 575.

94 Ayesha Jalal, *Democracy and Authoritarianism in South Asia A Comparative and Historical Perspective* (Cambridge University Press 1995) 63–65.

95 Renu Khator, 'The Political Party System of India: From One-Party Dominance to No-Party Dominance', in M Rimanelli (eds.) *Comparative Democratization and Peaceful Change in Single-Party-Dominant Countries* 339–361 (Palgrave Macmillan, New York 1999); Shaila Seshia, 'Divide and Rule in Indian Party Politics: the Rise of the Bharatiya Janata Party' (1998) 38(11) Asian Survey 1036.

96 Robert W Stern, 'India's Westminster System' in Haig Patapan, John Wanna and Patrick Weller (eds.), *Westminster Legacies: Democracy and Responsible Government in Asia and the Pacific* (University of New South Wales Press 2005) 17–20.

personalisation of powers, and heightened religious and caste conflicts have threatened the system's ability to continue performing its role to an expected level.[97]

Compared to India, the Dominion of Pakistan stumbled from the beginning. In 1947, Pakistan's founding leader, Mohammad Ali Jinnah, became the Governor-General instead of the Prime Minister. While the Governor-General, a mere figurehead, should have been a less attractive option for Jinnah, he would still prefer the office and start dominating the Cabinet and Constituent Assembly from that position. Jinnah placed himself in direct governance of the country, held ministerial positions, handpicked the Cabinet, overrode the Prime Minister, and even dismissed provincial ministries. Following Jinnah's death, the trend was carried forward by Governor General Ghulam Muhammad. An early-day Prime Minister, Liaquat Ali Khan, openly advocated the supremacy of one political party and termed the opponents of the Muslim League as traitors and enemy agents.[98] The League government frequently used the Public Safety Acts and other new draconian colonial laws to keep a check on political opponents.[99]

As Malagodi suggests, the early days of the Pakistan Republic saw the Governor-Generals and Presidents exercise ample powers to suspend cabinet government, dissolve constituent assemblies, or even the entire Constitution and assume direct powers under a so-called viceregal "power to remove difficulties".[100] They used the viceregal powers of the office controversially and to their subjective satisfaction. Those were in clear subversion of a key British constitutional principle (symbolic Monarchy limited by the advice of an elected government) and allowed the authoritarian political moves to go legally unchallenged.[101] Presidents later suspended the Constitution and promulgated martial laws at their sweet will. The military's persistent, direct, or indirect involvement in politics has put the country in a system of constitutionalised military rule – direct or indirect.[102] Pakistan got a constitution in

---

97 Stanley A Kochanek, 'Political Governance in India: the Challenge of Stability and Diversity' in A Shastri and AJ Wilson (eds.), *The Postcolonial States of South Asia*, 17–40 (New York: Palgrave Macmillan 2001) 37.

98 Mara Malagodi (n 34) 120.

99 Kamran Asdar Ali, 'The Enemy Within: Communism and the New Pakistani State' in Gyan Prakash, Michael Laffan and Nikhil Menon (eds.), *The Postcolonial Moment in South and Southeast Asia*, 31–47 (Bloomsbury Academic 2018) 33–34.

100 Mara Malagodi (n 34) 116.

101 ibid 122.

102 Samina Ahmed, 'The Fragile Base of Democracy in Pakistan' in A Shastri and AJ Wilson (eds.), *The Postcolonial States of South Asia*, 41–68 (New York: Palgrave Macmillan 2001).

1956 – nine years after its independence and became a Republic. The military suspended it within two years – in 1958. Pakistan's East and West wings were torn apart, and the military establishment took Pakistan towards an authoritarian presidentialism.[103]

The Pakistan formula of presidential abuses can be traced back to its colonial past and the political necessities of its post-independence political elites. Like their Indian counterparts, the Pakistani Muslim League leaders were well versed in the colonial viceregal hierarchical and centralised government system. However, the problem of representation was more acute in Pakistan. Jinnah and his cohort of Muslim League leadership were composed mainly of *muhajirs* (migrants) from North and West India, lacking any broad support base in the newly constituted State of Pakistan. So, the elites became insensitive to democratic opposition to their authority. During the anti-colonial movement, they preached the idea of an Islamic state with an "Islam-in-danger" rhetoric. Once Pakistan was realised, they found no social and economic policy to build the new State. So, governance became a political vice where the rulers continued manipulating the colonial laws and processes to stay in power. They started perpetuating colonial practices of viceregalism, fearing that representative institutions and devolved local governance would weaken their hold on political power.

Similarly, Myanmar derailed its Westminster system into pure military authoritarianism soon after its independence. Sri Lanka tried to stick to the Westminster procedure, institutions, and ceremonials in their formalities until 1972 but soon travelled towards a presidential system.[104] Bangladesh ceded from Pakistan and emerged as a sovereign peoples' republic in 1971. Bangladesh's revolutionary leaders understandably had a disdain for Pakistani presidentialism.[105] Hence, the Constitution of 1972 was structured in a Westminster way – a parliamentary form of government with a titular President. However, the

103 For a general appreciation of the political history of undivided Pakistan, see: Ayesha Jalal, *Democracy and authoritarianism in South Asia A comparative and historical perspective* (Cambridge University Press, 1995) 29–65.

104 Asanga Welikala, 'The Failure of Jennings' Constitutional Experiment in Ceylon' in A Welikala (ed) *The Sri Lanka Republic at 40: Reflections on Constitutional History, Theory and Practice* (Colombo: CPA 2012).

105 Ahmed Shafiqul Huque, 'The Impact of Colonialism: Thoughts on politics and governance in Bangladesh' (1997) 28(1) Asian Affairs 15, 24–25; Gyasuddin Molla, 'Democratic Institution Building Process in Bangladesh: South Asian Experience of a New Model of a "Caretaker Government" in a Parliamentary Framework' (*Heidelberg Papers in South Asian and Comparative Politics, Working Paper 3*, Heidelberg: South Asia Institute, University of Heidelberg, 2000) 2.

system soon faced an uphill journey against the country's problematic political party system,[106] personalised leadership culture and the party leaders' unwillingness to play by accepted parliamentary rules, whether in government or opposition.[107] Merely three years into independence, Bangladesh fell to an authoritarian one-party regime, followed by the phases of Pakistani-styled military rule, competitively authoritarian party governments, and a one-party monopoly.[108]

4 A Bagful of Problems

During the War of Independence in 1971, Bangladeshi revolutionaries formed a Constituent Assembly and opted for an absolutist presidential government as a wartime arrangement.[109] After the war, the Provisional Constitution Order of 1972 (PCO)[110] replaced the wartime presidential system with a parliamentary government. Under the PCO, the Prime Minister and his Cabinet were accountable to the Constituent Assembly. President became a symbolic Head of the State. A Parliament was, however, formally absent. Under the new arrangement, the Constituent Assembly was given the status of the legislature but was assigned the sole responsibility of framing the Constitution. The President, advised by the Prime Minister, continued to exercise the legislative power of the republic. It was argued that assigning the legislative and budgetary functions to the constituent Assembly could be suicidal. It would distract the Assembly from its principal mandate of framing the Constitution. By the time the Constitution was adopted on 4 November 1972,[111] the whole body of administrative and statutory public law was built by presidential orders and executive regulations. In this way, the legislative branch started with a very low profile. Professor Salimullah Khan called it a "false start".[112] Despite the Pakistan

106 Moudud Ahmed, *Bangladesh: Era of Sheikh Mujibur Rahman* (Dhaka: University Press Ltd, 1983).

107 D Hugh Evans, 'Bangladesh: an Unsteady Democracy' in A Shastri and AJ Wilson (eds.), *The Postcolonial States of South Asia*, 69–87 (New York: Palgrave Macmillan 2001) 86.

108 Ali Riaz, *Bangladesh: a Political History since Independence* (London: I.B. Tauris, 2016).

109 The Proclamation of Independence 10 April 1971 annexed to the Constitution of Bangladesh as the Seventh Schedule <http://bdlaws.minlaw.gov.bd/upload/act/367__Schedule.pdf> accessed 27 July 2024.

110 The Provisional Constitution of Bangladesh Oder, 1972.

111 The Constitution came into force on 16 December 1972, the first anniversary of the independence of Bangladesh.

112 Salimullah Khan, 'Bangladesh began badly: Remembering the roots of the impasse', *The Daily Star*, Constitution's 50 Anniversary Supplement (4 November 2022).

military's absolute presidentialism and "internal colonial rule"[113] encouraging a preference for a parliamentary system, the legislature was ironically not given as much importance as a Westminster parliament deserved. It was perceived and treated as a deliberative talking shop and an enabling, rather than oversight, institution. Throughout the next fifty years of Bangladesh's statehood, parliaments would remain so.

The PCO worked as a guideline for the Constitution drafting committee. After one year of deliberation and drafting, the Constitution of Bangladesh came into force on 16 December 1972, the first anniversary of the country's independence from Pakistan. Election to the First Parliament was held in March 1973. However, the legislative branch would soon face many other ground realities that would work to its detriment and ensure that it does not get the attention, respect and stature expected of a typical Westminster Parliament.[114] Though this book will address those repeatedly, at this initial stage, it is worth summarising the major political, cultural and institutional problems facing Bangladesh Parliament since its inception.

4.1 *Personalisation and Radicalisation of Politics*

The most pressing challenge came from the country's illiberal, clientelist, patrimonial and undemocratic political parties that would strike at the very root of the Parliament as an institution of democratic accountability.[115] Bangladesh Awami League (from now on, AL), the political party that spearheaded the liberation war, got an absolute majority in the first Parliament. Long before the liberation war, AL became a party of its benevolent leader, Bangabandhu Sheikh Mujibur Rahman- the Father of the Nation. The constitutional design adopted after the independence allegedly involved an all-powerful executive that would empower, rather than restrain, the country's undisputed leader, *Bangabandhu*.[116] Unfortunately, it "failed to be a befitting office for the successors, including the leader himself."[117]

---

113 Nizam Ahmed (n 25) 35.

114 A survey conducted in 2012 shows that the people of Bangladesh placed Parliament beneath the armed forces when they were asked about the amount of trust they have in the institutions. See: Steinar Askvik and Ishtiaq Jamil, 'The Institutional Trust Paradox in Bangladesh' (2013) 13(4) Public Organization Review 459, 466–470.

115 M Steven Fish, 'Stronger Legislature, Stronger Democracies' (2006) 17(1) Journal of Democracy 5.

116 M Jashim Ali Chowdhury, 'Constitution-making and Unmaking in Bangladesh' *The Daily Star* (Dhaka, 4 November 2022).

117 Md Lokman Hussain, "Constituting Limits and Accountability of the Executive Power in Bangladesh", in R Hoque, and R Chowdhury (eds.) *A History of The Constitution of*

The First Parliament would survive only two years (1973–75). Within months after Bangladesh's liberation war, the *Jatya Samajtantrik Dal* (from now on, JSD) emerged as the largest opposition party and started anti-government mobilisation. While JSD was touted as a leftist political party, other smaller and more hardline revolutionary leftist parties started murder, arson, looting and mayhem in the name of waging a so-called "class struggle" against the burgeons elites. It led the country into political, economic, and social instability. The Constitution was amended to bring in emergency powers and preventive detention clauses.[118] Not stopping there, the Constitution was amended again[119] to introduce a super-powerful presidential system, reducing the Parliament and judiciary into mere subordinates of the executive branch.[120] The way the first Parliament adopted the Fourth Amendment was a self-explanatory incident. While most of the ruling party members were not allegedly in favour of the proposed amendment, they had to give way to the personal wish of their leader.[121] The decision to radically transform the system was taken outside the Parliament and imposed upon its members.[122] It led to further radicalisation and polarisation and soon, an extra-constitutional intervention in politics.[123]

4.2 *Military Interventions*

The bloody overthrow of the country's first elected government in 1975 and the prolonged period of military intervention derailed the political processes and the prospects for civilian leadership.[124] The military dictators corrupted the political parties and processes aggressively.[125] In a bid to make "politics

---

Bangladesh: the Founding, Development, and Way Ahead, 129–144 (London: Routledge 2023) 142.

118 The Constitution (Second Amendment) Act 1973.

119 Famously known as BAKSAL (*Bangladesh Krishak Sramik Awami League*), the party was placed at the helm of a soviet style socialist system.

120 The Constitution (Fourth Amendment) Act 1975.

121 Md Morshedul Islam, 'The Politics behind the Passage of Fourth Amendment to the Constitution of the People's Republic of Bangladesh and its Provisions: a Modest Analysis' (2014) 4(9) Public Policy and Administration Research 55.

122 Moudud Ahmed, *Bangladesh: Era of Sheikh Mujibur Rahman* (University Press Ltd: Dhaka 1983) 208–209, 217, 233.

123 M Jashim Ali Chowdhury (n 116).

124 Talukder Maniruzzaman, 'The Fall of the Military Dictator: 1991 Elections and the Prospect of Civilian Rule in Bangladesh' (1992) 65(2) Pacific Affairs 203, 203–206.

125 Syed Imtiaz Ahmed, 'Civilian Supremacy in Democracies with 'Fault Lines': the Role of the Parliamentary Standing Committee on Defence in Bangladesh' (2006) 13(2) Democratization 283.

difficult for the politicians",[126] a direct impact of military officers interfering in politics was the corruption of political elites and mass intrusion of the business class and civil-military bureaucracy in the political process. The military dictators enthusiastically facilitated the rise of a bourgeois elite pumped up by illegally channelling state resources into private hands.[127] With career politicians driven out of politics, Bangladesh's post-1990 party system is dominated by the business elites and musclemen holding the reign of politics. This development discouraged open and fair access for all segments of society to the political process. Unlike the UK Parliament, where mostly full-time politicians rising from different walks of life dominate the process, the post-1975 parliaments of Bangladesh were filled up with business elites and make-shift politicians with little orientation and interest in democratic accountability and legislative oversight.[128] Most parliament members in Bangladesh have criminal records and well-founded corruption allegations against them.[129] For understandable reasons, these coteries of business and power elites prefer corruption, lobbying and backdoor settlement with their party bosses rather than a fair and transparent process of political selection from the grassroots.[130]

The military rulers altered the operational rules of the public administration, too. It entrenched the stronghold of the civil-military bureaucracy over the government machinery.[131] The post-1990 parliaments and civilian governments would fail to reassert democratic control over the armed forces and the bureaucracy.

126 Syed Badrul Ahsan, "Where politics has gone fugitive ...", *The Daily Star* (Dhaka, 15 December 2013).

127 Rounaq Jahan, 'Members of Parliament in Bangladesh' (1976) 1(3) Legislative Studies Quarterly 355.

128 Quamrul Alam and Julian Teicher, 'The State of Governance in Bangladesh: the Capture of State Institutions' (2012) 35(4) South Asia: Journal of South Asian Studies 858, 864.

129 ibid 866.

130 Rounaq Jahan, 'The Parliament of Bangladesh: Representation and Accountability' (2015) 21(2) The Journal of Legislative Studies 250, 252.

131 Muhammad A Hakim, 'Bangladesh: the Beginning of the end of Militarised Politics?' (1998) 7(3) Contemporary South Asia 283; Siegfried O Wolf, 'Civil-Military Relations and Democracy in Bangladesh' (2013) Spotlight South Asia Special Issue 1, 14–30; Aurel Croissant, David Kuehn, Philip Lorenz and Paul W Chambers, *Democratization and Civilian Control in Asia* (Palgrave Macmillan: London 2013) 118–135.

4.3 *Corrupt and Dynastic Political Parties*

As Craig Baxter argued, by the time the military regimes were overthrown in 1990, the survival of parliamentary democracy in Bangladesh depended on other issues directly impinging upon the Parliament.[132]

First, by the 1990s, Bangladesh's party system had firmly dynastic and patriarchic roots. *Bangabandhu*'s daughter, Sheikh Hasina, was now placed at the helm of AL. First military ruler General Zia's widow, Begum Khaleda Zia, got a similar hold over the Bangladesh Nationalist Party (from now on, BNP). The recently dethroned military ruler Ershad held a firm grip over his political party – the *Jatya Party* (from now on, JP). After the death of Ershad in 2019, his brother GM Quader would inherit the JP leadership. The emergence of this hereditary and personalistic leadership style would ravage the potential of intra-party democracy and executive accountability to the post-1990 parliaments.

Secondly, Bangladesh's anti-liberation war party *Jamaat e Islami* (from now on, JI), banned in independent Bangladesh, was revived during Zia's reign. By the 1990s, JI became the fourth largest party, with Ershad's JP in third place. The revival of JI and its natural ease with Begum Zia's BNP would later emerge as an irreconcilable dispute between the pro-liberation and secularist AL and the pro-Pakistan and religious nationalist BNP. Also, Zia's perceived involvement in the murder of *Bangabandhu* (1975) would create a deep hatred and distrust between AL and BNP. It laid the foundation for post-1990 confrontational politics that is marked by mutual distrust among the ruling and opposition parties, suppression of intra-party democracy, intolerance of democratic opposition, resort to violent street agitation, election rigging and back door conspiracies for ascending to or clinging on the power.[133] The patriarchic and personalising tendency of politics, apparent from the country's beginning, was only aggravated during military rule. The contrasting personalities, egos and political dynasties would block the prospect of internal democracy, mass-based recruitment, and merit-based promotion system within the political parties. The lack of intra-party democracy and excessively personalised leadership within the parties would effectively nullify the Westminster convention of Ministerial Responsibility.

---

132 Craig Baxter, 'Bangladesh a Parliamentary Democracy, if They Can Keep It' (1992) 91(563) Current History 132.

133 Shafi Md Mostofa and DB Subedi, 'Rise of Competitive Authoritarianism in Bangladesh' (2020) Politics and Religion 1.

While the subsequent chapters of this book will consider each of the problems mentioned above in greater detail, a brief historical account of the parliaments in Bangladesh is necessary at this stage.

5 A Brief History of Bangladesh Parliaments

Bangladesh Awami League (AL), the party that spearheaded the liberation war, got an absolute majority in Bangladesh's first parliamentary election in March 1973. However, the *First Parliament* (1973–75) was short-lived. It was constituted in a Westminster prototype but converted to a servile legislature under the one-party presidential government two years later. The Fourth Amendment, enacted in February 1975, made the President the Head of the State and government. Parliament's role and the judiciary's independence were substantially curtailed.[134]

Within months, a brutal *coup* on 15 August 1975 left *Bangabandhu* and his family murdered. Power passed to chaotic military factions. Then, a series of coups and countercoups placed Major General Ziaur Rahman (from now on, Zia) in the presidency. Martial law was proclaimed, and it continued till 1979. Zia continued the presidential system introduced by the Fourth Amendment but allowed multiple political parties to exist. Election to the *Second Parliament* (1979–81) was held in 1979. Zia's hastily formed Bangladesh Nationalist Party (BNP) got an absolute majority over *Bangabandhu*'s party – Awami League (AL). However, the status of the Parliament under Zia's presidential government remained unclear. While Zia's cohort boosted the Second Parliament as an "Independent and Sovereign" one, its inability to make the government answerable, Zia's absolute authority to dissolve it and its consistent by-passing through presidential ordinances earned it the badge of a "rubber stamp" parliament instead.[135] The Second Parliament allegedly legitimised rather than legislated.

In 1981, Zia was assassinated by a dissident section of the army. The then Army Chief Hossain Mohammad Ershad (from now on, Ershad) seized power in 1982. After four years of absolute Martial Law, Ershad followed his predecessor Zia's footsteps and sought to civilianise his regime. As part of the process, he formed his political party – Jatya Party (JP). Election to the *Third Parliament* (1986–88) was held in 1986. The result was widely believed to be

134 The Constitution (Fourth Amendment) Act 1975.

135 Azizul Haque, 'Bangladesh in 1979: Cry for a Sovereign Parliament' (1980) 20(2) Asian Survey 217, 221–222.

rigged in favour of JP. Facing a legitimacy crisis, Ershad dissolved it in 1988 and called the election to the Fourth Parliament the same year. This time, all major political parties boycotted the election. The *Fourth Parliament* (1988–90) faced a greater legitimacy crisis. Comprised of some otherwise unknown political parties mockingly termed "Domesticated Opposition Parties", Ershad had to dissolve it in 1990. Facing the violent agitation of AL and BNP, Ershad had to quit in late 1990.

Operating under Presidents hailing from the garrison, the second, third and fourth parliaments had little to offer in democratic legislation, oversight and policy formulation.[136] Apart from being used as a legitimising tool for presidential dictates, those parliaments barely existed in policy discourse. Ordinances promulgated by the presidents massively outnumbered the laws passed by the parliaments. Therefore, the insignificant existence of the Parliament as an institution during the first two decades of independent Bangladesh (1971–1991) constituted a raison *d'etre* for the combined opposition's anti-Ershad movement in 1990. Parties struggling for Ershad's demise promised to forestall the Parliament in the centre of democratic governance. However, at that phase of Bangladesh's political history, reviving parliamentary democracy was not the country's only challenge.[137] The challenges now rested on making the parliamentary system work on the ground, which had already been shaped during the martial law era.

Despite its thorny bedrock, the parliamentary system marked a promising restart in 1991. The fifth parliamentary election, held under the supervision of a non-political caretaker government formed after the resignation of Ershad, put Begum Zia's BNP in power. The *Fifth Parliament* (1991–1995) contributed substantially to ensuring a livelier, more participatory, and more vigilant legislative discourse. In 1991, this Parliament constitutionally restored the original scheme of the parliamentary system, sixteen years after it was abolished through the 1975 amendment.[138] Another hallmark of the Fifth Parliament was a brief but meaningful show of backbench autonomy and cross-party alignment on several contentious issues.[139] However, executive dominance over the legislative process followed the old martial law days trend. Begum Zia adopted a shortcut strategy of passing legislation through Ordinances and getting approved

136 Nizam Ahmed, 'Parliamentary Committees and Parliamentary Government in Bangladesh' (2001) 10(1) Contemporary South Asia 11, 13–14.

137 Maniruzzaman (n 124).

138 Ahmed (n 136) 15.

139 Nizam Ahmed, 'Parliamentary Opposition in Bangladesh: a Study of its Role in the Fifth Parliament' (1997) 3(2) Party Politics 147.

by the House. Over one-third of the bills passed in the Fifth Parliament owed their origin to Ordinances. Most of them, including the bulk of other regular parliamentary bills, did not receive committee-stage scrutiny.[140]

Enmity would soon grow between the opposition AL and the ruling BNP. A parliamentary by-election in 1994 was widely rigged in favour of the BNP.[141] The opposition parties then started continuous boycotting of Parliament and ultimately resigned *en masse*. They were demanding the introduction of an election-time non-party caretaker government. Opposition parties argued that elections in Bangladesh could not be fair under a political party government in power. With politics taken back to the streets again, the Fifth Parliament had to be dissolved before its tenure. Uncompromising BNP went for a one-party election to the Sixth Parliament and returned with a landslide victory.[142] The stubborn opposition also increased the scale of their violent agitation. Therefore, the *Sixth Parliament* (1996) lasted only a few months. BNP gave in to the opposition's demand. Before being dissolved, the Sixth Parliament passed the Thirteenth Amendment, introducing an election-time non-party caretaker government for Bangladesh.[143]

The seventh parliamentary election was held under a caretaker government headed by a retired Chief Justice of Bangladesh. The *Seventh Parliament* (1996–2001) saw Sheikh Hasina's AL in power and hosted the largest opposition party in Bangladesh's parliamentary history.[144] Later, it also became the first Parliament to fulfil its constitutional tenure. One of the Seventh Parliament's major successes was consolidating the institution and process of the parliamentary committee system.[145] For the first time in the history of Bangladesh, bills enacted in Parliament were referred to a special bills committee for scrutiny. After establishing different oversight committees, which shadowed the government ministries, bills were regularly referred to them. It marked a new beginning.[146] However, the largest opposition party – BNP – took a

140 Ahmed (n 25) 55.

141 Golam Hossain, 'Bangladesh in 1994: Democracy at Risk' (1995) 35(2) Asian Survey 171.

142 Adeeba Aziz Khan, 'Electoral Institutions in Bangladesh: a Study of Conflicts between the Formal and the Informal' (Ph.D. Dissertation: SOAS, London 2015) 27–38, 29.

143 Craig Baxter, 'Bangladesh: Can Democracy Survive?' (1996) 95(600) Current History 182.

144 In the Seventh Parliamentary Election, the main opposition party BNP secured 116 seats against the 146 seats of the government party AL. For statistical information on elections and other related parliamentary matters, see: Nizam Ahmed, *The Bangladesh Parliament: a Data Handbook* (BRAC University Press: Dhaka 2013).

145 Muhammad Mustafizur Rahman, 'Parliament and Good Governance: a Bangladeshi Perspective' (2008) 9(1) Japanese Journal of Political Science 39, 54.

146 Ahmed (n 25) 55.

retaliatory approach of non-participation, constant boycotts and walkouts from Parliament. The ruling party, AL, was also accused of circumscribing the opposition's role in Parliament.

BNP and its coalition partner JI dominated the *Eighth Parliament* (2001–2006). Apart from several committees working to some extent, this Parliament was marred by boycotting the opposition and a virtually dysfunctional committee system. The *Ninth Parliament* (2009–2014) institutionalised the committee system to some extent. Marginalised and consistently boycotting opposition, however, remained a continuing headache. This Parliament, dominated by AL, controversially scrapped the non-party caretaker government system. BNP refused to participate in the Tenth Parliamentary election held under the AL government in 2014. AL returned to power with a landslide in the one-party election. Since then, AL has continued successfully manipulating its ally JP to play the role of a dummy opposition. Several JP MPs, however, took cabinet positions. The election to the Eleventh Parliament was held on 30 December 2018. Though the BNP did not boycott it this time, AL men captured nationwide polling stations. The election being visibly rigged, the result saw another landslide for AL. An organizationally diminished BNP got routed out. AL's ally, the JP, again emerged as the main opposition party. With an ally pretending to be an opposition, the *Tenth* (2014–2018) and *Eleventh Parliaments* (2019–2024) have been the least effective in holding the government accountable. The other major political party, BNP, being essentially doomed, the institution of Parliament remains humble to the invincible premiership of AL's omnipotent leader, Sheikh Hasina. In the *Twelfth Parliament* (January-August 2024), BNP and like-minded political parties boycotted the election. The JP fielded candidates in 286 seats, while Awami League fielded 263 candidates leaving the others to its partners. Most curiously, 26 of those were left for the JP, in yet another show of an ally posing as an opposition. The most interesting characteristic of this election, however, was not the JP's role. It was rather the AL allowing its rebel candidates to stand as independents to challenge its and its allies' official nominees. 62 of the independent candidates, 58 of them AL party members, got elected in competitive constituencies. JP got only 11 seats, nonetheless, got the status of the main opposition party. On 5 August 2024, Prime Minister Sheikh Hasina left Bangladesh in the wake of a violent student protest which started initially demanding reform in the civil service recruitment system. President dissolved the Parliament the next day, the 6 August 2024. Like the Sixth Parliament, the Twelfth also booked its place in the history as a still born parliament surviving by months.

It brings us back to the dilemma of design raised at the beginning of this chapter. What logical explanation could make sense of all these cycles of instability in Bangladesh's parliamentary system? Does it have anything to do with the design's suitability to its host?

6 The "Eastminster Deviations"

Various theories have been offered to explain the struggle of the Westminster system in the East. Among those, Harshan Kumarasingham's "Eastminster system,"[147] pointing out the East's "five societal and cultural deviations"[148] from the West, represents a thoughtful proposition. Kumarasingham argues that the cultural dimension of society and politics in the East is qualitatively different from the West. Hence, in the non-white British colonies across Asia, Africa and the Pacific, the Westminster conventions and norms would roll in ways inconceivable at the Palace of Westminster in London.[149] Kumarasingham's is perhaps the only broad-based study of postcolonial constitution-making and the evolution of executive-legislature relations in the region.[150]

Kumarasingham continues to argue that, for the non-white colonies, who were not historically and culturally habituated to democratic self-governance, the Westminster system came more from elite preference than natural internalisation.[151] They were not ready for the political responsibilities that accompany the privilege of self-governance.[152] Despite their awareness of this significant cultural mismatch, the "unrepresentative and minuscule band" of political and intellectual elites that dominated the postcolonial nation-building in the East opted to implant the system for two obvious reasons.[153] First, as previously mentioned, the political elites trained and educated in the English legal system were at natural ease with the Westminster Parliamentary System. Secondly,

---

147 Harshan Kumarasingham, 'Eastminster: the Westminster Model in British Asia' (*The Constitution Unit*, Department of Political Science, University College London, 22 September 2016).

148 ibid.

149 Harshan Kumarasingham, *A Political Legacy of the British Empire: Power and the Parliamentary System in Postcolonial India and Sri Lanka* (I.B. Tauris: London, 2013) 1–24; Harshan Kumarasingham, 'Eastminster – Decolonisation and State-Building in British Asia', in Harshan Kumarasingham (ed.), *Constitution-Making in Asia – Decolonisation and State-Building in the Aftermath of the British Empire*, 1–35 (Routledge: London, 2016) 3–4; Kumarasingham, 'Eastminster: the Westminster Model' (n 147).

150 Kevin YL Tan and Ridwanul Hoque (n 55) 5.

151 Sir Ivor Jennings quoted in Kumarasingham, 'Eastminster – Decolonisation and State-Building' (n 88) 11.

152 ibid 12.

153 Sunil Khilnani, *The Idea of India* (Penguin 2004) 34.

the postcolonial elites incorporated the unwritten Westminster conventions in their constitutions either on the assumption that they would work in the same way as in Britain or with an understanding that those could be given a frozen seventeenth-century interpretation, ignoring Britain's democratic transformation since 1688.[154] While their first assumption is difficult to conceive, the second seems more probable.

The basic principles of the Westminster system – the constitutional conventions – were amendable to easy and purposeful manipulation. While scholars like Walter Bagehot saw Westminster's convention-based unwritten political norms as its "efficient" elements,[155] the political elites in non-white British colonies found those "malleable, moveable and mendacious"[156] enough to ensure executive aggrandisement and accretion of power in the party leaders and use those in "morally inappropriate, legally suspect, and politically fanatic"[157] ways. Therefore, the resultant political systems show distinctive characteristics of their own making.

Kumarasingham has underscored at least five cultural traits that differentiate a Westminster idealised from an "Eastminster" in action: a) elite-controlled "selective dictatorship" (opposed to Westminster's elective dictatorship),[158] b) a crude majoritarianism intolerant of the opposition (opposed to the Westminster's institutionalised opposition), c) a personalised perception of public power (opposed to the Westminster's institutionalised perception), d) an interfering Presidency (opposed to the Westminster's disengaged Monarchy),[159] and e) an "abusive viceregalism" (where the Westminster's convention-based discretionary powers are asserted in nakedly un-Westminster ways).[160] The first three of the five "Eastminster deviations" are especially relevant for the Parliament of Bangladesh – the subject of this book.

The first one, the Prime Minister and Cabinet's "Selective Dictatorship," is distinguishable from Westminster's "Elective Dictatorship". In 1976, Lord Hailsham called the British government an "elective dictatorship" that is

---

154 Malagodi (n 34) 120.

155 Walter Bagehot, *The English Constitution* (2nd Edition, London: HS King 1873) 61–92.

156 Kumarasingham, 'Eastminster – Decolonisation and State-Building' (n 149) 3–4.

157 Harshan Kumarasingham, 'Written Differently: a Survey of Commonwealth Constitutional History in the Age of Decolonisation' (2018) 46(5) The Journal of Imperial and Commonwealth History 874, 892.

158 ibid 892.

159 Kumarasingham, *A Political Legacy* (n 149) 25.

160 Kumarasingham, *A Political Legacy* (n 149).

"absolute in theory but tolerable in practice".[161] Lord Hailsham pointed towards Westminster's fusion of powers and executive dominance over the Parliament. The "tolerability" of the "dictatorship" seems to arise from the UK's party system. Despite a recent surge of presidential tendencies in the Prime Ministers,[162] 10 Downing Street has never been the UK's only locus of power. The UK's theoretical "elective dictatorship" operates within a practical chain of democratic delegation. The authority is primarily delegated from the people to the majority party, then to the Cabinet, then to the inner circle of the Cabinet members, and then to the Prime Minister. Within each delegation chain, there exists a corresponding chain of accountability. The Cabinet is answerable to the majority party backbench and, to some extent, the opposition. The Prime Ministers need to retain the confidence of their inner circle of cabinet members and the party.

In Eastminster, Kumarasingham argues, Westminster's "elective dictatorship" is replaced by a "selective dictatorship" system.[163] While Westminster's Executive dominance was a lucrative idea for Asia's postcolonial constitution-makers, the intellectual and political elites that rose to the helm of power in these countries were hardly "elected." The party system and hereditary leadership chain that followed in the postcolonial states were based on class and privilege-based selection rather than election. The selective dictators in Eastminster effectively subdue their cabinet colleagues and the parties. Absolutist leaders usually establish an alternative chain of delegation and selection from the reservoir of their relatives and retainers in family lines.[164] In the process, political dynasties in the East substituted the "British Raj" with some "Asian Rajs".[165] Families such as the Nehrus (India), Bandaranaikes and Rajapakshas (Sri Lanka), Sheikhs and Zias (Bangladesh), Bhuttos and Sharifs (Pakistan), and Koiralas (Nepal) exert insurmountable power over their states and party systems.[166] The emergence of these political gods and dynasties has been facilitated by a socially resonant preference for personalist and clientelist

161 Lord Hailsham, 'Elective Dictatorship' (*The Richard Dimbleby Lecture*, 14 October 1976, BBC, London).

162 Robert Blackburn, 'The Future of UK Constitutional Law', in Xenophon Contiades and Alkmene Fotiadou (eds.), *The Routledge Handbook of Comparative Constitutional Change* 369–387 (1st Edition, Routledge 2020) 374.

163 Kumarasingham, 'Eastminster: the Westminster Model in British Asia' (n 147).

164 Kumarasingham, *A Political Legacy of the British Empire* (n 149) 19–21.

165 ibid 15–16.

166 ibid 11.

– rather than institutionalist – public power.[167] The executive's selective nature deactivates the Westminsterial chain of the democratic delegation from electors to the political parties, from parties to the Cabinet and lastly, from the Cabinet colleagues to the Prime Minister. Thus, though the systems formally operate through competitive parties, the "neo-patrimonial states"[168] in the East make sure that the rules of the game and electoral processes perpetually operate to the ruling party's benefit, often leading to single-party dominations and parochial leaderships that rely on coercion rather than consent.[169]

The second one, a democratic bipartisanship, is a critical requirement for the Westminster Parliament's efficient working.[170] Arendt Lijphart famously distinguished the majoritarian Westminster Parliamentary System from the consociational democracies of continental Europe.[171] Westminster's majoritarian system features a bare majority government in control of the executive and legislature, excluding the opposition in the policymaking process.[172] Continental Europe's consociational or consensus system, on the other hand, looks for greater power-sharing between majority and minority parties and favours multi-party coalition governments over single-party governments. The current trend, however, favours various mixed majoritarian and consociational traits.[173] Nowadays, even some of Lijphart's pure or near-pure majoritarian systems (e.g., Belgium, Netherlands, and Switzerland) are adopting some

167 Andrew Harding, 'The Rulers and the Centrality of Conventions in Malaysia's 'Eastminster' Constitution' in Harshan Kumarasingham (ed.), *Constitution-Making in Asia – Decolonisation and State-Building in the Aftermath of the British Empire* (Routledge 2016) 257, 270, 272.

168 A neo patrimonial system is built upon a clientelist society where bureaucratic and administrative mechanism of the state is suitably manipulated to endorse, legitimise and perpetuate the personalist and clientelist rule. See: Mohammad Mozahidul Islam, 'The Toxic Politics of Bangladesh: a Bipolar Competitive Neo patrimonial State?' (2013) 21(2) Asian Journal of Political Science 148, 149–51; Sabina Sharmin and AKM Jamal Uddin, 'Characteristics of Political Culture in Bangladesh: a Critical Analysis from the perspective of Political Development and Underdevelopment' (2013) 1(1–2) Jagannath University Journal of Social Sciences 74, 77.

169 Kumarasingham, *A Political Legacy of the British Empire* (n 149) 26.

170 Peter Trubowitz and Nicole Mellow, '"Going Bipartisan": Politics by Other Means' (2005) 120(3) Political Science Quarterly 433, 434 (Bipartisan adversarial competition between the government party and opposition party is a key requirement for the Westminster Parliamentary System to be operative).

171 Arend Lijphart, *Patterns of Democracy* (Yale University Press 2012).

172 Saul Rose (n 91) 444.

173 Andrew Harding, 'The 'Westminster Model' Constitution Overseas: Transplantation, Adaptation and Development in Commonwealth States' (2004) 4 Oxford University Commonwealth Law Journal 143, 147–148.

consociational traits.[174] It is due to the recognition that the pure majoritarian and exclusionist tendency of Westminster majoritarianism carries with it a significant democratic deficit.

A Westminster minority party marks an institutional opposition and a government in waiting. Though the intra-party cohesion within Parliament weakens the opposition's influence over policymaking, the very presence of opposition in a standard Westminster parliament keeps the government alert to the pulse of its backbenchers. Also, sometimes a strategic opposition, instead of an outright one, exploits the exigencies of situations that may require the government to travel beyond the party line. Hence, in not-too-much-polarised parliaments or minority governments, the opposition can exert significant pressure upon the government, which is not an insignificant consociational element within the Westminster system.

In the "Eastminster", conditions supportive of a liberal-conservative bipartisanship are largely absent. The opposition there is seen as a matter of suspicion and destabilisation. Political opposition and societal minorities have always been secondary to the majority's ambitions. While the majoritarian tendencies embedded in the Westminster Parliamentary System were highly convenient for the ruling parties in "Eastminster", Westminster's common law and constitutional convention-based protections to the democratic minority and opposition were not.[175] Therefore, the crude majoritarianism that results from a Westminster system minus its conventions makes the Eastminster systems' bipartisan competition unprincipled and destructive.

The third characteristic of "Eastminster" is the personalisation of politics and public power. Kumarasingham argues that the East's political and legal relationships are built upon a "complex of personal relationships" different from the West's norms and cultures.[176] The "Eastminster" system functions within an "authoritarian framework of constitutionalism" where the rules of law are applied to a single or dominant party's favour and towards perpetuating

174 W Elliot Bulmer, *Constituting Scotland: the Scottish National Movement and the Westminster Model* (Edinburgh University Press 2016) (W Elliot Bulmer called the process the Westminster constitutionalised.); Julian Bernauer and Adrian Vatter, 'Can't get a satisfaction with the Westminster Model? Winners, Losers and the Effects of Consensual and Direct Democratic Institutions on Satisfaction with Democracy' (2012) 51(4) European Journal of Political Research 435; Akash Paun, 'After the Age of Majority? Multi-party Governance and the Westminster Model' (2011) 49(4) Commonwealth and Comparative Politics 440.

175 Kumarasingham, 'Eastminster – Decolonisation and State-Building' (n 149) 23.

176 ibid 11.

a particular person or group of persons' power.[177] Once the personalisation of power is accepted at the top echelon of a party structure, a series of personalities or dynasties take root at different stages of the party hierarchy. In the process, the prospects of intra-party democracy and the bottom-up leadership selection process wither away. Therefore, the MPs in an "Eastminster" Parliament play a mere partisan delegate (or mercenary) role.

While, at this point, these three of Kumarasingham's "Eastminster deviations" seem to make a powerful sense of the issues and problems of Bangladesh's parliamentary system identified earlier, Chapters 3–5 of this book will examine the Parliament's relationship with the executive, judicial and democracy branches in greater details. These chapters will try to make a case as to how the three "Eastminster Deviations" shape the legislature's structural relationship with the two other constitutional branches – the government and the courts – and the people. Chapter 6 will consider whether and how the same deviations stand in the way of reform and institutionalisation of the Bangladesh parliament.

7 Existing Literature and Contribution of This Book

There are many historical, institutional, and doctrinal studies on the parliament of Bangladesh, nearly all of which are consulted and referred to in the subsequent chapters of this book. A respectable number of researchers have studied the historical development, backsliding and rebuilding of parliamentary democracy in Bangladesh during distinct phases of its political journey. Some institutional studies have shed light on various institutional aspects such as the Parliament's procedure, party system, committee system, oversight mandate and weaknesses, etc. Some authors have examined the problems and prospects of parliamentary reform, particularly in light of the development assistance the multinational donor agencies offered during the post-1990 parliamentary stage, the most notable of those being ATM Obaidullah (2019).[178]

However, the vast range of works done by Nizam Ahmed of the Public Administration Department of the University of Chittagong, Bangladesh, stands out as the most prominent. Ahmed has written extensively on Parliament's history, institution, process, performance, and reform. He has studied specific

---

177 ibid 26.

178 ATM Obaidullah, *Institutionalization of the Parliament in Bangladesh: a Study of Donor Intervention for Reorganization and Development* (Palgrave McMillan, 2019).

parliaments (1995, 1998 and 2002),[179] parliamentary elections and election-time caretaker government (2003, 2004, 2010 and 2011),[180] committee system (2001),[181] parliamentary opposition (1997),[182] parliamentary parties (1994, 2003 and 2018),[183] backbench freedom (2018),[184] parliament-democracy nexus (2011),[185] Parliament and its members' relation with the people (2012 and 2018),[186] public participation in parliamentary and Committee process (2018 and 2019),[187] parliamentary reform (1998 and 2012),[188] comparative parliament and committee systems of the South Asian region (2001),[189] and Parliament's

179 Nizam Ahmed and Shahnaz Khan, 'The Development of Parliamentary Oversight in Bangladesh: a Research Note' (1995) 20(4) Legislative Studies Quarterly 573; Ahmed (n 25); Nizam Ahmed, *The Parliament of Bangladesh* (n 1).

180 Nizam Ahmed and SZ Ahmad, 'The Parliamentary Elections in Bangladesh, October 2001' (2003) 3(22) Electoral Studies 503; Nizam Ahmed, *Non-party Caretaker Government in Bangladesh: Experience and Prospect* (University Press Limited: Dhaka 2004); N Ahmed, 'Party Politics under a non-party Caretaker Government in Bangladesh: the Fakhruddin Interregnum (2007–09)' (2010) 48(1) Commonwealth and Comparative Politics 23; Nizam Ahmed, 'Critical Elections and Democratic Consolidation: the 2008 Parliamentary Elections in Bangladesh' (2011) 19(2) Contemporary South Asia 137.

181 Ahmed (n 136).

182 Ahmed (n 139).

183 Nizam Ahmed, 'Parliamentary Politics in Bangladesh' (1994) 32(3) Journal of Commonwealth and Comparative Politics 364; Nizam Ahmed, 'From Monopoly to Competition: Party Politics in the Bangladesh Parliament (1973–2001)' (2003) 76(1) Pacific Affairs 55; Nizam Ahmed, 'From Marginal to Minimal Legislature: Development of Parliament in Bangladesh (1991–2018)' (2018) South Asia Journal 120.

184 N Ahmed, 'Including the Excluded: Government Backbenchers and Opposition in the Parliamentary Process in Bangladesh' in Nizam Ahmed (ed.), *Inclusive Governance in South Asia: Parliament, Judiciary and Civil Service* (Palgrave McMillan 2018) 39–60.

185 Nizam Ahmed, 'Parliament and Democratic Consolidation in Bangladesh' (2011) 26(2) Australasian Parliamentary Review 53.

186 Nizam Ahmed, 'Parliament and Citizens in Asia: the Bangladesh Case' (2012) 18(3–4) The Journal of Legislative Studies 463; Nizam Ahmed, 'Parliament and Poverty Reduction in Bangladesh: Role of the MP' (2018) 25(1–2) South Asian Survey 163.

187 Nizam Ahmed, 'Parliament, Public Engagement and Legislation in Bangladesh: a case study of Domestic Violence Act of 2010' (2018) 24(4) The Journal of Legislative Studies 431; Nizam Ahmed and Sadik Hasan, 'Does Public Engagement Matter? Parliament, Public Engagement and the Budget Process in Bangladesh' (2019) 34(1) Australasian Parliamentary Review 28.

188 Nizam Ahmed, 'Reforming the Parliament in Bangladesh: Structural Constraints and Political Dilemmas' (1998) 36(1) Commonwealth and Comparative Politics 68; Nizam Ahmed, *Aiding the Parliament of Bangladesh: Experience and Prospect* (University Press Limited: Dhaka 2012).

189 Nizam Ahmed, 'Development and Working of Parliaments in South Asia' (2001) 9(1) Asian Journal of Political Science 18.

role in executive accountability (1995, 1996 and 2006).[190] While Ahmed classified the Bangladesh Parliament as a "marginal" one in his 2002 book,[191] two of his recent works (2018[192] and 2020[193]) indicate that it might have been reduced to a "minimal" one now.

Taiabur Rahman's comparative study of the Indian, Sri Lankan and Bangladeshi committee systems (2008)[194] argues that the institutional culture of clientelist and authoritarian leadership has hampered the accountability mandate of the parliamentary committees in the three jurisdictions, irrespective of whether the system is parliamentary or presidential.[195] While Rahman's "cultural institutionalism" has resounding relevance to the *Eastminster* perspective, the study was structurally limited to the parliamentary committees. Rahman did not frame his thesis within a postcolonial lens either.

Against these, this book contributes to Bangladesh's parliamentary literature in multiple ways.

First, it is a holistic institutional study of the history, making, functioning, weaknesses, and potentials of the Bangladesh Parliament framed within a quadrupole constitutional framework involving the executive, legislative, judicial, and democratic actors. It utilises Harshan Kumarasingham's "Eastminster" analogy to examine the institutional and operational logic of Bangladesh's "Westminster" parliament. Kumarasingham initially studied the Indian and Sri Lankan prime ministers' relationships with their cabinet colleagues and the working of cabinet government *vis-à-vis* the Heads of the States there. The study explained how the formal constitutional institutions of those countries were largely conditioned by informal and cultural value systems that spearheaded the personalisation of powers.[196] The thesis was later tested in various South and Southeast Asian states in an edited volume published in 2016.[197] It, however, has not been tested in Bangladesh yet. It is expected that the

190 Ahmed and Khan (n 179); N Ahmed and A Ahmed, 'The Quest for Accountability: Parliament and Public Administration in Bangladesh' (1996) 18(1) Asian Journal of Public Administration 70; Nizam Ahmed, *Limits of Parliamentary Control: Public Spending in Bangladesh* (University Press Limited: Dhaka 2006).

191 Ahmed, *The Parliament of Bangladesh* (n 1) 1–24.

192 Ahmed, 'From Marginal to Minimal' (n 183).

193 Nizam Ahmed, *Parliaments in South Asia India, Pakistan and Bangladesh* (Routledge 2020) 176–198.

194 Taiabur Rahman, *Parliamentary Control and Government Accountability in South Asia, A comparative analysis of Bangladesh, India and Sri Lanka* (Routledge 2008).

195 ibid 67–92.

196 Kumarasingham, *A Political Legacy* (n 149).

197 H Kumarasingham (ed.), *Viceregalism: the Crown as Head of State in Political Crises in the Postwar Commonwealth* (Palgrave Macmillan, 2020).

"Eastminster" logic framed within the landscape of South Asia's postcolonial constitutionalism would invite further interest in the study of Bangladesh *Jatya Sangsad* through a wider prism of postcolonial studies – which has not been attempted in Bangladesh to date.

Secondly, Bangladesh's parliamentary research is missing a legal and constitutional approach. So far, no legal academic in Bangladesh has seriously researched the Parliament. Bangladesh's legal academia has remained vastly busy with the executive and judicial branches.[198] This book addresses the gap by bringing in the much-needed constitutional and legal perspective in studying Bangladesh's legislative branch. It studies the constitutional position and contribution of the Bangladesh Parliament within a constitutional separation of powers and checks and balances framework involving the other constitutional branches – the executive and judiciary and the people – the ultimate constitutional sovereign of the country. The relationship between Bangladesh's legislative and judicial branches has been debated for a considerable time. While concerns have been frequently raised about the judiciary's intrusion into Parliament's terrains and *vice-versa*,[199] there has not been any attempt to examine how Bangladesh's judicial review system helps the two institutions relate or unrelate each other. This book addresses the relationship, questions the "antagonistic nature" of Bangladesh's judicial review system and proposes a "dialogic approach" to judicial review.

Thirdly, the book considers the problems and prospects of Bangladesh's parliamentary reform from a novel historical-institutional lens. Bangladesh's public administration and political science scholars have generally blamed "the lack of political will" in bringing in reforms and then wrapped up by calling

198 During the formulating years of the Republic, the constitutional researchers of Bangladesh focused on the Executive branch. Since the first two decades of Bangladesh's statehood (1971–1990) is marked by frequent restlessness in the epicentres of political powers, issues like presidentialism, controlled democracy, place and role of the military in the power structure and political party system were at the centre of the legal academic discourse. During the second and ongoing phase of Bangladesh's constitutional history (1991-present), legal intellectuals have turned eye towards two other constitutional institutions – the judiciary and the election commission. Among the most researched topic in these areas are judicial review, separation of judicial powers from the executive, judicial independence, judicial activism, politicization of judiciary and judicialization of politics. The legal scholars also paid attention to the electoral system of Bangladesh which was largely driven by the mid-1990s' political movement and constitutional amendment for non-party caretaker government.

199 M Jashim Ali Chowdhury, 'Judicial Review of "Internal Parliamentary Proceedings": the Dialogic and Non-Dialogic Approaches' (2021) 6(1) Comparative Constitutional Law and Administrative Law Journal 28.

for political mobilisation. What is missing in this discourse is an attempt to explain and make sense of why the modest reforms attempted from time to time have failed to yield their expected outcomes and how the reform initiatives themselves were ill-conceived and ill-implemented. Missing any reflection on why reforms attempted in the past did not uplift the institutional position of the Parliament and what could explain this cycle of cosmetic reform and failure, the existing literature on parliamentary reform in Bangladesh remains unhelpful. This book addresses the gap by considering a range of historical and institutional parliamentary reform theories as plausible yardsticks for understanding how politics play out the reforms.

Methodologically, this book adopts a comparative approach. While insights from other parliaments, such as the US Congress and the Indian Parliament, have been reflected in certain places, various chapters of this book consistently compared the Bangladesh Parliament's rules, conventions, and precedents with those of the British Parliament. The author has spent many hours observing the Westminster and Bangladesh parliaments at work. It was important because the book primarily investigates how the working of Bangladesh's "Westminster"-styled parliament is affected by its "Eastminster" traits.

8 Structure of the Book

This introductory Chapter dealing with the Parliament's constitutional design (Chapter 1) is followed by an introduction to the organisation, powers, and processes of the Bangladesh Parliament (Chapter 2). The next three chapters examine the Parliament's horizontal relationship with the Executive (Chapter 3) and Judicial branches (Chapter 4) and its vertical relationship with its electorate – the People (Chapter 5).

Chapter 3 (*A Subdued Legislature*) assesses the Bangladesh Parliament's capability to enforce the collective and individual ministerial responsibilities, the potentials and hurdles of parliamentary procedure in influencing and shaping the government's legislative proposals, the strengths and weaknesses of the parliamentary committees in scrutinising the government, and the nature and quality of opposition and backbench participation in the parliamentary processes. Initially, the Chapter considers the modern developments in the *Ministerial Responsibility Convention* and its contemporary critiques in the UK. It then tests the doctrine's utility in Bangladesh's parliamentary practices. Next, the Chapter evaluates the legislative procedure of the Bangladesh Parliament and examines how the parliamentary opposition could use the parliamentary procedures in politics sensitive ways – the "*Politics of Procedure*"[200] – to influence the government's legislative programs. The Chapter then deals with the role of parliamentary committees in enforcing executive accountability. This part evaluates whether Bangladesh's parliamentary committees *distribute or trade*[201] constituency benefits for the MPs or supply quality *information, scrutiny, and expertise*[202] to the House. This part also considers whether the *multi-party or coalition governments*[203] significantly empower the committees and how *partisan cartelisation*[204] of the committees impacts their scrutiny power. The next section of the chapter examines how Bangladesh's political party system fares within Anthony King's *party modes of executive-legislature relation*[205] and Edmund Burke's *delegate and trustee modes of representation.*[206] King's theory is applied to evaluate Bangladesh's inter-party and intra-party parliamentary behaviour, and Burke's theory is utilised to examine the nature of Bangladeshi MPs' representative functions.

Chapter 4 considers the Parliament's relationship with the judiciary, particularly the Supreme Court of Bangladesh (SCB). Bangladesh is a constitutional supremacy where the written rules and principles of the Constitution limit the legislative and judicial branches. Under the Constitution, the legislature and judiciary are locked in a chain of mutual deference (comity) and accountability. However, the lived reality of Bangladesh's parliament-judiciary relationship

---

200 Robert Blackburn, 'The Politics of Parliamentary Procedure at Westminster' (2017) The Journal of International and Comparative Law 279; Robert Blackburn, 'The Politics of Parliamentary Procedure at Westminster Revisited' in TBC. (ed.), TBC: Volume of Essays in honour of Emeritus Professor Kostas Mavrias (Sakkoulas 2020). Robert Blackburn, 'The Nature and Importance of Parliamentary Procedure' in Robert Blackburn, Arianna Carminati and Lorenzo Spadacini (eds.), *Parliament as the Cornerstone of Democracy: Studies on the UK and Italian Parliaments in commemoration of Magna Carta's 800th Anniversary* (Kings College London, University of Brescia and Magna Carta 800th Anniversary Commemoration Committee 2018).

201 Kenneth A Shepsle and BR Weingast 'Political Preferences for the Pork Barrel: a Generalization' (1981) 25 American Journal of Political Science 96.

202 Keith Krehbiel, *Information and Legislative Organization* (University of Michigan Press 1991).

203 Lanny W Martin and Georg Vanberg, *Parliaments and Coalitions: the Role of Legislative Institutions in Multiparty Governance* (Oxford University Press 2011).

204 Gary W Cox and Mathew D McCubbins, *Legislative Leviathan: Party Government in the House* (Cambridge University Press 2007).

205 Anthony King, 'Modes of Executive-Legislative Relations: Great Britain, France and West Germany' in Philp Norton (ed.), *Legislatures* (Oxford University Press 1990) 186–207; John P Mackintosh, *The British Cabinet* (Stevens and Sons Ltd: London 1977).

206 Edmund Burke, *Speech to the Electors of Bristol,* 3 November 1774 <https://press-pubs.uchicago.edu/founders/documents/v1ch13s7.html> accessed 28 July 2024.

suggests that the Parliament's role in ensuring *judicial accountability* and the judiciary's role in keeping the Parliament within its constitutional boundaries are shaped by the antagonistic tune of the country's *Strong Form of Judicial Review.*[207] In this context, the two constitutional branches often transgress each other's boundaries. The last part of the Chapter then considers whether a *Democratic Dialogue Model of Judicial Review* [208] could be an alternative route to explore.

Chapter 5 evaluates the Parliament and its members' vertical and political accountability[209] to their electorate – the people. It examines the Bangladesh Parliament's representational legitimacy, its continued accountability to the people and public support for the institution. Analysing Bangladesh's struggle with electoral fairness, parliament's detachment from its electorates, the meagre level of public participation in parliamentary processes, and the MPs' clientelist relationship with their constituents, contribute to the Parliament's declined institutional strength vis-à-vis the executive and judiciary.

Chapter 6 identifies the political and attitudinal problems that resist the Bangladesh Parliament's institutionalisation. This chapter offers a *history*,[210]

207 Mark Tushnet, 'New Forms of Judicial Review and the Persistence of Rights- and Democracy-based Worries' (2003) 38 Wake Forest Law Review 813; Mark Tushnet, *Weak Courts, Strong Rights* (Princeton University Press 2008).

208 Peter Hogg and Allison Bushell, 'The Charter Dialogue Between Courts and Legislatures (Or perhaps The Charter of Rights isn't such a bad thing after all)' (1997) 35 Osgoode Hall Law Journal 75; Philip Norton, 'A Democratic Dialogue? Parliament and Human Rights in the United Kingdom' (2013) 21(2) Asia Pacific Law Review 141; Catherine A Fraser, 'Constitutional Dialogues between Courts and Legislatures: Can We Talk?' (2005) 14(3) Forum Constitutionnel 7; Alison L Young, *Democratic Dialogue and The Constitution* (Oxford University Press 2017) 180; TRS Allan, 'Constitutional Dialogue and The Justification of Judicial Review' (2003) 23(4) Oxford Journal of Legal Studies 563, 582–584; Tom R Hickman, 'Constitutional Dialogue, Constitutional Theories and the Human Rights Act 1998' (2005) Public Law 306.

209 Mark Bowens, 'Two Concepts of Accountability: Accountability as a Virtue and as a Mechanism' (2010) 33(5) West European Politics 946; Mark Bennister and Phil Larkin, 'Accountability in Parliament' in Cristina Leston-Bandeira and Louise Thompson (eds.), *Exploring The Parliament* (Oxford 2018); GA O'Donell, 'Delegative Democracy' (1994) 5(1) Journal of Democracy 55; Staffan I Lindberg, 'Accountability: the Core Concept and its Subtypes' (2013) 79(2) International Review of Administrative Sciences 202; JM Ackerman, 'Co-governance for Accountability: Beyond 'Exit' and 'Voice'' (2004) 32(3) World Development 447; A Fung, and E Wright, 'Deepening Democracy Innovations in Empowered Participatory Governance,' (1998) 26(4) Politics and Society 15.

210 Jürgen Deeg, 'Organizational Discontinuity: Integrating Evolutionary and Revolutionary Change Theories' 2009 20(2) Management Revue 190.

attitude[211] and *institution*[212]-sensitive explanation of why major reform initiatives attempted in distinct phases of Bangladesh's political history have failed to uplift the institutional stature of the Parliament. It shows that reforms fail in Bangladesh either because they are either ill-conceived, short-term interest driven, or they do not align with the regime's personal, temporal, and power-perpetuating interests. Standing at the root of the problems are Bangladesh's dynastic, patriarchal and clientelist party system, the absolutist Monarchic authority of the Prime Ministers and party leaders over their respective parties and the resultant lack of participatory political processes.

Chapter 7 revisits the issues identified in chapters 1–6 and tries to make an overall argument as to how Bangladesh's three distinctive "*Eastminster Traits*" – "selective dictatorship" within the government; patriarchal, dynastic and clientelist political selection within the political parties; and an illiberal antagonistic two-party system – control the Parliament's performance and contribution within the country's constitutional system. The chapter predicts that Bangladesh's competitively parochial political parties and their leaders will continue to resist the drastic realignment of the *status quo*. Therefore, the future of parliamentarism in Bangladesh seems to hinge on some moderate and incrementally bound reforms within the procedural realm of parliamentary activities that could enhance its voice and profile as an accountability institution. First, the Parliament and its committees need to reinvigorate their public relations, participation, and trust-building activities. Continuous engagement with the citizens, civil society and other "fourth branch" organisations should build its independent public support base. Parliament's own public support base should gradually challenge the dynastic political parties' exclusive claim to democratic representation and pave the way for the Parliament's institutional assertiveness. Secondly, the parliamentary reform agenda may emphasise some moderate demands such as the demands for the Speakers to renounce their party affiliations and the amendment of the Constitution's widely framed anti-defection clause that chokes the backbench voices in Parliament. These procedural and relatively moderate changes may help the Parliament gradually reassert its standing as an independent constitutional organ. Thirdly, a strategic contribution by the Supreme Court could be to shun its current policy of distancing itself from the legislature and engage

---

211 Philip Norton, 'Reforming Parliament in the United Kingdom: the Report of the Commission to Strengthen Parliament' (2000) 6(3) The Journal of Legislative Studies 1.

212 Alexandra Kelso, *Parliamentary Reform at Westminster* (Manchester University Press 2013); Peter Dorey and Alexandra Kelso, *House of Lords Reform Since 1911 Must the Lords Go?* (Palgrave McMillan 2011).

with the Parliament in a spirit of "democratic dialogue". This should further strengthen the parliament's standing as a co-equal constitutional branch *vis-à-vis* the executive and judiciary. Lastly, if Bangladesh's parliamentary system continues to survive notwithstanding its vulnerability to recurring military or extra-constitutional interventions, the suggested incrementalism should prepare grounds for more fundamental reforms once the current equilibrium of the political party system breaks apart and a realignment arrives.

CHAPTER 2

Organisation, Position and Powers

1 Introduction

The Parliament of Bangladesh is officially known as The *Jatya Sangsad* (House of the Nation). It is a unicameral legislature established under Article 65 of the Constitution of the People's Republic of Bangladesh. The Parliament is entrusted with legislative powers, constitutional amendment powers, financial and budgetary powers, and the powers of democratic oversight over the government. Parliament elects, removes, and impeaches the President, a ceremonial head of the State. Executive powers of the State are entrusted to the Prime Minister. The Prime Minister and the Cabinet are drawn from the majority parliamentary party. The government remains in power so long as it bears the confidence of Parliament. As Bangladesh recognises constitutional supremacy, parliamentary laws remain subject to judicial review. The Supreme Court of Bangladesh is considered the guardian of the written Constitution and, hence, has the power of judicial review over executive and legislative actions. The Supreme Court has expanded its judicial review power even on the constitutional amendments. Parliament, in turn, regulates the laws and qualifications of the appointees to the Supreme Court. Recently, there has been substantial debate regarding the parliamentary removal and impeachment of Supreme Court judges, though the original Constitution of 1972 gave the legislature such powers. Parliament is officially elected by the people through a universal adult franchise.

Fairness and processes of the elections, however, have always been questionable. Added to the legitimacy question over the Parliament's representative claim is a concern about how the MP candidates are selected at the party level. Bangladesh's political parties are internally undemocratic and clientelist. The Parliament's political selection process is, therefore, hardly democratic, and it directly impacts the legislature's relationship with its electorate. The Parliament is not well connected with the people. As the peoples' purported representatives, its members do not engage them constructively. Partisan iron grip over the MPs and their parliamentary businesses negatively impacts the legislature's law-making, budgetary and scrutiny functions. In any standard appraisal of the institution, Bangladesh Parliament appears to have mostly

 | DOI:10.1163/9789004720831_003

abdicated its core functions to the convenience of the party governments and, in the process, lost the 'dignity and morale' in the eyes of the people.[1]

2 Composition of the Parliament

Article 65 of the Constitution has fixed the number of directly elected Members of Parliament (the MPs) at three hundred. In addition, Parliament today includes fifty women MPs indirectly elected by the three hundred MPs.[2] Known as the 'reserved seat' MPs, these seats are proportionally distributed among the parties represented in the Parliament. Before introducing the proportional distribution system in 2004,[3] the majority parties usually took all the reserved seats unless they agreed to share some with coalition or strategic partners.

While women's organisations have generally welcomed the reservation of women member seats, they have raised concern over the trend of ad-hoc changes made in consecutive constitutional amendments.[4] It has also been argued that apart from consolidating the numerical majority of the ruling parties,[5] reserved seat MPs have played a negligible role in the parliamentary

1 Abdullah Al Faruque, 'Role of Parliament in Ensuring Democratic Accountability in Bangladesh: Setting the Agenda for a Strengthened Parliamentary System' in M Rafiqul Islam and Muhammad Ekramul Haque (eds.) *The Constitutional Law of Bangladesh: Progression and Transformation at its 50th Anniversary,* 121–137 (Singapore: Springer Nature 2023) 123.

2 The Constitution of the Peoples Republic of Bangladesh 1972, art. 65(3) <http://bdlaws.minlaw.gov.bd/act-367.html> accessed 30 July 2024. The manner and form of the indirect election were then regulated by the Representation of People (Seats for Women Members) Order 1973.

3 Presently, the Parliament (Reserved Women Seats) Election Act 2004 provides for proportional distribution of reserved seats among the parliamentary parties.

4 In 1972, the original Article 65(3) reserved fifteen women's seats for ten years beginning in 1973. In 1978, a military ruler increased the number of seats to thirty, and the reservation was extended for another ten years. It was later made part of the Constitution through the Constitution (Fifth Amendment) Act 1979. The Constitution (Tenth Amendment) Act of 1990 extended the reservation period for another ten years. The Constitution (Fourteenth Amendment) Act of 2004 once again extended the reservation by another ten years. This time, however, the number of seats was increased to forty-five. The Constitution (Fifteenth Amendment) Act of 2011 extended the reservation for another ten years. It, however, raised the number of reserved seats to fifty. Lastly, the Constitution (Seventeenth Amendment) Act of 2018 extended the reservation for another twenty-five years.

5 In 1991, for example, Bangladesh Nationalist Party (BNP) won 140 seats out of three hundred. Falling eleven seats short of a majority, BNP had to rely on Jamaat e Islami (JI), which won 18 seats. Once the government was formed, it took twenty-eight reserved seats and gave two seats to JI. Through this process, BNP secured the required majority, and

process.[6] While the framers of the Constitution adopted the reservation policy as a temporary arrangement, the successive extensions of its tenure without any serious commitment to women's empowerment in the national political discourse did not escape criticism.[7] A Bench of the High Court Division of the Supreme Court of Bangladesh (HCD) questioned the reservation policy in *Shamima Sultana Seema v Bangladesh*.[8] Though the case was related to reserved women seats in City Corporations, the petitioner also questioned the parliamentary reservation system.[9] The Court accordingly made some *obiter* comments on the doubtful constitutionality of the reservation in Parliament.[10] Calls for direct elections to the women's reserved seats have intensified since then.[11]

2.1 *Parliamentary Election Process*

Article 65 of the Constitution does not regulate the manner of parliamentary elections. It simply states that MPs shall be elected "in accordance with law" and "from single territorial constituencies ... by direct election."[12] Article 124 of the Constitution authorises the Parliament to pass laws determining constituencies, electoral rolls, and the process, manner, etc., of elections. The principal

---

its government no longer relied on the support of JI. Similarly, in 1996, Awami League (AL) won 146 seats out of three hundred. Falling five seats short of a majority, AL had to rely on Jatya Party (JP), who had thirty-two seats. Once the AL formed the government, they took twenty-seven reserved seats and left three seats for JP. It, however, gave AL the required majority, and its government no longer required the support of JP. For statistical data on various election results in Bangladesh, see Nizam Ahmed, 'Bangladesh' in Dieter Nohlen, Florian Grotz and Christof Hartmann (eds.) Elections in Asia and the Pacific: a Data Handbook, Volume I (OUP 2001), 535–538.

6 Nizam Ahmed and Sadik Hasan, 'Alangkar or Ahangkar? Reserved-Seat Women Members in the Bangladesh Parliament' in Nizam Ahmed (ed.) Women in Governing Institutions in South Asia, Parliament, Civil Service and Local Government (Springer 2018) 17–39; Pranab Kumar Panday, 'Representation without Participation: Quotas for Women in Bangladesh' (2008) 29(4) International Political Science Review 489; Jannatul Ferdous, 'Representation of Women in Parliament of Bangladesh: Is it Hopeful?' (2019) 6(2) Journal of Governance and Public Policy 110.

7 SM Masum Billah, 'Reserved seats for women, Constitutionality and human rights issues' *The Daily Star*, Law and Our Rights (Dhaka, 7 February 2009).

8 *Shamima Sultana Seema* v. *Bangladesh* 57 DLR (2005) 201.

9 ibid, para 50.

10 ibid, para 58 (per ABM Khairul Haque J).

11 Mahbuba Sultana, 'Reserved Seats and Women's Representation in Bangladesh Parliament: Gaps between Expectations and Reality' (2018) 3(1) Premier Critical Perspective 41.

12 Constitution (n 2), art. 65(1).

election law of Bangladesh – the Representation of the Peoples' Order 1972 (the RPO) – was issued under Article 124 and has been amended several times.

Articles 72 and 123 of the Constitution provide some guidance about the timing of the parliamentary general election. As per Article 123(3), a general election to the Parliament is held within ninety days before the expiry of the tenure of a sitting Parliament. If the President dissolves the Parliament before the end of its tenure, election to the next Parliament is held within ninety days after such dissolution. Article 72(3) states that a parliament's tenure is five years from its first sitting after a general election. If the Republic is at war, the Parliament's tenure may be extended up to six months after the termination of the war. A limitation, however, is that the Parliament's tenure cannot be extended by more than one year at a time.[13] In a war situation, the President may call a dissolved Parliament back into session.[14] Though it has not yet been applied, this provision could lead to the controversial intervention of the President in the electoral process. Recalling an already dissolved Parliament would postpone the election to the next Parliament. As per Article 48(3) of the Constitution, the President may act only following the advice of the Prime Minister. Hence, the President's decision to recall a dissolved Parliament could be the decision of the outgoing Prime Minister, who, as per Article 57(3) of the Constitution, might be waiting for his successor to be elected in the ensuing election.

Besides the general parliamentary elections, mid-term vacancies are filled through by-elections to the concerned constituencies. Article 123(4) of the Constitution provides that a by-election to fill the vacancy in any seat will be held within ninety days of its official notification. In some cases, the Chief Election Commissioner (CEC) may extend that deadline by another ninety days if they think the election could not be held within the first ninety-day period due to an "Act of God".

2.1.1 Qualification of the MP Candidates

As per Article 66(1) of the Constitution, any citizen of Bangladesh eligible to be registered in the Electoral Roll and who has attained twenty-five years of age may be a candidate in parliamentary elections. Though educational background or personal disposition are not listed as qualifications, there have been growing calls for better information sharing about the candidates' criminal, financial and educational records. This movement drew inspiration from an

13 ibid art 72(3).

14 ibid art 72(4).

Indian Supreme Court decision requiring the candidates to supply information about their criminal records.[15] The Bangladesh Supreme Court later made the disclosure of such information compulsory.[16]

2.1.2 Disqualification of the Candidates and Elected MPs

As per Article 66(2) of the Constitution, a person shall be disqualified from serving, or to continue, as a Member of Parliament if they are declared a person of unsound mind, an insolvent, a dual citizen of another country, or is convicted of a criminal offence involving "moral turpitude", sentenced to imprisonment for at least two years for the offence and five years have not passed since he served a sentence. Article 66(2)(f) provides that any person holding any office of profit in the service of the Republic will be disqualified from being an MP. The Constitution (Fifteenth Amendment) Act of 2011 added that persons convicted under the Bangladesh Collaborators (Special Tribunals) Order, 1972, will also be disqualified as MPs.

Apart from the constitutional disqualifications in Article 66(2), Article 12(1) of the RPO contains additional statutory grounds for disqualifications, including certain restrictions on civil and military staff, leaders of foreign fund-receiving NGOs and candidates switching party affiliations. Article 12 also disqualifies those who defaulted on bank loans, utility bills, etc. These disqualifications were introduced during the late 1990s and early 2000s in response to various public mobilisations for fairer politics and cleaner candidatures.[17]

2.1.3 Vacation of Seats by the Sitting MPs

Parliamentary seats may be vacated by resignations or the dissolution of Parliament. MPs may also vacate their seats when any disqualifications mentioned in Article 66(2) of the Constitution arise. Article 67(1) provides some additional grounds for vacation. Three of those deserve mention. First, an MP-elect will vacate their seat if they fail to take an oath of office within ninety days of a newly elected Parliament's first meeting. Second, an MP will lose their seat if they remain absent from Parliament without the Speaker's leave for ninety consecutive sitting days. Third, a seat will be vacated if an MP resigns from or votes against their political party or abstains from voting by disregarding the party instruction under Article 70(1).

---

15 *Union of India v Association for Democratic Reforms* (2002) 3 SCR 294.

16 *Abdul Momen Chowdhury and* others *v Bangladesh and* others 2005, 34 CLC (HCD); *Md Abu Safa v Abdul Momen Chowdhury and others* V ADC (2008) 64.

17 Abu Sufian Shamrat, 'Electoral Reform in Bangladesh (1972–2014): an Assessment' (*South Asia Journal Blog*, 23 October 2016).

2.2 *The Speaker and Deputy Speaker*

As per Article 74(1) of the Constitution, the Speaker and Deputy Speaker are elected at the first sitting of Parliament after every general election. The Speaker election process is governed by Rules 8–10 of the Parliamentary Rules of Procedure (the RoP). Though the RoP requires individual MPs to propose other colleagues for the post, the nomination is usually pre-determined along partisan lines. The practice is that the majority party proposes its preferred MPs as the Speaker and Deputy Speaker. Knowing that their members cannot win, the opposition parties usually do not propose their candidates for the post. Formal voting then follows, and the Speaker and Deputy Speaker are elected. Article 74(3) of the Constitution permits the Deputy Speaker to assume the role in the absence of the Speaker. The RoP requires the Speaker to nominate, at the commencement of each parliamentary session, a panel of five such MPs who would preside over the House in order of precedence if both the Speaker and Deputy Speaker are unavailable.[18]

2.2.1 Powers and Functions of the Speaker

As per Article 148(2) of the Constitution, the Speaker administers the oath to Members of Parliament. The RoP has detailed the powers and functions of the Speaker. When a Speaker is reelected as a member of a new Parliament, Rule 5(3) of the RoP allows them to take an oath to themselves first and then administer it to newly elected MPs.[19] Apart from administering the oath, the Speaker can make MPs behave orderly. They may punish grossly disorderly behaviour by ordering an MP to withdraw immediately and for the rest of a sitting day from the House.[20] In extreme cases, they may name an MP who obstructs the business of the House by persistently and willfully disregarding the Chair's authority or abusing the House's rules and suspend that MP for the duration of a whole session after a motion being passed in the floor.[21]

Subject to the President calling and proroguing the Parliament, the day-to-day sitting and adjournment of parliamentary business is directed at the discretion of the Speaker.[22] The Speaker, however, may constitute a Business Advisory Committee (BAC),[23] which, if constituted, would include the Prime Minister, the Leader of the Opposition, and the Chief Whips of the majority and

18 The Rules of Procedure (RoP) of Bangladesh Jatya Sangsad 1973, rule 12.
19 *Fazlur Rahman v Md Abdul Hamid and Ors* (2004) 56 DLR (HCD) 448.
20 RoP (n 18) r. 15.
21 ibid r 16.
22 ibid, rr 20, 22, 23.
23 ibid r 219.

opposition parties. This high-powered Committee could potentially contribute to more democratic management of the parliamentary business. However, absent any mandatory language in the RoP, the composition and conduct of such Committee remain the Speaker's privilege. So far, the BAC has remained an underutilised tool. The BAC's weaknesses apart, several other rules require the Speaker to consult the Prime Minister in setting the parliamentary agenda.[24] For example, while private member businesses are scheduled for Thursdays, the Speaker, in consultation with the Prime Minister, who is also the Leader of the House, may direct such business on any other day.[25]

It is expected that once elected, the Speaker sets aside their partisan loyalty. However, Bangladeshi Speakers' partisan tendencies have been a constant source of frustration for opposition parties in Bangladesh.[26] The frustration was reflected in an *obiter* comment from a Supreme Court judge in *Anwar Hossain Monju v Bangladesh*[27] where ABM Khairul Haque J urged Speakers "to risk their wooden chair to uphold the dignity of their office by beginning completely impartial and remain independent and aloof of browbeating of their party bosses in conducting the proceedings of the House."[28]

3 Parliament's Relation with Other State Organs

Bangladesh Parliament's relationship with the executive branch mirrors the British parliamentary system. However, the judicial branch, particularly the Supreme Court, is separated from the legislative and executive branches. Hence, despite being modelled in a Westminster set-up, the American doctrine of Separation of Power and Checks and Balances is seen as a 'Basic Structure' of the Constitution,[29] and the judiciary uses it to seek a higher level of detachment, autonomy and independence from the representative and executive branches.[30] Particularly, the Supreme Court's strong desire to avoid any sort of

24 ibid rr 25, 26, 30.

25 ibid, r 25.

26 Jalal Firoj, 'Forty Years of Bangladesh Parliament: Trends, Achievements and Challenges' (2013) 58(1) Journal of the Asiatic Society of Bangladesh (Humanities) 83, 98–100.

27 *Anwar Hossain Monju v Bangladesh* 16 *BLT* (HCD) 86.

28 ibid 97.

29 M Jashim Ali Chowdhury, *An Introduction to the Constitutional Law of Bangladesh* (Chittagong: Book Zone Publications, 3rd edition, 2016) 252–257.

30 Ali Mashraf and Tahseen Lubaba, 'Public Interest Litigation and the Constitution of Bangladesh: Past, Present, and Future' in M Rafiqul Islam and Muhammad Ekramul Haque (eds.) *The Constitutional Law of Bangladesh: Progression and Transformation at its 50th Anniversary*, 401–420 (Singapore: Springer Nature 2023).

parliamentary engagement in the judicial accountability process[31] has often led to antagonism and mutual distrust between the two organs.[32]

3.1 *Parliament and the Government*

The President invites the Leader of the parliamentary majority party to be the Prime Minister and form a government.[33] The PM and Cabinet have no fixed term or tenure, nor do they hold their office at the pleasure of the President. The Prime Minister serves so long as they hold the confidence of a majority of MPs.[34] Suppose a motion of no confidence is passed in the Parliament. In that case, the Prime Minister has to resign, and the President must invite another MP, who might have the confidence of the majority, to form the government. If no such MP is found, the President shall dissolve the Parliament. The Prime Minister would continue in office until the next election when a successor enters the office.[35]

Bangladesh's Prime Minister (PM) retains the Leader of the House position. Considering the government's tight grip over parliamentary businesses, the Prime Minister's House leadership position, atop her parochial grip over her party, restrains the scope of backbench influence on the government's legislative preferences. The Prime Minister's leadership position also inhibits the Speaker from conducting parliamentary business. The Speaker is elected on the party line. They remain in office until the subsequent Parliament elects its Speaker in its first sitting.[36] There is no conventional understanding that the Speaker would return to the next Parliament unopposed. Nor is the Speaker required to formally denounce their party allegiance upon their election. Though the Speakers are expected to discharge their function party-neutrally,[37] successive Bangladeshi Speakers have remained abjectly partisan in conducting parliamentary business.[38]

---

31 Sarkar Ali Akkas, 'Mechanisms for Judicial Accountability in the Contemporary World: Whither Bangladesh?' in M Rafiqul Islam and Muhammad Ekramul Haque (eds.) *The Constitutional Law of Bangladesh: Progression and Transformation at its 50th Anniversary*, 156–172 (Singapore: Springer Nature 2023) 165–167.

32 M Jashim Ali Chowdhury, 'The Antagonistic Style of Judicial Review in Bangladesh: a Good Candidate for the Dialogic Model?' (2021) 15 Journal of Parliamentary and Political Law, 549.

33 Constitution (n 2) art 56.

34 ibid art 57(2).

35 ibid art 56(4).

36 ibid art 74(6).

37 ibid art 75(1)(b).

38 Mizanur Rahman Khan, 'Speaker's Questionable Neutrality' *The Daily Star* (Dhaka, 22 May 2012).

The backbench members of the government and opposition parties are constitutionally restrained from voting against their respective political parties.[39] The Constitution of 1972 introduced an anti-defection clause – Article 70. As per the clause, an MP elected through the nomination of a political party would be barred from voting against that party on the floor of Parliament. It has remained a "Damocles' sword"[40] upon the backbenchers of the ruling and opposition parties, paving the way for the Prime Minister and the Opposition Leader to exert dictatorial control over their parliamentary parties.[41] It reduced the MPs' conscientious participation in parliamentary debates, questions and committee work.[42]

3.2 *Parliament and the Judiciary*

Parliament's relationship with the judiciary marks a curious mix of institutional comity, aggressive judicial review and strong distrust of each other. Like the UK, the internal parliamentary proceedings are formally insulated from judicial interference.[43] However, the Supreme Court of Bangladesh (SCB) has made substantial inroads into the parliamentary spheres under the cloak of its guardianship of Bangladesh's constitutional supremacy. The SCB has a constitutionally granted power of judicial review of statutes.[44] Again, it took clues from the Indian Supreme Court and expanded its judicial review power toward constitutional amendments. Bangladesh Supreme Court's approach to judicial power has been generally expansive, and there is a perception that the judiciary frequently airs a "supremacist's voice"[45] in its pursuit. It often places the judiciary in confrontation with the Parliament.

Next, the Parliament's participation in judicial accountability is practically absent. Article 95 of the Constitution grants Parliament law-making authority in determining the qualifications for appointing judges. The President formally appoints judges on the recommendation of the Prime Minister and the Chief

39 Lokman Bin Nur, "Constitutionalism in shaping political order of Bangladesh', in *Asian Constitutional Law: Recent Developments and Trends Vol 1* (Conference Proceedings, 8th Asian Constitutional Law Forum, Hanoi, Vietnam, 6–7 December 2019) 205, 210.

40 Badrul Haider Chowdhury, Former Chief Justice of Bangladesh quoted in AKM Shamsul Huda, *Constitution of Bangladesh Vol 2* (Rita Court: Chittagong, Bangladesh, 1997) 560.

41 Constitution (n 2) art 70.

42 Ziaur Rahman, 'Democracy: Freedom of Speech and Floor-crossing Interface' (2010) 1 The Northern University Journal of Law 24.

43 Constitution (n 2) art 78.

44 ibid art 26, 95, 96 & 102.

45 Ridwanul Hoque, 'Can the Court Invalidate an Original Provision of the Constitution?' (2016) 2 University of Asia Pacific Journal of Law and Policy 13, 15.

Justice.[46] Like the appointment of Supreme Court judges, the appointment of other constitutional officers like the Election Commissioners,[47] Comptroller and Auditor General,[48] and members of the Public Service Commission[49] are controlled by the government. While the Parliament is given a general law-making power of prescribing the qualifications and other requirements for candidates to such offices,[50] the President appoints these office bearers as per the advice of the Prime Minister. So, the resultant position is that the Parliament is theoretically entitled to make laws regulating the appointment of judges, their salaries, and other terms and conditions of service. However, it has practically no say in the actual appointment process. Appointment to the higher judiciary has remained an exclusive privilege for the executive branch.

Though the original Constitution of 1972 provided for the parliamentary removal of judges, it was later removed from the Constitution. The original Constitution of 1972 provided for a significant parliamentary role in removing judges. As with presidential impeachment, judges were to be removed by a two-thirds majority in Parliament. This system was substituted in 1977 by a military ruler, who instituted the Supreme Judicial Council system. The Council comprised the Chief Justice and two of his colleagues in the Appellate Division. In 2014, the Sixteenth Amendment to the Constitution sought to revive the original parliamentary removal system.[51] In 2016, the Supreme Court declared the Sixteenth Amendment unconstitutional in *Advocate Asaduzzaman Siddiqui v Bangladesh.*[52] This judgement has been a matter of contentious constitutional debate in Bangladesh.[53] While the government's review petition against the

46 The requirement of consultation with the Chief Justice was incorporated in the original Article 95(1) of 1972. It was later omitted, but the consultation continued as a matter of convention. Later, the Supreme Court of Bangladesh declared the consultation mandatory in *Advocate Idrisur Rahman v Bangladesh* 60 DLR (2008) (HCD) 714.

47 Constitution (n 2) art 118.

48 ibid art 127.

49 ibid art 137.

50 ibid arts 118 (1), 127(2), 137 and 138(1).

51 Asano Noriyuki and Minato Kazuki, 'Politicization of the appointment and removal of judges in a declining democracy: the case of Bangladesh' (Institute of Developing Economies, Japan External Trade Organization Discussion Paper, 2019).

52 *Advocate Asaduzzaman Siddiqui v Bangladesh* 10 ALR (AD) 03 (2017).

53 Anisur Rahman, '16th Amendment of the constitution: Another view' *The Daily Star* (Dhaka, 23 September 2014); SM Masum Billah, 'Faith, Hope and Promise' *Dhaka Tribune* (Dhaka, 17 August 2014); Md Yasin Khan Chowdhury, 'Removal of Judges under 16th Amendment of Bangladesh Constitution: a Euphemism to curb on Judiciary' (2015) 3 DIU Journal of Humanities and Social Science 89; M Jashim Ali Chowdhury and Nirmal Kumar Saha, 'Advocate Asaduzzaman Siddiqui v. Bangladesh: Judiciary's Dilemma with Impeachment' (2017) 3(3) Constitutional and Administrative Law Quarterly 7; Ridwanul

judgement is still pending in the Appellate Division, the invalidated Sixteenth Amendment remains in the printed pages of the Constitution. Unlike the previous invalidation of constitutional amendments, the AL government did not reprint the Constitution by omitting the Sixteenth Amendment and restoring the Supreme Judicial Council system. Thus, there is confusion about the current status of the Sixteenth Amendment.[54] In 2019, some judges of the Supreme Court facing allegations of misconduct were told by the Chief Justice to refrain from judicial work. They were not investigated by the Supreme Judicial Council nor removed by the Parliament.[55] On 10 August 2024, six of the seven Appellate Division judges, including the Chief Justice, was forced to resign by the student protesters ousting Sheikh Hasina's government couple of days earlier. In his resignation letter, the Chief Justice mentioned fear of the life and security of his colleagues. The fate of the Sixteenth Amendment is important for another reason as well. The Constitution provides that other constitutional office bearers like the Election Commissioners, Comptroller and Auditor General, and Members of the Public Service Commission shall be removed on the same grounds and under the same procedures as Supreme Court judges.[56]

3.3 *Parliament and the People*

Bangladesh Parliament and its members' public relations are not straightforward. People elect the Parliament. However, considering Bangladesh's problematic history of electioneering, most parliaments' electoral legitimacy remains questionable.[57] Concerns surrounding a free, fair, and credible parliamentary election continue to haunt the Parliament's democratic legitimacy.[58] Though an apolitical system of election-time-caretaker-government was introduced in 1996,[59] it later became controversial for the rampant politicisation of the judiciary. The controversy is partially attributable to the Chief Justices

---

Hoque, 'Can the Court Invalidate' (n 52); Po Jen Yap and Rehan Abeyratne, 'Judicial self-dealing and unconstitutional constitutional amendments in South Asia' (2021) 19(1) International Journal of Constitutional Law 127.

54 Haroon Habib, 'Bangladesh: Judiciary v. Parliament', *The Hindu, Frontline* (New Delhi, 18 August 2017); M Rafiqul Islam, 'Judging apex judges by parliamentarians', *The Daily Star, Law and Our Rights* (Dhaka, 18 July 2017); Tribune Report, 'High Court hears argument over existence of contempt law', *Dhaka Tribune* (Dhaka, 10 March 2014).

55 The Business Standard Report, 'A catch 22 for the Supreme Court', *The Business Standard* (Dhaka, 25 August 2019).

56 Constitution (n 2) arts 118(5), 129(2), 139(2).

57 Ali Riaz, 'Bangladesh's Failed Election' (2014) 25(2) Journal of Democracy 119, 121.

58 Nizam Ahmed, 'Critical Elections and Democratic Consolidation: the 2008 Parliamentary Elections in Bangladesh' (2011) 19(2) Contemporary South Asia 137, 149.

59 The Constitution (Thirteenth Amendment) Act, 1996.

leading the caretaker government. The caretaker government was declared unconstitutional[60] and abolished[61] in 2011. Since then, Bangladesh's politicised and severely incapacitated Election Commission continues to prove an unconvincing alternative.[62]

On the institutional level, once elected, the Parliament becomes detached from and inaccessible to the people. The people of Bangladesh have shown little interest in petitioning the Parliament and participating in its legislative and Committee works.[63] Apart from showing interest in the leaders' political point-scoring speeches in the House, the people have practically no interest in Parliament's legislative and scrutiny businesses. Individually, the MPs' relations with their constituents do not follow the standard parliamentary norms. Though they remain excessively engulfed with local development issues, it interferes with the local government bodies and reduces the quality of their parliamentary works.

4 General Powers and Functions of the Parliament

Typical of a Westminster parliament, the Parliament of Bangladesh has three broad categories of powers – first, the law-making power, including the constitutional amendment power; second, the power of the purse – the power to approve taxation and expenditure; and third, the power to enforce the collective and individual ministerial responsibilities of the government.

4.1 *Law Making and Constitutional Amendment Powers*

The Parliament of Bangladesh possesses plenary legislative[64] and constitutional amendment power.[65] Though statute laws are passed by a simple majority of the members present in the parliamentary session, constitutional amendments require a two-thirds majority of the total membership. The Parliament's law-making power is subject to constitutional limits. Statutes inconsistent with fundamental rights or any provision of the Constitution are

60 *Abdul Mannan Khan v. Bangladesh* 64 DLR (AD) (2012) 107.

61 The Constitution (Fifteenth Amendment) Act, 2011.

62 M Rafiqul Islam, 'Constitutionality of Army Deployment in Parliamentary Elections' *The Daily Star, Law and Our Rights* (Dhaka, 17 April 2018).

63 Nizam Ahmed, 'Parliament and Citizens in Asia: the Bangladesh Case' (2012) 18(3–4) The Journal of Legislative Studies 463, 467–68.

64 Constitution (n 2) art 65.

65 ibid art 142.

unconstitutional. The judiciary has also gained the power to review constitutional amendments. The original Constitution of 1972 did not limit the amendment power. The amendment power was free of any other limitation except for a procedural requirement of a two-thirds majority.[66] In *Anwar Hossain Chowdhury v Bangladesh*, the Supreme Court of Bangladesh borrowed the "basic structure doctrine" from the Indian Supreme Court's *Keshavananda Bharati* judgment.[67] Under this doctrine, certain parts of the Constitution constitute basic structures of the document and, therefore, could not be altered through constitutional amendments. The Constitution (Fifteenth Amendment) Act of 2011 recently expressly endorsed the basic structure doctrine. Article 7B of the Constitution now provides that the "basic structures" cannot be amended. It also identifies certain parts and provisions[68] – an unusually long list of provisions[69] – which are not amendable.

Since the *Anwar Hossain Chowdhury* judgment, judicial review of constitutional amendments has been the norm rather than the exception in Bangladesh. So far, the Supreme Court has invalidated, in whole or in part, the fifth, seventh, eighth, thirteenth, and sixteenth amendments to the Constitution. The Eleventh, Twelfth and Fourteenth Amendments were challenged, but those challenges failed on substantive grounds. Parliament has almost always acquiesced to Supreme Court judgments on constitutional amendments, except in the case of the Sixteenth Amendment. That case resulted in combative exchanges between the Parliament and the Court and caused the Chief Justice to resign.[70]

4.2 *Financial Powers*

Article 83 of the Constitution lays down the Parliament's financial powers. It unequivocally provides that no tax may be imposed, and no revenue may be collected from the people without parliamentary authorisation.[71]

---

66 ibid art 26(3).

67 Jafar Ullah Talukder and M Jashim Ali Chowdhury, 'Determining the Province of Judicial Review: a Re-evaluation of 'Basic Structure of the Constitution of Bangladesh' (2009) 2(2) Metropolitan University Journal 161.

68 Article 7B of the Constitution provides that apart from the "basic provisions" of the constitution, the Preamble, all articles of Part I and II, subject to the provisions of Part IXA all articles of Part III, and the article 150 of Part XI are not amendable. On a rough estimate, this list has made more than one-third of the Constitution unamendable.

69 Ridwanul Hoque, 'Eternal Provisions in the Constitution of Bangladesh: a Constitution Once and for All?' in Richard Albert and Bertil Emrah Oder (eds.) *An Unamendable Constitution?* (Springer 2018) 195, 224.

70 Ashutosh Sarkar, 'Chief justice steps down' *The Daily Star* (Dhaka, 12 November 2017).

71 Constitution (n 2) art 83.

Appropriation laws passed by Parliament regulate payments into and withdrawals from the public account.[72] The President may regulate this area only where the Parliament makes no law.[73]

At the beginning of each financial year, the government presents an Annual Financial Statement (budget) before the Parliament.[74] It contains the government's fiscal policy, priorities, and proposals for expenditure and taxation for the coming fiscal year.[75] Parliament engages in a general debate on the budget.[76] However, the budget as such is not passed into law. The government must submit separate Demands for Grants for each expenditure proposal in the budget statement.[77] Parliament reserves the power to discuss and vote to approve, modify, or reject these demands.[78] There is, however, one exception. Demands for Grants related to the "Charges upon the Consolidated Fund" are debatable but not amendable. Parliament may discuss but cannot vote on those.[79] Charges upon the Consolidated Fund mainly include the remunerations payable to constitutional office holders like the President, Speaker, Deputy Speaker, Judges of the Supreme Court, Comptroller and Auditor General, Election Commissioners, and the Members of the Public Service Commission, and the administrative expenses of their offices.[80] This provision is an important safeguard of the institutional independence of these offices. It ensures that these constitutional institutions are secure from the arm-twisting of hostile political governments.

There are, however, some other unwelcome restraints on the Parliament. Unlike the British Parliament, the Bangladesh Parliament does not send the annual budget for committee scrutiny. Also, three procedural devices known as Votes on Accounts, Votes of Credit and Withdrawal by Presidential Ordinance work to the advantage of the government. Sometimes, the government may secure advanced monetary grants through the "Votes on Accounts" process before the Parliament approves its budget.[81] The "Vote of Credit" allows a government facing an adversarial parliament to withdraw money through presidential orders for a maximum of sixty days.[82] The government can thereby

72 ibid art 90(3).
73 ibid art 85.
74 ibid art 87(1).
75 ibid art 87.
76 ibid art 89.
77 ibid arts 81–82.
78 ibid art 89(2).
79 ibid art 89(1).
80 ibid art 88.
81 ibid art 92(1).
82 ibid art 92(3).

pressure a parliament unwilling to pass its demands for grants to come to terms with it. In extreme cases, the President may even dissolve the Parliament and withdraw money from the public account through their Ordinance power.[83] Though Parliament must ratify such ordinances within thirty days of its reconstitution,[84] this process may allow the governments to propose budgets and get them approved by the President indefinitely. Such a situation may arise when a parliament is dissolved, but the election to the next Parliament is deliberately deferred beyond the ninety-day time limit. From 2007–2007, a military-backed caretaker government refused to hold elections for around two years and utilised this provision to publish their budgets in large press conferences and later approve those budgets through presidential ordinances.[85]

4.3 *Accountability Powers*

Typical of a Westminster Parliament, the Parliament of Bangladesh is dominated by the government. It is called into session by the President[86] upon written advice of the Prime Minister.[87] The Prime Minister and other ministers in the Cabinet have the "right" to speak and participate in parliamentary business. The Cabinet largely determines the parliamentary agenda. Government business has priority over private member business. While the government's collective responsibility is expressed in the Parliament's power of tabling a no-confidence motion, there is no express provision regarding individual ministerial responsibility in the Constitution.[88] Article 58(2) of the Constitution makes the ministers responsible to the Prime Minister. They serve at the Prime Minister's pleasure. Parliament, however, can make ministers answer questions, debate their actions, and scrutinise their departments through parliamentary committees.

4.3.1 Parliamentary Questions

Parliamentary questions are asked and answered during the first hour of each sitting day. Ministers take turns answering parliamentary questions on a rotational basis. The Prime Minister's question time takes place on Wednesdays.

---

83 ibid art 93(3).

84 ibid art 93(4).

85 Mashihur Rahman, 'Budget, Ordinance and Constitutional Government', *The Dhaka Courier* (Dhaka, 11 May 2007) 10, 12.

86 Constitution (n 2) art 72(1).

87 ibid art 72(1) (further proviso).

88 M Jashim Ali Chowdhury, 'Ministerial 'non-responsibility'', *The Daily New Age* (Dhaka, 31 May 2019).

The questions consist of two types – starred and unstarred. Ministers must give an oral answer to the starred questions. Supplementary questions can follow those. Ministers must give written answers to the unstarred questions, and no further supplementary questions are permitted there. Parliamentary questions have serious efficacy concerns in Bangladesh.[89] There are procedural complexities in tabling questions.[90] Ministers have near-absolute discretion in answering or ducking questions.[91] The Speakers show a partisan attitude in entertaining questions and a tendency to refuse urgent questions.[92] Under the RoP, the Speaker has wide powers regarding the admission, rejection or amendment of Parliamentary questions.[93] The MPs also avoid accountability questions and focus on their constituency demands instead.[94] Prime Minister's Question Time has failed to generate any meaningful accountability. Questions asked to the Prime Minister usually lack a critical bent. The RoP gives the Prime Minister absolute discretion of whether or not to answer a particular question.[95] Prime Ministers have usually faced comfortable and friendly questions and used the platform to score political points by attacking the opposition rather than answering for their government's actions and policies.[96]

4.3.2 Parliamentary Debate

As mentioned earlier, the government largely dominates the Parliament's agenda and debates. Individual members and opposition parties have very limited scope to initiate and sustain debate in the House unless the government allows them. Still, the MPs can serve Call Attention Notices[97] on matters of public interest. These are usually directed towards a Minister. While the Speaker usually allows these, MPs often use the motions to press a minister over their constituency issues. Apart from permitting a two or three-minute speech

89 M Jashim Ali Chowdhury, 'Parliamentary Questions in Bangladesh' *The Daily Observer, Law and Justice* (Dhaka, 20 July 2019); M Jashim Ali Chowdhury, 'Procedural modernisation of Prime Minister's Question Time in Parliament', *The Daily Observer, Law and Justice* (Dhaka, 09 November 2019).

90 RoP (n 18) rr 41–59.

91 Nizam Ahmed, *The Parliament of Bangladesh: a Data Handbook* (Institute Governance Studies, BRAC University, Dhaka 2013) 219–20.

92 Institute of Governance Studies, BRAC University, *State of Governance in Bangladesh 2008* (BRAC University 2008) 42.

93 ibid rr 45, 55.

94 Mustafizur Rahman, 'Parliament and Good Governance: a Bangladesh Perspective' (2008) 9(1) Japanese Journal of Political Science 39, 48.

95 RoP (n 18) r 48.

96 Jalal Firoj (n 26).

97 RoP (n 18) r. 71.

by the concerned MP, these notices rarely result in any follow-up debate in the House. MPs may also move for half-an-hour discussions on answers given by the Ministers during the question hour.[98] Speakers rarely allow the half-an-hour discussion motions. The MPs may sometimes request short discussions[99] on matters of public importance. The RoP, however, requires the Speaker to consult the Prime Minister before approving such requests.

MPs may also move private member resolutions on matters of public importance.[100] These resolutions are discussed on the private member business days. Absent the endorsement of the government, they rarely pass. MPs can also move points of order. Such points of order may draw the Speaker's attention to procedural irregularities, such as a lack of quorum on the House floor. Otherwise sidelined in parliamentary agenda setting, opposition parties in Bangladesh usually table motions for adjournment of any day's parliamentary business and demand discussion on matters they consider important and urgent.[101] Government parties have historically viewed these motions as disruptive tactics. Indeed, opposition parties have abused these motions to create chaos, stage walkouts, and parliament boycotts.[102] Unlike the UK House of Commons, the Bangladesh parliament does not reserve any opposition day in parliamentary business.

4.3.3 Parliamentary Committees

There are three types of committees in the Bangladesh Parliament – standing, select, and special committees.[103] Standing committees are constituted permanently and for a parliamentary term. Special committees are constituted to handle special issues or matters coming to the Parliament occasionally.[104] Select committees are mainly formed to scrutinise a specific bill. However, bills

98 ibid r 60.

99 ibid rr 68–70.

100 ibid rr 130–31.

101 ibid rr 60–67.

102 Until recently, walk-outs from sessions and boycotts of parliament by the opposition parties were a regular and painful part of Bangladesh's parliamentary practice. For more insight on this problem see Elora Shehabuddin, 'Bangladesh in 1999: Desperately Seeking a Responsible Opposition' (2000) 40(1) Asian Survey 181.

103 RoP (n 18), r 189(1).

104 ibid, r 266; To take an example, in 2010, an All-Party Parliamentary Committee on Constitutional Amendment was formed to examine all the past amendments of Bangladesh Constitution. See: Library of Congress, *'Bangladesh: Special Parliamentary Committee on Constitution Formed to Review All Past Amendments'* <https://www.loc.gov/item/global-legal-monitor/2010-08-13/bangladesh-special-parliamentary-committee-on-constitution-formed-to-review-all-past-amendments/> accessed 28 July 2024.

may be sent to standing committees instead of a select committee. Until the seventh Parliament of 1996–2001, no select committee was ever established for scrutinising a particular bill. The seventh Parliament established a select committee to review the bills tabled in the House.[105] Earlier parliaments would usually send bills to the relevant standing committees.

The Constitution lists the public accounts and parliamentary privileges committees as two standing committees.[106] Other standing, select, and special committees are formed at the discretion of Parliament as per the RoP.[107] Apart from subject-wise committees, such as parliamentary privileges, government estimates, and public accounts standing committees, ministerial standing committees oversee the ministries continuously. Before a reform in the fifth Parliament (1991–1996), ministerial standing committees could only scrutinise government bills relating to the Ministry under its oversight. Since the reform, the ministerial standing committees also oversee, investigate, and report on the operation and policies of the Ministry concerned.[108] Since the ministerial standing committees mirror government ministries, their number varies from term to term.

Committee work is, however, severely compromised due to structural issues surrounding the committee system. The core of the problem is the lack of appreciation for the system itself.[109] Until the Ninth Parliament (2009–2013), parliaments often finished over half their tenures without constituting committees.[110] In some instances, committee formation was delayed due to the opposition parties' refusal to submit their list of nominees.[111] When formed, the committees are constituted of members on partisan lists supplied by the leadership. Members and Chairs of the committees are distributed among the parties in proportion to their seats in Parliament. The RoP also designates some *ex officio* members – the Speaker, the Leader of the House, the Leader

105 Nizam Ahmed, *The Parliament of Bangladesh* (Ashgate Publishers 2002).

106 Constitution (n 2) art 67.

107 ibid art 76(1).

108 Constitution (n 2) art 76(2)(c); RoP (n 18) rr 246–48; Taiabur Rahman, *Parliamentary Control and Government Accountability in South Asia: a Comparative Analysis of Bangladesh, India, and Sri Lanka* (Routledge 2008).

109 Nizam Ahmed (n 105) 131.

110 Jalal Firoj (n 26); Farheen Alamgir, Tanvir Mahmud and Iftekharuzzaman, 'Corruption and Parliamentary Oversight: Primacy of The Political Will' (Transparency International Bangladesh 2006).

111 Nizam Ahmed, 'From Monopoly to Competition: Party Politics in the Bangladesh Parliament (1973–2001)' (2003) 76(1) Pacific Affairs 55, 68–69; Quamrul Alam and Julian Teicher, 'The State of Governance in Bangladesh: the Capture of State Institutions' (2012) 35(4) Journal of South Asian Studies 858.

of the Opposition, etc.[112] The House usually adopts a resolution confirming the partisan committee placements. The RoP designates some on an *ex officio* basis. For instance, the Speaker chairs the Business Advisory Committee.[113] Other chairs are decided by the party leadership,[114] though, formally, either the House or the committees themselves elect the chairs.[115] Historically, the majority parties have claimed almost all the chairs.[116] Though the chairs are now distributed among the parties on a proportionate basis, the government party decides which committee chairs will be allotted to members of other parties. Unless the government is exceptionally generous, chairs of important committees like the Public Accounts, Public Undertaking, and Estimate committees are unlikely to be given to the opposition members.[117] Until a reform in the seventh Parliament (1996–2001), the ministerial standing committees were chaired by the Minister of the relevant Ministry.[118] Since the rule is amended, general MPs are appointed to the chairs, but the Ministers remain *ex officio* members of standing committees overseeing their Ministry. There is now a perception that committee chairs – whose salaries and amenities are equal to government ministers – are distributed among ministerial aspirants who could not be accommodated in the Cabinet. In this process, expertise and accountability are mostly ignored.[119] Packed with partisan chairs and members, the committees rarely display an interest in holding the government accountable to Parliament.[120]

4.3.4 The Comptroller and Auditor General

Bangladesh's Comptroller and Auditor General (CAG) is a constitutional post. As an officer of Parliament, the CAG is required to report to the Parliament through the President.[121] The CAG places its audit report before the Public

---

112 RoP (n 18), rr 219, 225, 231, 239, 240, 245, 246, 249, 257, 264, 266.

113 ibid rr 219, 257, 264.

114 Nizam Ahmed, 'Parliament-executive relations in Bangladesh' (1997) 3(4) The Journal of Legislative Studies 70, 85–88.

115 RoP (n 18) r 191(1).

116 KM Mahiuddin, 'The Parliamentary Committee System in Bangladesh An Analysis of its Functioning' (Ph.D. Thesis, Ruprecht-Karls-Universität Heidelberg 2009) 104–106.

117 ATM Obaidullah, *Institutionalization of Parliament in Bangladesh: a study of the donor intervention for reorganization and development* (Palgrave Macmillan 2019) 107–138.

118 Nizam Ahmed, 'Parliamentary committees and parliamentary government in Bangladesh' (2001) 10(1) Contemporary South Asia 11, 24.

119 ATM Obaidullah (n 117) 338.

120 Philip Norton and Nizam Ahmed, 'Legislatures in Asia: Exploring Diversity' in Philip Norton and Nizam Ahmed (eds.) *Parliaments in Asia* (Frank Cass 1999) 51–52.

121 Constitution (n 2) art 132.

Accounts Committee, which considers it, recommends corrective actions, and investigates anomalies in government expenditure that the report may unearth.[122] The CAG attends the PAC meetings and sends representatives to the Public Undertaking Committee and Estimate Committee meetings.

Functional autonomy and the institutional separation of the CAG from the government bureaucracy are substantially compromised in Bangladesh.[123] While their status as a parliamentary officer is expressly mentioned in the Constitution, appointment to the office has paradoxically been entrusted to the President and Prime Minister.[124] Governments have traditionally appointed senior bureaucrats to the post. While the audit mandate of CAG constitutionally extends to the public accounts of the State[125] as well as to the accounts of all courts of law and other authorities and officers of the government,[126] section 3A of the Comptroller and Auditor General (Additional Functions) Act of 1974 empowers the government to exclude any office from CAG jurisdiction. The Bangladesh government's Rules of Business (1996) also requires the CAG to contact the Prime Minister's office. Despite Article 128(4)'s express requirement that the CAG "shall not be subject to the direction or control of any other person or authority,"[127] the office is administratively dependent on the Ministry of Finance. The Ministry controls the appointment, promotion, and terms and conditions of all the staffers at the CAG office.

4.3.5 Ombudsman

Article 77 of the Constitution permits the Parliament to create an office of the Ombudsman who will work as a parliamentary officer and "investigate any action taken by any Ministry, a public officer or a statutory public authority." The Ombudsman receives direct complaints from citizens, investigates them, and reports to the Parliament. Though the Ombudsman Act 1980 was passed in pursuance of Article 77, the law left it to the government to decide when to allow the office to assume its function. Due to the bureaucracy's resistance, the Ombudsman office has not yet been created.[128]

---

122 ibid art 76.

123 M Jashim Ali Chowdhury and Md Abdullah Al Mamun, 'The Comptroller and Auditor General of Bangladesh: Arguments for "Substantial Independence"' (2016) 21 The Chittagong University Journal of Law 159.

124 Constitution (n 2) art 127.

125 ibid art 84.

126 ibid art 128(1).

127 ibid art 128(4).

128 Nadim Zawad Akil, 'Absence of the office of Ombudsman: 48 years and counting', *The Daily Star, Law and Our Rights* (Dhaka, 10 November 2020).

5 Conclusion

While the executive-legislature relationship in the Westminster system is admittedly a "dominant-dormant one",[129] the general discussion above reveals that the Bangladesh Parliament's position *vis-à-vis* the executive branch is especially weak. Though the Constitution and the RoP have empowered the Parliament in many significant ways, the non-institutionalisation of the committee system and the MPs' lack of freedom from their partisan whips have undermined the textual powers of the institution. While a Westminster Parliament's legislative process is naturally subject to government dominance, the Bangladeshi Speakers' failure to distance themselves from their partisan bonds has further eroded the legislative autonomy of the Parliament.[130] Given the lack of necessary tools and space for the parliamentary opposition,[131] the Parliament's capability to ensure executive, legislative, budgetary and policy scrutiny has remained largely nominal.[132] Moreover, the government has practically co-opted parliamentary officers like the Comptroller and Auditor General. The Ombudsman has never even been established. The recent Sixteenth Amendment controversy shows that Parliament's relationship with the judiciary is antagonistic. Finally, the Parliament have mostly detached itself from its electoral base – the people. Though the MPs maintain a close tie with their localities, this does not constructively add to the Parliament's public relations. There are questions of electoral fairness and legitimacy.

---

129 MM Khan, *Dominant Executive and Dormant Legislature: Executive-Legislature Relations in Bangladesh* (South Asian Publishers India 2006).

130 Philip Norton, 'Playing by the Rules: the Constraining Hand of Parliamentary Procedure' (2011) 7(3) Journal of Legislative Studies 13, 15.

131 M Jashim Ali Chowdhury, 'In Search of Parliamentary Opposition in Bangladesh' *IACL-AIDC Blog* (University of Melbourne, 21 January 2021).

132 M Jashim Ali Chowdhury and Raihan Rahman Rafid, 'Parliaments during the Pandemic: a "Dual State" Explanation of Bangladesh Parliament (Jatya Sangsad)' (2020) 18(1–2) Bangladesh Journal of Law 25.

CHAPTER 3

A Subdued Legislature

1 Introduction

A Westminster parliament's capacity to enforce governmental accountability is generally doubted. In 1921, Lord Bryce famously branded the British parliament a declined legislature.[1] Nelson Polsby called the British Parliament a mere "arena type legislature" where the government's programs and policies are given theatrical scrutiny without leaving any substantial scratch over those.[2] Several factors structurally undercut the Westminster parliament's control over the executive branch. Parliament's *law-making function* is affected by the specialisation of legislative drafting, limitations over the parliamentary timetable and the government's power in setting the parliament's agenda etc.[3] In written constitutional systems like Bangladesh, its law-making power is further restrained by judicial review.[4] Parliament's *financial oversight* is affected by the magnitude and intricacy of budgetary policies, which are beyond the grasp of individual legislators and non-financial experts in parliamentary committees. The mass-based and cohesive political parties and their policies affect Parliament's *accountability function*. Cohesive political parties prevent the Parliament from using its controlling devices like votes of confidence, motions of censure, impeachment, etc. Beyond the parties, mass media has overtaken the bulk of the public agenda-setting tasks.[5] Interest groups and non-governmental organisations have partially relieved the MPs from their *representative roles* by directly linking the government and the people.[6] There

1 Lord Bryce quoted in Philip Norton (ed.), *Legislatures* (Oxford: Oxford University Press 1992) 47.

2 Nelson W Polsby, 'Legislatures' in Norton, P (ed.), *Legislatures*, 130–148 (Oxford: Oxford University Press 1990).

3 Ann E Snyder, 'Britain and the European Economic Community: the Decline of Parliamentary Sovereignty in the International Legal Arena' (1991) 18 Ohio Northern University Law Review 131, 151–152; Robert Elgie and John Stapleton, 'Testing the Decline of Parliament Thesis: Ireland, 1923–2002' (2006) 54 Political Studies 465, 466.

4 Jeffrey Goldsworthy, *Parliamentary Sovereignty Contemporary Debates* (Cambridge University Press 2010) 106–140.

5 Valentine Herman and Juliet Lodge, 'The European Parliament and the "Decline of Legislatures" Thesis' (1978) 13(1) Politics 10, 11–12.

6 John P Macintosh MP 'Introduction: Attitude to the Representative Role of Parliament' in *People and Parliament* (Saxon House 1979) 1–10 (Macintosh argues that there is a shift

 DOI:10.1163/9789004720831_004

is also the problem of technocracy, where the decisions are taken, presented, and shaped by a few political elites who bypass the people's representatives in parliament.[7]

Still, scholars like Mezey and Norton refuse to underestimate the strength of a Westminster parliament vis-à-vis the executive branch. They argue that Britain's so-called "golden age of parliamentary sovereignty" is mythic[8] and simplistic.[9] Even during the heydays of parliamentary sovereignty, parliaments carried significant democratic and political restraints. So, Mezey would call the Westminster parliament a "reactive", if not active, institution that responds to the government policies rather than making them by itself. However, he agrees that even within the Westminster system, there may be some "minimal" or "marginal",[10] "low viscosity/controlled,"[11] and "mere arena style"[12] prototypes. Philip Norton perceives the UK parliament as a "policy influencing" legislature that modifies or sometimes rejects government policies which is much different from being a "little or no policy impact"[13] parliament. A more contemporary work by Matthew Flinders and Alexandra Kelso argues that Lord Bryce and his followers' declinist views are too focused on the coercive aspect of parliamentary businesses. To Flinders and Kelso, a Westminster parliament is "not designed, intended or resourced to play the kind of proactive scrutiny role that the declinists appear to demand".[14] Mainly a policy influencing body,

---

towards the plebiscitary approach to political decision-making in the Westminster which undermines the parliament's authority. In a plebiscitary approach, decisions are made through negotiations between outside bodies and the governmental agencies).

7 JJ Richardson and AG Jordan, *Governing Under Pressure: the Policy Process in a Post-Parliamentary Democracy* (Martin Robertson 1979) 122.

8 ML Mezey, 'Parliament in the New Europe', in J Hayward and E Page (eds.), *Governing the New Europe* (Polity Press 1995) 196, 196 (Mezey argues that the premise that at some time in the past a golden age of parliaments existed is largely unsubstantiated).

9 Philip Norton, 'Parliament in the United Kingdom: Balancing Effectiveness and Consent?' (1990) 13(3) West European Politics 10, 31; Philip Norton, 'Introduction: the Institution of Parliaments', in P Norton (ed.), *Parliaments and Governments in Western Europe* (London: Frank Cass 1998) 1–15; Philip Norton, *Parliament in British Politics* (2nd Edition, Palgrave 2013) 5–7.

10 Michael L Mezey, *Comparative Legislatures* (Duke University Press 1979).

11 Jean Blondel, 'Party Systems and Patterns of Government in Western Democracies' (1968) 1(2) Canadian Journal of Political Science 180.

12 Polsby (n 2).

13 Philip Norton (1990), 'Parliaments: a framework for analysis' (1990) 13 (3) West European Politics 1, 4–5.

14 Matthew Flinders and Alexandra Kelso, 'Mind the Gap: Political Analysis, Public Expectations and the Parliament' (2011) 13(2) The British Journal of Politics and International Relations 249, 256.

a Westminster parliament's "control of the executive manifests itself in procedures and processes that lie beneath the visible lithosphere of parliamentary activity."[15]

From a minimalist point of view, the mere existence of a parliament should serve an important purpose of democracy – regular and periodic turnover of powers and the stability of a state.[16] The mere existence of the parliamentary opposition should ensure that the government's programs and policies are regularly debated, and alternative policies are laid for public appreciation. While the government remains electorally accountable for its broader programs and policies, broad-based political parties should remain alert to the intra-party concerns raised inside and outside the parliament.

In the case of Bangladesh, though several authors categorised the parliament as a "marginal"[17] or "minimal"[18] legislature, they have not offered much analytical justification for the categorisation. While the Bangladesh parliament is not expected to be immune from the structural disadvantages of a typical Westminster parliament, this chapter will consider what unique realities of the country prevent its legislature from being a policy-influencing body at the minimum. Subsequent parts of this chapter will examine the efficiency of the Bangladesh parliament, particularly its question, debate, law-making and committee-level scrutiny functions. It argues that the legislative and scrutiny roles of the parliament vis-a-vis the government are affected by various procedural and structural flaws and by the political parties to such an extent that they essentially reduce the parliament's position to a subdued constitutional organization.

1.1 *Questioning and Debating the Government*

Ministers are responsible to the Parliament.[19] The responsibility has both individual and collective dimensions.[20] Collective responsibility means that the Prime Minister and the Cabinet remain in power so long as they retain the

---

15 ibid, 261–64.

16 Deane E Neubatjer, 'Some Conditions of Democracy' (1967) American Political Science Review 1002; Gerhard Loewenberg, 'The Influence of Parliamentary Behavior on Regime Stability: Some Conceptual Clarifications' (1971) 3(2) *Comparative Politics* 177.

17 Nizam Ahmed, *The Parliament of Bangladesh* (Ashgate 2002 Routledge reprint 2018)1–24.

18 Nizam Ahmed, 'From Marginal to Minimal Legislature: Development of Parliament in Bangladesh (1991–2018)' (2018) South Asia Journal 120; Nizam Ahmed, *Parliaments in South Asia: India, Pakistan and Bangladesh* (Routledge 2020)176–198.

19 Keith Dowding and Won-Taek Kang, *'Ministerial Resignations 1945–1997'* (1998) 76 Public Administration 411.

20 Rodney Brazier, *Constitutional Practice* (Oxford: Clarendon 1994) 140.

confidence of the majority members of parliament. While the removal of a Prime Minister through a motion of no confidence is unusual in the UK's Palace of Westminster, a relatively strong culture of intra-party democracy and institutionalisation of parliamentary party groups like the 1922 Conservative Party Committee[21] and Parliamentary Labour Party[22] make sure that intra-party leadership challenge to a sitting prime minister always remains a possibility.

As per as individual ministerial responsibility is concerned, four features of the Westminster system place it on a very shaky foundation. First, the ministers' individual responsibility is generally seen more as a responsibility to the Prime Minister than to Parliament. The cohesiveness of the Cabinet and the Prime Ministers' moral obligation to shield their colleagues from parliamentary criticism makes individual ministerial responsibility difficult to achieve.[23] However, the ministers are bound by a Ministerial Code of Conduct. In appropriate cases, egregious failure or impropriety in public dealings may render even the Prime Minister unable to defend a colleague.[24] So, absent such a strongly adverse public opinion, ministers are unlikely to be removed for mere parliamentary disapproval of their performances. As Griffith and Ryle put it:

> Unless some measure of culpability can be attached to the Minister or a scapegoat is needed, he can usually expect to be retained or moved to another equivalent post, so long as he has the Prime Minister on his side.[25]

Secondly, a minister's responsibility is limited to answering the parliament members on the floor, orally or in writing, for their department's "policies, decisions and actions".[26] This responsibility, again, is limited to giving "accurate and truthful information, [and] correcting any inadvertent error at the earliest

---

21 Philip Norton, *The 1922 Committee: Power Behind the Scenes* (Manchester University Press 2023); Stuart Ball, 'The 1922 Committee: the Formative Years, 1922–45' (1990) 9(1) Parliamentary History 129.

22 Andrew Scott Crines, David Jeffery and Timothy Heppell, 'The British Labour Party and leadership election mandate(s) of Jeremy Corbyn: patterns of opinion and opposition within the parliamentary Labour Party' (2018) 28(3) Journal of Elections, Public Opinion and Parties 361.

23 AW Bradley and KD Ewing, *Constitutional and Administrative Law* (13th Edition, Longman 2002).

24 Diana Woodhouse, 'Ministerial responsibility in the 1990s: when do ministers resign?' (1993) 46(3) Parliamentary Affairs 277.

25 Robert Blackburn, Andrew Kennon and Michael Wheeler-Booth (eds.) *Griffith and Ryle on Parliament: Functions, Practice and Procedures* (Sweet and Maxwell 2003) 37.

26 The Ministerial Code 2015, Cabinet Office, The United Kingdom.

opportunity."[27] Though the ministers deliberately misleading the parliament are expected to resign, there is no hard and fast rule that sets the parameters of "deliberately misleading".

Thirdly, the individual responsibilities of the ministers cover their "a) personal conduct, b) general conduct of their departments and c) conduct of the civil servants working under the ministers".[28] While the ministers' personal conduct and departmental performances are relatively easy to attribute,[29] they may sometimes refuse to take responsibility for the conduct of the civil servants. The emergence of "Next-Step Agencies"[30] has complicated the matter further. The Next-Step Agencies are entrusted with operational responsibilities under the broader principles framed by the Ministers. The problem with this formulation is that ministers may now deflect responsibilities[31] by asserting that while they made the policies, the operational side of public functions rested with the Next Step Agencies or bureaucracies.[32] The 1995 dismissal of Derek Lewis by Home Secretary Michael Howard after Sir John Learmont's Report on the Parkhurst Prisoners' Escape is a standard example. The Learmont Report aptly showed how Mr Derek Lewis's operational process was dictated by the then Home Minister, who did not take responsibility.[33]

Fourthly, a recent UK practice of allowing the bureaucrats to answer the parliament on behalf of ministers – known as the "Osmotherly Rule"[34] – has further camouflaged the ministers' actual role in their departmental operations. The agency Heads are also required to face the departmental select committees on behalf of the ministers.[35] A minister would need to step in only

---

27 ibid, para 1.2.

28 Brazier (n 20) 147.

29 Margaret L Liu, 'Ministerial Responsibility and Constitutional Law' (2002) 7(2) Coventry Law Journal 25.

30 Charles Polidano, 'The Bureaucrat Who Fell under a Bus: Ministerial responsibility, executive agencies and the Derek Lewis affair in Britain' (1999) 12(2) Governance 201.

31 Carol Harlow, 'Accountability, New Public Management, and the Problems of the Child Support Agency' (1999) 26(2) Journal of Law and Society, 150, 151.

32 Matthew Flinders, 'Chapter 2: Parliamentary Accountability: Demoralized or Revitalized?' in *The Politics of Accountability in the Modern State* (Ashgate 2001, Routledge Revival 2019).

33 Prison Security: Learmont Report, HL Deb 16 October 1995 vol 566 cc600–14.

34 It is named after EBC Osmotherly, a civil servant who first drew up the concept in 1980. See: Thomas Erskine May, 'Evidence from Civil Servants' in *Treatise on the Law, Privileges, Proceedings, and Usage of Parliament* Part VI, Chapter 38, Paragraph 38.35 (25th Edition Online 2019).

35 Departmental Evidence and Response to Select Committees 2009, Cabinet Office, UK; The UK Government Resource and Accounts Act 2000; The Osmotherly Rules 2009 and The Ministerial Code 2010 (para 5.3.-5.5).

when a member of parliament feels that the Agency Head's answer is insufficient. It has been argued that the executive Heads answering MP's questions and giving evidence before select committees might prevent the disclosure of the actual role played and intervention done by the ministers in the operational process.[36] As Diana Woodhouse argues, "[I]t perpetuates the belief that the [ministerial responsibility] convention is simply a facade behind which the government can hide."[37]

Despite these structural and procedural weaknesses, a Westminster parliament's power to question the government and debate its policies, if utilized strategically, could go a long way in delivering democratic accountability. Parliamentary Question Time (PQT) has special significance in enforcing ministerial responsibility.[38] MPs ask questions to extract information from the government,[39] demanding accountability,[40] sponsoring constituency interests,[41] and sometimes enhancing the MPs' visibility.[42] Asked and answered mostly on an individual ministry basis and at the beginning of each day's parliamentary business, parliamentary questions are important because individual and private members mostly dominate these. Since the question time is not controlled by the parliamentary agenda-setting power of the ruling party,[43] the opposition and individual MPs may project a 'spotlight upon every corner'[44] of the administration. An additional advantage of the question time is that, unlike the motions for scheduled or unscheduled debates and motions of no

---

36 Second Report from Public Service Committee, *Ministerial Accountability and Responsibility*, HC 313-I, 1995–96.

37 Diana Woodhouse, 'Ministerial Responsibility: Something Old, Something New' (1997) 2 Public Law 262.

38 Frances H Ryan, 'Can Question Period be Reformed?' (2009) Canadian Parliamentary Review 18, 22.

39 Oliver Rozenberg, Oliver Chopin and Catherine Hoeffler et el, 'Not Only a Battleground: Parliamentary Oral Questions Concerning Defence Policies in Four Western Democracies' (2011) 17(3) The Journal of Legislative Studies 340.

40 Shane Martin, 'Parliamentary Questions, the Behaviour of Legislators, and the Function of Legislatures: an Introduction' (2011) 17(3) The Journal of Legislative Studies 259.

41 Michael Kellermann, 'Electoral Vulnerability, Constituency Focus, and Parliamentary Questions in the House of Commons' (2016) 18(1) The British Journal of Politics and International Relations 90.

42 Stefanie Bailer, 'People's Voice or Information Pool? The Role of, and Reasons for, Parliamentary Questions in the Swiss Parliament' (2011) 17(3) The Journal of Legislative Studies 302, 303.

43 Nizam Ahmed, 'Development and Working of Parliaments in South Asia' (2001) 9(1) Asian Journal of Political Science 18, 29.

44 Michael Cole, 'Accountability and quasi-government: the role of parliamentary questions' (1999) 5(1) *The Journal of Legislative Studies* 77, 83.

confidence, MPs wishing to table parliamentary questions would not need a parliamentary majority behind their move.[45] If selected through balloting, both the government and opposition members get scopes to ask questions and solicit information and accountability.[46] It is perhaps the most important reason why parliamentary questions usually get more attention than other parliamentary works at Westminster.

Questions apart, parliament debates and criticizes the government's legislative proposals, budgetary and economic policies, day-to-day administration of the bureaucracy, and the country's ongoing political developments and public interest issues.[47] Suppose the private members and opposition parties are allowed meaningful avenues to raise the matters that the government might be willing to avoid discussing. In that case, parliamentary debates may go a long way towards enforcing the ministerial responsibilities.

The next paragraphs of this part will consider how and why Bangladesh's Parliamentary Question Time (PQT), Prime Minister's Question Time (PMQT), and debate practices generally fail "in ensuring responsible (ministerial) behaviour".[48]

1.2 *Parliamentary Questions*

Sceptics argue that the output of parliamentary questions as an accountability tool and a method of extracting information is considerably circumscribed in the Westminster system.[49] Apart from being used as part of the wider political confrontation,[50] its efficacy as an accountability tool is in decline.[51] There are some procedural hurdles for the PQT to leave its mark on the parliamentary process. There are also institutional contexts (structural issues) and attitudinal problems that may reduce its efficacy. *Procedurally,* the limits on short notice or spontaneous questions could prevent the MPs from extracting

45 Nizam Ahmed (n 43).

46 Nizam Ahmed, *Parliament and Public Spending in Bangladesh: Limits of Control* (Bangladesh Institute of Parliamentary Studies: Dhaka, 2000).

47 Blackburn, Kennon and Booth (n 25) 10.

48 Nizam Ahmed and Aftab Ahmed, 'The Quest for Accountability: Parliament and Public Administration in Bangladesh' (1996) 18 Asian Journal of Public Administration 70, 92.

49 Franklin and Norton, 'Questions and Members', in Franklin and Norton (eds.), *Parliamentary Questions* (Oxford: Clarendon Press 1993) 10; J Mackintosh, *The Government and Politics of Britain* (London: Hutchinson 1970) 27.

50 N Johnson, 'Parliamentary Questions and the Conduct of Administration' (1961) 39(2) *Public Administration* 131, 144–146.

51 Mackintosh (n 49).

useful information.[52] *Structurally,* an absence of bipartisan spirit and obligation upon the ministers to answer the questions faithfully and routinely could substantially reduce the PQT's dent. *Attitudinally,* loyalist MPs' partisan motive to manipulate the session by asking friendly questions,[53] lack of backbench assertiveness,[54] the Ministers' tendency to offer evasive and vague answers[55] and the Speaker's inaction or partisan leniency towards the Ministers could disserve the purpose of PQT.[56] The PMQT is particularly vulnerable to theatrics and political point-scoring rather than showcasing a genuine commitment to accountability.[57]

1.2.1 Procedural Hurdles

In Bangladesh, Parliamentary Questions are asked and answered during the first hour of every sitting day (PQT) except the day the budget is presented. On Wednesday, the Prime Minister answers for an extra half an hour (PMQT).[58] It started in 1997 when the then Prime Minister Sheikh Hasina offered *ex-gratia* to face and answer parliamentary questions.[59] Accordingly, the Business Advisory Committee of the Seventh Parliament (1996–2001) recommended its introduction.[60]

Members of the Bangladesh Parliament are required to submit at least fifteen days' notice of their questions.[61] Questions are categorised as Starred

52 M Wiberg, 'Parliamentary Questionings: Control by Communication?' in H Doring (ed.), *Parliaments and Majority Rule in Western Europe* (St. Martin Press 1995) 179, 183.

53 John Bercow, 'Prime Minister's Questions in the United Kingdom' (2012) Canadian Parliamentary Review 9.

54 S Lazardeux, 'The French National Assembly's Oversight of the Executive: Changing Role, Partisanship and Intra-Majority Conflict' (2009) 32(2) West European Politics 287; David Judge, 'Backbench Specialisation- A study in Parliamentary Questions' (1973) 27(4) Parliamentary Affaires 171, 171.

55 N Johnson (n 50).

56 Parameswary Rasiah, 'Does Question Time fulfil its role of ensuring Accountability?, *Australian Audit, Discussion Paper 16/2006* (Analysis and Policy Observatory, Australia 2006).

57 P Dunleavy and G Jones, 'Leaders, Politics and Institutional Change: the Decline of Prime Ministerial Accountability to the House of Commons, 1868–1990' (1993) 23(3) British Journal of Political Science 267; GT Thomas, 'United Kingdom: the Prime Minister and Parliament' (2004) 10 (2–3) The Journal of Legislative Studies 4; RK Alderman, 'The Leader of the Opposition and Prime Minister's Question Time' (1992) 45(1) Parliamentary Affairs 66.

58 The Rules of Procedure (RoP) of Bangladesh *Jatya Sangsad* 1973, rule 41.

59 Jalal Firoj, 'Forty Years of Bangladesh Parliament: Trends, Achievements and Challenges' (2013) 58(1) Journal of the Asiatic Society of Bangladesh (Humanities) 83, 118.

60 RoP (n 58) r. 76.

61 ibid, r. 42.

Questions requiring an oral answer on the floor or Unstarred Questions sufficing with written answers.[62] On the given day for a Starred Question, the member asks the question by merely referring to its number. Questions will be printed in advance, but the Minister shall reply orally. The Ministers in Bangladesh usually parrot the written answer prepared by their ministries. The member concerned, and then any other member permitted by the Speaker may ask supplementary questions.[63] Unstarred Questions are not answered orally, but printed answers are laid before the floor, and there is no scope for supplementary questions over that.[64] If a Starred Question is not called on the scheduled day, the supplied written answer will be considered laid on the table, and no supplementary question will be allowed.[65]

Urgent or short notice questions require at least five days' notice, and the admission of those depends on the Minister's good grace. The Speaker may allow such questions only when a Minister agrees.[66] Historically, the Speakers have shown unwillingness to allow spontaneous questions or questions that have not been pre-scripted and vetted by the party leadership. It prevents meaningful questioning of the government.

Next, the questions for the Prime Minister are selected through an unclear process. As per the RoP, those do not go through balloting.[67] Rather, the Prime Minister would decide which questions are answered and which are not.[68] The Prime Ministers are naturally reluctant to accept questions with a critical tune. Among the Prime Minister's questions submitted in the Seventh Parliament (February 1997 to May 1999), slightly more than 10% have been accepted and answered.[69]

1.2.2 Structural Hurdles

Unlike the UK House of Commons, the PQT in Bangladesh *Jatya Sangsad* is not conducted in a bipartisan spirit. Parliaments worldwide recognise the importance of the partisan environment for meaningful accountability. For example, questions in the Canadian House of Commons are reserved exclusively

---

62 ibid, r. 44.
63 ibid, r. 56.
64 ibid, r. 51.
65 ibid, r. 52.
66 ibid, r. 59.
67 ibid, r. 48.
68 Nizam Ahmed, 'Reforming the Parliament in Bangladesh: Structural Constraints and Political Dilemmas' (1998) 36(1) Commonwealth and Comparative Politics 68, 85.
69 Nizam Ahmed (n 43), 34.

for the opposition members.[70] The New Zealand Parliament also allows members from different parties to ask questions in proportion to their strength in the Parliament.[71] While the Speaker of the UK Parliament would generally maintain a balanced ratio of government and opposition members called to ask questions, the Bangladeshi balloting system does not achieve partisan balancing.

In the case of the PMQT, the Bangladesh Parliament does not treat the Leader of the Opposition as the UK Parliament does. Bangladesh's Leader of the Opposition has never asked or debated with the Prime Minister during the PMQT.[72] In the Seventh Parliament (1996–2001), where the PMQT started, the opposition party continuously boycotted the session. The Prime Minister in the Eighth Parliament (2001–2006) would allegedly reject any question tabled by the Opposition Party members.[73] With a face-to-face debate between the Prime Minister and the opposition leader missing, Bangladesh remains deprived of the Opposition Leader's service to the nation as the Prime Minister-in-waiting.[74] While there is a danger that such face-to-face engagement might hyper-sensitise the political competition in Bangladesh, regular occurrences of the event could have reduced much of the heat. The country could have benefitted from a show of alternative personalities and leadership styles. It could also have brought the Parliament to public attention and increased its institutional value. Unfortunately, the Bangladesh Parliament's PMQT has remained a political monologue of "symbolic value",[75] and the system has not faced significant demand for modernisation.[76]

Next, there is no mention in the RoP of a member's power to compel an answer. Since a member cannot compel a Minister to answer questions, "the ultimate fate of a question depends greatly on both the Speaker's satisfaction and the Minister's willingness to consider it".[77] Ministers can ignore the members' questions in two ways. They may request delaying a question towards a subsequent day reserved for their Ministry.[78] It would effectively kill the

70 R Marleau and C Montpetit (eds.), *House of Commons Procedure and Practice* (House of Commons: Ottawa 2000), 422.

71 Standing Order 391(2) of the New Zealand Parliament, 2020.

72 Nizam Ahmed (n 17) 122.

73 All Answers Ltd, 'Balancing Power of President and Prime Minister' (Lawteacher.net, June 2019).

74 Nizam Ahmed (n 68), 86.

75 ibid, 76.

76 ibid, 77.

77 Institute of Governance Studies, *State of Governance in Bangladesh 2008: Confrontation, Competition & Accountability* (BRAC University: Dhaka, 2009) 42.

78 RoP (n 58) r. 52.

question by causing it to lapse.[79] Secondly, they may request to table their oral answers to Starred Questions. It essentially converts a Starred Question into an Unstarred one and prevents the instantaneous supplementary questions from being asked. In the Third Parliament (1986–1988), the rate of tabling oral answers reached as many as 90 per cent.[80] Though the members' interest in asking questions has increased,[81] statistics until the Ninth Parliament suggest that not more than 50 per cent of the accepted ministerial questions were answered. It starkly contrasts with the 4 per cent unanswered questions in the UK Parliament.[82]

1.2.3 Attitudinal Problems

Some attitudinal problems also affect the parliamentary questions in Bangladesh. First, the questions posed by the lawmakers mostly concern their constituency demands, and those lack critical reflection on the public administration of Bangladesh.[83] A study of 500 questions from each session of the First to Fourth Parliaments (1972–1990) showed that 55.65 per cent of questions were exploratory. 34.30 per cent of them were concerned with the day-to-day functioning of public administration. Only 10.05 per cent of questions had accountability tunes.[84] Another study of 130 selected questions from the Eighth Parliament (2001–2006) indicates that around 40.77 per cent of the questions involved constituency issues. Thirty-nine per cent of those concerned with contentious political debates involving the opposite parties. 29.23 per cent of questions were aimed at knowing the government's steps on various issues. Importantly, no critical questions 'seeking clarification on administrative lapses' were asked in that Parliament.[85] Another study covering the Eighth and Ninth Parliaments (2001–2013) found that only 4.3 per cent of the

79 Rounaq Jahan and Amundsen, *The Parliament of Bangladesh: Representation and Accountability* (Centre for Policy Dialogue and Chr. Michelsen Institute, Dhaka and Bergen, 2012) 54.

80 Nizam Ahmed, *The Bangladesh Parliament A Data Handbook* (Institute of Government Studies (IGS), BRAC University, Dhaka, 2013) 219.

81 Nizam Ahmed (n 43) 33.

82 Frances H Ryan, 'Can Question Period be Reformed?' (2009) Canadian Parliamentary Review 18, 22.

83 Muhammad Mustafizur Rahaman, 'Parliament and Good Governance: a Bangladeshi Perspective' (2008) 9(1) Japanese Journal of Political Science 39.

84 Salahuddin Aminuzzaman, 'Institutional Processes and Practices of Administrative Accountability: the Role of *Jatiyo Sangsad* of Bangladesh' (1993) 10(2) South Asian Studies 44, 55.

85 Mustafizur Rahman (n 83) 48.

oral questions and 12.4 per cent of supplementary questions had accountability tunes. Nearly 40 per cent of the questions involved constituency issues.[86]

Secondly, the quality of questions asked, and the responses made by the Prime Minister are doubtful. Until recently, it was believed in the UK that there might be an illiberal process of "syndication" in questioning.[87] Under the syndication process, party whips pass favourable questions to backbenchers who would raise those on the floor. Understandably, those lack critical tunes. Though Bangladesh does not have any recorded evidence for such practice, the general character of the questions asked to the Prime Ministers suggests that the MPs would "request" the Prime Minister for something rather than "demand" or "ask" for accountability. MPs are seen asking questions about how a particular foreign tour went, how the Prime Minister see a certain political or national issue, or an issue involving the opposition party, etc.[88] Statistics compiled by Nizam Ahmed suggest that around 91 per cent of the oral and supplementary questions asked to the Prime Minister during the Seventh, Eighth, and Ninth Parliaments (1996–2013) were about requesting constituency benefits. Only 9.8 per cent of the questions during this period called for remedial actions against some administrative or governmental lapses. Ahmed's statistics also show that 9.4 per cent of the total supplementary questions asked during this period were about blame-shifting or vilifying the Opposition rather than asking the Prime Minister.[89] Bangladeshi Prime Ministers have taken their chance to utilize the PMQT as a platform to talk over the "failures" of the past government/s and the current Opposition rather than reflecting on their own deficiencies.[90]

Thirdly, the Rules of the Bangladesh Parliament cannot tackle the Ministers' tendencies to provide misinformation and even disinformation to the Parliament. While "misleading the Parliament" is considered contempt in the UK,[91] the best the Bangladesh Parliament once could do in this regard was to "alert the secretaries of different ministries" to be more careful in supplying information to the Parliament.[92] In the Fifth Parliament (1991–1995), the

---

86 Nizam Ahmed, '*Jatiya Sangsad*: the Parliament of Bangladesh' 3 <https://www.psa.ac.uk/sites/default/files/Parliament%20of%20Bangladesh.pdf> accessed 22 July 2024.

87 Philip Norton, 'Introduction: Parliament since 1960', in Mark Franklin and Philip Norton (eds.), *Parliamentary Questions* (Oxford, 1993) 14–15.

88 Jalal Firoj (n 59) 117–119.

89 Nizam Ahmed (n 80), 229–231, Tables 6.16, 6.17.

90 Nizam Ahmed (n 68) 84–86.

91 Thomas Erskine May (n 34) Part II, Chapter 15, Paragraph 15.27 (Members deliberately misleading the House: a Minister inadvertently misleading the parliament is required to correct the mistake and apologise).

92 Nizam Ahmed and Aftab Ahmed (n 48) 90.

opposition leader "warned" the government Ministers against supplying incorrect information on one occasion.[93] On another occasion, the ruling party's Deputy Leader challenged the authenticity of information supplied by one of the ministers belonging to his party.[94] On another occasion, a member moved a motion alleging that two Ministers breached the parliamentary privilege by providing incorrect information to the House.[95] The motion was referred to the Standing Committee on Privileges, and the Committee never reported back to the House.

Fourthly, the Speaker's willingness to increase the number of questions, stop friendly questions[96] and encourage supplementary questions largely determines the outcome of the PQT. In Bangladesh, the Speaker is given wide discretion in approving or rejecting questions. S/he may disallow a question on subjective considerations like "obstructing or prejudicially affecting the procedure of the House",[97] "matters not falling within the primary concern of the government", "matters under active consideration of a parliamentary committee", and "matters involving policy too large to deal within the time limits"[98] etc. Since Bangladesh has a demonstrated problem with the Speakers' neutrality, these grounds are susceptible to misuse. Statistically, the rejection of questions on procedural grounds is alarmingly high. Around 53.9, 44.5 and 58 per cent of questions were rejected by the Speaker on procedural grounds in the Seventh (1996–2001), Eighth (2001–2006) and Ninth (2009- up to December 2010) Parliaments, respectively.[99]

1.3 *Parliamentary Debate*

The post-World War II modernisation process in the UK House of Commons has resulted in innovative tools that allow the MPs to initiate debates on issues of critical accountability concerns. Standing Order 14 of the UK House of Commons allots twenty days of exclusive opposition businesses. Out of the twenty, the leader of the principal opposition party would determine the House agenda for seventeen days, while the leader of the second-largest

---

93 ibid, 91.

94 ibid, 92.

95 Bangladesh Parliament, *Summary of the Proceedings of the Tenth Session of the (Fifth) Parliament* (Dhaka: Parliament Secretariat 1993) 32.

96 Parameswary Rasiah (n 56) 5.

97 RoP (n 58) r. 55.

98 ibid, r 53.

99 Rounaq Jahan and Amundsen (n 79) 53–56.

opposition would determine the rest of the three days' agenda.[100] Thirty-five more days are allotted for debates chosen by the ruling party and opposition backbenchers.[101] A dedicated Backbench Business Committee chooses from topics suggested by the MPs. Backbench days ensure that important but uncomfortable issues are not kept off the agenda by the government.[102]

There is additional scope for participation in the *Westminster Hall Debate*.[103] Westminster Hall is an informal extension of the House of Commons to reduce pressure upon parliamentary time. Issues raised by MPs, public petitions and select committee reports are debated in the Hall without voting.[104] A concerned Minister of the government would reply to the concerns.[105] Any other MP interested in the topic may participate in the debate. If a need for voting arises, the matter is referred to the House.[106]

Apart from these collective tools, individual members may submit non-binding internal petitions to the House of Commons. Members' petitions are known as *Early Day Motions* (*EDM*).[107] These are scarcely debated on the floor. Still, they have a very strong signalling potential when members express independent opinions separate from their government or party policy.[108] An MP may also raise issues of concern in the Half-an-hour *Adjournment Debate* at the end of each day's session.[109] Also, Standing Order 24 allows individual MPs to request *Emergency Debate* on any matter of urgent importance. If the Speaker allows, the application will be submitted to the House. If the House agrees, a full debate usually follows the next day.[110]

---

100 Thomas Erskine May (n 34) Part II, Chapter 18, Paragraph 18:13 (Public business: Opposition time).

101 ibid, Part II, Chapter 18, Paragraph 18:14 (Backbench business).

102 Mark Shephard and Jack Simson Caird, The Role of Backbench MPs, in Cristina Leston-Bandeira, Louise Thompson (eds.), *Exploring Parliament* 187–195 (Oxford University Press 2018) 191–92; David H Foster, 'Going 'Where Angels Fear to Tread': How Effective was the Backbench Business Committee in the 2010–2012 Parliamentary Session?' (2015) 68(1) Parliamentary Affairs 116.

103 Thomas Erskine May (n 34) Part III Chapter 23 (Sittings in the Westminster Hall).

104 ibid, Part III Chapter 23 Paragraph 23.3 (Business which may be taken).

105 ibid, Part III Chapter 23 Paragraph 23.11 (Speaking time limits and distribution of time within debate).

106 ibid, Paragraph 23.8 (Participation and quorum).

107 ibid, Part III Chapter 20 Paragraph 20.17 (Early Day Motions).

108 Michael Kellermann, 'Sponsoring Early Day Motions in the British House of Commons as a Response to Electoral Vulnerability' (2013) 1(2) Political Science Research and Methods 263.

109 Thomas Erskine May (n 34), Part III Chapter 18 Paragraph 18.36 (Daily Adjournments).

110 ibid, Part III Chapter 19 Paragraph 19.22 (Proposals to hold an emergency debate under Standing Order No 24).

Compared to the UK House of Commons, the scope of private member and opposition-initiated debates in the Bangladesh Parliament is significantly low.

1.3.1 Private Member Initiated Debates

As per the RoP of Bangladesh Parliament, MPs can move motions for adjournment, call attention, short discussions and half-an-hour discussions.[111] The Thursday is reserved for private member businesses.[112] However, the Leader of the House – the Prime Minister – may advise the Speaker to reschedule the private member days.[113]

MPs may demand a *Half-an-hour Discussion* when they feel that a Minister's answer to any parliamentary question involves a matter of public importance and needs further clarification.[114] MPs would need to give a three-days-notice of such motion. The required three days' notice may be waived if the Minister agrees.[115] There is no formal motion or voting on a Half-an-hour discussion. It includes a short statement from the member and a reply from the Minister concerned. Upon prior intimation of their interest, the Speaker may allow two other members of the Parliament to participate in the discussion by asking questions.[116] The Speaker is allowed a wide discretion to accept or reject such notice if they feel that it "seeks to revise the policy of the Government".[117] Statistics show that the Speakers have traditionally used their discretion in the government's favour, and *Half-an-hour Discussions* are rarely allowed.[118] Until the Ninth Parliament (2009), only 2.9 per cent of Half-an-Hour Discussion motions were accepted and discussed. 81.4 per cent of the motions were rejected straight, while the others got lapsed or withdrawn. Most disappointingly, no half-an-hour discussion occurred in the Seventh (1996–2001) and Eighth (2001–2006) parliaments.[119]

Individual MPs may also move a *Call Attention Motion*. As per the rule, once admitted, the sponsoring MP would be given a fixed time, usually two to three minutes, to discuss and bring any matter of urgent public importance to a minister's attention. There cannot be any instant debate on the statement of the

---

111 MN Kaul, *Parliamentary Institutions and Procedures* (New Delhi: National Publishing House 1979).

112 RoP (n 58) rr 25, 74–75.

113 ibid, r 25.

114 ibid, r 60.

115 ibid, r 60(2) proviso.

116 ibid, r 60(6).

117 ibid, r 60(5).

118 Nizam Ahmed and Aftab Ahmed (n 48) 79.

119 Nizam Ahmed (n 80) 223.

Minister made in reply to such a motion.[120] It is seen that MPs bring the Call Attention Motions to press their locality or constituency-based demands.[121] While the Ministers generally respond with assurances and promises about the demands,[122] there is no effective system of auditing the implementation of the assurances given.[123]

MPs may also request *Short Discussion* on "urgent public importance" matters.[124] However, the RoP requires the Speaker to take the advice of the House Leader – the Prime Minister – before accepting such a motion.[125] This consultation requirement is similar to the Private Member Resolutions.[126] *Private Member Resolutions* usually address important issues of public policy and government accountability.[127] MPs wishing to move such a resolution must give ten days of advance notice.[128] The responsible Minister of the government is, by rules, required to inform the Parliament of any government action that may have been taken in furtherance of a private member resolution passed by it.[129]

1.3.2 Opposition Initiated Debates

While there are no designated Opposition Day in Bangladesh Parliament, members of the Opposition parties may use the private member business days and other individual tools mentioned above. The opposition parties have traditionally used the *Motion for Adjournment* of parliamentary business to discuss matters they consider urgent and important.[130] Such motions, however, are scarcely admitted or passed in the House.[131] Moved two hours before every day's business, the government usually considers the adjournment motions as tools of willful disruption of parliamentary businesses. There is also evidence

---

120 RoP (n 58) r. 71.
121 Nizam Ahmed (n 80) 3.
122 MM Huq, 'Call Attention Motions and Accountability of Public Corporations in the Bangladesh First Parliament' (1991) 12(1) Dhaka University Studies Part-C 101.
123 Nizam Ahmed and Aftab Ahmed (n 48) 91.
124 RoP (n 58) r 68.
125 ATM Obaidullah, *Institutionalization of the Parliament in Bangladesh: a Study of Donor Intervention for Reorganization and Development* (Palgrave McMillan, 2019) 150.
126 RoP (n 58) rr 135, 150, 156–58.
127 ibid, r 130.
128 ibid, r 131.
129 ibid, r 143.
130 ibid, r 61.
131 Nizam Ahmed and Aftab Ahmed (n 48).

of the opposition parties abusing the tool to disrupt the House business and score political points.[132]

The motion for Unscheduled Debates is another popular route for the opposition parties. Until the Seventh Parliament (1996–2001), the motions for *Unscheduled Debate* – were being moved as a matter of custom. Around 29 unscheduled debates occurred in the Fifth Parliament (1991–1995). The Seventh Parliament (1996–2001) legalized the tradition. Following the then Speaker's visit to the Palace of Westminster, the Business Advisory Committee took the initiative to include 'unscheduled debates' as a regular parliamentary process. In June of 1998, it was announced that there would be regular half-an-hour unscheduled debates at the end of every sitting day. The treasury and the opposition will be given an equal fifteen minutes each. The Seventh Parliament saw 51 such debates.[133] However, the Speaker later complained that the opposition parties were using the device as a disruption tool, and it was terminated in the eleventh session of the Seventh Parliament.[134]

To conclude the discussion on ministerial responsibility, Bangladesh has not recorded any incident of parliament enforcing the collective ministerial responsibility by causing the government's fall through a non-confidence motion or intra-party rebellion against the Prime Minister. There is no constitutional provision directly referring to individual ministerial responsibility either. There is no UK-styled Ministerial Code of Conduct. Article 58(2) of the Constitution makes a minister personally responsible to the prime minister.[135] It means that parliament may not enforce a minister's resignation until and unless the prime minister – also the party leader – agrees. Given the prime minister's dictatorial control over the party, it is almost unthinkable that a minister in the good book of the prime minister would ever have to resign in the face of any parliamentary or opinion pressure.

Additionally, the Constitution allows the prime minister to choose someone as a minister who might not be an elected MP. Known as the "technocrat" ministers, they cannot be more than one-tenth of the total number of ministers.[136] However, they must sit in parliament and answer the MPs' questions relating to their ministry.[137] Technocrat ministers apart, there grew a recent practice

132 Nizam Ahmed, 'Parliament-executive Relations in Bangladesh' (1997) 3(4) The Journal of Legislative Studies 70, 80.

133 Nizam Ahmed (n 17) 193.

134 Jalal Firoj (n 59) 122.

135 The Constitution of the Peoples Republic of Bangladesh, 1972 art. 58(2).

136 ibid, art 56(2).

137 ibid, art 73A (1).

of appointing Advisers to the Prime Minister who are assigned portfolios of different policy areas and supervision of various ministries. They are accorded salaries and amenities comparable to the ministers and dictate the activities of relevant ministries. However, these "Ministers beyond the Cabinet"[138] do not sit in parliament, nor do they answer the parliamentary committees. Therefore, the overall impact of parliamentary questions and debates in Bangladesh presents a system of "ministerial non-responsibility".[139]

2 Legislative Processes as Tools of Accountability

The procedural rules of a Westminster parliament are designed to advance, rather than hinder, the government's legislative and fiscal programs. As Philip Norton puts it, "[P]urely in terms of observable decision-making, there is little evidence of parliament affecting policy outcomes regularly and significantly".[140] However, despite the government's powerful agenda-setting role, the Westminster legislative process – from the first reading through the second reading, committee, report, and finally the third reading stages – allows the opposition parties and backbench members ample opportunities to influence and, in certain cases to limit, the government's dominance in law-making. Robert Blackburn has called this the "politics of parliamentary procedure".[141] Blackburn argues that the opposition and backbench MPs may utilise the legislative processes in politically sensitive ways to challenge the government's monopoly over the parliament's legislative business. He identified at least seven rules, norms and practice-based avenues which allow the "politics" to roll within the realm of the procedure.

First, the governmental practice of announcing legislative policies through the Queen's annual speech to the Parliament[142] allows the departmental select

138 M Jashim Ali Chowdhury, "Ministers' beyond the Cabinet: Accountability concerns' *The Daily Star* (Dhaka, 1 May 2010).

139 M Jashim Ali Chowdhury, 'Ministerial Non-responsibility' *The Daily New Age* (Dhaka, 31 May 2019).

140 Norton, *Parliament in British Politics* (n 9) 130.

141 Robert Blackburn, 'The Politics of Parliamentary Procedure at Westminster' (2017) 4(2) Journal of International and Comparative Law 279; Robert Blackburn, 'The Nature and Importance of Parliamentary Procedure' in Robert Blackburn; Arianna Carminati; Lorenzo Spadacini (eds.), *Parliament as the Cornerstone of Democracy: Studies on the UK and Italian Parliaments in commemoration of Magna Carta's 800th Anniversary* (Kings College London, University of Brescia and the Magna Carta 800th Anniversary Commemoration Committee 2018) 45.

142 Blackburn, 'The Politics of Procedure' (ibid) 287.

committees to scrutinise those even before the government tables any bill in parliament. There is also a convention allowing the Leader of the Opposition to decide the agenda of the debate on the Queen's Speech. It means that the controversial aspects of the government's legislative programme will be discussed in Parliament at length.

Secondly, Westminster's conventional "confidence and supply agreements"[143] between a minority government and its coalition or working majority partners put a powerful coalition clog on the government's monopoly in policymaking.

Thirdly, the legislative journey of most government bills is determined by a programming motion agreed upon between the party whips in advance through the "Usual Channel".[144] Usual channels preserve the trust and confidence in the parliamentary process, avoid the government's need to force its way through the Parliament, and allow the opposition adequate opportunity to air their grievances and views.[145]

Fourthly, the conventional gentlemen's agreement of pairing between the government and opposition concluded at the beginning of each parliament hands the opposition party strong leverage in cases of extreme difference of opinion with the government. The agreement pairs a government member with an opposition one. If one of the pairs informs the other that they may not be present in Parliament to vote on a bill or motion, the other will graciously refrain from voting. While such understanding helps the parliamentary equilibrium in most cases, it also empowers the opposition parties. They may renounce it in extreme cases and create significant inconveniences for the government. The inconvenience heightens when the government enjoys a slim or mere working majority in parliament.[146]

Fifthly, the UK parliament's legislative procedure recognises various opposition rights. Opposition parties may schedule a debate and determine the agenda for around twenty business days. They may also call for an emergency adjournment debate under Standing Order 24. Another weapon for them is, of course, the motion of censure. While most opposition motions are likely to be defeated in voting, they allow the opposition parties the scope to air their major disagreement with the government and popularise the debating points.

Sixthly, the Westminster system recognises some important backbench member rights. Establishing the Backbench Business Committee, providing

143 Blackburn, Kennon and Booth (n 25) 318–345.

144 Blackburn, 'The Politics of Procedure' (n 141) 290.

145 ibid, 288.

146 ibid, 289.

thirty-five backbench business days, regularising the e-petition system, etc., have created significant scopes of backbench input in the parliamentary process. Moreover, the traditional avenues like parliamentary questions are further strengthened by the Speakers' increasing willingness to entertain short-notice questions, urgent questions, instantaneous supplementary questions, etc.[147] Private members have also benefitted from the "ten minutes rule bills",[148] which would allow them short speeches in the Chamber. While the ultimate possibility of these bills making their way to the statute books is very slim, members may use this to attract public attention to pressing issues of concern. Apart from their select committee activism, the members also greatly benefit from introducing the Westminster Hall Debate, which allows parallel sittings of the House.[149]

Seventhly, but perhaps the most important, the British Speakers' detachment from their political parties has added a visible value to the Palace of Westminster.[150] The Speaker is empowered in numerous ways to facilitate meaningful scrutiny of the government's legislative procedure. Speakers facilitate backbench participation by allowing urgent questions, opposition amendment proposals, etc. They may refuse the government's Closure Motion, likely to infringe the opposition's right to have an adequate debate or which could otherwise abuse the House rules.[151]

Besides Robert Blackburn, Megg Russel's studies on the Westminster law-making process also show that the UK Parliament – individual MPs and the Opposition combined – influences the legislation in six ways.[152] Firstly, non-government members frequently change the direction of legislative policies by securing concessionary amendments from the government.[153] Secondly, the select committees' investigative works at pre-legislative stages generate in the government an apprehension of parliamentary resistance to controversial

---

147 M Jashim Ali Chowdhury, 'The Way John Bercow redefined the Speakership' (*DUCSU Law and Politics Review* (*DUCSU LPR*) *Blog*, University of Dhaka, 02 January 2020).

148 Thomas Erskine May (n 34), Part III, Chapter 18, Paragraph 18.40: 'Motions under Standing Order No 23 (the 'Ten-minute Rule').

149 Blackburn, 'The Politics of Procedure' (n 141) 296.

150 Richard Berry and Sean Kippin, 'Choosing the Speaker of the House of Commons: some proposals for change' (*Democratic Audit* 2013) <https://www.democraticaudit.com/2013/08/27/choosing-the-speaker-of-the-house-of-commons-some-proposals-for-change/> accessed 29 July 2024.

151 Thomas Erskine May (n 34) Part III, Chapter 20 Paragraph 20.53.

152 Meg Russell, D Gover and Kristina Wollter, 'Does the Executive Dominate the Westminster Legislative Process? Six Reasons for Doubt' (2016) 69 Parliamentary Affairs 286, 301.

153 Meg Russell and Daniel Gover, *Legislation at Westminster: Parliamentary Actors and Influence in the Making of British Law* (Oxford University Press 2017) 267.

legislative proposals.[154] Thirdly, the government considers the pulse of their party backbencher before finalizing its legislative proposals on controversial issues.[155] Fourthly, the private members and the opposition frequently politicize the controversial legislative issue through the "usual channel" process and mass media activism.[156] Fifthly, the government not infrequently concedes to non-government amendment proposals at a bill's report stage.[157] Sixth, MPs and the associated pressure groups create extra-parliamentary pressure upon the government.[158]

In Bangladesh, within the different stages of legislative procedure, relatively few avenues of "politics" may play towards the advantage of the backbench members and the opposition parties and allow them to influence the government's legislative proposals. Legislative procedure in Bangladesh broadly mirrors the Westminster process. However, a comparison of Bangladesh's legislative procedure with the UK's parliament's legislative stages shows that the absence of Westminster-like conventions and practices prevents the "politics of procedure" from rolling in the way Blackburn and Meg Russel perceived it in Westminster. The law-making process of the Bangladesh Parliament lacks meaningful scope for private members or opposition parties to have a say in legislation. Parliamentary committees also play a very formal and minimal role. The government's agenda-setting power and purely majoritarian approach to parliamentary business have placed it in the leading role for passing legislation and circumscribed the Parliament's institutional power to influence proposed laws.

2.1 *Pre-legislative Stage*

Before finding their place in the statute book, laws go through pre-legislative and legislative stages. In Bangladesh, legislative proposals usually arise from a cluster of sources like the government's electoral manifesto, demands from executive departments, judicial directives, law commission reports, and public demands crystalized through mass media, civil society, professional bodies, etc. The UK governments usually publish White Papers ahead of each parliamentary session that explains its legislative program for the session. The government's annual legislative plan is also included in the King's Speech. The speech is debated in both Houses. It gives the select committees a meaningful

154 ibid, 269.
155 ibid, 270.
156 ibid, 271.
157 ibid, 272.
158 ibid, 273.

signal to start their pre-legislative studies. On many occasions, select committees criticize the government's position and achieve surprising modifications in the government's legislative agenda.[159] Select committee reports can generate a huge amount of opinion force behind its position by gathering public testimonies and reflecting on it cross-party. By law, the government must respond to all select committee reports, forcing the government to anticipate "how the committees will react" to particular legislative policy.[160] Therefore, a defiant government is more likely to face stiff opposition while passing a bill.

Like that of the British King, the President of Bangladesh's annual parliamentary speech should include the government's legislative programs. Unfortunately, the Presidential speech in Bangladesh rarely contains a comprehensive legislative agenda except parroting the government's political and administrative policies and actions. Therefore, the general debate on the presidential speech does not allow members to consider the broader principles of the government's legislative program.[161] There is also no White Paper style declaration of the government's legislative intent. Bangladesh, therefore, completely misses the scope of debating the government's legislative program, if any, at its root.[162] The government of Bangladesh rather initiates legislation on an as-the-idea-comes-in basis. Governments in Bangladesh instead bring forth their legislative proposals on an *ad hoc* basis. Bureaucratic proposals for law-making are initiated in the relevant department or Ministry. Three departments are usually involved in the process. These are (1) the Legislative Drafting Wing of the Ministry of Law, Justice and Parliamentary Affairs; (2) the Ministry of Finance; and (3) the Cabinet Division. The Legislative Drafting Wing writes the bill. The Ministry of Finance opines on draft bills if they require government expenditure. During this process, a draft bill may travel back and forth between Law, Finance, and other relevant ministries. At this stage, government departments or ministries may invite input from expert bodies such as the Law Commission, Attorney General, individuals, civil societies, or other stakeholders. The Cabinet Division, headed by the Prime Minister and including all the Ministers of the government, is the final body that considers the draft and signals its readiness for the bill to be placed before the Parliament.[163] After

---

159 ibid, 212.

160 ibid, 228–230.

161 R Jahan and I Amundsen, *The Parliament of Bangladesh: Representation and Accountability* (CPD-CMI 2012) <http://www.cpd.org.bd/pub_attach/CPD_CMI_WP2.pdf> accessed 29 July 2024.

162 Jahan and Amundsen (n 79).

163 Administration of the Government of Bangladesh operates under the Rules of Business 1996 framed as per Article 55(6) of the Constitution of Bangladesh.

the Cabinet approves a draft bill, the relevant Minister, called the Minister-in-charge, tables the bill in the House.[164]

Individual or private members have to draft their bills. However, the research assistance, office, interns, and logistics support for individual members are so inadequate that they struggle to produce high-quality legislative drafts.

2.2 *Legislative Stage*

During the legislative phase, a bill goes through a first reading (reading the title of a bill and tabling it on the floor), a second reading (discussion on the principles of the bills, committee stages, clause-by-clause reading and amendment proposals) and the third reading (motion to pass the bill).

2.2.1 First Reading (Tabling the Bill)

A bill starts with the Minister or private member giving notice to the parliament secretariat of their intention to table a "motion for leave to introduce" the bill. The Minister-in-charge would need to give seven days' notice for government bills. For private member bills, the Member-in-charge must provide fifteen days' notice.[165] They would also give a brief statement on the purposes of the bill. If the bill involves expenditure from the public purse, such as the budget, the Minister-in-charge would need to certify that it was presented before the President and that the President recommended the bill's introduction.[166] On private member bills, the Member-in-charge must attach the written recommendation of the President, which they must secure through a relevant ministry.[167] This onerous requirement means private members are practically barred from introducing money bills or bills with monetary implications without the government's consent.

The first reading starts on the day scheduled for tabling the motion for leave to introduce the bill. Except in cases where another member opposes this motion, the first reading is usually a formality. It is very brief, involving only the tabling of the motion for the introduction of the bill. When a motion for leave to introduce the bill is moved, any other member may oppose it. If any opposition is raised, the Speaker will allow the opposing member a brief time to explain why they oppose the bill's introduction. The Minister/

---

164 Md Abu Saleh, 'Law Making Process in Bangladesh Parliament' (2013) 6 Jahangirnagar Journal of Administrative Studies 143, 249–151.

165 ibid rr 72, 74, 75.

166 Constitution (n 135) art. 82, 89(3); See also: Gavin Murphy, 'How Legislation is Drafted and Enacted in Bangladesh' (2006) 27(3) Statute LR 133.

167 RoP (n 58) r 73.

Member-in-charge of the bill then replies to the objection. Without any further debate, the Speaker then puts the matter to a vote. The leave to introduce the bill will usually be decided through a voice vote. Once the leave is granted, the first reading ends and the second reading is reserved for a different day.

It is important to note that parliamentary time for private member businesses is limited. While government business is conducted throughout the week, Thursdays are reserved for private member business.[168] In consultation with the Prime Minister, the Speaker may vary the private member business days at his discretion.[169] There is a separate parliamentary committee on private member bills and resolutions. It examines and recommends the timetable for discussion of private member bills.[170] In post-independence Bangladesh, only seven private member bills have been passed, indicating that backbench members lack the scope, logistics, and interest in passing extra-governmental legislation.[171]

2.2.2 Second Reading (Discussion of General Principles)

The second reading involves discussing a bill's general principles rather than a clause-by-clause discussion of its contents. Once introduced through the first reading, a bill is published in the Parliament's official gazette. On the day of the second reading, the Minister or Member-in-charge of the bill will propose that the House consider it on the floor, refer it to a standing or select committee or circulate it to elicit wider public opinion.[172] Once they propose one of these options, any other MP may oppose it and propose one of the alternatives. During the discussion of these proposals and counterproposals, the general purpose and principles of the legislation are discussed. No amendments or clause-by-clause reading, and debate occur at this stage.[173] Once the discussion is over, the question is put to the vote, and the appropriate course – direct consideration on the floor, sending to a committee, or circulating for public opinion – of the bill is decided. Once the appropriate course is determined, the next stage – Committee Stage – begins.

---

168 RoP (n 58) rr 74, 75.

169 ibid r 25.

170 ibid, rr 222–24.

171 Abdul Latif Mondol, 'What will happen to the bills?', *The Daily Star* (Dhaka, 14 September 2009).

172 RoP (n 58) r 77.

173 ibid r 78.

2.2.3 Committee Stage Amendments and Clause-by-Clause Discussion

Under the UK House of Commons Standing Orders, bills are referred to a Public Bill Committee (PBC), Departmental Select Committee, Grand Committee or the Committee of the Whole House.[174] The Private Bill Committee considers the bills brought by individual MPs.[175] Regarding scrutiny of legislative proposals, the PBCs are hamstrung by partisan committee appointments and strict pre-programming of their works by the House. PBCs are relatively small and formed ad hoc to consider particular bills. The PBC stage usually starts around one week after the second reading of the bill in the House. A Programme Motion determines how much time the PBCs would get to accomplish their task. The biggest problem of the PBCs is their partisan members – 'cannon fodder' attendees[176] – who are primed to vote on a party line in almost all circumstances.[177] There are, however, signs of development. According to the 2006 Modernisation Committee report titled *The Legislative Process*, the PBCs have been given the power to "send for persons, papers and records" in the manner of a select committee. It has permitted the PBCs to call for experts, citizen groups and outsiders to contribute to the legislative process. As their participation grows, the scope of the consensual approach to legislative scrutiny grows with it.[178] Though there is still much powerlessness in selecting the witnesses and timetabling the scrutiny work,[179] it has also helped the members gain more expertise, socialisation and interest in committee work.[180] Additionally, Ministers in charge of bills are increasingly persuaded and sometimes forced to assure the PBCs about bringing amendments at the report stage.[181]

Compared to this, the governments in Bangladesh traditionally hastened their legislative proposals through the floor and frequently bypassed the

---

174 General Committees, Factsheet L6 (The UK House of Commons Information Office 2009) 4.

175 Meg Russell, Bob Morris and Phil Larkin, *Fitting the Bill: Bringing Commons legislation committees into line with best practice* (University College London Constitution Unit, June 2013) 10–13.

176 Blackburn, Kennon and Booth (n 25) 387.

177 SA Walkland, 'Government Legislation in the House of Commons' in SA Walkland (ed.), *The House of Commons in the Twentieth Century: Essays by Members of the Study of Parliament Group* (Oxford: Clarendon Press, 1979) 247, 251.

178 Jessica Levy, 'Public Bill Committees: an Assessment Scrutiny Sought; Scrutiny Gained' (2010)63(3) Parliamentary Affairs534, 539.

179 L Thompson, 'More of the Same or a Period of Change? The Impact of Bill Committees in the Twenty-First Century House of Commons' (2013) 66 Parliamentary Affairs 459, 470.

180 L Thompson, 'Debunking the Myths of Bill Committees in the British House of Commons' (2016) 36(1) Politics 36, 45.

181 Thompson (n 179).

committee stage altogether.[182] Before the Seventh Parliament (1996–2001), bills were rarely sent for committee scrutiny.[183] In the Seventh Parliament, the House started sending bills to a special parliamentary bill committee for scrutiny. Bills are now routinely referred to ministerial standing committees and occasionally to ad hoc legislative select committees established for a specific bill.[184] If a motion to refer the bill to a select committee is passed during the second reading, the House will constitute such a committee through a separate motion.[185] The House, however, may still send any bill to a ministerial standing committee.[186] Private member bills are referred to the Standing Committee on Private Members' Bills. At the committee stage, the opposition and backbench members are expected to have more opportunities to debate and propose amendments. The committees can decide on any issue or agenda by simple majority, and dissenting members may note their dissents in the committees' report.[187] After a clause-by-clause deliberation, the committees may return the bill with or without amendment proposals.[188] Quality of deliberation within the committees remains a concern, however. Problems of the parliamentary committees will be discussed in detail in the next part of this Chapter.

2.2.4 Third Reading, Passage, and Presidential Assent

One a bill is returned to the House with or without amendments, the Minister or Member-in-charge may then move to consider the bill along with the report of the Committee.[189] Once taken into consideration, the Speaker fixes a day for clause-by-clause reading and discussion of the bill. Decisions on amendment proposals are taken by vote. The Speaker usually puts the motion to a vote without additional debate. At this stage, debate, if there be any, concerns on whether the bill as a whole should be passed or rejected. Details of the bill are not touched upon again at this stage.[190]

2.2.5 Filibustering and the Closure and Programme Motions

Participation and opposition input in the legislative process become acutely important during the second reading stage. In an extreme disagreement

182 Nizam Ahmed (n 132) 77–8; Nizam Ahmed (n 68) 71.
183 Nizam Ahmed (n 68) 77.
184 Nizam Ahmed (n 80) 134.
185 ibid r 225.
186 Constitution (n 135) art 76(2)(a); RoP (n 58) r 77.
187 RoP (n 58) r 228(5).
188 ibid rr 80, 81.
189 ibid, r. 81–88.
190 ibid, r. 91.

between the government and the opposition, the opposition party may try to dislodge the government's legislative programme by proposing many amendments and prolonging debates. To handle this pressure, the government uses tools like Closure Motion, Guillotine Motion, and Programme Motion to tackle opposition obstructionism. The UK House of Commons has detailed rules and norms regulating the use of the Closure, Guillotine and Programme Motions.

In a *Closure Motion*, the government moves a motion named "That the question now be put". It means that parliament would now end the discussion and proceed to vote. The Speaker of the UK House of Commons, who is traditionally party-neutral, would allow the motion only when he is sure that the Closure is not being invoked to infringe the rights of the House minority.[191] A Closure Motion passes if at least 100 members of parliament vote in its support. In the case of *Guillotine Motions*, the debate must end, and voting is arranged within three hours of the passage of the motion.[192]

However, a third device, "Programme Motion",[193] is popular among the government and opposition parties. Initiated since the 2003–04 session of the UK House of Commons, programming motions are usually proposed through the Usual Channel and carried out immediately after the initial second reading stage. It would specify the time allowed to complete each stage of the bill. While the programme motion primarily works to the government's advantage, the opposition and backbenchers are more likely to concede to such a time-structured formula instead of being subject to a more uncertain and sudden Closure or Guillotine Motion. However, failure to secure a Programme Motion may be fatal to a government whose majority is slim and who faces an opposition threat of withdrawal from the pairing agreement. In 2012, the failure to agree on a Programme Motion forced the Conservative-Liberal Coalition Government to withdraw its House of Lords Reform Bill.[194]

In Bangladesh, the RoP does not formally recognise filibustering. Nevertheless, the opposition parties may propose many amendment proposals to indefinitely prolong the debate on a bill. In that case, the Speaker may choose and order the amendment proposals to be raised on the floor of the House.[195] As a rule of thumb, unless the government party have shown

191 Thomas Erskine May (n 34) Part III Chapter 25 Paragraph 25.54 (The Closure).

192 ibid, Part IV Chapter 28 Paragraph 28.26 (Allocation of time orders (guillotines)).

193 ibid, Part IV Chapter 28 Paragraph 28.59 (Programme Motion).

194 Liam Laurence Smyth, Glenn McKee, Matt Korris, 'The Legislative Cycle', in Cristina Leston-Bandeira, Louise Thompson (eds.), *Exploring Parliament* 67–79 (Oxford University Press 2018) 71.

195 RoP (n 58) rr 286, 287.

leniency, successive Speakers of Bangladesh have tended to ignore opposition amendments.[196]

The government, in turn, invokes Closure Motion or pre-programming of legislative business through the Business Advisory Committee. Unlike the British Parliament, there is no tradition of an informal agreement between the government and opposition parties on the timetabling of bills.[197] The Business Advisory Committee, headed by the Speaker, may decide the timeline for each stage.[198] The Committee, however, is dominated by ruling party members, and the opposition has little chance there. Moreover, the Speaker is not bound to form a Business Advisory Committee. Rather, the Speaker is required by the RoP to consult the Leader of the House – the Prime Minister – in almost every aspect of parliamentary timetabling.[199]

A *Closure Motion*, when passed, halts the debate and puts the question to a vote.[200] While the Speaker is empowered to judge whether the motion is invoked to "infringe the Opposition's right of reasonable debate",[201] Bangladeshi Speakers have never questioned the ruling party's Closure Motions on this ground. Unlike the British Parliament, there is no tradition of an informal agreement between the government and opposition parties on the timetabling of bills.[202]

Additionally, in a prolonged debate on the floor, the Speaker is permitted to "take the sense of House" and vary the timetable for discussion at any stage of a bill.[203] It empowers the Speaker to end the debate and put the matter to voting "forthwith".[204] Suppose the opposition party members propose an excessive number of amendments. In that case, the Speaker can choose and order the amendment proposals to be raised on the floor of the House.[205] Faced with a reservation from the ruling party, successive Speakers of Bangladesh have tended to ignore opposition amendments.[206]

---

196 Nizam Ahmed (n 43) 29.

197 Michael Rush and Clare Ettinghausen, *Opening up the Usual Channel* (Hansard Society 2002).

198 RoP (n 58) r 219.

199 ibid, r 220.

200 ibid, r 290(2).

201 ibid, r. 290(1).

202 For a plain idea about the UK parliament's informal communication practices, see Michael Rush and Clare Ettinghausen, *Opening up the Usual Channel* (Hansard Society 2002).

203 RoP (n 58) r 291(1).

204 ibid r 291(2).

205 ibid r 286, 287.

206 Nizam Ahmed (n 43) 29.

2.2.6 Presidential Assent

Bills considered and passed by the Parliament of Bangladesh are sent to the Head of the State (the President) for assent.[207] President's options are very limited. They either assent to the bill within fifteen days or send it for reconsideration by the Parliament.[208] If Parliament passes the bill again with or without modification, the President must assent to it within seven days of its second presentation.[209] In the case of Money Bills, the President's power to send them back is further curtailed. They must assent to the bill within fifteen days.[210] Otherwise, the bill is automatically passed.[211]

To sum up, the executive-legislature relation in the Westminster system is a dominant-dormant one.[212] However, the comparative analysis presented above reveals that Westminster's procedural safety valves and protections of the backbench and opposition rights are missing in Bangladesh. While a Westminster parliament is not designed to obstruct the government's legislative program, parliamentary procedure is verily expected to play a preventive role, making the government anticipate possible parliamentary and popular reactions to its legislative proposals.[213] On the other hand, the Bangladesh Parliament can barely generate any fear of reaction in the government and shape the government's legislative proposals.

3 Scrutiny by the Parliamentary Committees

Described as its "eyes and ears",[214] committees do three important jobs[215] for parliament. They oversee executive accountability continuously. They facilitate public participation in the parliamentary process. They offer expertise and alternative career prospects to the backbench MPs. These three tasks,

207 Constitution (n 135) art. 80(2).

208 ibid, art. 80(3).

209 ibid, art. 80(4).

210 President Justice Shahabuddin Ahmed famously sent a controversial bill titled the Public Safety Act 2000 back to the parliament. The government however argued that the bill was a Money Bill and hence the President was not entitled to return it.

211 Constitution (n 135) art 80(3).

212 MM Khan, *Dominant Executive and Dormant Legislature: Executive-Legislature Relations in Bangladesh* (New Delhi: South Asian Publishers India, 2006).

213 M Moran, *Politics and Governance in the UK* (London: Palgrave 2015) 111.

214 Michael Jogerst, *Reform in the House of Commons: the Select Committee System* (Kentucky: University Press of Kentucky 1993) 215–216.

215 Martin Indyk, 'Making government responsible: the role of parliamentary committees' (1980) 15(1) Australian Journal of Political Science 93.

however, risk putting the committees at odds with parliamentary political parties. Assertive parliamentary committees may invite the wrath of the governing party by seeking information and revision of governmental policies.[216] They may question the government's sole representative claim by creating an independent public relations route for the Parliament.[217] They may trouble the parliamentary parties by fending off crude partisanship in parliamentary business and encouraging expertise-based work by the MPs.[218] The majority parties may see them as a reservoir of backbench revolts. The opposition parties may see them as harmful to their oppose-everything-and-propose-nothing approach. Therefore, the committee system's relationship with the political parties is not straightforward.

The impact of a parliamentary committee system largely depends on the nature of the parliament itself. The U.S.-styled congressional and the Westminster-styled parliamentary systems offer significantly different political and institutional contexts that shape the work and impact of the committee system. Party cohesion is relatively loose in the congressional model. Therefore, committee assertiveness and individual member activities draw visible public attention there.[219] On the other hand, a Westminster parliament is a party, and Cabinet dominated. Hence, committee activism is relatively harder to achieve.[220]

Four leading committee theories[221] explain how the parliamentary committees are organised across the congressional and parliamentary systems, why they behave in particular ways, and how the political parties influence their formation and work. These theories are known as the "distributive or gains from trade theory"; "information, scrutiny and expertise supply"; "coalition"; and "partisan cartel" theories.

---

216 Gareth Griffith, *Parliament and Accountability: the Role of Parliamentary Oversight Committees* (New South Wales: Parliamentary Library Service 2005) 11.

217 Michael Jogerst (n 214).

218 Bert A Rockman, 'Legislative-Executive Relations and Legislative Oversight' (1984) 9(3) Legislative Studies Quarterly 387, 394.

219 Malcolm Shaw, 'Parliamentary Committees: a global perspective' (1998) 4(1), Journal of Legislative Studies 225, 227.

220 Lawrence D Longley and Roger H Davidson, 'Parliamentary committees: Changing perspectives on changing institutions' (1998) 4(1) Journal of Legislative Studies 1, 2.

221 Thomas Zittel and Eric M, 'Uslaner, Comparative Legislative Behavior' in Robert E Goodin (ed.) *The Oxford Handbook of Political Science* (Oxford: Oxford University Press 2009), 392–408.

3.1 *Committee Work for Constituency Benefits, Re-election, and Career Prospects*

Shepsle and Weingast[222] have offered "the distributive and gains from trade theory" of committee activities focusing on individual committee members. They argue that committee members seek committees that best serve their constituency interests and re-election prospects.[223] Members engage in policy trade or pork-barrel politics with colleagues from the same or other committees to ensure that decisions most favourable to their constituents are supported and adopted in return for their concession to measures that might be less relevant for theirs but important for the other colleagues' constituents.[224] This behaviour allows the members to distribute material benefits to their constituents and increases their re-election prospects.[225] However, the distributive theory assumes that the legislature is highly decentralised[226] and has policymaking capability comparable to the US Congress. Members also can self-select into their preferred committees[227] without much dictation from their parties.[228]

In parliamentary systems, the scope of pressing constituency issues through committee work is limited. MPs' constituency works here are primarily linked with government departments rather than parliamentary committees.[229] Also, parliamentary elections have a strong partisan tendency. People tend to elect the Prime Minister and the governing party rather than their constituency MPs.[230] Therefore, the parliamentary system does not offer substantial constituency benefits or re-election prospects for the committee members. Also,

222 Kenneth A Shepsle and BR Weingast, 'Political Preferences for the Pork Barrel: a Generalization' (1981) 25 American Journal of Political Science 96.

223 D Rohde and Kenneth A Shepsle, 'Democratic Committee Assignments in the House of Representatives: Strategic Aspects of a Social Choice Process,' (1973) 67 American Political Science Review 889.

224 Kenneth A Shepsle, *The Giant Jigsaw Puzzle: Democratic Committee Assignments in the Modern House* (University of Chicago Press 1978).

225 Ingvar Mattson and Kaare Strom, 'Parliamentary Committees' in Herbert Dohring (ed), *Parliament and Majority Rule in West Europe* (University of Mannheim 1995) 249–307.

226 Shane Martin and Tim A Mickler, 'Committee Assignments: Theories, Causes and Consequences' (2019) 72(1) Parliamentary Affairs 77.

227 Shepsle (n 224).

228 Martin and Mickler (n 226) 79.

229 Philip Norton, 'The Growth of the Constituency Role of the MP' (1994) 4(1) Parliamentary Affairs 705.

230 Andrew Eggers and Alexander Fischer, 'Electoral Accountability and the UK Parliamentary Expenses Scandal: Did Voters Punish Corrupt MPs?' *Political Science and Political Economy Working Paper 8/2011* (London: London School of Economics 2011).

unlike the US Congressional system, the scope of private member legislation is very limited in parliamentary systems.[231] MPs can rarely press constituency issues by sponsoring legislative proposals in Parliament. All these make the MPs' self-selection to their preferred committees difficult.

Despite the constraints, the Distributive/Gains from Trade Theory is growing in relevance in the party-centred parliamentary model. While the committee works may not guarantee direct constituency benefits and re-election prospects for the MPs, the Committee works help them enhance their career prospect in particular areas of public policy. Growth of expertise begets reputation and profile for the MPs, making their involuntary or party-directed removal from a committee harder. The post-1979 development of the select committee system in the UK has created avenues for non-partisan if not fully autonomous, committee assignments.[232] Some recent studies by Lord Norton[233] show that party dominance has eroded significantly after the 1979 and post-2000 reforms.[234] Most senior British MPs now acquire expertise and reputation[235] in their respective policy areas that offer them a choice – call it a choice to self-appoint – on the type of Committee they want. Select Committee chairs and members thereby garnish an autonomous identity outside the traditional framework of partisanship.[236] Therefore, while the British MPs may not pursue their committee assignments for their re-election prospects or

231 Russel and Gover (n 153) 272–275.

232 Lucy Atkinson, *Select Committee and the UK Constitution* (The Constitution Society 2017) 40.

233 Philip Norton, 'Power behind the Scenes: the Importance of Informal Space in Legislatures' (2019) 72 Parliamentary Affairs 245; Philip Cowley and Philip Norton, 'Rebels and Rebellions: Conservative MPs in the 1992 Parliament' (2002) 1(1) British Journal of Politics & International Relations 84.

234 Michael A Jogerst, 'Backbenchers and select committees in the British House of Commons: Can Parliament offer useful roles for the frustrated?' (1991) 20 European Journal of Political Research 21, 35; Michael A Jogerst (n 214), 7–8, 31–35; Mathew Flinders, 'Shifting the Balance? Parliament, the Executive and the British Constitution' (2002) 50(1) Political Studies 23; The Reform of the House of Commons Committee was a Select Committee established by the UK Parliament. It is unofficially known after the name of its Chairman Tony Wright.

235 In 2001, around 100 Labour MPs revolted against the Tony Blair government's attempt to de-select Gwyneth Dunwoody and Donald Anderson as the chairs of transport and foreign affairs committees of the House of Commons. See Hannah White, *Select Committees under Scrutiny: the Impact of Parliamentary Committee Inquiries on Government* (London: Institute for Government 2015) 7.

236 Alexandra Kelso, 'Political Leadership in Parliament: the Role of Select Committee Chairs in the UK House of Commons' (2016) 4(2) Politics and Governance 115, 123–24; Rogers and Walters, *How Parliament Works* (London: Routledge, 2015) 333.

constituency interests, they still choose their select committees for reasons beyond their party leaders' control.

On the other hand, committee assignments in Bangladesh do not offer direct constituency benefits for the MPs. MPs would rather utilise parliamentary question time and personally lobby with the ministers for constituency benefits.[237] Similarly, the nomination of the MP candidates is an exclusive privilege of the party high-ups rather than the grass-root party units. Hence, the committee work rarely relates to the MPs' re-election prospects in Bangladesh.[238] Committee work is also considered an unattractive career or expertise development route for the MPs. The unwillingness of Bangladeshi political parties to appreciate the recent development in parliamentary models like that of the UK has reduced the relevance of the distributive theory's premise in Bangladesh.

3.2 *Committees as Suppliers of Information, Expertise and Scrutiny*

A second perspective on the committee system is that of Keith Krehbiel.[239] Krehbiel perceives the committees as suppliers of information, scrutiny and policy expertise to the main Chamber. Applicable to both congressional and parliamentary models, Krehbiel's theory argues that committees improve the quality of the policy process by capitalising on the varied expertise of the large pool of legislators. This theory invokes an "economy of operation logic"[240] and a "rational choice institutionalism"[241] argument where specialisation and expertise are encouraged on a cost-benefit basis. If a member incurs the cost of applying his knowledge to a specific public domain, s/he should gain authority and deference in that policy area. It also enhances their chance of getting a ministerial position when their party comes to power. Parliament's interest in generating "an incentive structure that induces members to take the trouble of acquiring expertise."[242] is understandable. In return, the Parliament will

---

237 Zahir Ahmed, 'From Shape Shifting to Collusion in Violence: an Ethnography of Informal Relationships Between Bangladeshi Members of Parliament and Their Constituents' (2019) 42(1) Legal and Political Anthropology Review (PoLAR) 5, 11–13.

238 Mohammad Mozahidul Islam, 'The Toxic Politics of Bangladesh: a Bipolar Competitive Neo-patrimonial State?' (2013) 21(2) Asian Journal of Political Science 148, 149–51.

239 Keith Krehbiel, *Information and Legislative Organization* (University of Michigan Press 1991).

240 Mattson and Strom (n 225).

241 Thomas W Gilligan and Keith Krehbiel, 'Organization of Informative Committees by a Rational Legislature' (1990) 34 American Journal of Political Science 531, 544–47.

242 Thomas W Gilligan and Keith Krehbiel, 'Collective Decision-Making and Standing Committees: an Informational Rationale for Restrictive Amendment Procedures' (1987) 3 Journal of Law, Economics and Organization 287; Thomas Gilligan and Keith Krehbiel,

benefit from the expertise, diversification of the workload, and increased legislative output.[243] The plenary of the House draws apolitical, objective and technical information from the committees. The support enhances the Parliament's capability to make up at least some of its expertise, information and knowledge gaps vis-à-vis the bureaucrats and technocrats in the government.

3.2.1 Supply of Expertise and Information

In the UK, a decisive moment came in 1979 when the detailed and permanent system of select committees was established. The new select committee system of 1979 is aligned with the departmental line.[244] There is usually at least one select committee assigned the task of monitoring the work of each government department. The UK committees are empowered to determine their agenda, gather written and oral evidence, sometimes by travelling through the country or beyond, and employ specialist advisers outside the Parliament.[245] Recent evaluations of select committees have been largely positive.[246] Select Committees also maintained a high media profile, perhaps comparable to the US congressional committees.[247] However, the expertise valued in the UK Public Bill Committees is primarily procedural.[248]

Compared to the expertise-driven work of the UK select committees, the ministerial standing committees in Bangladesh have not been able to build expertise and legal or public support bases. They have paper powers to inquire into irregularities and serious complaints against the administration and recommend corrective measures. They also have the authority to review and recommend necessary measures for due enforcement of laws passed by Parliament.[249] They have plenary power of subpoena,[250] examination on oath, and production of documents, papers and records.[251] However, the committees lack the power to follow up with their reports and recommendations. The

---

'Asymmetric Information and Legislative Rules with a Heterogeneous Committee' (1989) 33 American Journal of Political Science 459.

243 Martin and Mickler (n 226) 81–82.

244 Atkinson (n 232) 27.

245 The UK House of Commons Standing Order No. 152 (4a).

246 Meg Russell and Meghan Benton, *Selective Influence: the Policy Impact of House of Commons Select Committees* (University College London Constitution Unit 2011) 9–29.

247 Marek Kubala, 'Select Committees in the House of Commons and the Media' (2011) 64(4) *Parliamentary Affairs* 694.

248 Russell, Morris and Larkin (n 175) 43.

249 Constitution (n 135) art. 76(2)(b).

250 ibid, art. 76(2)(c).

251 ibid, art. 76(3); RoP (n 58) r. 202–204.

responses are generally evasive, even in rare cases of the government responding to committee reports. The minority members in the committees are usually not allowed to prepare and submit their report except to record a brief "note of dissent", which is appended to the committee report.

Once the committees are formed, the MPs show extreme inertia in discharging their duties and mandates. The lacklustre approach the committee members show to their committee assignments is reflected in statistics. The First Parliament (1973–1975) received only one report from a committee.[252] The Second Parliament (1979–1981) witnessed committee chairs as condolence gifts to people who could not be included in the Cabinet otherwise.[253] The Third Parliament (1986–1988) constituted some general standing committees but did not form ministerial or departmental standing committees. The Public Accounts Committee of that Parliament produced only three reports. The Fourth Parliament (1988–1990), for the first time in the history of Bangladesh, established a detailed range of committees. However, all the committees produced only five reports – two by the Public Accounts, each by the Estimate, Public Undertaking and Governmental Assurance committees.[254] In the Fifth, Seventh and Eighth parliaments, thirty, twenty-nine, and ten committees, respectively, did not produce any report at all. There is a rule that every standing Committee would meet at least once a month.[12]. It is rarely followed.[255] A very recent study on the works of the committees on the Ministry of Finance and Agriculture confirms the dismal state of affairs in terms of meeting frequency, attendance and quality of the reports produced by the committees.[256]

3.2.2 Supply of Legislative Scrutiny

Unlike the UK Public Bill Committees' legislative stage scrutiny and the Departmental Select Committee's pre-legislative scrutiny, the bill committees' contribution to Bangladesh's legislative scrutiny process is modest. The RoP stipulates sending bills to a select committee created for the specific bill or a related ministerial standing committee.[257] The use of select committees for specific bills started in the Seventh Parliament (1996–2001). Before 1996, bills

252 Dilara Choudhury, *Constitutional Development in Bangladesh: Stresses and Strains* (Oxford University Press 1994) 122.

253 Ahmed (n 17) 133.

254 Salahuddin Aminuzzaman (n 84).

255 Nizam Ahmed, 'Parliamentary Committees and Parliamentary Government in Bangladesh' (2001) 10(1) Contemporary South Asia 11, 15.

256 Navid Saifullah, 'Effectiveness of the Parliamentary Standing Committees in Bangladesh' (Masters in Governance and Development Thesis: BRAC University Dhaka 2006) 41.

257 RoP (n 58) r. 77, 80.

were rarely sent to committees after the second reading. Since the Seventh Parliament, however, most bills have been sent to the bill committees or ministerial standing committees. Absent pre-legislative scrutiny by any ministerial standing committee, the bill committees are left alone in dealing with the law. Unlike the UK, where the bill's journey is programmed in the House,[258] Bangladeshi rules of procedure provide that committees should report back within a month if the House prescribes no time limit. If the Committee requests further time, the House may extend it.[259] While this might appear a good opportunity for Bill Committees to do detailed work, they usually waste the chance by dilly-dallying their work. Lapse of bills in the committee stage and never returning to the House is not rare in Bangladesh. Although the committee members may propose amendments to a bill, its acceptance or rejection depends on the attitude of the government party. Traditionally, no major changes are proposed, tolerated or accepted by the House. Also, the finance committees do not have any scope for discussion or deliberation on budget, financial or appropriation bills. It means the committees have no say, let alone control, over the government's budgetary and fiscal policies.[260] It is in clear contrast with the practice of the House of Commons, where the Commons Treasury Select Committee and Lords' Economic Affairs Sub-committee do significant scrutiny over the budget.

To sum up, while the UK Parliament has acquired a laudable level of specialisation, information generation capability, and scrutiny mandate over the years, Bangladesh refuses to recognise the parliamentary committees as a reservoir of expertise, information and scrutiny. Without this recognition, committeemen are not unlikely to show poor commitment to the Committee works[261] and remain loyal "lobby fodders" of their parties who would select or de-select them at their sweet will.[262]

3.3 *Coalition Logic for Committee Assertiveness*

A third perspective on the committee activities is that of Martin and Vanberg. Their "coalition theory"[263] argues that the organisation of a legislature follows

258 Russell, Morris and Larkin (n 175).

259 RoP (n 58) r. 209(1).

260 ibid, r. 111(3).

261 Taiabur Rahman, *Parliamentary Control and Government Accountability in South Asia: a Comparative Analysis of Bangladesh, India and Sri Lanka* (Routledge 2008) 110–129.

262 Nizam Ahmed (n 68) 88.

263 Lanny W Martin and Georg Vanberg, *Parliaments and Coalitions: the Role of Legislative Institutions in Multiparty Governance* (Oxford University Press 2011).

governments' formation and is, in particular, influenced by the frequency of coalition governments. The theory builds on the tension between coalition partners who govern jointly but remain accountable to the people separately. Therefore, parties try to keep a tab on their coalition partners through coalition agreements to minimise the risk of being seen as overly accommodating.[264] The coalition government has important ramifications for the organisation and the assertiveness of parliamentary committees. A series of empirical studies show that multiparty governments significantly imbue committee autonomy.[265] In turn, a strong committee system provides an added layer of intra-coalition scrutiny over the one existing under the coalition agreement. Martin and Vanberg[266] have tested the logic in Danish, German, Dutch, Irish and French parliaments and found that a strong committee system better facilitates coalition bargains.[267] Another study by Martin and DePauw in Ireland shows a similar result.[268] Zubek shows that a coalition government trying to temper the committee's autonomy is less likely to succeed than a majority government.[269]

In institutionalised parliamentary systems, coalition governments are usually formed under a negotiated Coalition Pact between the partners. Coalition partners use the pact as a powerful political tool of mutual restraint. They usually appoint Junior Ministers to shadow the Ministers appointed from another coalition partner. Partners also negotiate an agreement on the day-to-day government businesses and the role the collation ministers would play within the government.

Within the Parliament, coalition party members use parliamentary questions, and the Committee works to scrutinise their partners.[270] Committees

264 Mark Bennister and Richard Heffernan, 'Cameron as Prime Minister: the Intra-Executive Politics of Britain's Coalition Government' (2012) 65 Parliamentary Affairs 778, 748–85.

265 Tim A Mickler, 'Committee autonomy in parliamentary systems – coalition logic or congressional rationales?' (2017) 23(3) The Journal of Legislative Studies 367.

266 Lanny W Martin and Georg Vanberg, 'Coalition Policymaking and Legislative Review' (2005) 99(1) American Political Science Review 93, 97–131.

267 ibid, 132–155; Lanny W Martin and Georg Vanberg, 'Policing the Bargain: Coalition Government and Parliamentary Scrutiny' (2004) 48 American Journal of Political Science 13.

268 Shane Martin and Sam DePauw, 'Coalition Government and the Internal Organization of Legislatures' (Annual Meeting of the American Political Science Association, Toronto, September 2009).

269 Radoslaw Zubek, 'Coalition Government and Committee Power' (2015) 38(5) West European Politics 1020, 1032.

270 Kaare Strøm, Wolfgang C Muller and Daniel Markham Smith, 'Parliamentary Control of Coalition Governments' (2010) 13 Annual Review of Political Science 517, 527–528; Lanny W Martin and Georg Vanberg, 'Coalition Government, Legislative Institutions, and

serve the best sort of accountability when the Minister and Committee chairs belong to different coalition parties.[271] Kim and Loewenberg's study on several German coalition governments indicates that majority and minority partners distribute committee chairs in a way that allows one partner to shadow the ministries controlled by another partner(s).[272] This factor has important ramifications for the organisation and the assertiveness of committees. A series of empirical studies show that multiparty governments significantly imbue committee autonomy.[273] A strong committee system appears to better allow the coalition partners to police their coalition bargain. Government Bills on divisive issues get rigorous scrutiny by coalition partners sitting on committees.[274]

A study on the dataset of parliamentary questions during David Cameron and Nick Clegg's coalition government (2010–2015) has shown that the coalition party backbenchers have extensively used the parliamentary question times in the UK as a tool of intra-coalition accountability.[275] The Cameron-Clegg Cabinet was based on the Coalition Agreement that placed a "coalition committee" at the "top of the government's collective decision-making machinery".[276] Governmental policies were outlined in the "Coalition Programme for Government". Working within the agreed structure, Prime Minister David Cameron dealt with an added "intra-party rivalry" layer.[277]

Bangladesh has seen at least four – two official and two unofficial – coalition governments so far.[278] In 1991, the majority party BNP fell eleven seats

Public Policy in Parliamentary Democracies' (2020) 64(2) American Journal of Political Science 325.

271 M Hallerberg, 'The Role of Parliamentary Committees in the Budgetary Process within Europe' in RR Strauch, J Von Hagen (eds.) *Institutions, Politics and Fiscal Policy* (Kluwer 2000) 87–106; M Hallerberg, 'Electoral Laws, Government, and Parliament' in H Doring and M Hallerberg (eds.) *Patterns of Parliamentary Behavior* (Aldershot Ashgate 2004) 11–33.

272 DH Kim and G Loewenberg, 'The role of Parliamentary Committees in Coalition Governments: Keeping tabs on Coalition partners in the German Bundestag' (2005) 38 Comparative Political Studies 1104.

273 Tim A Mickler (n 265).

274 Lanny W Martin and Georg Vanberg, 'Coalition Policymaking and Legislative Review' (2005) 99(1) American Political Science Review 93.

275 Martin and Richard Whitaker, 'Beyond Committees: Parliamentary Oversight of Coalition Government in Britain' (2019) 42(7) West European Politics 1464.

276 Akash Paun, *United We Stand: Coalition Government in the UK* (Institute for Government. London 2010).

277 Mark Bennister and Richard Heffernan, 'Cameron as Prime Minister: the Intra-Executive Politics of Britain's Coalition Government' (2012) 65 Parliamentary Affairs 778.

278 M Moniruzzaman, 'Parliamentary Democracy in Bangladesh: an Evaluation of the Parliament during 1991–2006' (2009) 47(1) Commonwealth and Comparative Politics 100.

short of a majority (140 out of 300).[279] They formed a government with the tacit support of *Jamaat e Islami* (JI), which had eighteen seats. Though they did not make any political pact or express coalition-making, it is understood that the coalition was based on some tactical voting arrangement during the election.[280] However, after the government's formation, the BNP took 28 of the 30 reserved seats for women. JI got the rest of the seats. Once the reserved seat election was over, BNP no longer needed JI's support to sustain its majority. Hence, the electoral coalition ended there. JI later joined the combined opposition parties, pressing for the introduction of the caretaker government. The combined opposition resigned from Parliament in 1994 to press their demand home.[281] A similar thing happened in the Seventh Parliament when AL got 146 seats and formed a government with the Jatya Party's (JP) support.[282] Unlike BNP, AL offered a Ministry to the JP in its "Government of National Consensus".[283] Absent any declared political pact between the AL-JP, the intra-partner accountability relations remained unclear. Like the BNP government of 1991, the AL government secured its absolute majority through the reserved women's seats. The JP Minister acted like a loyal associate of the AL Prime Minister.[284] The JP leader, HM Ershad, later joined the opposition parties and went against the government. The JP Minister, however, refused to resign from the Cabinet.[285]

Bangladesh's first-ever official coalition government took power in 2001. This time, BNP-JI formed an electoral alliance and won the election as a coalition.[286] The JI was given two ministries. However, the election result itself

---

279 Craig Baxter, 'Bangladesh in 1991: a Parliamentary System' (1992) 32(2) Asian Survey 162.

280 Taj Hashmi, 'Islamic Resurgence in Bangladesh: Genesis, Dynamics and Implications', in Satu P Limaye, Mohan Malik and Robert G Wirsing (eds.), *Religious Radicalism and Security in South Asia* (Honolulu, Hawaii: Asia pacific Center for Security Studies 2004) 35–75, 54.

281 Golam Hossain, 'Bangladesh in 1994: Democracy at Risk' (1995) 35(2) Asian Survey 171.

282 Mohammad Mohabbat Khan and Syed Anwar Husain, 'Process of Democratization in Bangladesh' (1996) 5(3) Contemporary South Asia 319.

283 Stanley A Kochanek, 'Bangladesh in 1996: the 25th Year of Independence' (1997) 37(2) Asian Survey 136; M Rashiduzzaman, 'Political Unrest and Democracy in Bangladesh' (1997) 37(3) Asian Survey 254.

284 Immigration and Refugee Board of Canada, 'Bangladesh: the estrangement between Jatiya Party (JP) cabinet minister Anwar Hussain Manju and the leadership of the JP (since June 1996)' (Canada: September 1998).

285 Elora Shehabuddin, 'Bangladesh in 1999: Desperately Seeking a Responsible Opposition' (2000) 40 (1) *Asian Survey* 181.

286 Moazzem Hossain, 'Home-Grown' Democracy' (2006) 40(9) Economic and Political Weekly 791.

was not conducive to any intra-coalition bargain. In the 2001 election, BNP got 193 seats, and JI got 17. Left without a necessity for JI's continued support to sustain its majority, BNP did not need to bother much about its coalition partner. The JI Ministers largely offered a blank check to the majority partner and co-operated it throughout the tenure.[287] A similar thing happened in the ninth parliamentary election of 2008. AL got 230, and its Grand Alliance partner JP got 33 seats. Some Ministries were given to different coalition partners, but no intra-coalition pact of accountability was declared. Coalition Ministers behaved as though they all were from the majority partner AL.[288] It, therefore, is not unsurprising that the parliamentary literature of Bangladesh has so far overlooked this "intra-coalition" aspect of parliamentary accountability. Therefore, Martin and Vanberg's coalition logic seems less relevant for Bangladesh.

3.4 *Partisan Cartelisation of Parliamentary Committees*

Cox and McCubbins have proposed the partisan cartel theory to appreciate the political parties' role in shaping the parliamentary committee systems. They argue that distributive and expertise theories unduly ignore the phenomenon of party politics within legislatures.[289] Cox and McCubbins also reject the self-selection thesis. They argue that though the member preferences for committee assignments are important in the US Congress and determine much of actual assignments, party involvement in the process is no less significant. If non-partisanship is so strong, there is a risk that committees will become equally unpopular among the government and the Opposition.[290] Governments might see a committee-oriented parliament as a threat to party discipline and a potential reservoir of backbench revolts. The Opposition also might feel forced by a consensual committee system to co-operate with the government rather than oppose it. It, therefore, makes sense that parties would like to influence the committee members' behaviour and agenda.[291] Hence, Martin and Mickler

287 Ishtiaq Hossain and Noore Alam Siddiquee, 'Islam in Bangladesh politics: the role of Ghulam Azam of Jamaat-I-Islami' (2004) 5(3) Inter-Asia Cultural Studies 384; Rounaq Jahan, 'Bangladesh in 2002: Imperiled Democracy' (2003) 43(1) Asian Survey 222.

288 Sandeep Bhardwaj, *Bangladesh in 2009: Challenges After Elections* (Institute of Peace and Conflict Studies IPCS: Issue Brief No 90 January 2009).

289 Gary W Cox and Mathew D McCubbins, Legislative Leviathan: Party Government in the House (Cambridge University Press 2007).

290 Rockman (n 218).

291 JH Aldrich and DW Rohde, 'Measuring conditional party government' (Annual Meeting of the Midwest Political Science Association, Chicago, April 1998).

claim that political parties "cartelise" the Parliament's legislative power by shaping the committees.[292]

Political parties – government or opposition – have a strong interest in cartelising the committees. They do so because they feel that too assertive committee activists harm the internal party. Party control in committee assignment is unavoidable even in the congressional system. Partisan control over the committee formation process is more obvious in the parliamentary system, where the Heads of the party governments and their Cabinet are drawn from the Parliament. The UK Parliament, however, seems to defy Cox and McCubbins' cartelisation logic. Despite the system's inherent proneness to partisan cartelisation, the UK House of Commons has opted for a less partisan committee assignment process and injected a very strong policy influencing and scrutiny capability into the committees. As mentioned earlier, the 1979 select committees in the UK and their subsequent reforms in 2006 and 2010 have facilitated a shift from crude partisanship[293] to a consensual approach in non-party or cross-party dealings.[294]

On the other hand, political parties in Bangladesh are not culturally receptive to non-partisan and reconciliatory approaches. The absence of command decentralisation and decisional autonomy for the party members affects the committee system directly. The selection of members and committee chairs in Bangladesh is an absolute privilege of the party leadership. As per the RoP, the number of members in different committees is either fixed or subject to a ceiling.[295] The RoP does not deal with the methods of appointment as such. The Speaker chooses the members of committees concerning the administration of Parliament, *e.g.*, House, Petition and Library Committees.[296] In other cases, it is the party high-ups who decide who is to be placed where. Membership is distributed among parties in proportion to their seats in the House. Though the political parties usually gather their members' interests and preferences before they are pencilled for a committee, committee members are ultimately chosen from the partisan lists. The House moves a formal resolution confirming the appointment.

292 Martin and Mickler (n 226) 82–83.

293 Michael Rush, 'Parliamentary Scrutiny' in Robert Pyper and Lynton Robins (eds.), *Governing the UK in the 1990s* (St Martin's Press 1995) 108–30; Gavin Drewry (ed), *The New Select Committees: a Study of the 1979 Reforms* (Clarendon Press 1985).

294 Atkinson (n 232).

295 RoP (n 58) r. 219, 225, 231, 239, 240, 245, 246, 264, 266.

296 ibid, r. 231, 249, 257.

In some cases, opposition parties allege that the Speaker, instructed by the government party, had ignored their list of members. For example, the new party in power dropped an opposition MP who appeared assertive in the Seventh Parliament's defence committee from the same Committee in the Eighth Parliament. He was offered a relatively less significant committee instead.[297]

Regarding the appointment of Committee chairs, RoP allocates the chair of some committees on an *ex officio* basis.[298] Other chairs may be appointed through the resolution of Parliament or elected, formally at least, by the committees concerned.[299] Instead of MPs pursuing an extra-governmental route of a political career, committee chairs in Bangladesh are distributed by the party high-ups as compensation for those party men who could not be offered ministerial positions in the first place.[300] As a result, Bangladesh allegedly has more than necessary parliamentary committees. Those work as sources of patronage for the government rather than as sources of government accountability.[301] Ruling parties have traditionally claimed chairmanship of most committees, and the appointment of opposition members to the chair is rare.[302] Once in the Fifth Parliament (1991–1995), the chair of a sub-committee established by a committee was assigned to an opposition party member as a good gesture – the first of its kind in Bangladesh's history. Since the Ninth Parliament, chairs have been distributed among the parties on a *pro-rata* basis. As mentioned earlier, allocation of the chairs, however, remains an absolute privilege of the party leaders, *i.e.*, the Prime Minister and the Opposition Leader.[303]

To sum up the comparative discussion on the UK and Bangladesh's parliamentary committee systems, it appears that while the House of Commons committees have substantially circumscribed crude partisanship and are drawing from the committees' expertise and intra-coalition accountability regimes, Bangladesh remains engulfed by a degenerated version of partisanship that fits in with the partisan cartel theory alone. While recent developments in the UK House of Commons have paved the way for non-partisan,

---

297 Rahman (n 261); Mustafizur Rahaman (n 83) 54–56.

298 RoP (n 58) r. 219, 257, 264.

299 ibid, r 191(1).

300 ATM Obaidullah, 'Standing Committees on Ministries in the Bangladesh Parliament: the Need for Reorganisation' (2011) 18(2) South Asian Survey 317, 338.

301 Philip Norton and Nizam Ahmed, 'Legislatures in Asia: Exploring Diversity' in Philip Norton and Nizam Ahmed (eds.), *Parliaments in Asia* (Frank Cass 1999) 51–52.

302 KM Mahiuddin, 'The Parliamentary Committee System in Bangladesh An Analysis of its Functioning' (Ph.D. Thesis, Ruprecht-Karls-Universität Heidelberg 2009) 104–106.

303 Nizam Ahmed (n 132) 85–88.

if not fully autonomous, selection to the committees, Bangladesh's strictly partisan selection process makes the re-election and career prospect-driven selection theory unsuitable. The UK parliamentary committees have gained a laudable level of specialisation, information generation and scrutiny capability over the years. Bangladesh Parliament, however, is refusing to move in that direction. Next, Bangladesh's several "tactical electoral coalitions" have miserably failed to generate the minimum relation of intra-coalition accountability between the partners.

In general, Bangladesh's committee-related rules of the RoP were "mostly honoured in the breach".[304] The Fifth Parliament could not establish parliamentary committees until half its tenure passed.[305] Due to the opposition party's refusal to put their list of nominees, the Seventh Parliament (1996–2001) took two years to form all the parliamentary committees.[306] However, the same Parliament amended the RoP to ensure that committees are constituted within the first session of each Parliament. Still, the next Parliament (2001–2006) took over 20 months to set up all the committees.[307] It took the UNDP to threaten the withdrawal of funds from its "Strengthening Parliamentary Democracy" project to convince the ruling party to form committees and allow them to operate.[308] However, the ninth (2009–2013), tenth (2014–2018) and eleventh (2019-present) parliaments have constituted their committees within the first session of their tenure. The Eleventh Parliament (2019- 2023) created a record of the fastest possible formation within the first ten sitting days of its first session. Apparently, the absence of meaningful opposition in those parliaments facilitated such unusually fast law-making.[309] Therefore, Bangladesh's parliamentary committees continue to serve a mere ceremonial purpose, and their accountability roles remain mostly unrealised.

---

304 Nizam Ahmed (n 17) 131.

305 Jalal Firoj (n 59).

306 Nizam Ahmed, 'From Monopoly to Competition: Party Politics in the Bangladesh Parliament (1973–2001)' (2003) 76(1) Pacific Affairs 55, 68–69.

307 Quamrul Alam and Julian Teicher, 'The State of Governance in Bangladesh: the Capture of State Institutions' (2012) 35(4) Journal of South Asian Studies 858.

308 Farheen Alamgir, Tanvir Mahmud and Iftekharuzzaman, 'Corruption and Parliamentary Oversight: Primacy of The Political Will' (Transparency International Bangladesh 2006).

309 M Jashim Ali Chowdhury, '11th Parliament: Rays of hope for the Committee System' *The Daily Star Law and Our Rights* (Dhaka, 05 March 2019).

4 Political Parties as the Agents of Accountability

In one of his recent papers, Jeremy Waldron called for the revival of a "*political* political theory"[310] that would bring the political parties, their structures, representation and competition for power to the forefront of the "empirical political science".[311] Political parties have shaped the Westminster parliamentary system so drastically that the system now essentially depends on the existence of at least two main and stable political parties that alternate in government within a reasonable frequency. The politicisation of the UK Parliament evolved through competition between the Whigs and Tories (the 1710s-1880s), the Liberals and Tories (the 1880s-1920s) and then the Tories and the Labours (the 1920s-present).[312] By the end of the nineteenth century, parliamentary elections, processes and oversight functions became identifiable exclusively within a partisan environment.[313] Partisan competition within a parliamentary framework begets stability in the system. Regular and orderly alteration of power incentivises the opposition and government parties to preserve and defend the model, expecting that all will benefit from it eventually.[314] Within the parliament, political parties shape how the institution performs its oversight role and legislative mandate.

Professor Anthony King examined the patterns of executive-legislature relations in Britain, France, and West Germany within a partisan environment.[315] King found that parliamentary party groups interact in intra-party, inter-party (opposition), non-party, and cross-party modes. *The intra-party mode* is about how party leadership and backbenchers interact and hold each other accountable. In *the opposition mode,* competing political parties debate and oppose each other's policies and actions.[316] *The cross-party and non-party*

310 Jeremy Waldron, 'Political Political Theory' (2013) 21 Journal of Political Philosophy 1.

311 ibid, 17.

312 Leslie Lipson, 'The Two-Party System in British Politics' (1953) 47(2) The American Political Science Review 337.

313 Philip Norton, 'Old Institution, New Institutionalism? Parliament and Government in the UK' in Philip Norton (ed.), *Parliaments in Contemporary Western Europe* 16–43 (Routledge 1998) 18.

314 Gregoire Webber, 'Loyal Opposition and the Political Constitution' (2017) 37(2) Oxford Journal of Legal Studies 357.

315 Anthony King, 'Modes of Executive-Legislative Relations: Great Britain, France and West Germany' in Philp Norton (ed.), *Legislatures* (Oxford University Press 1990) 186–207; John P Mackintosh, *The British Cabinet* (Stevens and Sons Ltd: London 1977).

316 Robert Leonardi, Raffaella Nanetti and Gianfranco Pasquino, 'Institutionalization of Parliament and Parliamentarization of Parties in Italy' (1978) 3(1) Legislative Studies Quarterly 161.

modes mainly operate in parliamentary committees where abject partisanship is relatively relaxed. The *Non-party Mode* thrives in expertise-driven committee activities where party members focus on specialised and technical matters rather than political controversies. *The cross-party mode* flourishes when coalition partners of government or even the ruling party and opposition parties work within the limits of a pre-negotiated political pact.[317] Individual MPs also caucus on issues, principles and interests that may call for *cross-party* collaboration or *non-partisan* positions. The next few paragraphs will examine how the behaviour of political parties shapes the modalities of parliamentary opposition and intra-party accountability in the Bangladesh Parliament.

4.1 *Inter-party Relations within the Parliament*

Recognition of the opposition's right to exist and act within the system has been characterised as the "polyarchic"[318] quality of democracy. The opposition's meaningful participation in the parliamentary process largely depends on the competing political parties' recognition of each other's existence as mutually reinforcing. The presence or absence of this recognition differentiates the democracies from the "illiberal or non-democratic regimes".[319] The leading Westminster systems, including the UK, have successfully institutionalised the opposition and installed it as a government-in-waiting and the most important safety valve against constitutional breakdown or extra-constitutional interference in politics.[320] The institutionalisation of the opposition has resonance beyond the internal parliamentary processes. In the UK, the Prime Minister and the Leader of the Opposition occasionally sit around the table on the Privy Councilor's terms to consult and inform each other on issues of particular national interest.[321] Within the House, despite the government's upper hand in controlling the agenda, there are a significant number of avenues through which the opposition contributes and influences the parliamentary scrutiny (Parliamentary Question), agenda (Parliamentary Debate) and law-making (The 'Politics of Procedure'). As Meg Russel and David Gover's study shows,

317 ibid.

318 Robert A Dahl, *Polyarchy: Participation and Opposition* (Yale University Press 1971).

319 Ludger Helms, 'Studying Parliamentary, Opposition in Old and New Democracies: Issues and Perspectives' (2008) 14(1–2) The Journal of Legislative Studies 6, 6–9.

320 Philip Norton, 'Making Sense of Opposition' (2008) 14 (1–2) The Journal of Legislative Studies 236, 237.

321 Rodney Brazier, 'The Constitutional Role of the Opposition' (1989) 40 Northern Ireland Legal Quarterly 131, 133–134.

the opposition's information-seeking and politicizing strategies contribute to the parliament's influence over the government's legislative agenda.[322]

However, in illiberal democracies like Bangladesh, the Westminster system's formal and procedural marginalisation of the opposition has resulted in excessive ruling party dominance and total suppression of the parliamentary and political oppositions. The reasons behind this are historical, cultural and institutional.

From a *historical perspective*, political parties in Bangladesh have been indoctrinated in local, regional, and global geopolitical interest lines. They have fallen prey to India and Pakistan's enduring geopolitical and military rivalry.[323] Major political groups of Bangladesh are strongly believed to be sponsored, or at least supported,[324] by the opposing sides of the rivalry. Therefore, not based on broad ideological competition, Bangladeshi political blocks are featured by personal hatred and mutual distrust fuelled by strong regional players. *Secondly,* the military rulers have critically wounded the prospect of an ideologically competitive bipartisanship in Bangladesh. To build up an anti-Awami League support base, the post-1975 military rulers installed the pro-Pakistani and anti-liberation war forces into the mainstream of Bangladesh politics. Political parties like JI and AL's Pakistan-era arch-rival Muslim League and their leaders, accused of openly collaborating with the Pakistani military forces during the liberation war, were rehabilitated by Ziaur Rahman within ten years of Bangladesh's liberation from Pakistan.[325] Awami League strongly believes that Ziaur Rahman and later his wife, Begum Khaleda Zia, were harbouring militant, fundamentalist and anti-liberation war forces like Jamaat Islami as a matter of deliberate policy.[326] *Thirdly,* the personal relationship between Khaleda Zia and Sheikh Hasina is deeply touched by Ziaur Rahman's

322 Russel and Gover (n 153) 274.

323 TV Paul, 'Why has the India-Pakistan Rivalry Been so Enduring? Power Asymmetry and an Intractable Conflict' (2006) 15(4) Security Studies 600.

324 Md Abdul Mannan, 'Islamo-nationalism, domestic politics, and Bangladesh's policy of balancing against India since the 1990s' (2018) 21(4) International Area Studies Review 340.

325 Kamal Hossain, *Bangladesh: Quest for Freedom and Justice* (Karachi: Oxford University Press 2013).

326 Stanley A Kochanek, 'Governance, Patronage Politics, and Democratic Transition in Bangladesh' (2000) 40(3) Asian Survey 530, 531–33 (as Stanley A Kochanek explains it BNP is drawn upon "a broad-based coalition of political forces opposed to the Awami League drawn from the military, the bureaucracy, the business community, pro-Chinese radicals, pro-Islamic elements, and former members of the League who opposed Mujib's one-party state. Many of these groups had been banned by the organization and ostracized as collaborators because of their pro-Pakistani sympathies").

perceived involvement with the plotters of the 15 August 1975 killing of Sheikh Mujibur Rahman and his family members.[327] On Khaleda Zia's part, there was distrust of the Awami League for the entente Hasina maintained with Ershad, who was widely believed to be involved in the assassination of Ziaur Rahman.[328] Therefore, the post-1990 clashes between Bangladesh's ruling and opposition parties go beyond a mere ideological conflict between liberal and conservative forces. The liberal-conservative bipartisanship envisaged by the Westminster Model is understandably not meant to deal with this personal and emotional conflict.

Beyond this saga of a personal misfit between the two leaders, *the cultural* context of Bangladeshi society makes the competing political parties reluctant to see their existence as mutually reinforcing and an important safeguard for democracy. It has hurt the development of liberal-conservative bipartisanship in Bangladesh. It also might partially explain why the famous "two turn-over of power test"[329] for democratic consolidation did not work in post-military era Bangladesh.[330] Absent the "parliamentarisation of conflict",[331] and in the contentious winner-takes-all politics of Bangladesh,[332] being a peaceful institutional opposition is as unattractive as recognising the opposition. Ruling parties have been comfortable in Parliament minus a strong Opposition. Opposition parties also found the Parliament "useless" and showed comfort outside of it. They remained reactive, disruptive and unforgivingly extra-parliamentary.[333] Parliament boycotts and walkouts,[334] street agitation, violence and backdoor conspiracies have been very common in Bangladesh.[335] The Opposition parties boycotted 135 out of 400 sitting days in the Fifth Parliament (1991–1996), 163 out of 382 days in the Seventh Parliament (1996–2001), 223 out of 373 days

327 Nizam Ahmed, 'Non-Party Caretaker Governments and Parliamentary Elections in Bangladesh: Panacea or Pandora's Box?' (2004) 11(1) South Asian Survey 49, 69.

328 ibid.

329 Samuel P Huntington, *The Third Wave: Democratization in the Late Twentieth Century* (University of Oklahoma Press 1991) 266–67; G O'Donnell, 'Illusions about Consolidation' (1996) 5(3) Journal of Democracy 35.

330 Nizam Ahmed, 'Party Politics under a Non-party Caretaker Government in Bangladesh: the Fakhruddin Interregnum (2007–09)' (2010) 48(1) Commonwealth and Comparative Politics 23, 39–40; Nizam Ahmed (n 306) 59.

331 Nizam Ahmed (n 17) 11–14.

332 Muhammad Mustafizur Rahaman, 'Origins and Pitfalls of Confrontational Politics in Bangladesh' (2007) 14(1) South Asian Survey 101.

333 M Jashim Ali Chowdhury, 'In Search of Parliamentary Opposition in Bangladesh' (*IACL-AIDC Blog*, University of Melbourne, 21 January 2021).

334 Jalal Firoj (n 59) 122–23.

335 Nizam Ahmed (n 306) 55.

in the Eighth Parliament (2001–2006) and 316 out of 370 days in the Ninth Parliament (2009–2013).[336] Though the Opposition parties usually blame the discriminatory treatment and failure to get a floor in parliament as the reasons for walkouts and boycotts, there is a reasonable perception that most walkouts have been pre-planned as part of street mobilisation against the government.[337]

Institutional difficulties faced by the opposition in Bangladesh are no less aggravated. First, they remain seriously disadvantaged regarding parliamentary time allocated to them. Unlike the UK House of Commons, there is no tradition of Usual Channel negotiation between the government and the opposition for pre-programming a legislative process. A Business Advisory Committee headed by the Speaker looks into timetabling the various stages of a bill. Though it has representation from the opposition, the numerical strength of the government party in the committee, chairmanship of a partisan Speaker and an express requirement for the Speaker to consult the Leader of the House would prevent any meaningful consideration of the timetable proposed by the opposition. However, the Speaker is not bound to form the Business Advisory Committee.[338]

At the committee stage, the opposition and backbench members should ideally have a greater chance of debating and proposing amendments. Though the Rules of Procedure require recording minutes of dissents by individual members, the overall quality of the deliberation at the committee stage remains disappointing. Subject to a few rare exceptions, members from the government backbench and opposition alike have traditionally failed to utilise the select committee on bills to the fullest.[339] The select committee's power to take evidence from representatives of special interest groups has also not been widely reported. Back in the House, the opposition's amendment proposals will most likely be voted down without serious consideration.

Therefore, it is unsurprising that the opposition in Bangladesh has remained invariably obstructionist.[340] Beyond strictly opposing every government policy and action, the opposition parties hardly sponsored legislative proposals

336 Shahidulla Kaiser, 'Culture of Parliament Boycott and the Future of Parliamentary Democracy in Bangladesh' (2015) 19(2) Himalayan and Central Asian Studies 44; Dilara Choudhury, 'Culture of Parliament Boycott in Bangladesh' *The Daily Star* (Dhaka: 18 March 2013).

337 Shahidulla Kaiser (ibid) 47–49.

338 RoP (n 58) rr. 219–221.

339 Nizam Ahmed (n 80) 134–136.

340 Nizam Ahmed (n 306) 70–71.

and policy debates inside or outside the Parliament.[341] Though there was an exceptionally encouraging period of institutionalised opposition during the early 1990s, the opposition mode of parliamentary politics did not thrive in institutional ways.

For three years (1991–1994) in the Fifth Parliament, the opposition members and the government party backbenchers showed some commitment to parliamentary scrutiny and legislative assertiveness. MPs of the Fifth Parliament (1991–1996) initiated 82 private member bills, more than the total of all the previous four parliaments.[342] Out of those, around 80 per cent of the motions seeking an explanation for the government's policy failure and 90 per cent of the motions seeking an explanation for administrative malpractices were moved by the opposition MPs.[343] The initial years of parliamentary politics in the Fifth Parliament (1991–1994) soon fell into disarray. A rigged by-election in 1994 reminded the opposition parties of the farce elections of the 1980s under the military rulers.[344] It also rang an alarm that the ruling party would rig the next general election.[345] The opposition parties demanded the introduction of an election-time caretaker government, resigned from parliament and took to the streets.[346]

Interestingly, the Tenth (2014–2018), Eleventh (2019–2024) and Twelfth (Jan-Aug 2024) parliaments did not see any opposition in the rightful sense of the term. With the main opposition party, BNP, boycotting the Tenth parliamentary election and being marginalised since then, the current official Opposition party, Jatya Party (JP), a political ally of the ruling party, is "pretending"[347] to be an opposition while receiving benefits from the ruling party AL through tacit understanding.[348]

---

341 Nizam Ahmed, 'Parliamentary Opposition in Bangladesh: a Study of its Role in the Fifth Parliament' (1997) 3(2) Party Politics 147, 155.

342 Nizam Ahmed (n 132) 82–83.

343 ibid.

344 M Jashim Ali Chowdhury, 'Elections in 'Democratic' Bangladesh', in Mark Tushnet and Madhav Khosla (eds.), *Unstable Constitutionalism: Law and Politics in South Asia* (Cambridge University Press 2015) 192–229.

345 Golam Hossain (n 281).

346 Md Morshedul Islam, '1996's Non-party Caretaker Government Movement and the Role of Opposition in Bangladesh: a Politico-legal Analysis' (2016) 3(6) Global Journal of Political Science and Administration 20.

347 Jashim Ali (n 333).

348 RB Andeweg, 'Parties in Parliament: the Blurring of Opposition' in Müller W, Narud H (eds.), *Party Governance and Party Democracy* (New York: Springer 2013) 99–114.

4.2 *Intra-party Accountability*

The relationship between political parties and their members has been consistently debated. The debate may be traced back to Edmund Burke's *Trustee v. Delegate Models of Representation* thesis. In 1774, the question for Burke's consideration was whether the MPs represented their constituents' will or their independent judgment. Burke perceived the dilemma as a tension between the MPs' trusteeship over the gross national interest and their role as delegates of their constituencies. The more a representative follows his self-judgement, the more he endorses a Trustee Model.[349] The more he follows the view of an aggregate, such as his constituencies, the more he embodies the Delegate Model.[350] Burke's famous speech to the electors of Bristol in 1774 runs as follows:

> Parliament is not a congress of ambassadors from different and hostile interests, which interests each must maintain, as an agent and advocate, against other agents and advocates, but Parliament is a deliberative assembly of one nation, with one interest, that of the whole – where not local purposes, not local prejudices, ought to guide, but the general good, resulting from the general reason of the whole.[351]

Recently, conflicting views have been expressed about whether the Burkean dilemma of representation is still valid.[352] Thomassen and Schmitt argue that Burke's views were meant for the political transition from a pre-modern government based on absolute Monarchy to one based on parliamentary sovereignty.[353] Before the parliamentary revolution, the members individually represented their geographic constituencies.[354] Once the parliament gained

349 David Judge, 'Representation in Westminster in the 1990s: the Ghost of Edmund Burke' (1999) 5 The Journal of Legislative Studies 12, 13.

350 AH Birch, *Representation* (London: Macmillan 1972) 15.

351 ibid 39.

352 Heinz Eulau, John C Wahlke, William Buchanan and Leroy C Ferguson, 'The Role of the Representative: Some Empirical Observations on the Theory of Edmund Burke' (1959) 53(3) The American Political Science Review 742, 746, 751–52.

353 J Thomassen, 'Empirical Research into Political Representation: Failing Democracy or Failing Models?' in MK Jennings and T Mann (eds.), *Elections at Home and Abroad* (Michigan: University of Michigan Press 1994) 238–239; J Thomassen and H Schmitt, 'Political Representation and Legitimacy in the European Union' in Schmitt, H and Thomassen, J, (eds.), *Political Representation and Legitimacy in the European Union* (Oxford: Oxford University Press 1999)3–24, 14.

354 H Pitkin, *The Concept of Representation* (Berkeley, CA: University of California Press 1967) 176.

sovereignty, it became responsible for the aggregate national interest. Though they maintain a strong local tie,[355] the UK's post-1688 parliamentarians have not confined themselves within pure geographical blocks. With the emergence of the internet and industry-based demographics, the members of parliament now represent a diverse range of constituencies, interests, and issues.[356] While all these developments could have ideally facilitated a Trustee Model of Representation, an eighteenth-century development seems to keep Burke's representational dilemma alive.

The emergence of the political party system at Westminster has reignited the debate on trustee vs delegate models of representation.[357] It is argued that people can better judge political parties for their policies and programmes when party members subordinate their personal views to those of their parties.[358] Studies confirm that the British voters have generally attached less importance to the individual performances of the MPs. They usually frame the elections as a choice between the parties and leaders competing for the No 10 Downing Street rather than between MPs vying for their parliamentary seats.[359] The UK electors' overwhelmingly partisan approach to voting was further confirmed in the wake of the infamous Expenses Scandal of 2009. It was seen that the MPs charged with financial improprieties did not face significant backlash in the 2010 election.[360] On the other hand, conscientious rebels of political parties are usually de-selected in the next general election.[361] Despite these, the MPs' *intra-party assertiveness and conscientious position* are significantly visible in Westminster. Recently, British MPs have shown increased willingness to cross their party lines to embrace a trustee model of representation. They do this,

---

355 Philip Norton, 'Parliament and Citizens in the United Kingdom' (2012) 18 (3–4) The Journal of Legislative Studies 403, 404–405.

356 Cristina Leston-Bandeira, 'Towards a Trustee Model? Parliamentary Representation in the Internet Era: the Portuguese Case' (2012) 65 (2) Parliamentary Affairs 425, 427–428.

357 Philip Norton (n 355) 404.

358 CJ Kam, *Party Discipline and Parliamentary Politics* (Cambridge: Cambridge University Press 2009); WC Müller, 'Political Parties in Parliamentary Democracies: Making Delegation and Accountability Work' (2000) 37(3) European Journal of Political Research 309.

359 P Mitchell, 'Voters and their representatives: Electoral institutions and delegation in parliamentary democracies' (2000) 37(3) European Journal of Political Research 335.

360 Andrew Eggers and Alexander Fisher, Electoral Accountability and the UK Parliamentary Expenses Scandal: Did Voters Punish Corrupt MPs?' Political Science and Political Economy Working Paper No 8/2021 (Department of Government London School of Economics 2011).

361 Nick Vivyan and Markus Wagner, 'Do Voters Reward Rebellion? The Electoral Accountability of MPs in Britain' (2012) 51 European Journal of Political Research 235, 259.

especially when their parties do not present well-defined or distinguishable policy alternatives to the voters.[362]

This rise of backbench assertiveness in the UK is paradoxical to some extent. While the electors in Westminster tend to vote for the Party or the Prime Minister they want to be in the government; they also expect their MPs to maintain strong constituency links and take a position on matters that affect them.[363] The post-1979 modernisation of Parliament and the internal party democracies also facilitate the trustee-type behaviour of the MPs. Philip Norton argues that the UK Parliament does not pose significant structural constraints on MPs unless they "themselves subscribe to a (...) limited conception of democracy".[364] As the MPs' rebellious floor speeches and voting behaviour are less likely to hurt the parties in the general election,[365] parties do not need to strictly control the floor.[366] They can also allow "free votes" when major partisan interests are not at stake. Backbenchers would dissent from their party leaders based on their expertise, reputation and constituency interests.[367] Statistics show that backbench rebelliousness is consistently growing in the UK,[368] and open challenges from the backbench are more common than they used to be.[369] MPs doing it once usually make it a habit later.[370] In the 2015

362 M Kent Jenning and Thomas E Man, *Elections at Home and Abroad Essays in Honour of Warren Miller* (Michigan University Press 1994) 243, 252.

363 Philip Norton (n 229) 706; Philip Norton, 'The United Kingdom: Building the link between Constituent and MP' p 19–42 in Philip Norton (ed.), *Parliament and Citizens in Western Europe* 19–42 (London: Routledge 2002) 25–26; Michael Rush, *The Role of the Member of Parliament Since 1868: From Gentlemen to Players* (Oxford 2001); David Judge and Rebecca Partos, 'MPs and their Constituencies: Parties and MPs' in Cristina Leston-Bandeira and Louise Thompson (eds.), *Exploring Parliament* 67–79 (Oxford University Press 2018) 267–269.

364 P Norton, *The Commons in Perspective* (Oxford: Martin Robertson 1981); Alan Beattie, 'Why the Case for Parliamentary Reform in Britain is so Weak' (1998) 4(2) The Journal of Legislative Studies 1, 13–14.

365 Sevn Oliver Prosch and Jonathan B Slapin, *The Politics of Parliamentary Debate: Parties, Rebels and Representation* (Cambridge University Press 2015) 123.

366 ibid, 65.

367 ibid, 35.

368 Philip Cowley, *The Rebels: How Blair Mislaid His Majority* (London: Politico's 2005); Philip Cowley and Mark Stuart, 'In the Brown stuff? Labour Backbench Dissent Under Gordon Brown, 2007–10' (2014) 28(1) Contemporary British History 1.

369 Russel and Gover (n 153) 275, 276.

370 Mark Stuart, 'Whips and Rebels' in Cristina Leston-Bandeira and Louise Thompson (eds.), *Exploring Parliament* 67–79 (Oxford University Press 2018) 256; Philip Cowley, 'The Coalition and Parliament' in A Seldon and M Finn (eds.), *The Coalition Effect 2010–2015* (Cambridge: Cambridge University Press 2015) 136–156.

Parliament, 35 per cent of MPs rebelled, 28 per cent in 2005–2010 and 21 per cent in 2001–5.[371]

As per as Bangladesh is concerned, the Bangladeshi electorate, like their British counterpart, mainly elect their prime ministers but expect their MPs to serve the constituencies.[372] There is, however, an important qualitative difference between the electors' motives in the two countries. Unlike their UK counterparts, Bangladeshi electors do not show much "cognitive awareness of the MPs' role orientation".[373] Hence, the nature of constituency expectations is different in the two countries. Apart from the flow of development and cash allocation through clientelist channels,[374] electors in Bangladesh do not bother much about their MPs' policy positions. MPs need to maintain the channel in which wealth, success, and opportunities are distributed from the higher echelon of the parties rather than from institutions and administrative due process.[375] Therefore, the Bangladeshi MPs have practical reasons and contextual compulsions to follow the partisan delegate's role. Some of those reasons may be summarised as follows:

First, the political parties lack the key ingredients of intra-party democracy, *i.e.*, democratic election of party leadership and grassroots participation in party policymaking.[376] The structural calculus within the parties revolves around the personality cult and patrimony of the dynastic leaders.[377] It has been called a "One Kingdom Two Dynasties"[378] system. Bangladesh's two major political parties – AL and BNP – are held in the absolute grip of two hereditary leaders. Within the parties, the chiefs are final regarding the nomination of MP candidates, although 'eyewash' attempts are undertaken by convening a formal nomination board.[379] The party, anticipating coming to power,

371 Mark Stuart (ibid) 257.

372 Nizam Ahmed, 'Parliament and Poverty Reduction in Bangladesh: Role of the MP' (2018) 25(1–2) South Asian Survey 163, 171–177; Zahir Ahmed (n 237), 11–13.

373 Muhammad Sayadur Rahman, '*Upazila Parishad* in Bangladesh: Roles and Functions of Elected Representatives and Bureaucrats' (2012) 11 Commonwealth Journal of Local Governance 100, 112.

374 S Aminul Islam, 'The Predicament of Democratic Consolidation in Bangladesh,' (2006) 3(2) Bangladesh e-Journal of Sociology 4; Mustafizur Rahaman (n 332) 106–107.

375 Mushtaq Khan, 'Class, Clientelism and Communal Politics in Contemporary Bangladesh', in KN Pannikar, TJ Byres, and U Patnaik (eds.), *The Making of History: Essays Presented to Irfan Habib* (New Delhi: Tulika, 2000) 17–18.

376 Inge Amundsen, 'Democratic Dynasties? Internal Party Democracy in Bangladesh' (2016) 22(1) Party Politics 49.

377 Nizam Ahmed (n 306) 71–76.

378 Ali Riaz, *Bangladesh: a Political History since Independence* (London: I.B. Tauris, 2016).

379 Sadiat Mannan, Md Harun-Or-Rashid, Jens Stanislawski and Niaz Ahmed Khan, 'Realpolitik: Democratic Embeddedness within Major Political Parties in Bangladesh'

would benefit its local representatives through budgetary allocations or purely personal favours like the nomination.[380] In return, the successful nominees would fund the parties[381] and back their rule by suppressing the opposition through muscle and money in their constituencies.[382] Once the bond of reciprocity is disturbed, the MPs might fall out of favour, and a new candidate emerges. The disgruntled candidate may defect to a rival party, which is more common, create a new one that is unlikely to thrive, or gradually perish, which is inevitable. Absent the ideological defections, factional wrangling within the parties reinforces the inevitability of the dynastic leaders as symbols of party "unity and sustenance".[383]

Secondly, the political dynasties thrive on the commercialisation of politics bolstered by the business elites' flooding into politics. While the businessmen constituted only 13 per cent of the MPs in the First Parliament (1973–1975), it rose to 48 per cent in the Seventh (1996–2001), 53 per cent in the Eighth (2001–2006)[384] and 61 per cent in the Eleventh (2019- 2023) Parliament.[385] It has made politics a highly rent-seeking profession in Bangladesh.[386] Unlike the UK, the parliamentarians in Bangladesh conspicuously lack representation from intellectuals, civil society, professional groups and the working class.[387] This routing out of the conscientious societal groups from politics has enabled

---

Working Paper Series No 25 (BRAC Institute of Governance and Development, BRAC University, Dhaka 2015) 27–28.

380 Mozahidul Islam (n 238) 149–51, 156; Sabina Sharmin and AKM Jamal Uddin, 'Characteristics of Political Culture in Bangladesh: a Critical Analysis from the perspective of Political Development and Under development' (2013) 1(1–2) Jagannath University Journal of Social Sciences 74, 77.

381 Md Rajib Hasnat Shakil and Kaniz Marzia, 'Problems of Party Funding and Expenditure Political Parties and Good Governance: Bangladesh Perspective' (2013) 8(5) IOSR Journal of Humanities and Social Science (IOSR-JHSS) 37, 42.

382 Stanley A Kochanek (n 326) 547–49; Abeeba Aziz Khan, 'Power, Patronage, and the Candidate-nomination Process: Observations from Bangladesh' (2020) 54(1) Modern Asian Studies 314; Md Saidur Rahman, 'Institutionalization of Democracy in the Political Parties in Bangladesh Does Culture Matter?' (LL.M. Dissertation, North South University, Dhaka 2010) 33–36.

383 Mahfuzul H Chowdhury, 'Dynamics of Political Parties in Bangladesh' (1995) 2 South Asian Survey 63.

384 Shakawat Liton, 'Business factor in our politics' *The Daily Star* (Dhaka: 15 October 2015).

385 Citizens for Good Governance (Shujan), 'Parliament of millionaires' *The Daily Star* (Dhaka: 07 January 2019).

386 Rounaq Jahan, 'Members of Parliament in Bangladesh' (1976) 1(3) Legislative Studies Quarterly 355; Rounaq Jahan, 'The Parliament of Bangladesh: Representation and Accountability' (2015) 21(2) The Journal of Legislative Studies 250.

387 Jahan and Amundsen (n 79).

the dynastic leaders to ruthlessly suppress the ideological dissidents within their parties if there are any.[388]

Thirdly, parliamentary parties do not facilitate systematic consultation between front and backbenchers. None of the parties in the Fifth and Seventh parliaments held parliamentary party meetings routinely.[389] The backbenchers lack the opportunity to discuss the issues the party leadership would raise in the House. There is no serious demand for that type of participation either. Backbenchers understand the obvious danger of making such demands on the top party leadership.[390]

Fourthly, the Constitution of Bangladesh strictly restricts rebellious voting in Parliament. As per Article 70 of the Constitution – popularly known as the anti-defection clause – an MP, elected as a nominee of a particular party, cannot vote against their party, nor can s/he abstain from voting in defiance of party directives.[391] In 1972, the insertion of Article 70 was informed by Bangladesh's political experiences of the pre-independence era. Continuous and amoral defections by the MPs and consequent fall of governments – some within days and weeks of formation – during the 1950s created a huge credibility crisis in the political parties. It later created a fertile ground for the intervention of the Pakistani military in politics.[392]

Later, Article 70 was identified as the sole troublemaker in Bangladesh's parliamentary life. The Supreme Court considered it on four occasions. In *Abdus Samad Azad v. Bangladesh*, the Court justified the article by branding it as "a self-imposed restriction in the Constitution itself."[393] On the second occasion, in *Secretary, Parliament Secretariat v. Khandker Delwar Hossain,*[394] a judge, though he did not question its constitutionality, expressed a wish that it would not be necessary to be in the Constitution in future.[395] In *Advocate Asaduzzaman Siddiqui v Bangladesh*, the Court again criticised it for suppressing conscientious contribution from the MPs.[396] On the fourth and final

388 ibid.

389 Nizam Ahmed (n 306) 74.

390 ibid, 75.

391 Nizam Ahmed, 'In Search of Institutionalisation: Parliament in Bangladesh' (1998) 4(4) The Journal of Legislative Studies 34, 42.

392 Sabbir Ahmed, 'Article 70 of the Constitution of Bangladesh: Implications for the Process of Democratisation' (2010) 31 (1) BIISS Journal 1, 3–7.

393 *Abdus Samad Azad v. Bangladesh* (1992) 44 DLR 354 (Per Anowarul Hoque Chowdhury J Para 26).

394 1999 BLD (AD) 276.

395 ibid, 288 (Per Justice Mustafa Kamal).

396 (2016) 10 ALR (AD) 03.

occasion, the Court held that it "safeguards the democracy".[397] While there is a perception that the total removal of Article 70 from the Constitution might cause sudden disintegration in the major political parties of Bangladesh,[398] it appears that the article is not the only reason for the lack of backbench assertiveness. The Constitution and the Parliament's Rules of Procedure do not prevent the MPs from debating their government's policies on the floor and scrutinising the government in the committees.

The backbench assertiveness and intra-party mode of parliamentary activities appear more a matter of the political context discussed above than a single provision of the Constitution.[399] It has been evidenced in the Fifth Parliament (1991–1996). During that period, the backbench push made the ruling party rethink its legislative proposal several times.[400] For example, the then ruling party, BNP, nominated Abdur Rahman Biswas, controversial for his anti-liberation war role during 1971, for the Presidency. Though the ruling party high-ups ignored the repeated calls from the main opposition Awami League (AL) to nominate an acceptable candidate for the post, the government backbench seemed to hear the call. Though sure of its candidate's defeat, the AL nominated Justice Badrul Haider Chowdhury, an ex-Chief Justice of Bangladesh, for the post. Many of BNP's pro-liberation war MPs were allegedly considering voting against Biswas.[401] In the election, the ruling party candidate narrowly escaped defeat. Out of 330 votes, Biswas secured 172 (the least votes needed were 166), and AL-backed Justice Chowdhury got 92 votes. A total of 66 ruling party backbenchers refrained from voting.

In 1992, the Fifth Parliament witnessed another backbench rebellion over whether Bangladesh should return to the Parliamentary government outlined in the original Constitution of 1972 or retain the post-1975 presidential system installed by the deposed military rulers. Though the ruling BNP high-ups were reluctant to respect its pre-election promise to revive the parliamentary government, the backbench MPs joined their voice with the opposition parties

---

397 Staff Report, 'High Court issues split order on the legality of Article 70 of constitution' *Dhaka Tribune* (Dhaka, 15 January 2018); Staff Report, 'Article 70 safeguards democracy: HC', *The Daily Star* (Dhaka, 25 May 2018).

398 Zahed Iqbal, 'Article 70 of the Constitution: a Critical Analysis (In Bangla)' Presented at the Eighth Monthly General Meeting of The Asiatic Society of Bangladesh (Dhaka: 8 April 2021) 15.

399 Hasanuzzaman, 'To amend Article 70 or not', *The New Age* (Dhaka, 22 April 2011).

400 ibid.

401 Nizam Ahmed (n 17) 233.

in the BNP Parliamentary Party meeting held in June 1991.[402] The government was almost forced to respect its electoral promise and pass the Constitution (Twelfth) Amendment Act 1991.[403]

While the initial years of the Fifth Parliament presented an encouraging picture, the vibe, unfortunately, could not be carried through. Once the opposition party resigned from the Fifth Parliament, started agitating in the streets, and political violence ensued, the backbenchers strongly coalesced behind their respective party leadership.[404] The next phase of illiberal bipartisanship and competitive authoritarianism[405] led the government and the opposition backbenchers towards a Burkean model of delegate-type representation.[406] However, a major departure from Burke is that the Bangladeshi MPs act as the delegates of their parties, not their geographical constituencies.

5 Conclusion

This chapter considered the Parliament of Bangladesh as an institution of horizontal accountability *vis-a-vis* the executive branch. The parliament's question and debate practices seem less conducive to the enforcement of individual and collective ministerial responsibility conventions meaningfully. Analysis of the procedural, structural and attitudinal issues of Parliamentary Question Time and Prime Minister Question Time suggests that several procedural rigidities (*e.g.,* short notice questions), structural deficiencies (*e.g.,* the absence of a bipartisan approach to the sessions, parliament's inability to punish inaccurate or misleading information) and attitudinal problems (*e.g.,* lack of the Speaker's neutrality and lacklustre commitment of the ministers and MPs, too much focus on constituency demands) have reduced the question hours' effectiveness drastically. The lack of adequate opportunity for the opposition and

---

402 Nizam Ahmed, 'Parliamentary Politics in Bangladesh (1994) 32(3) The Journal of Commonwealth and Comparative Politics 364, 375.

403 Zillur R Khan, 'Bangladesh in 1992: Dilemmas of Democratization' (1993) 33(2) *Asian Survey* 150.

404 Nizam Ahmed (n 17) 226–227.

405 Shelley Feldman, 'Bangladesh in 2014: Illusive Democracy' (2015) 55(1) Asian Survey 67.

406 Thomas A Hockin, 'The Roles of the Loyal Opposition in Britain's House of Commons: Three Historical Paradigms' (1971) 25(1) *Parliamentary Affairs* 50 (Britain's Old Tory time parliamentarians were not recognised opposition, critique or watchdogs of the Crown. They were rather delegates of local and constituency interests without any say whatever in the "Great Matters of the State").

private members to initiate debates and the strict government control over the parliamentary calendar have reduced the dent of parliament's scrutiny power.

Secondly, like the UK parliamentary rules and procedures, the Bangladesh parliament recognises the government's right to pass its legislation. Still, parliamentary procedures should have "consequences for policy outcomes."[407] When the procedures are long-established and extensive, governments may not change them whimsically.[408] Very often, the mere existence of parliamentary procedure guarantees that there are institutional restraints on the government's legislative program. Discussion in this chapter has shown that while the UK House of Commons has adopted several important procedural devices to maximise restraint, the Bangladesh parliament's legislative procedure is largely missing the pro-committee, pro-opposition, and pro-backbench rules.

Thirdly, while the UK parliamentary committees have overcome most of the partisan barriers over their activities and amassed great institutional strength in terms of supplying expertise, information and scrutiny, the Bangladeshi committee system has fallen hostage to pervasive partisan cartelisation. It makes Bangladesh's parliamentary committees hardly the tools of executive accountability.

Next, there seem to be issues with the parliamentary parties' behaviour and the nature of the MPs' representation works. The political parties in Bangladesh are highly personalised, centralised and patrimonial, and this obnoxious culture of clientelism and illiberalism has handicapped intra-party accountability. A conspicuous lack of intra-party democracy and accountability has pushed the Bangladeshi parliamentarians towards a partisan delegate's role. Again, suppression and intolerance of parliamentary opposition and the agitative and street violence-based political opposition have subsided the government's accountability to the legislature. The opposing political parties' traditional reliance on political violence and agitation as the only route of governmental accountability has created a system of bipartisan competitive authoritarianism[409] in Bangladesh.

---

407 Philip Norton, 'Playing by the Rules: the Constraining Hand of Parliamentary Procedure' (2001) 7(3) Journal of Legislative Studies 13, 17.

408 ibid, 30.

409 Shafi Md Mostofa and DB Subedi, 'Rise of Competitive Authoritarianism in Bangladesh' (2021) 14(3) Politics and Religion 431.

Overall, Bangladesh's illiberal and inherently undemocratic party system has largely spoiled the accountability role of parliamentary questions, debates, legislative procedure and committee scrutiny. Therefore, Bangladesh's marginal, dormant and subdued parliament could hardly be called an institution meant for democratic accountability of the government.[410]

---

410 Nizam Ahmed (n 86).

CHAPTER 4

A Defiant Judiciary

1 Introduction

Parliament's relationship with the judiciary requires mutual deference and scrutiny. Parliament refrains from debating *sub-judice* matters and the judges' official conduct. The judiciary refrains from using parliamentary debates in their statutory interpretation processes. It also refrains from judging the internal parliamentary proceedings, including the members' speech within the House.[1] As a matter of mutual scrutiny, Parliament regulates, by law, the judges' appointment and removal and the courts' jurisdictions. Judges are invited to engage with the parliamentary committees on judicial and law reform issues. In constitutional supremacies, the judicial review of statute laws seeks to restrain the Parliament within its constitutional boundaries.[2] Even within the UK's parliamentary sovereignty system, the judiciary has got the power to declare certain statute laws incompatible with human rights.[3] This chapter examines the Bangladesh Parliament's relation with the Supreme Court by focusing on the two branches' approaches to inter-institutional comity, the Parliament's role in judicial accountability processes and the judicial review's dent on parliamentary laws.

The first part of this chapter argues that the Bangladesh Parliament's commitment to the *sub judice* rule is weak. The judiciary's respect for the exclusionary rule of interpretation and the internal parliamentary proceedings is also inconsistent. Though the Court has shown general deference to the debates in Parliament, they have shown a willingness to lift the veil of those "internal proceedings" that might involve constitutional questions. The Bangladesh Supreme Court sees the internal proceedings doctrine through a self-aggrandised perception of its sole guardianship over the Constitution. British judiciary's approach in this regard is largely conciliatory.

1 Anne Twomey, 'Can Parliamentary Privilege be Used to Shut-Down Parliamentary Accountability?' *Australian Public Law Blog* (University of New South Wales, Sydney, 22 January 2020).

2 Rivka Weill, 'Reconciling Parliamentary Sovereignty and Judicial Review: On the Theoretical and Historical Origins of the Israeli Legislative Override Power' (2011) 39 Hastings Constitutional Law Quarterly 457.

3 The Human Rights Act (HRA) 1998 (UK), sec. 4.

 | DOI:10.1163/9789004720831_005

The second part considers the role of the Bangladesh Parliament in various areas of judicial accountability systems, such as the appointment and removal of judges and the democratic oversight of the overall affairs of the judiciary. Though the British Parliament does not participate in the judicial appointment process, it can impeach and remove the judges for misconduct. Until recently, the judges' appearance before the parliamentary committees and their hearing was relatively rare. British judges now almost routinely attend committee hearings in the Palace of Westminster. In contrast, this chapter shows that Bangladesh's higher court judges deeply distrust the legislative branch and hypersensitivity to parliamentary participation in the judicial accountability process, including the judges' removal. Judges' appearance before the parliamentary committees is also unknown.

The last part of this chapter considers the nature of Bangladesh's judicial review system and its implication for the legislature-judiciary relation. It argues that Bangladesh's "strong form" and "antagonistic" judicial review negatively impact the inter-institutional relations between the judiciary and Parliament. Compared to this, the UK's "dialogic" judicial review tends to generate a healthy institutional relationship between the organs. Within the UK's parliamentary sovereignty system, the judiciary does not have the power to review the statute laws.[4] However, two important constitutional realignments have changed the understanding drastically – The Constitutional Reform Act (CRA) 2005 and the Human Rights Act (HRA) 1998. Even before those, the UK judiciary had slowly but consistently widened the boundaries of judicial review of royal prerogatives[5] and statute laws.[6] The entry into force of the CRA seems to have to speed up the process.[7] The HRA 1998 marked the judiciary's entry into an era of 'democratic dialogue'[8] where the Court could enter into a direct conversation with the Parliament regarding the human rights compatibility of its

4 Paul Craig, 'Proportionality and Judicial Review: a UK Historical Perspective' in Stefan Vogenauer and Stephen Weatherill (eds.), *General Principles of Law European and Comparative Perspectives* 145–166 (Hart Publishing 2017).

5 *Council of Civil Service Unions v Minister for the Civil Service* [1984] UKHL 9; *M v Home Office* [1994] 1 AC 377; *R v Secretary of State for Foreign and Commonwealth Affairs, ex parte Bancoult (No 2)* [2008] UKHL 61; *R (Miller) v Secretary of State for Exiting the European Union* [2017] UKSC 5; *R (Miller) v The Prime Minister* and *Cherry v Advocate General for Scotland* [2019] UKSC 41.

6 *R (Jackson) v Attorney General* [2005] UKHL 56 and *AXA General Insurance v HM Advocate* [2011] UKSC 46.

7 Ian Turner, 'Judicial Review, Irrationality, and the Limits of Intervention by the Courts' (2010) 21(2) King's Law Journal 311.

8 Philip Norton, 'A Democratic Dialogue? Parliament and Human Rights in The United Kingdom' (2013) 21(2) Asia Pacific Law Review 141.

statutes. The "Democratic Dialogue" approach of judicial review may arguably help Bangladesh's Parliament and higher judiciary to reconcile their mutual boundaries and accountabilities.

2 Parliament and the Judiciary's Inter-institutional Comity

In written constitutions like Bangladesh, the Parliament's relation with the judiciary and other coordinate branches of the government should be guided by the principles of separation of power and checks and balances. Constitutional organs work for each other's accountability. They respect each other's autonomy and exclusive institutional spaces, too. Observing the *sub judice* rule, Parliament must refrain from deliberating on the judges' official conduct and the cases pending in their dockets. The judiciary, in its turn, refrains from intruding into the Parliament's privileges and immunities, particularly its internal proceedings. An exclusionary rule of judicial interpretation discourages the courts from using parliamentary debates while interpreting a statute. The judiciary also does not entertain cases or complaints arising from something said or done on the parliament floor.

2.1 *Bangladesh Parliament's Position on the* sub judice *Rule*

The *sub judice rule* reflects a longstanding convention of comity between the two organs. It means the legislature does not intrude in the judges' territory and undermine their authority.[9] Such non-intrusion is important for unencumbered enforcement of the rule of law and the citizens' right to have a fair trial without undue influence from the outside. However, it is understood that the *sub judice* rule is not absolute. The Speaker of the UK House of Commons enjoys the discretion to permit such matters to be discussed, particularly when the right of Parliament to legislate on any matter is asserted. In 1999, the Joint Committee on Parliamentary Privilege asserted that the *sub judice* rule must be balanced against "the Parliament's constitutional right to discuss any matter it pleases."[10] Though there have been occasional violations of the *sub judice* rule by the Ministers and parliament members, those violations are not pervasive enough to overshadow the general adherence to the rule.[11] The UK Parliament,

9 Philip A Joseph, 'Parliamentary Privilege Developments in New Zealand: the Good, the Bad and the Ugly' (2015) 30(2) Australasian Parliamentary Review 115.

10 Joint Committee on Parliamentary Privilege, Session 1998–1999, *Parliamentary Privilege*, HL 43-I / HC 214-I, section 192.

11 Lord Burnett of Maldon, 'Parliamentary Privilege – Liberty and Due Limitation' (21st Commonwealth Law Conference 2019 Livingstone, Zambia, 9 April 2019) 14–15.

in its turn, has generally been respectful of the *sub judice* rule, though there are occasional "attacks upon the courts [mostly] for public consumption and short-term political gain".[12]

In Bangladesh, Article 78(3) of the Constitution guarantees freedom of speech within the House. On the other hand, the Parliament's Rules of Procedure (RoP) bar the *sub judice* matters and the judges' conduct from being discussed on the floor.[13] The application of the *sub judice* rule, however, is not nuanced. On many occasions, the government Ministers and MPs have shown insensitivity towards the greater stake behind the rule. Several contempt petitions were lodged based on the Ministers' speeches on the floor, including the two cases named *Ataur Rahman*[14] and *Cyril Sikdar*.[15] Though the Supreme Court dismissed those cases on the basis of internal proceedings doctrine (discussed in part 2.3. below), there was a clear disgust that the MPs did not respect the sub judice rule.

Though the Bangladesh Parliament's position on the *sub judice* rule appears incoherent, the Supreme Court's position on the other rules of comity – *e.g.*, exclusion of parliamentary debate in statutory construction and non-intrusion in the internal proceedings of the Parliament – is similarly incoherent too.

2.2 *Bangladesh Supreme Court's Incoherence over the Exclusionary Rule*

Parliamentary debates on the House floor during the passage of law should ideally help the Court understand the purpose for which the Parliament passes a law. Still, an *Exclusionary Rule of Statutory Construction* provides that parliamentary debates are not used in statutory interpretation.[16] It is argued, among others, that consultation of parliamentary debates during the passage of law might invite the Court to sit over the judgment of the Parliament's internal proceedings, parliament members' motivation and rationality behind a legislative policy. However, despite a long tradition of respecting the Parliament's privileges and immunities and its internal proceedings, the British judiciary has asserted a right to determine the scope of the immunity and privilege

---

12 M Lavarch, 'Fighting the Friends from Finance' in H Stacy, M Lavarch (ed.), *Beyond the Adversarial System* (The Federation Press, Sydney, 1999) 15 quoted in Stephen Colbran, 'The Limits of Judicial Accountability; the Role of Judicial Performance Evaluation' (2003) 6(1) Legal Ethics 55, 61.

13 The Rules of Procedure (RoP) of Bangladesh *Jatya Sangsad* 1973, r. 270 <https://mrdibd.org/wp-content/uploads/2021/04/Rules-of-Procedure.pdf> accessed 17November 2024.

14 *Ataur Rahman Khan v. Md. Nasim* 52 DLR 16.

15 *Cyril Sikdar* v. *Nazmul Huda* 46 DLR 555.

16 Stefan Vogenauer, 'A Retreat from Pepper v Hart? A Reply to Lord Steyn' (2005) 25(4) Oxford Journal of Legal Studies 629.

claims.[17] The modern-day courts, however, disfavour a total exclusion of the parliamentary materials in statutory construction. Ascertainment of the intention of Parliament now constitutes an essential ingredient of statutory construction.[18] A judgment of the Appellate Committee of the UK House of Lords – *Pepper v Hart*[19] – argued that the courts might consider the parliamentary debates in very limited circumstances, requiring them to know the intention of the Parliament in enacting a particular law. Though the debate regarding the reach of *Pepper* persists, the judgment represents the judiciary's willingness to engage the Parliament in the statutory construction process. As Lord Browne-Wilkinson put it in the 1992 case of *Pepper v Hart*, the modern courts' purpose of using parliamentary debates in the construction of statutes is "far from questioning the independence of Parliament". It rather works to give "effect to what is said and done there",[20] he argued.

In *Pepper v. Hart*, Lord Browne-Wilkinson argued that a Ministerial or sponsor statement regarding the purpose of a bill might be used in interpretation when – a) the usual means of interpretation yield absurd, obscure or ambiguous result; b) the statement sought to be used was made by the promoter of the law or amendment concerned and c) the statement clarifies what the law or amendment was designed for, and the Parliament approved the law or amendment without further amendment.[21] Apart from these "triple locks",[22] Lord Wilkinson further constrained the admissibility of such statements by requiring those to be considered along with "such other Parliamentary material as is necessary to understand such statements and their effect".[23] This additional proposition was intended to ensure that consideration of ministerial statements does not make the Parliament's intention subservient to the government's or the promoters' intention.

Interestingly, the post-*Pepper* case laws in the UK show that Lord Browne Wilkinson's conditions are sometimes ignored. Hansard has allegedly become "an open book"[24] for ascertaining the meaning and purposes of statutes. In

17 *Bradlaugh v. Gossett* [1884] 12 QBD 271; *Stockdale v. Hansard* [1839] 9 Ad &El 1 96; *R v. Chaytor* [2010] UKSC 52.

18 Stephane Beaulac, 'Parliamentary Debates in Statutory Interpretation: a Question of Admissibility or of Weight?' (1998) 43(3) McGill Law Journal 288, 314–21.

19 *Pepper (HM Inspector of Taxes) v Hart and related appeals* [1992] BTC 591.

20 ibid, 614 [Per Lord Browne-Wilkinson].

21 ibid, 615 [Per Lord Browne-Wilkinson].

22 Stefan Vogenauer (n 16) 636.

23 Mark Keith Heatley, 'Devolution: a New Breath of Life for Pepper v Hart?' (2017) 38 Liverpool Law Review 287, 305.

24 Stefan Vogenauer (n 16) 636.

2001, Lord Steyn vehemently contested *Pepper v. Hart*.[25] The UK courts then started taking clues from Lord Steyn and attempted occasional retreats from *Pepper's* position.[26] For example, in *Wilson v First County Trust* (2),[27] the House of Lords, in its judicial capacity, argued that such materials could be used only to determine the meaning of an ambiguous term. Beyond this, it will be unacceptable to use the parliamentary debates to ascertain the aim and purposes of law and to consider the Parliament's justification of the means it took towards the purpose.[28]

Despite the *Wilson*'s conditioning of *Pepper v. Hart*, the UK judiciary has not completely retreated to the pre-*Pepper* position of total exclusion of parliamentary debates in the statutory construction process.[29] Courts have referred to parliamentary materials to understand the state of the law before an enactment, ascertain the aims of the enactment, the *mischief* the enactment wanted to remove,[30] and its practical effect.[31] In the process, the British courts have consulted ministerial statements,[32] parliamentary committee reports,[33] ministerial conference reports,[34] and departmental explanatory notes.[35] Common law jurisdictions like the USA, Australia, and Canada have "either moved or are going towards" such jurisprudential positions.[36]

Compared to this, the Bangladesh Supreme Court has remained oblivious to the *Exclusionary Rule* and taken inconsistent positions without offering coherent reasoning. While the Bangladesh Supreme Court has generally refrained from using parliamentary debates in statutory construction, it does not appear that the Court did this in full awareness of the *Exclusionary Rule*. Occasionally,

---

25 Lord Steyn, 'Pepper v Hart; A Re-examination' (2001) 21(1) *Oxford Journal of Legal Studies* 59.

26 Stefan Vogenauer (n 16) 663.

27 *Wilson v First County Trust* (2) [2003] UKHL 40, [2004] 1 AC 816; Alison Young, *Democratic Dialogue and the Constitution* (Oxford: Oxford University Press) 204–06.

28 *Wilson v First County* (ibid) para 52–53 [Lord Nicholls], 116 [Lord Hope] and 143 [Lord Hobhouse].

29 Mark K Heatley (n 23).

30 *Wilson v First County* (n 27) para 118 [Lord Hope].

31 ibid, para 60 [Lord Nicholls], 142 [Lord Hobhouse].

32 *R v Secretary of State for the Home Department, ex parte Brind* [1991] 1AC 696.

33 *Black Clawson International Ltd v. Papierwerke AG* [1975] AC 591.

34 *Attorney-General's Reference (No 1 of 1988)*, [1989] 2 WLR 729.

35 *R (Westminster City Council) v National Asylum Support Service* [2002] UKHL 38.

36 Stephane Beaulac (n 18) 321; Robert G Vaughn, 'A Comparative Analysis of the Influence of Legislative History on Judicial Decision-Making and Legislation' (1996) 7(1) Indiana International and Comparative Law Review 1.

the judges have referred to parliamentary conduct or debates without addressing whether such use was permissible.

For example, in *Anwar Hussain Chowdhury v Bangladesh,*[37] there was a challenge to the Eight Amendment to the Bangladesh Constitution. The amendment sought to introduce Islam as the State Religion of Bangladesh and decentralise the Supreme Court by establishing divisional benches outside the capital city. One of the petitioner's lawyers claimed that the MPs voting for the amendment only knew about the State Religion. The long title of the amendment bill did not mention that it would also decentralise the Court.[38] Shahabuddin Ahmed J[39] Muhmammod Habibur Rahman J[40] and ATM Afzal J[41] rejected the argument by asserting that no MPs had objected to the long title during the debate on the floor. This reasoning appears problematic because it shows that the judges might have accepted the argument had the MPs raised the issue during the floor debate. Had the judges done this, it would have been a clear violation of the *Exclusionary Rule*. The three judges in *Anwar Hossain Chowdhury* apparently did not show their awareness of the rule while deciding the question.

Similar examples can be found in the Fifth,[42] Seventh[43], Thirteenth,[44] and Sixteenth Amendment cases,[45] the declaration of independence case,[46] and the case about preserving places of historic importance.[47] Bangladesh's Constituent Assembly debates and parliamentary committee deliberations were used as historical materials in these judgments. However, the judgments do not offer much insight into the desirability or permissibility of such use from a statutory construction perspective. It appears that Bangladesh's judicial standing on the use of parliamentary debate in statutory construction is

---

37 *Anwar Hossain Chowdhury v Bangladesh* (1989) 18 CLC (AD) 1/ (1989) BLD (Spl) 1.

38 ibid, para 395–96, 449, 454.

39 ibid, para 397 [Per Shahabuddin Ahmed J].

40 ibid, para 455 [Per Muhmammod Habibur Rahman J].

41 ibid, para 652 [Per ATM Afzal J].

42 *Bangladesh Italian Marble Works Ltd v Bangladesh* 2006 (Special) BLT 1 (HCD); *Khandker Delwar Hossain v Bangladesh* 62 DLR (AD) (2010) 298.

43 *Siddique Ahmed v Bangladesh* (2011) 33 BLD (HCD) 84; *Siddique Ahmed v Bangladesh* (Appellate Division) <www.supremecourt.gov.bd/resources/documents/563864_CA48.pdf> accessed 08 August 2023.

44 *Abdul Mannan Khan v Bangladesh* (2012) 64 DLR (AD) 1.

45 *Advocate Asaduzzaman Siddiqui v Bangladesh* (2016) 10 ALR (AD) 03.

46 *Dr. MA Salam v Bangladesh* 18 BLT (Spl) (2010) 1 <http://www.clcbd.org/document/584.html> accessed 08 August 2023.

47 *Major General AKM Shafiullah v Bangladesh* W/P No 4313/2009 <http://www.clcbd.org/document/585.html> accessed 07 August 2023.

guided by the temporal necessity of a case in hand rather than any serious consideration of the legislature and judiciary's institutional relations.

2.3 *Internal Process Doctrine*

Parliamentary privileges and immunities – particularly the sanctity of its internal proceedings – are inherent to the legislature's representative character. MPs' freedom of speech and deliberation within the House and its committees were established through the House of Commons' struggle against the Crown and its courts, including the House of Lords.[48] Its trademark doctrine of parliamentary sovereignty also bolsters these privileges and immunities.[49] Article 9 of the UK Bill of Rights, 1689 contained an express guarantee that the speeches, debates and proceedings in Parliament would not be impeached or questioned in any court or place outside the Parliament. The courts will not question the propriety of the parliamentary process and the Speaker's rulings concerning the process or order within the House. There are, however, debates in the UK about the scope of the privileges and immunities and how the judiciary should approach those.[50] British courts argue that it has the power to determine the scope of its jurisdiction, *i.e.*, the power to decide whether something qualifies as the Parliament's internal proceeding.[51] However, in these cases, the British judiciary usually takes a conciliatory approach, invites the Speaker's Counsel to submit their views and then considers those seriously.

Landmark British cases on the internal parliamentary proceedings are *Stockdale v. Hansard*[52] and *Bradlaugh v. Gossett.*[53] In *Bradlaugh v. Gossett*, Lord Coleridge CJ and Stephen J held that the Parliament has "exclusive power of interpreting" the boundaries of its internal proceedings.[54] The courts may intervene when a rights-related question needs to be answered independently

48 Richard Gordon and Malcolm Jack, *Parliamentary Privilege: Evolution or Codification?* (The Constitution Society 2013) 13–22; Nicholas Garforth and Peter Leyland, *Accountability in the Contemporary Constitution* 270–78 (Oxford University Press 2013); Chuks Okpaluba, 'Can a court review the internal affairs and processes of the legislature? Contemporary developments in Southern Africa' (2015) 48(2) Comparative and International Law Journal of Southern Africa 183, 186–9.

49 S Lakin, 'Parliamentary privilege, Parliamentary sovereignty, and Constitutional Principle' (*UK Constitutional Law Blog*, 11 February 2013).

50 A Twomey, 'Article 9 of the Bill of Rights 1688 and Its Application to Prorogation' Principle' (*UK Constitutional Law Blog*, 4 October 2010).

51 DC Jain, 'Judicial Review of Parliamentary Privileges: Functional Relationship of Courts and Legislatures in India' (1967) 9(2) Journal of the Indian Law Institute 205.

52 *Stockdale v. Hansard* (n 17).

53 *Bradlaugh v. Gossett* (n 17).

54 ibid, para 280 [Per Lord Coleridge C. J. & Stephen J.].

of the House.[55] For example, the right of a general citizen to sue any person who might have sat and voted in the House unlawfully must be interpreted by the Court independently of the House.[56] The courts might also be called to adjudicate cases where the Parliament expels or suspends any of its members, summons anyone from the public to appear before its committees, or punishes anyone for its contempt.[57] In such cases, the courts must see whether the matter is still internal to the Parliament.[58]

While deciding on an "internal proceedings" question, the British courts usually follow a "core and essential function" test. Courts consider something as the Parliament's internal proceeding when they find that such thing is "appropriate and necessary for the operation of the legislature."[59] The UK Supreme Court has reiterated this longstanding rule in the cases of *R v. Chaytor*[60] and *Cherry-Miller II*.[61] In *Chaytor,* the question was whether irregularities in claiming parliamentary expenses by the MPs could be prosecuted in courts.[62] The defendant parliamentarians argued that the expenses claim for their parliamentary services were privileged and internal to the Parliament and thus out of the Court's jurisdiction.[63] The Court framed the question as to whether the criminal proceedings would harm the "core or essential business of Parliament" and whether it would "inhibit debate or freedom of speech" within the Parliament.[64] Lord Philips opined that "the only thing that [the criminal prosecution] would inhibit [in the expense case] would be the making of dishonest claims."[65] In *Cherry-Miller II* (2019),[66] the UK Supreme Court did not give in to the government's "*blunt argument of no-go area*"[67] of

55 ibid, para 283.
56 The Constitution of the Peoples' Republic of Bangladesh, art. 69 (Punishment for sitting in Parliament unlawfully).
57 *Powell v. McCormack*, 395 US 486, 506 (1969) (Expulsion of a US House of Representative member); *Kielly v. Carson* (13 E.R. 225, May 23, 1842) (Canada's Newfoundland legislature punishing one of its members); Enid Campbell, 'Expulsion of Members of Parliament' (1971) 21(1) University of Toronto Law Journal 15.
58 Lord Burnett of Maldon (n 11).
59 Russell Keith, 'Judicial Intervention in Parliamentary Proceedings: the Implications of Egan v Willis' (2000) 28(3) Federal Law Review 549, 570.
60 *R v. Chaytor* (n 17), para 14–16.
61 *R (Miller) v. Prime Minister* (n 5).
62 *R v. Chaytor* (n 17) para 5–7.
63 ibid, para 12–13.
64 ibid, para 8.
65 ibid, para 48.
66 *R (Miller) v Prime Minister* (n 5).
67 Lord Mance DP 'Justiciability' (40th Annual FA Mann Lecture, 27 November 2017) 22.

internal proceedings.[68] In this case, a dubious prorogation of Parliament in the wake of the Brexit crisis was challenged. The Court found that a prorogation issued by the Crown under the Prime Minister's advice and "imposed upon the parliament from outside" could not constitute an internal proceeding of Parliament.[69]

Chaytor and *Cherry-Miller II* confirm that parliamentary privileges do not substantively bar the Court from judging the breadth of any privilege claim.[70] Rather, it is a procedural bar that comes into effect only after the Court determines the scope of the privilege claimed.[71] Once a matter is found to fall within the scope of internal parliamentary proceedings, the courts would stop there, and the Parliament would reserve its exclusive authority over the matter.[72]

However, one of the important characteristics of the UK's internal proceedings jurisprudence is the British judiciary's alertness to its relationship with the Parliament and keenness to take the Parliament's perspective seriously. For example, in *Warsama and Gannon v. Foreign and Commonwealth Office,*[73] the question was whether the judiciary could consider the findings of a non-statutory inquiry report about child abuse allegations in some governmental institutions. The government published the inquiry report under a motion for an Unopposed Return. In the UK parliamentary practice, Unopposed Returns are the procedure through which the government or Ministers publish papers in their hands.[74] While the papers are essentially government documents, publication through the Unopposed Return procedure gives them protection equal to parliamentary papers.[75] In England and Wales High Court, Judge McCloud found the report covered by "proceeding in parliament."[76] She, however, permitted an appeal against her decision by noting some observations about the Unopposed Return procedure.[77] She noted that motions for Unopposed Returns could not be debated in Parliament. It was a device that allowed the government to publish papers under the cloak of parliamentary privileges.[78]

68 *R v. Chaytor* (n 17) para 63.

69 ibid, para 66–68.

70 Thomas Erskine May, 'The Opposing Views' in *Treatise on the Law, Privileges, Proceedings, and Usage of Parliament* Part II Chapter 16, Paragraph 16.1 (25th Edition Online 2019).

71 *Prebble v. Television New Zealand Ltd* [1995]1 AC 321(N.Z.).

72 *Bradlaugh v. Gossett* (n 17).

73 *Warsama v. Foreign and Commonwealth Office* [2018] EWHC 1461 (QB).

74 Erskine May (n 70) 'Unopposed Return', Part I Chapter 7, Paragraph 7.32.

75 Barry K Winetrobe, 'The Autonomy of Parliament', in Dawn Oliver and Gavin Drewry (eds.), *The Law and Parliament* 14–32 (Butterworths 1998) 16.

76 *Warsama* (n 73) para 107, 116, 117.

77 ibid, para 129–130.

78 ibid, para 103.

Master McCloud invited the Speaker's office to comment on the status of Unopposed Return as an internal parliamentary proceeding.[79] The Speaker's counsel, Ms. Saira Salimi's written submission, supported the Unopposed Returns' internal proceeding status.[80] In appeal, the UK Court of Appeals endorsed the Speaker's view. It argued that an Unopposed Return would qualify as Parliament's internal proceeding despite the lack of debate on the motion to publish a document.[81] The invitation to the Speaker's office to aid the Court in finding the right answer to the question at hand showed its preparedness to give it due weight and, if necessary, show deference to the legislature's view on a matter that is essentially within the legislative branch's purview. The Court of Appeal noted:

> Although we are not bound to accept the view of counsel for the Speaker on what is or should be the scope of the privilege, we should 'pay careful regard' [...] to her view, reflecting that of the Speaker on behalf of the House of Commons, as a person in a position to speak on the matter with authority.[82]

In Bangladesh's constitutional supremacy, however, parliamentary privileges and immunities are accepted within the limits of the written Constitution. Interestingly, the Bangladesh Supreme Court's "internal proceedings" jurisprudence is highly influenced by a "sole constitutional guardianship" approach borrowed from the Indian Supreme Court.[83] It occasionally delivers judgments that are overly intrusive and indefensible within a separation of power context. Some of the Court's decisions drew antagonistic reactions from the Parliament. On some other occasions, the Court avoided deciding concrete constitutional questions, fearing that the legislature may not comply.

2.3.1 Bangladesh Supreme Court's Intrusive "Sole Guardianship Approach"

Judicial consideration of internal parliamentary proceedings is barred by Article 78(1) of the Constitution of Bangladesh. However, the Bangladeshi

79 ibid, para 42–43.

80 ibid, para 83.

81 *Foreign and Commonwealth Office v. Warsama & Anor* [2020] EWCACiv 142, para 60.

82 ibid, para 56 [Per Lord Burnett of Maldon, Lord Justice Coulson and Lady Justice Rose].

83 M Jashim Ali Chowdhury, 'Judicial Review of "Internal Parliamentary Proceedings": the Dialogic and Non-Dialogic Approaches' (2021) 6(1) Comparative Constitutional Law and Administrative Law Journal 28, 39.

Supreme Court does not shy away from judging internal parliamentary businesses if a constitutional question is involved. It has tested the boundary of Parliament's internal proceedings in cases relating to parliament boycotts, resignations, floor-crossing and the Speakers' rulings.

The first reported cases of judicial inquiry into the Parliament's internal proceedings are the *Ataur Rahman Khan* and *Cyril Sikder* cases mentioned earlier. In *Ataur Rahman Khan v. Md. Nasim,* the then Home Minister criticised the Supreme Court judges over granting bail to numerous arrestees in various criminal cases. The Minister commented, "Sitting on a high pedestal to ensure justice in the society, they (Judges) are patronising terrorism".[84] Though the Minister's comment was labelled "unfortunate", the Court rejected the petition by holding that the parliamentary freedom of speech guaranteed in article 78(3) of the Bangladesh Constitution covers "anything said in Parliament". The word "anything" is of the widest import and covers "everything" said therein.[85]

A similar judgment came in *Cyril Sikdar* v. *Nazmul Huda*, where a Minister remarked on "corruption" in the lower judiciary.[86] The High Court Division Bench initially issued an order upon the Parliament Secretariat to send copies of the proceedings of Parliament to the Court. The furious MPs from the government and opposition parties in the Fifth Parliament pressed the Speaker to discuss the matter in Parliament. Taking exception to the *sub judice* rule, the Speaker agreed to discuss by observing: "The hands of the High Court Division are long. The question is whether they are too long to stretch to Parliament."[87] Anticipating an institutional tussle, the High Court Division recalled its order and decided that the proceedings of Parliament were unnecessary for the case. The Court, again, dismissed the contempt petition by holding that the remedy for such wrong lies with the Parliament, not the Court.[88]

In 1994, the opposition-party MPs of the Fifth Parliament (1991–1996) demanded the introduction of an election-time caretaker government.[89] At one stage, the MPs started boycotting the parliament sessions continuously.[90]

84 *Ataur Rahman* (n 14), para 2.

85 ibid, para 23.

86 *Cyril Sikder* (n 15), para 2.

87 Nizam Ahmed, *Parliaments in South Asia: India, Pakistan and Bangladesh* (Oxon and New York: Routledge 2020) 140.

88 *Cyril Sikder* (n 15), para 17.

89 Golam Hossain, 'Bangladesh in 1994: Democracy at Risk' (1995) 35(2) Asian Survey 171; Md Morshedul Islam, '1996's Non-party Caretaker Government Movement and the Role of Opposition in Bangladesh: a Politico-Legal Analysis' (2016) 3(6) Global Journal of Political Science and Administration 20.

90 Md Nazrul Islam, 'Non-Party Caretaker Government in Bangladesh (1991–2001): Dilemma for Democracy?' (2013) 3(8) Developing Country Studies 116, 120.

The boycott was challenged in *Anwar Hossain Khan v. Speaker Jatya Sangsad*.[91] The High Court Division bench held that abstention from the parliamentary sessions without leave of the Speaker could not be an internal matter for Parliament.[92] That being a question of "constitutional obligation to represent the people", the Court ordered the opposition MPs to return to the Parliament immediately.[93] However, the Division Bench did not elaborate on how the Court could enforce the MPs' constitutional obligation to represent the people and how the absence or presence of MPs in the House could not be internal to the Parliament. The opposition parties vehemently criticised the Court order, saying it was a politically motivated judgment and amounted to invading the Parliament's "sovereignty".[94] In the face of criticism, the Appellate Division stayed the order of the High Court Division and instructed the opposition parties to appeal against that order formally.[95] The Court's decision was appealed, and it would take another thirteen years to be decided.[96]

Before the appeal would be decided, the boycotting MPs approached their ninety consecutive sitting days of absence without leave.[97] As per Article 67(1)(b) of the Bangladesh Constitution, MPs would lose their seat if they remained in unauthorised absence for ninety consecutive sitting days. The President of Bangladesh then sent a Special Reference to the Appellate Division of the Supreme Court.[98] *Special Reference No 1 of 1995*[99] asked whether the MPs' boycott would mean an absence without leave. Some legal experts urged the Court not to answer the reference. They argued that the vacation of parliamentary seats was an internal matter of Parliament.[100] The Appellate Division rejected the argument and held that the questions referred to it were related to the interpretation of a few words of Article 67(1)(b) of the Constitution, *i.e.*, the meaning of "absent without leave".[101] Interpretation of the Constitution is the Court's responsibility, and it has nothing to do with the internal proceedings

91 *Anwar Hossain Khan v. Speaker of Bangladesh Sangsad Bhaban* 47 DLR (HCD) (1995) 42.
92 ibid, para 20.
93 ibid, para 41.
94 Nizam Ahmed (n 87) 149.
95 ibid, 141.
96 *Moudud Ahmed v. Anwar Hossain Khan*, 60 DLR (2008) (AD) 108.
97 Nizam Ahmed, 'Parliamentary Opposition in Bangladesh: a Study of its Role in the Fifth Parliament' (1997) 3(2) Party Politics 147,151.
98 *Special Reference No. 1 of 1995*, 47 DLR (1995) (AD)111.
99 ibid, para 2.
100 ibid, para 85.
101 ibid, para 84.

of the Parliament.[102] Justice Latifur Rahman, however, took a step further and observed:

> The internal and proper business of the proceedings of the Parliament is beyond the purview of the Constitutional Court, but while acting in the name of internal proceedings, if any violation of the constitutional provision takes place, then this Court is certainly competent to interfere.[103]

The High Court Division's view in *Anwar Hossain Khan v Speaker* and the Appellate Division's view in *Special Reference No 1 of 1995* suggest that the Supreme Court is willing to limit the defence of the internal proceedings in cases involving constitutional questions. However, as will transpire thirteen years later, the Court was unsure what it could do in concrete cases of internal proceedings.

Thirteen years later, in 2008, the Appellate Division disposed of the appeal against *Anwar Hossain Khan v. Speaker.* However, in the appeal – *Moudud Ahmed v. Anwar Hossain Khan*[104] – the Appellate Division avoided the "internal proceedings" issue. It overturned the High Court Division's order to the MPs to return to Parliament by simply observing that the appearance/non-appearance and participation/non-participation was a matter of personal choice and volition of the MPs. While the Court could order an MP to attend the Parliament, it might not enforce the actual attendance. Therefore, the Appellate Division observed that since the Court's order would serve no purpose, the High Court Division should not have made such an order.[105]

Now, the *Moudud Ahmed* court seems to wash its hands off in cases where MPs' personal choice and volition would determine the outcome. It was decided apparently on an apprehension that MPs would not follow the Court's order. This tendency to tailor-making suitable arguments to fit the necessity of a given case is detrimental to the jurisprudential strength of the Court. This tendency is hardly based on consistent appreciation of the constitutional doctrines involved.[106]

The Court's hesitation and lack of confidence become even more evident in cases where the Speaker's rulings or actions were challenged. In 1995, after

102 ibid, para 33.

103 ibid.

104 *Moudud Ahmed v. Anwar Hossain* (n 96).

105 ibid, para 70.

106 M Jashim Ali Chowdhury, 'Bangladesh's Inconsistency with the Prospective Invalidation', in Po Jen Yap (ed.), *Constitutional Remedies in Asia* (London: Routledge 2019) 33–46.

the High Court Division ordered them to join the Parliament in *Anwar Hossain Khan v. Speaker*, 147 MPs belonging to the opposition parties resigned from Parliament *en masse*.[107] They sent their resignation letters to the Speaker through their party leaders.[108] A political deadlock followed when the Speaker kept the resignation letters on his table for over two months and did not issue any official notification of the event.[109]

Article 66(4) of the Bangladesh Constitution[110] and Rule 178 of the Parliament's Rules of Procedure (RoP)[111] require the Speaker to inform the Election Commission about any such incident in Parliament. The Members of Parliament (Determination of Dispute) Act 1980 has entrusted the Election Commission to decide whether the seats had become vacant.[112] In case of vacancy, the Election Commission is required by Article 123(4) of the Constitution to arrange a by-election within ninety days of such vacancy.

With everything pending at the Speaker's table, two writ petitions were moved to the High Court Division. The validity of *en masse* resignation was challenged in *Rafique Hossain v. Speaker*. On the other hand, the Speakers' inaction was challenged in *Alauddin Khalid v. Speaker.* The Court heard and decided the cases together, and the judgment is reported as *Rafique Hossain and Alauddin Khalid v. Speaker*.[113] This time, the High Court Division issued a show-cause notice upon the Speaker asking about the validity of the MPs' *en masse* resignation. The notice also directed the Speaker not to act against the resignation letters for ten days until the Court's next hearing occurs.[114] The government party MPs, particularly the Chief Whip of the government party, seriously objected to the Court's order. The Speaker was allegedly in favour of raising the matter on the floor and expressed his deep frustration with the Court's ordering the Speaker about something internal to the Parliament.[115] However, the senior leaders of the government party persuaded the Speaker not to discuss the matter in the Parliament, and the Speaker accordingly replied to the Court, stating his view of the matter.[116]

107 Golam Hossain, 'Bangladesh in 1995: Politics of Intransigence' (1996) 36(2) Asian Survey 196.

108 Nizam Ahmed, *The Parliament of Bangladesh* (Routledge 2017) 196.

109 ibid, 207.

110 Constitution of Bangladesh (n 56), art. 66(4).

111 RoP (n 13) r 178.

112 The Members of Parliament (Determination of Dispute) Act, 1980 sec 3.

113 *Rafique Hossain v. Speaker Bangladesh Parliament*, 47 DLR 361 (1995).

114 Nizam Ahmed (n 87) 141.

115 ibid, 142.

116 M Humaiyun Rashid (ed.) *Rulings of the Speaker* (Dhaka: Institute of Parliament Studies 2000) 106.

At the hearing, the MPs argued that resignation was internal to the Parliament and out of the judicial review.[117] The Court was unconvinced and held that the "act of submission of resignation" did not form part of the proceedings of Parliament until and unless the Speaker officially brought it to the notice of Parliament following Rule 178(3) of the RoP.[118] *Mr. Alauddin Khalid*, on the other hand, argued that the inaction of the Speaker was *mala fide* and he was, thereby, intentionally withholding from his constitutional duty.[119] Against this, the Speaker's counsel argued that under Article 67(2) of the Constitution of Bangladesh, the Speaker had some roles to play.[120] He had to see whether the resignation had been submitted duly, whether the member resigning had assigned any reason for their resignation, whether the resignation letter contained any extraneous matters,[121] and whether the resignation letters were in line with the related constitutional provision.[122] The Court was unconvinced by this argument, too. It held that the Speaker's only role if there be any, was to be sure whether the signatures of the resigning MPs were genuine.[123] Apart from this, no provision of the Constitution empowered the Speaker to accept or reject any MPs' resignations on any other technical grounds.[124]

Interestingly, despite all these observations, the Court refused to give any order in the case, arguing that the petitioner had no *locus standi* to challenge the *en masse* resignation or the Speaker's inaction. Compared to the Bangladesh Supreme Court's strong favour of Public Interest Litigation and the expansion of the *locus standi* rule from the mid-1990s (discussion on judicial review below), this decision appears confusing. The decision was perhaps motivated by the Court's attempt to distance itself from the ongoing political tussle between the government and opposition parties. Soon after the decision, the then Speaker issued a ruling holding that the *en masse* resignation of the MPs was not valid in his judgment. He, therefore, refused to forward the matter to the Election Commission.

The Supreme Court was again asked to judge the Speaker's authority in parliamentary business around five years later. The *Khandker Delwar Hossain v. Speaker*[125] was a case relating to floor crossing by two opposition party MPs

117 *Rafique Hossain v. Speaker* (n 113) para 7.
118 ibid, para 67 [Per Kazi Ebadul Haque J].
119 ibid, para 5.
120 ibid, para 38.
121 ibid, para 19.
122 ibid, para 13.
123 ibid, para 72.
124 ibid, para 64 [Per Kazi Ebadul Haque J].
125 *Khandker Delwar Hossain v. The Speaker* 51 DLR 1 (1999).

in the seventh Parliament (1996–2001). The opposition MPs did not officially resign from their party but joined the so-called "national consensus government" led by the ruling party and accepted ministerial positions.[126] The Opposition Chief Whip wrote the Speaker about his party's disapproval of the defection. Article 70 of the Bangladesh Constitution states that MPs defecting from their parties would lose their parliamentary seats (See: Chapter 3). The letter requested the Speaker to refer the matter to the Election Commission. The Speaker, however, remained silent for around two months. After that, he ruled that the concerned MPs had not resigned from their parties, nor did they vote or abstain from voting against their party's decision. Absent these conditions, no constitutional dispute under Article 70 needed to be referred to the Election Commission.

The matter went to Court. In the hearing, the government disputed the Court's power to direct the Speaker to do anything.[127] It was also argued that the Speaker's ruling in Parliament was its "internal proceedings".[128] The Speaker's office even refused to tender any representation to the Court. It also did not supply a copy of the Speaker's ruling as requested by the Court.[129] Facing a non-cooperative Parliament, the High Court Division tried to avoid confrontation. It held that the Court did not need to judge the validity of the Speaker's ruling in that case.[130] It was rather concerned with the Speaker's constitutional duty in the matter. Like *Rafique Hossain and Alauddin Khalid v. Speaker* (1995), the Court held that the Speaker did not have any role except forwarding the matter to the Election Commission.[131] Accordingly, the Speaker was directed to refer the matter to the Election Commission. The government appealed. The Appellate Division confirmed the High Court Division's position.[132] Compared to the direction in this case, the Court's refusal to issue an order in *Rafique Hossain and Alauddin Khalid v. Speaker* (1995) appears opportunistic.

The latest, and perhaps the most egregious, example of judicial overreach is, perhaps, the *A. K. M. Shafiuddin v. Bangladesh*.[133] In this case, a Bangladeshi MP moved a motion to discuss a High Court Division judgment regarding a property named *Sarak Bhaban*. In that judgment, a High Court Division bench

126 ibid, para 2–4.
127 ibid, para 22.
128 ibid, para 23.
129 ibid, para 61.
130 ibid, para 62.
131 ibid, para 57.
132 *Secretary, Parliament Secretariat, Dhaka v. Khandker Delwar Hossain*, 19 BLD (AD) 276 (1999).
133 *AKM Shafiuddin v. Bangladesh* (2012) 41 CLC (HCD), para 2–15.

ordered the government to deliver the possession of disputed *Sarak Bhaban* to the Registrar of the Supreme Court.[134] The Speaker accepted the motion, and during the discussion, she allegedly commented that the judges of the Supreme Court act exceptionally swiftly when matters of their interest come to the docket.[135] This observation of the Speaker on the floor of the Parliament was later brought to the notice of the relevant High Court Division bench during a subsequent hearing of the *Sarak Bhaban* case. The sitting judge then commented that the Speaker's speech amounted to "sedition", and she should be punished for that.[136] Infuriated by the comment, the MPs reacted harshly in a subsequent parliamentary debate. The Speaker then ruled that the concerned judge violated his constitutional oath by breaching the Parliament's privileges. She also commented that Parliament would support it should the Chief Justice take action against the concerned judge.[137] That ruling of the Speaker is now challenged in this *A. K. M. Shafiuddin* case. It was argued that the Speaker's ruling was unconstitutional as it amounted to an attack on the independence of the judiciary.[138]

The High Court Division bench disposed of the petition without passing any order but did not miss a chance to remind the Speaker that parliamentary privileges are "not unlimited" under the Bangladesh Constitution[139] and, also that the Speaker's ruling, particularly the comment on the Chief Justice's disciplinary action, was unconstitutional and "*non est in the eyes of the law*."[140] This position of the High Court Division is clearly against the historical position of the Court in not questioning the Speaker's ruling, which is an internal proceeding of the Parliament.

The second argument of the High Court Division was that Judges' discipline is a matter for the Supreme Judicial Council, and the Speaker "must not" comment on this.[141] As mentioned earlier in this part, the Supreme Judicial Council is a disciplinary body activated by the President and comprises the Supreme Court judges themselves.[142] No rule in the Constitution says that nobody could complain to the President or the Chief Justice about any Supreme Court judges. Rather, such a complaint or information is a requirement for the President to

134 ibid, para 3.
135 ibid, para 2.
136 ibid, para 21.
137 ibid, para 12–13.
138 ibid, para 1.
139 ibid, para 41.
140 ibid, para 33.
141 ibid, para 26.
142 Constitution of Bangladesh (n 56) art 96.

trigger an investigation by the Supreme Judicial Council.[143] Given the situation, even an ordinary citizen of Bangladesh should be able to call upon the Chief Justice or the President to initiate a Supreme Judicial Council process. Without such scope, the Supreme Judicial Council could never be activated. Therefore, the "Speaker-must-not" argument of the High Court Division appears unexplainable in any constitutional sense.

Regarding the "sedition comment" made by one of their fellow judges, the High Court Division rested the case by making a brief but evasive description of it as "unfortunate". In doing this, the Court practically ignored a sitting judge's disrespectful comment about the head of the legislative branch. Instead, the Court defended it on a technical excuse that it did not "call in question the validity of a proceeding of Parliament".[144] In the end, however, the Court itself called into question the validity of the Speaker's ruling and declared it "*non est* in the eyes of the law". Unsupported by the Constitution, the High Court Division's argument, in this case, represents a classic example of judicial self-dealing and its refusal even to tolerate lawful criticism of the judges' conduct.

Considering all the cases together, the Bangladesh Supreme Court's position on the Internal Proceedings Doctrine appears to be incoherent, indecisive, opportunistic, deflective and, in extreme circumstances, clear transgressions of limits. While the Court's jurisprudential incoherence might be influenced by the overt or covert political influence upon the judges,[145] the antagonistic approach of the members and office-bearers of the Parliament also forced the Court to surrender its adjudicatory responsibility sometimes. In cases of aggressive exchange, the Court and judges are guided by their ego and institutional protectionism. Compared to this, the British Parliament and the judiciary's conciliatory approach to the rules of comity forges a delicate balance between the judicial power of interpretation and the Parliament's claim of exclusivity over its internal affairs.

3 The Concept of Judicial Accountability

Judicial accountability is traditionally seen as contradictory to judicial independence. However, there are reasons to question the attitude. First, within a

143 ibid, art. 96(5) reads: "Where, upon any information received from the Council or from any other source, the President has reason to apprehend that a Judge."

144 *AKM Shafiuddin* (n 133) para 31.

145 Ridwanul Hoque, 'The Recent Emergency and the Politics of the Judiciary in Bangladesh' (2009) 2(2) NUJS Law Review 183.

liberal constitutional order, judicial accountability should be as important as its independence. Accountability brings a chain of discipline within the institution and establishes a foundation for public trust. Secondly, greater legislative engagement and role play in the judicial accountability process must be encouraged rather than disputed. The Parliament's engagement in the process invites openness and democratic deliberation and imposes a significant restraint on the possibility of non-transparent back-door pressure an opportunist executive branch might be interested in putting on the judiciary. Thirdly, apart from the democratic quality that Parliament brings, some institutional rationale calls for parliamentary engagement with the judiciary. Parliament finances the judiciary. It determines the courts' composition and jurisdictions and the judges' privileges, immunities, appointment, tenure, removal, and discipline. In congressional and parliamentary models, the judiciaries report their overall activities and finances to the legislative branch.[146] Courts are also generally responsive to information requests from parliaments. If invited, the judges in the UK and elsewhere tend to appear to answer the parliamentary committees. They sometimes proactively engage the legislature in policies affecting the judiciary.[147]

Therefore, scholars like Mark Tushnet argue for recognising the importance of the judiciary's institutional accountability and balancing it against the individual judges' functional independence.[148] Tushnet argues that while the judges' decisional autonomy and institutional independence must be strictly guarded, their collective behaviour and non-judicial or social conduct affecting their institution's prestige and position must also be open to inter-institutional scrutiny.[149]

However, the higher courts in the Indian subcontinent, including Bangladesh, generally distrust politicians and try to resist parliamentary involvement in the issues they consider "internal" to the judiciary. Under this approach, any argument for inter-institutional checks and balances is usually

146 David Harper, 'Parliament and Judiciary: Judicial Independence and Nature of the Relationship between Parliament and the Judiciary' (2015) 30(2) Australasian Parliamentary Review 8.

147 Robert Hazell and Patrick O'Brien, 'Meaningful Dialogue: Judicial Engagement with Parliamentary Committees at Westminster' 25 August 2015 <https://discovery.ucl.ac.uk/id/eprint/10051319/1/Hazell_Meaningful%20Dialogue%20v%2014%20RH%20copy%20for%20UCL%20RPS%20Aug%202015.pdf> accessed 30 July 2024.

148 Mark Tushnet, 'Judicial Accountability in Comparative Perspective' in Nicholas Bamforth and Peter Leyland (eds.), *Accountability in the Contemporary Constitution* (Oxford 2013).

149 Stephen Burbank, 'Judicial Independence, Judicial Accountability and Interbranch Relations' (2007) Faculty Scholarship at Penn Law 98.

seen as an invitation to interfere with judicial independence.[150] Judges like to see the scopes of appeals, reviews and revisions by the higher courts as sufficient for their decisional accountability.[151] While they do not reject the existence of its democratic[152] and explanatory[153] accountability to the people, the involvement of the people's representatives in enforcing those accountabilities is received with hesitation and confusion. Subsequent paragraphs of this part will consider the Bangladesh Supreme Court's attitude to parliamentary participation in the judicial accountability process and critique how the judiciary self-deals on matters that relate to it and shows a generally dismissive attitude towards the Parliament.

3.1 *Judges' Democratic Accountability to the Parliament*

As Professor Tushnet argues, the judiciary's independence may cohabit with its accountability when there is a carefully articulated balance between political or democratic accountability (accountability to the people and their representatives) and legal accountability (accountability to the law, professional regulatory authorities, appellate and provisional authorities and professional codes of conducts).[154] The judiciary's legal accountability is intra-branch, which can reduce potentially inappropriate inter-branch influences.[155] Democratic accountability to the public, on the other hand, is channelled through their representatives.[156]

The Parliament's involvement in the judicial accountability process is defensible on functional grounds also.[157] It finances the judiciary. It determines, by law, the Court's composition, jurisdiction and the judges' privileges, immunities and terms and conditions of services.[158] In congressional and

---

150 AP Shah, 'A Manifesto for Judicial Accountability in India' *The Wire* (New Delhi, 19 July 2019).

151 Lord Phillips, 'Judicial Independence' (*Commonwealth Law Conference*, Nairobi, Kenya, 12 September 2007).

152 Paul D Carrington, 'Judicial Independence and Democratic Accountability in Highest State Courts' (1998) 61(3) Law and Contemporary Problems: Judicial Independence and Accountability 79, 80.

153 A Le Sueur, 'Developing Mechanisms for Judicial Accountability in the UK' (2004) 24 Legal Studies 73.

154 Mark Tushnet (n 148) 58–59.

155 Stephen B Burbank, Judicial Independence, Judicial Accountability, and Interbranch Relations (2006–2007) 95 The Georgetown Law Journal 909, 914–916.

156 C Geyh, 'Rescuing Judicial Accountability from the realm of Political Rhetoric' (2006) 56(4) Case Western Reserve Law Review 911, 917–919.

157 Stephen Colbran (n 12) 59–62.

158 Mark Tushnet (n 148) 61–63.

parliamentary models,[159] the judiciaries report their overall activities and finances to the legislative branch.[160] The judicial branch is generally responsive to information requests from parliaments.[161] If invited, the judges tend to appear on the parliamentary committees. In some jurisdictions, the judges would proactively engage the Parliament over policies affecting their institution.[162] Parliamentary participation in judicial appointment and removal is also recognised in leading constitutional systems.

3.1.1 Parliament's Role in Judicial Appointments

It is said that the UK has "a blurring concept of separation of powers but a strong concept of judicial independence".[163] The judges' appointment is largely independent of parliamentary and executive control. Previously, the Lord Chancellor appointed the judges in consultation with the Lord Chief Justice.[164] After the CRA 2005, an independent appointment commission controls the process. During the passage of the CRA, some advocated introducing a US-styled system of the confirmation hearing for the higher court judges or appearances before a select committee soon after an appointment. The suggestion was rejected and continues to draw the judges' irritation.[165]

On the other hand, Bangladesh's judicial appointment is solely controlled by the Executive branch – the Prime Minister and the President.[166] There is, however, a conventional primacy of the Chief Justice's recommendation regarding the candidates. Apart from its legislative power to prescribe the qualification and process of appointment, the Parliament has no participation in the judges' appointment process. In 2008, there was an attempt to establish an independent appointment commission named the Supreme Judicial Commission.

159 David Harper (n 146) 8.

160 The UK House of Lords Constitution Committee, 'Sixth Report, Chapter 3: Parliament and Judiciary' (*House of Lords*, 11 July 2007) para 136.

161 Stephen Burbank (n 149) 917–922.

162 RJD Hazell and PC O'Brien, 'Meaningful Dialogue: Judicial Engagement with Parliamentary Committees at Westminster' (2016) Public Law 54–73.

163 ibid, 55–57.

164 Lord Philips (n 151) 3.

165 Lords Constitution Committee (n 160) para 132–135.

166 Constitution of Bangladesh (n 56) arts 48(3), 95(1) and 98(1) empowers the President to appoint permanent and ad hoc judges to the High Court Division and Appellate Division of the Supreme Court of Bangladesh. Except in case of the Chief Justice, the President is bound by the advice of the Prime Minister.

However, the Supreme Court invalidated it on the excuse that it might inhibit the primacy of the Chief Justice's opinion in the candidate selection process.[167]

3.1.2 Parliament's Role in Judges' Removal

Regarding the judges' removal, the necessity of a process through which allegations of misconduct and incapacity can be made and investigated is not disputed. There is, however, a debate as to what could be the best model for such a process. In the UK, impeachment and removal of the higher court judges are done by the petition of both Houses of Parliament.[168] This power originated from the 1701 Act of Settlement and is now contained in section 11(3) of the Supreme Court Act 1981. However, it never had to be exercised in England and Wales. In Ireland, an Irish High Court of Admiralty judge was removed in 1830 for corruption.[169]

On the other hand, the Constitution of Bangladesh originally provided for the parliamentary removal of judges. The system was substituted in 1977 by a military ruler with a Judicial Council system. The Council comprised the Chief Justice and two of his senior colleagues. Under the system, the President would send any allegation of misconduct or incapacity against a Supreme Court judge to the Council. The Council would investigate the allegations and report on them. Based on the Council's express recommendation for removal, the President will remove the judge.

In 2009, the Supreme Court declared the military ruler's access to power and constitutional amendments unconstitutional.[170] However, the Court, "in a supremacist's voice",[171] "condoned" the Judicial Council system. It was observed, without any explanation, that the Council system was more transparent and pro-judiciary than the original one involving the Parliament.[172] Absent any other explanation, it appears that the judges were comfortable with the

167 *Idrisur Rahman* v. *Bangladesh* 60 DLR (HCD) 714; *Bangladesh & Justice Syed Dastagir Hossain* v. *Idrisur Rahman* 15 BLC (AD) 49; M Jashim Ali Chowdhury, 'Supreme Judicial Commission needs readjustment' *The Daily Star* (Dhaka, 10 May 2008).

168 Lord Phillips, 'Judicial Independence and Accountability: a View from the Supreme Court' (*Gustave Tuck Lecture*, 8 February 2011) 6–7.

169 Lord Philips (n 151) 6.

170 *Khandker Dlewar Hossain* (n 42).

171 Ridwanul Hoque, 'Can the Court Invalidate an Original Provision of the Constitution?' (2016) 2 University of *Asia Pacific* Journal of Law and Policy 13, 15.

172 *Khandker Dlewar Hossain* (n 42) "These substituted provisions being more transparent procedure than that of the earlier ones and also safeguarding independence of judiciary, are to be condoned" (p 177 of the Full Text Judgment) <http://www.dwatch-bd.org/5th%20Amendment.pdf> accessed on 06 August 2023.

Council members' (the judges themselves) exclusive power of investigation and recommendation for the potential removal of any of their colleagues.

However, the practical efficiency of the Council system has always been doubtful. The political government being the dominant controller of the whole process, the Council remained grossly dysfunctional and ineffective during its entire existence.[173] Political governments have shown reluctance to trigger the Council proceedings against their appointees. It was considered unhelpful to their political interests.[174] The Council system was used only once to remove a High Court Judge. That, again, was done under the pressure of a very intense public exposure of bribery by the judge concerned.[175] The most interesting case of non-use of the system was seen during the military-backed caretaker government of 2007–2008. While a military ruler introduced the Judicial Council System in the late 1970s, the 2007 military regime found it unhelpful to their cause. This time, there might have been apprehension that the Supreme Court judges comprising the Council would favour their colleagues had the President triggered an investigation process. Accordingly, several judges were invited to "tea" at the President's House – *Banga Bhaban* and were allegedly pressured to resign. While some quietly complied, others did not.[176]

In 2014, the Parliament passed the Sixteenth Amendment to the Constitution and sought to revive the original parliamentary removal system.[177] In 2016, the Supreme Court declared the amendment unconstitutional.[178] Despite the argument that parliamentary removal of judges would install the so-far missing institutional balance between these two organs,[179] judges were excessively concerned with the MPs' abject partisanship and lack of conscience

173 Anisur Rahman, '16th Amendment of the constitution: Another view' *The Daily Star* (Dhaka,23 September 2014).

174 *Bdnews24.com*, Justice Shamsuddin Choudhury seeks Chief Justice SK Sinha's removal' (Dhaka, 13 September 2015).

175 Anisur Rahman, 'Citizens' concern over appointment of judge in Supreme Court' *The Daily Star law and Our Rights* (Dhaka, 11 February 2003).

176 Hindustan Times, 'Former Bangladesh president tried to remove judges', 17 July 2009 <https://www.hindustantimes.com/world/former-bangladesh-president-tried-to-remove-judges/story-um1yiQxa2lougYmPmbRjfO.html> accessed 17 November 2024.

177 Asano Noriyuki and Minato Kazuki, 'Politicisation of the appointment and removal of judges in a declining democracy: the case of Bangladesh' (2019) Institute of Developing Economies, Japan External Trade Organization (IDE-JETRO) Discussion Paper <https://core.ac.uk/download/pdf/288469659.pdf> accessed 31 May 2023.

178 *Advocate Asaduzzaman Siddiqui* (n 45).

179 SM Masum Billah, 'Faith, Hope and Promise' *Dhaka Tribune* (Dhaka, 17 August 2014).

autonomy – mainly blaming Article 70.[180] Also, the judgment's institutional arguments were problematic. The Court insubstantially argued that the Bangladesh constitution separates the higher judiciary from the executive and legislature "entirely and absolutely", and the legislature's "poking of the nose" into the judges' removal process would threaten judicial independence.[181]

The Court also ducked the judiciary's democratic accountability question by superficially arguing that "nowhere in [the] Constitution is there a provision to the effect that the Judiciary shall be responsible or accountable to the parliament".[182] It also argued that since the Bangladeshi President, whom the Parliament elects, triggers the Supreme Judicial Council and removes a judge under the Council's recommendation, it should be enough of the judiciary's democratic accountability.[183] At the end of all these arguments, the Supreme Court of Bangladesh extraordinarily declared the parliamentary removal system of Bangladesh's original Constitution as violating the basic structures of that same Constitution. In doing this, the Supreme Court simply ignored that even India – whose Basic Structure Doctrine it relied on[184] to decide the case – has a system of parliamentary removal.[185]

While the Supreme Court could have reclaimed its representation in the investigative body to be formed under the revived parliamentary removal process, the denial of the Parliament's authority altogether seems to be inspired by the Court's general distrust of the politicians and resistance to parliamentary involvement in issues it considers "internal" to itself.[186] Under this approach, any argument for inter-institutional checks and balances is mostly seen as an invitation to interfere with judicial independence.[187]

180 Md Yasin Khan Chowdhury, 'Removal of Judges Under 16th Amendment of Bangladesh Constitution: a Euphemism To Curb On Judiciary' (2015) 3 DIU Journal of Humanities and Social Science 89.

181 M Jashim Ali Chowdhury and Nirmal Kumar Saha, '*Advocate Asaduzzaman Siddiqui v. Bangladesh*: Judiciary's Dilemma with Impeachment' (2017) 3(3) Constitutional and Administrative Law Quarterly 7.

182 Ridwanul Hoque (n 171) 20–21.

183 ibid, 21.

184 *Keshavananda Bharati v. State of Kerala* (1973) 4 SCC (India) 225 (Establishing the Basic Structure Doctrine); *Anwar Hossain Chowdhury v Bangladesh* (n 37) (Endorsing the doctrine in Bangladesh).

185 The Constitution of India, art 124(4).

186 Chowdhury and Saha (n 181).

187 AP Shah (n 150).

3.2 *Judges' Explanatory Accountability to the Parliamentary Committees*

In the common law world, except in the US, the Judges' appearances before the parliamentary committees are generally discouraged. Some argue that the Commonwealth judiciaries' discomfort about appearances before the parliamentary committee might be linked to the popular perception of the Ministers' *sacrificial* accountability to the Parliament.[188] In the public gaze, the idea of government Ministers losing the confidence of Parliament and resigning as a consequence feeds the image of sacrificial accountability to the legislature that is suitable for political office bearers only.

However, this "sacrificial" sense of accountability must be distinguished from the judiciary's "explanatory" accountability to the people.[189] When the judges appear before the parliamentary committees, they explain how the justice system operates and respond to common criticisms (such as delays, human rights sensitivity, sentencing, lack of efficiency and lack of equal access) against it.[190] Lord Chief Justice Lord Thomas once summed this up in one of his annual appearances before the House of Commons Justice Committee, saying, "I feel that we owe a duty to tell you how we are administering the system and how people are being appointed".[191]

The judges' parliamentary engagement has a strong dialogic value. The judges' evidence to parliamentary committees benefits both sides. Parliament is interested in knowing how the laws it has passed work in practice and how a proposed law might work. Evidence given by the judges to the parliamentary committees lends "jurists' prestige"[192] to their inquiries. By engaging the committees, the judges, in turn, get an important opportunity to influence legislation that may impact the judiciary's work at their drafting stages.

The recent surge of judicial appearances before the UK parliamentary committees is a notable development.[193] In the UK, the judges now routinely

188 Vernon Bogdanor, 'Parliament and the Judiciary: the Problem of Accountability' (Third Sunningdale Lecture on Accountability, 9 February 2006).

189 A Sengupta, 'Judicial Accountability: a Taxonomy' (2014) Public Law 245.

190 A Le Sueur, 'Parliamentary Accountability and the Judicial System' in N Bamforth and P Leyland (eds.) *Accountability in the Contemporary Constitution* 200–230 (Oxford, OUP 2013) 208.

191 Lord Chief Justice Lord Thomas's answer to the Question No 18 posed by the UK House of Commons Justice Committee, 2 April 2014 quoted in Hazell and O'Brien (n 147) 57.

192 H Rishikof and B Perry, '"Separateness but Interdependence, Autonomy but Reciprocity": a First Look at Federal Judges' Appearances before Legislative Committees' (1995) 46(2) Mercer Law Review 667, 687.

193 Sir Jack Beatson, 'The New Model Judiciary and the Other Two Branches of the State' (2015) 20(2) Judicial Review 63, 65–67.

appear before parliamentary committees and testify on issues involving the administration of justice, statutory interpretation and legal development.[194] The practice has been internalised by section 5 of the CRA 2005, which permits the Lord Chief Justice to "lay before Parliament written representations on matters that appear to him to be matters of importance relating to the judiciary, or otherwise to the administration of justice".

Though the parliamentary committees may, in theory, summon a judge to appear, the process generally works voluntarily. Previously, the judges called to the committee would seek advice and support from their respective offices. The UK Judiciary has now developed a formal guideline for the judges' appearance. As per the guideline, the judges do not comment on (a) the merits of individual cases; (b) their fellow judges, politicians, or other public officials; (c) the merits of future laws or government policies; and (d) the matters awaiting a formal consultation between the executive and the judicial branches.[195]

The judges, however, may advise the committees on a proposed law's practical and technical aspects if it impacts how the judicial process works. For example, the judges' appearances before the Joint Committee on Human Rights have paved the way for the judiciary to participate in the committee's post-legislative scrutiny work. The Joint Committee conducted two inquiries into how the courts define the terms "public authority" and "function of a public nature" found in section 6 of the HRA.[196] Janet L Hiebert has branded the system as a 'Parliamentary (Human Rights) Protection Model'[197] that creates a dialectical relationship between the Parliament and the judiciary.[198]

However, as discussed earlier, the Supreme Court of Bangladesh has aggressively resisted the Parliament's participation in the judges' removal process. There is also no precedent of the parliamentary committees calling the judges or the judges answering them. Considering the heightened level of judicial protectionism showcased in the judges' appointment and removal cases of India,[199]

---

194 Hazell and O'Brien (n 147) 63–64.

195 The Judicial Executive Board, 'Guidance to Judges on Appearances before Select Committees' (London, October 2012) Paragraph 3.

196 The Seventh Report of Session 2003–04, *The Meaning of Public Authority under the Human Rights Act* (HL Paper 39/HC 382); The Ninth Report of Session 2006–07, *The Meaning of Public Authority under the Human Rights Act* (HL Paper 77/HC 410).

197 Janet L Hiebert, 'Parliament and the Human Rights Act: Can the JCHR help facilitate a Culture of Rights?' (2006) 4(1) International Journal of Constitutional Law 1, 2–3.

198 ibid, 5.

199 Rehan Abeyratne, 'Upholding Judicial Supremacy in India: the NJAC Judgment in Comparative Perspective' (2017) 49 George Washington International Law Review 101.

Pakistan[200] and Bangladesh[201] Supreme Courts, the non-engagement between the Bangladesh Parliament and Supreme Court is not surprising either. Absent any serious call for institutional dialogue between the representative and counter-majoritarian branches, the subcontinent courts and parliaments are likely to continue the way of mutual distrust and disengagement.[202] An exemplary case from the Bangladesh Supreme Court might help understand the magnitude of the non-relation between the two organs.

4 Judicial Review of the Statute Laws and Constitutional Amendments

Bangladesh has constitutional supremacy rather than a parliamentary one.[203] The written rules of the Constitution limit the Parliament's legislative powers.[204] "Basic structures" of the Constitution limit its amendment power.[205] In the face of recent democratic decay in Bangladesh, judicial activism enthusiasts tend to project the judiciary as the sole guardian of the country's constitutional supremacy.[206] This approach tends to justify[207] the judicial review of parliamentary laws, constitutional amendments and sometimes, the parliamentary privileges and immunities – including its internal proceedings as a crucial "reactive"[208] accountability tool against the ruling elite's "majoritarian assault"[209] on the rule of law and fundamental rights. However, this part will argue that the Bangladesh Supreme Court's jurisprudence of *Strong Form*

200 Saroop Ijaz, 'Judicial Appointments in Pakistan: Coming Full Circle' (2014) 1 LUMS Law Journal 86.

201 Ridwanul Hoque (n 171).

202 M Jashim Ali Chowdhury, 'A simple amendment un-simplified' *The Daily New Age* (Dhaka, 25 August 2017).

203 Constitution of Bangladesh (n 56) arts 7(2) and 26(2) expressly provides that laws consistent with the constitution or the fundamental rights within are invalid and without any effect.

204 ibid, arts 65(1) & 7.

205 *Anwar Hossain Chowdhury v Bangladesh* (n 37).

206 Kawser Ahmed, 'The Supreme Court's Power of Judicial Review in Bangladesh: a Critical Evaluation' (SSRN, 16 April 2015) <https://ssrn.com/abstract=2595364> accessed 31 July 2024.

207 Ridwanul Hoque, 'Taking justice seriously: judicial public interest and constitutional activism in Bangladesh' (2006) 15(4) Contemporary South Asia 399.

208 M Flinders, 'Mechanisms of judicial accountability in British central government' (2001) 54(1) Parliamentary Affairs 54, 62.

209 Samuel Issacharoff, 'Constitutional Courts and Democratic Hedging' (2011) 99 Georgetown Law Journal 961; Sujit Choudhury, '"He Had a Mandate": the South African

Judicial Review is informed by a self-aggrandised posture of guardianship over the Constitution that frequently places it in confrontation with the legislative and political branches.

4.1 *"Strong" and "Weak" Forms of Judicial Review*

Mark Tushnet has classified the judicial review systems into two broad categories – the *Strong Form and Weak Form Judicial Review Systems.*[210] This classification later became an influential way of understanding the difference between the US-influenced hard judicial review systems working in a constitutional supremacy context and the UK-influenced soft judicial review systems working in a parliamentary sovereignty context.[211] Tushnet has categorised the US system as a Strong Form Judicial Review and the British, Canadian and New Zealand systems as Weak Form Judicial Review.[212] He argues that the Strong Form of judicial review places the Court above the legislature and people. It creates what is known as 'counter-majoritarian difficulty'[213] when the unelected judges interpret the Constitution or laws in a way that most people may reasonably think is mistaken. In such cases, the people and their representatives in the legislature have little to do except "amend the Constitution or wait for judges to retire or die and replace them with judges who hold the better view of what the Constitution means."[214]

Compared to the US, the New Zealand Bill of Rights 1990 gives the judiciary an *interpretative mandate* to interpret the law or legal provisions in rights compatible way but bars the Court from declaring one as incompatible straight or refusing to enforce it on this ground. Tushnet calls it the weakest of the Weak Form judicial review systems.[215] Again, the UK Human Rights Act 1998 allows the Court an *augmented interpretative mandate* whereby the Court can declare a statute or its provision "incompatible" with the citizen's human rights.[216] The

---

Constitutional Court and the African National Congress in a Dominant Party Democracy' (2009) 2 Constitutional Court Review 1.

210 Mark Tushnet, *Weak Courts, Strong Rights* (Princeton University Press 2008).

211 Aileen Kavanagh, 'What's so weak about "Weak-Form Review"? The case of The UK Human Rights Act 1998' (2015) 13(4) International Journal of Constitutional Law 1008.

212 Tushnet (n 210) 22–31.

213 LR Barroso, *'Counter majoritarian, Representative, and Enlightened: the Roles of Constitutional Courts in Democracies'* (2019) 67(1) *The American Journal of Comparative Law* 109 (a supporter of counter majroitarianism, Luis R Barroso argues that apart from serving the interest of the unpopular minorities in a majoritarian democratic system, courts may enlighten non-liberal societies by its liberal and progressive judgments).

214 Tushnet (n 210) 22.

215 ibid, 25.

216 HRA (n 3).

Court, however, cannot refuse to enforce the statute. The statement of incompatibility would rather invite the Parliament to rectify the situation.[217] The Canadian Charter of Rights 1982, on the other hand, allows the Court a *dialogic judicial review power* that allows it to declare any rights restrictions inconsistent with the Charter (Section 1 of the Charter) and suspend its operation until and unless the legislature makes it enforceable for a maximum of five years "notwithstanding" the inconsistency (Section 33 of the Charter).[218]

4.2 *Bangladesh's "Strong Form" Judicial Review*

Within Bangladesh's written constitutional framework, invalidation of parliamentary statutes contrary to fundamental rights[219] or other written constitutional provisions[220] has been a relatively straightforward exercise of judicial review. Since the mid-1990s, the Supreme Court started liberalising the *locus standi* rule.[221] The Court's Public Interest Litigation (PIL) jurisprudence ensued from there, and it started issuing activist judgments touching upon the judicially unenforceable Fundamental Principles of State Policies of the Bangladesh Constitution.[222] The Supreme Court also adopted the Indian "basic structure doctrine" to claim a right to review the constitutional amendments judicially.[223] The Supreme Court's activist entanglement with constitutional amendments, laws contravening the constitutional "Principles",[224] and PIL has drawn forceful counter-majoritarian critique.[225] Generally, Bangladesh

---

217 Tushnet (n 210) 28.

218 ibid, 31.

219 Constitution of Bangladesh (n 60) art 26(2) restricts the Parliament from enacting laws inconsistent with the constitution. If such laws are in fact enacted those laws shall be declared void to the extent of the inconsistency.

220 ibid, art 7(2) is about constitutional supremacy. Clause 2 of article 7 declares that laws inconsistent with any part of the Constitution will be void to the extent of such inconsistency.

221 *Dr Moohiuddin Faruque v Bangladesh and Ors* 49 DLR 1997 (AD) 1 (FAP 20 Case).

222 M Jashim Ali Chowdhury, 'Claiming a 'Fundamental Right to Basic Necessities of Life': Problems and Prospects of Adjudication in Bangladesh' (2011–12) 5 Indian Journal of Constitutional Law 184, 196–205.

223 *Anwar Hossain Chowdhury v. Bangladesh* (n 37).

224 Constitution of Bangladesh (n 56) art 8(2) that the Fundamental Principles of State Policies in Part II of the Constitution are guiding principles for the governance of the state but not judicially enforceable.

225 Muhammad Ekramul Haque, 'The Concept of "Basic Structure": a Constitutional Perspective from Bangladesh' (2005) 16(2) The Dhaka University Studies, Part-F 123; Mohammad Moin Uddin and Rakiba Nabi, 'Judicial Review of Constitutional Amendments in Light of the "Political Question" Doctrine: a Comparative Study of the Jurisprudence of Supreme Courts of Bangladesh, India and the United States' (2016) 58(3) Journal of the Indian Law Institute 313; Md Abdul Malek, 'Vice and Virtue of the

and its South Asian neighbours' Strong Form Judicial Review system have generated an antagonistic relationship between the parliaments and the courts.[226]

4.2.1 Enforcement of Fundamental Rights

Bangladesh Supreme Court's power to strike down statute laws for infringement of fundamental rights is based on Article 26(2) of the Constitution, which declares that laws contrary to the constitutionally articulated fundamental rights will be unconstitutional. In fundamental rights cases, the Court has applied a strict scrutiny test and declared discriminatory laws, laws capable of being used in a discriminatory way, laws missing detailed guidelines for their application,[227] laws seeking to *ex post facto* criminalise something,[228] and laws involving legislative judgement[229] unconstitutional. In relevant cases, the Parliament reacted to the judgment by bringing remedial amendments to the laws. However, such responsiveness has not been a regular phenomenon. There are many cases where the Supreme Court came out with specific recommendations on necessary amendments in-laws and sometimes even quasi-legislative guidelines with the force of laws. The Parliament refused to act and amend the laws accordingly.[230]

4.2.2 Constitutional Amendment Review

The Parliament of Bangladesh is given plenary legislative power[231] and the power to amend the Constitution.[232] Though the Constitution has recognised

---

Basic Structure Doctrine: a Comparative Analytic Reconsideration of the Indian Subcontinent's Constitutional Practices' (2017) 43(1) Commonwealth Law Bulletin 48.

226 Chintan Chandrachud, Balanced Constitutionalism: Courts and Legislatures in India and the United Kingdom (Oxford University Press 2017).

227 *Dr Nurul Islam v Bangladesh* 1 BLD (1981) (AD); *Muhibur Rahman Manik v Bangladesh and others* 23 BLD (High Court Division of the Supreme Court) 26.

228 Constitution of Bangladesh (n 56) art 35(1) provides that no person shall be convicted of any offence except for violation of a law in force at the time of the commission of the act charged as an offence, nor be subjected to a penalty greater than, or different from that which might have been inflicted under the law in force at the time of the commission of the offence.

229 There is a limitation on the power of the Parliament to pass "legislative judgments". It is a well-established judicial principle that the legislature cannot make direct inroad into the judicial power of the State. When the court declares a law to be invalid, Parliament cannot pass a law declaring that judgment to be invalid or that the action taken under the invalid statute shall be deemed to be valid retrospectively. *Mofizur Rahman v Bangladesh* 34 DLR (Appellate Division of the Supreme Court) 321.

230 Abdullah Al Faruque, *Analysis of Decisions of the Higher Judiciary on Arrest and Detention in Bangladesh* (National Human Rights Commission of Bangladesh, January 2013).

231 Constitution of Bangladesh (n 56) art 65.

232 ibid, art 142.

judicial review of statute laws, judicial review of constitutional amendments is controversial. The original Constitution of 1972 contained no limitation on the Parliament's power of amendment. As per Article 142 of the Constitution, an amendment could be done through a bill passed by a two-thirds majority of the members of Parliament. As mentioned earlier, Article 26(2) of the Constitution provides for the invalidity of statutes contravening fundamental rights. However, Article 26(3) provides that this limitation would not apply to constitutional amendments.[233] While the framers' intention of keeping the constitutional amendments out of judicial review was clear in Articles 142, 26(2) and (3), the Bangladesh Supreme Court, in *Anwar Hossain Chowdhury v Bangladesh,*[234] claimed for itself a power of judicially reviewing constitutional amendments under the so-called doctrine of "Basic Structures",[235] which is borrowed from the Indian *Keshabanandha Bharati* case.[236] The Basic Structure doctrine claims certain provisions and principles of the Constitution as its basic structures that are not amendable by the Parliament.

There is debate about whether the Supreme Court could give itself such power, especially when the Parliament passes amendments through a special super-majority and under its constituent rather than plenary legislative authority.[237] Despite these, judicial review of constitutional amendments has been a rule rather than an exception in Bangladesh. So far, out of the nine challenged constitutional amendments, the Court has invalidated five.[238] The legislative response to the invalidated amendments was an initial protest and then a quiet acquiescence, except in the latest invalidation of the sixteenth amendment, which resulted in an intensely combative exchange.

The first-ever invalidation of any constitutional amendment involved part of the Eighth Amendment in *Anwar Hossain Chowdhury* (1989). It was an amendment seeking to decentralise the Supreme Court and establish around eight

233 ibid, art 26(3).

234 *Anwar Hossain Chowdhury v Bangladesh* (n 37).

235 Salimullah Khan, 'Leviathan and the Supreme Court: an Essay on the *'Basic Structure' Doctrine'* (2011) 2 Stamford University Journal of Law 89.

236 Jafar Ullah Talukder and M Jashim Ali Chowdhury, 'Determining the Province of Judicial Review: a Re-evaluation of 'Basic Structure of the Constitution of Bangladesh' (2009) 2(2) Metropolitan University Journal 161.

237 M Jashim Ali Chowdhury and Nirmal Kumar Saha, 'Amendment Power in Bangladesh: Arguments for the Revival of Constitutional Referendum' (2020) 9 Indian Journal of Constitutional Law 38; Uddin and Nabi (n 225).

238 Ridwanul Hoque (n 171).

circuit benches of the High Court Division. The Court invalidated it, holding that Bangladesh's unitary character was a basic feature of the Constitution[239] and could not be destroyed by decentralising the Supreme Court.[240] The Fourth Parliament (1988–1989) MPs discussed the judgment under an adjournment motion, seriously objected to the Court's assertion of judicial review in a constitutional amendment and regarded it as aggression on Parliament's "sovereignty".[241] A 22-member parliamentary committee was formed to recommend that the President promulgate some guidelines specifying the boundaries of judicial review. The committee, however, did not report.[242] After minimising the political heat, the government quietly submitted to the Court's view. The Ministry of Law reprinted the Constitution by restoring the former version of the relevant provision. Later, the ruling party – the *Jatya Party* (JP) – tried to claim political credit for the judgment by projecting it as a sign of an independent judiciary's presence in the country.[243]

The Fifth Amendment was invalidated by a High Court Division bench in *Bangladesh Italian Marble Works Company Ltd v Bangladesh* in 2005.[244] The amendment invalidated the assumption of power and subsequent activities by martial law rulers, including Major Zia. This decision came around one year before the Eighth Parliament's tenure ended. The then ruling party – BNP – was the Fifth Amendment's direct beneficiary in the late 1970s. Expectedly, the government reacted fiercely, appealed the decision to the Appellate Division immediately and secured a stay over the High Court judgment.[245] The government, however, could not finish the appeal hearing. Coming to power in 2009, the AL government withdrew the appeal. Though the subsequent proceedings continued by adding a BNP leader as the Appellant, the Appellate Division upheld the High Court Division's judgment.[246]

Similarly, the Seventh Amendment was invalidated by the Court in *Siddique Ahmed v Bangladesh* in 2010.[247] This time, it demoralised the political base of

239 *Anwar Hossain Chowdhury v Bangladesh* (n 37) para 419, 420.

240 Rokeya Chowdhury, 'The Doctrine of Basic Structure in Bangladesh: From 'Calfpath' to Matryoshka Dolls' (2014) 14 Bangladesh Journal of Law 43.

241 Nizam Ahmed (n 87) 145–146.

242 ibid, 146.

243 Syed Rahman, 'Bangladesh in 1989: Internationalization of Political and Economic Issues' (1990) 30(2) Asian Survey 150, 154.

244 *Bangladesh Italian Marble Works Ltd* (n 42).

245 Ali Riaz, 'Bangladesh in 2005: Standing at a Crossroads' (2006) 46(1) *Asian Survey* 107, 111.

246 *Khondhker Delwar Hossain v Bangladesh Italian Marble Works Ltd and Others* (2010) 62 DLR (AD) 298.

247 *Siddique Ahmed v Bangladesh* (2011) 33 BLD (HCD) 84.

JP, whose leader, Lt. General HM Ershad, sponsored the amendment in the 1980s. Like Zia's Fifth Amendment, Ershad's Seventh Amendment validated his accession to power and subsequent activities. This time, again, the ruling AL government did not appeal the judgment. BNP and JP, however, criticised the judgment as an unnecessary reopening of the country's foreclosed history.[248]

The invalidation of the Thirteenth Amendment in 2011 was politically controversial. The Thirteenth Amendment of 1996 introduced the system of an election-time caretaker government. Despite critical questions about the democratic legitimacy and efficiency of the caretaker government system,[249] it had been minimally successful in ensuring three orderly and periodic power transfers during the 1990s and 2000s. Some have argued that the Supreme Court was doing the ruling party AL's bidding this time by prematurely invalidating the system.[250] In a face-saving observation, the Court opined that two subsequent national elections could be arranged under the invalidated caretaker government system beyond which the system would stand nullified. However, the AL government ignored this observation and used the judgment as an excuse to remove the caretaker government system from the Constitution.[251]

In 2011, the AL government reprinted the Constitution to comply with the Fifth, Seventh and Thirteenth amendments.[252] However, the government cherry-picked some parts of the judgments to ignore in the reprint. For example, the government found it politically inconvenient to erase the religious clauses introduced through the Fifth and Seventh Amendments. So, it kept those intact in the reprinted Constitution. Parliament entered the scene after the controversial reprint. An All-Party Parliamentary Constitutional Review Committee was assigned to revise the Constitution and recommend the pathways to restore the fundamentals of Bangladesh's 1972 Constitution.

---

248 Abdul Halim, 'The 7th Amendment Judgment by the Appellate Division: Judicial Politics or Judicial Activism' (2012) The Counsel Law Journal 19.

249 M Rafiqul Islam, 'The supreme court ruling on the CTG' *The Daily Star, Law and Our Rights* (Dhaka, 21 May 2011); Md Zakir Hossain and M Jashim Ali Chowdhury, 'The Caretaker Government: a Constitutional Evaluation and Search for Alternatives' (In Bangla) (2014) 19 The Chittagong University Journal of Law 228.

250 *Saleem Ullah v Bangladesh* (2005) 57 DLR (HCD) 171; *Abdul Mannan Khan* (n 48).

251 Maimul Ahsan Khan, 'Constitutional Disaster & 'Legal' Impunity: Constitutional Amendments in Perspective' *Asian Human Rights Commission* <http://www.humanrights.asia/resources/journals-magazines/article2/special-report-inexistent-rule-of-law-in-bangladesh/04-2/> accessed 30 July 2024.

252 M Jashim Ali Chowdhury, 'The dilemma of constitution reprint' *The Daily New Age* (Dhaka, 15 April 2011).

Later, the Fifteenth Amendment was passed in pursuance of the committee's recommendations.

One of the interesting features of the Fifteenth Amendment Act is that a newly inserted Article 7B recognised the "basic provisions of the Constitution" as unamendable. It meant the Parliament officially accepted the Court's right to review the constitutional amendments.[253] However, if the Fifteenth Amendment constitutes the Parliament's official approval of the judicial power of amendment review, the Sixteenth Amendment case[254] presents a strikingly opposite position.

The Sixteenth Amendment sought to restore the parliamentary removal system for the Supreme Court judges. While some reasonably accuse the Parliament of doing the government's bid to further choke up Bangladesh's already marginalised judiciary,[255] the Supreme Court's bullish response to the amendment exposed it to a confrontation with the political and legislative branches.[256] While judicially reviewing it, the Supreme Court passed a scathing rebuke of the Parliament and invalidated the Sixteenth Amendment.[257] The High Court Division ruling of 5 May 2016 infuriated the Ministers and MPs. The full-text judgement allegedly contained some derogatory remarks on the general character and disposition of the Parliament members. It took the matter to a direct institutional confrontation between the Parliament and the Court. MPs scrambled the floor and heavily criticised the Court for refusing to submit itself to the Parliament's removal power.[258]

The High Court Division judgment was immediately appealed against, and the Appellate Division rejected the government's appeal on 3 July 2017. Another round of infuriated criticism ensued on the floor of the House on 9 July 2017. Full-text judgement of the Appellate Division came out on 1 August 2017. While the High Court Division's comments were already fuelling the fire, the opinion of the Chief Justice in the appeal verdict was full of attacks on the

253 Ridwanul Hoque, 'Eternal Provisions in the Constitution of Bangladesh: a Constitution Once and for All?' in Richard Albert and Bertil Emrah Oder (ed), *An Unamendable Constitution?* (Springer 2018) 195, 224.

254 *Advocate Asaduzzaman Siddiqui v Bangladesh* 2012 CLC (HCD) 41.

255 M Rafiqul Islam, 'Parliamentary impeachment of senior judges amid powerful executive: a paradox?' *The Daily Star* (Dhaka, 26 August 2014).

256 Rizwanul Islam, 'Impeachment of Judges: a suggestion' *The Daily Star* (Dhaka, 27 August 2014).

257 Chowdhury and Saha (n 181).

258 Ashutosh Sarkar and Shakhawat Liton, 'JS's authority to impeach SC Judges: Bangladesh High Court scraps 16th amendment to Constitution Govt to appeal' *The Daily Star* (Dhaka, 11 November 2017).

politicians and the morale of Parliament.[259] It put him in a straight hot seat. He was accused of bias,[260] and a demand for his resignation started to echo on the political spectrum. While the AL government was preparing for a review petition against the judgement,[261] Chief Justice SK Sinha declared the Sixteenth Amendment dead and hurriedly tried to revive the pre-sixteenth amendment system of the Supreme Judicial Council within two days of publishing the full-text verdict.[262]

In reaction, the offended lawmakers called the government not to reprint the Constitution as per the Appellate Division verdict. On 13 September 2017, Parliament unanimously passed a resolution for taking "proper" legal steps towards cancelling the verdict and expunction of the Chief Justice's "unconstitutional, objectionable and irrelevant" observations therein.[263] Scenes changed swiftly after that, and by 11 November 2017, Chief Justice Sinha was forced to leave the country "for treatment" and later resigned as the Chief Justice.[264]

The review petition against the Appellate Division judgement is still pending. The government has not reprinted the Constitution as it did in the cases of the Eighth, Fifth, Seventh and Thirteenth Amendment judgments. The subsequent Chief Justices also did not call any meeting of the Supreme Judicial Council. Later, three judges of the Supreme Court facing misconduct charges were instructed by the then Chief Justice to refrain from their respective benches. It was unclear whether the Supreme Judicial Council would investigate them, or the judges would be subject to the parliamentary removal process.[265] So, Bangladesh's current law on judges' removal is unclear.

---

259 Chowdhury (n 202).

260 Nazrul Khasru, 'Justice Sinha's "Broken Dream": a Death Knell of the 16th Amendment Judgment' (*Bangladesh Law Digest Blog*, 11 December 2018).

261 Ashutosh Sarkar, 'Chief justice steps down' *The Daily Star* (Dhaka, 12 November 2017).

262 Tribune Report, 'Supreme Judicial Council reinstated, SC judges get their own code of conduct' *The Dhaka Tribune* (Dhaka, 03 August 2017).

263 New Nation Report, 'JS Will Again Pass 16th Amendment' *The New Nation* (Dhaka, 05 August 2017).

264 DS Report, 'PM critical of CJ's remarks' *The Daily Star* (Dhaka, 22 August 2017); DS Report, 'AL leaders now calling for CJ to step down' *The Daily Star* (Dhaka 23 August 2017); DS Report, 'I am completely well, says Chief Justice SK Sinha as he leaves country' *The Daily Star* (Dhaka, 13 October 2017); DS Report, 'Chief justice steps down' *The Daily Star* (Dhaka, 12 November 2017); DS Report, 'Forced to quit: BNP, No pressure: AL' *The Daily Star* (Dhaka, 12 November 2017).

265 TBS Report, 'A catch 22 for the Supreme Court' *The Business Standard* (Dhaka, 25 August 2019).

5 Importance of "Democratic Dialogue"

The dialogic premise of the judicial review found its root in a 1997 article by Peter Hogg and Allison Bushell.[266] Hogg and Bushell's ideas were based on the 'notwithstanding clause' of sections 1 and 33 of the Canadian Charter of Rights 1982. They argued that section 1's requirement of "demonstrable justification" behind any parliamentary restriction of rights[267] created a scope for the judiciary to sit over the judgment of Parliament's right-limiting statutes. Once the Court declares a statute's unconstitutionality, the legislature would correct the fault or override it through a Section 33 declaration. Hogg and Bushell argued that Parliament's penultimate law-making authority against a judicial invalidation marked a brand-new regime of "Charter dialogue" in Canada. Their article drew incredible attention from Canadian judges and academia. By 2007, when Hogg and Bushell revisited their dialogue thesis,[268] the Canadian judges had applied the dialogic logic in a series of high-profile cases and issued several straight or deferred declarations of invalidity under Section 1, assuming that the legislature would respond by correcting the faults.[269] Later, the British scholars invoked this 'dialogic premise'[270] to explain the limited judicial review introduced by the Human Rights Act 1998.[271]

The Human Rights Act 1998 created a scope for limited judicial review of statutory laws. Though Mark Tushnet has called it an "augmented interpretative mandate",[272] most British constitutional scholars see it as a Canada-styled democratic dialogue model.[273] Sections 3, 4, and 19 of the HRA 1998 have created

266 Peter W Hogg and Allison A Bushell, 'The Charter Dialogue Between Courts and Legislatures (Or perhaps The Charter of Rights isn't such a bad thing after all)' (1997) 35 Osgoode Hall Law Journal 75.

267 Section 1 of the Canadian Charter of Rights and Freedoms 1982 runs as follows: "The Canadian Charter of Rights and Freedoms guarantees the rights and freedoms set out in it subject only to such reasonable limits prescribed by law as can be demonstrably justified in a free and democratic society."

268 Peter W Hogg, Allison A Bushell Thornton and Wade K Wright, 'Charter Dialogue Revisited: Or "Much Ado About Metaphors"' (2007) 45(1) Osgoode Hall Law Journal 1.

269 ibid 7–25.

270 Philip Norton, 'A Democratic Dialogue? Parliament and Human Rights in the United Kingdom' (2013) 21 Asia Pacific Law Review 141.

271 Catherine A Fraser, 'Constitutional Dialogues between Courts and Legislatures: Can We Talk?' (2005) 14(3) Forum Constitutionnel 7.

272 Tushnet (n 210) 28.

273 Alison L Young, *Democratic Dialogue and The Constitution* (Oxford University Press 2017) 180: TRS Allan, 'Constitutional Dialogue and The Justification of Judicial Review' (2003) 23(4) Oxford Journal of Legal Studies 563, 582.

the opportunity for Dialogue between Parliament and the courts. Section 19(1) of the HRA requires a minister sponsoring any bill to make "a statement of compatibility" during the bill's second reading stage. The Minister must state that, in his view, "the provisions of the bill are compatible with (European) Convention rights". If he cannot make such a statement, he will need to say that the government wants the House to proceed without such a statement being made. Next, section 3(1) obliges the courts to read, as far as possible, a law compatible with the European Convention on Human Rights (ECHR) 1950. In cases where a statute appears clear, and the Court's interpretative engineering fails to do a compatible reading, section 4 would require the Court to declare its incompatibility with ECHR.

The Court, however, will not declare the law invalid. Once a declaration of incompatibility is made, an "institutional dialogue" would ensue. The Joint Committee on Human Rights (JCHR) and the government would carry on the dialogic project.[274] As per section 10 of the HRA, the government must respond to a declaration of incompatibility, and the JCHR would oversee the governmental response. The JCHR works in a spirit of backbench assertiveness and non-partisanship.[275] JCHR's contribution towards the House of Commons deliberation and the House of Lords' judicial intervention in counterterrorism[276] and immigration and asylum bills[277] shows that the HRA's dialogic project can be processed in non-partisan and expert-driven avenues.[278] Janet L Hiebert has described it as a "Parliamentary Protection Model"[279] for human rights.

The HRA-styled institutional dialogue between the judiciary and legislature involves a conversation between Parliament and the judiciary.[280] Though the penultimate voice is reserved for the legislature, the judicial voice adds a qualitative value to the law.[281] This model of judicial review may be "weak",[282] but it

274 Janet L Hiebert (n 197).

275 ibid, 16, 22.

276 ibid, 28–30.

277 ibid, 31–35.

278 ibid, 36.

279 ibid, 2–3.

280 FF Davis, 'Parliamentary Supremacy and the Re-Invigoration of Institutional Dialogue in the UK' (2012) 67 Parliamentary Affairs 137, 141–142.

281 Mark Tushnet, 'The Hartman Hotz Lecture: Dialogic Judicial Review' (2008) 61 Arkansas Law Review 205; Janet L Hiebert, 'Interpreting A Bill of Rights: the Importance of Legislative Rights Review' (2005) 35(2) British Journal of Political Science 235.

282 Richard Bellami, 'Political Constitutionalism and the Human Rights Act 1998' (2011) 9(1) International Journal of Constitutional Law 86, 109 (The Political Constitutionalism favours a rights protection regime that entrusts the rights interpretation responsibility with the political branches of the State).

gives the judiciary a chance to request additional parliamentary consideration of controversial laws. Historically, the UK parliament has respected the Court's views and showed clear inertia to overturn judicial positions expressly.[283]

5.1 *Potentials of Dialogic Judicial Review in Bangladesh*

The UK and Canadian model of Democratic Dialogue has attracted interest across the Commonwealth.[284] Yap Po Jen has studied Asia's three weak judicial review systems – Singapore, Malaysia, and Hong Kong.[285] He argues that despite having no power to strike down legislation, those courts have engaged in a "thin dialogic review" by utilising various sub-constitutional tools like signalling, rather than straight declaring, a statute's unconstitutionality[286] or issuing delayed declarations of invalidity that allowed the legislature to react and the political momentum for change to gather.[287] Similarly, Rehan Abeyratne and Dion Misri considered the Indian Parliament's response to various activist judgments of the Indian Supreme Court in socio-economic rights cases[288] and argued that a constitutional dialogue does happen in India when the Court draws up quasi-legislative guidelines which remain in force until the Parliaments legislate on a matter.[289] Tom R Hickman also supports the proposition that the Indian Supreme Court's PIL framework fosters a cooperative mode of constitutionalism participated by all three branches of government.[290]

As mentioned earlier, Bangladesh's judicial review system is a "strong form"[291] one, and the legislature and judiciary have remained two distant,

283 Kavanagh (n 211) 1025–26.

284 Christine Bateup, 'Expanding the Conversation: American and Canadian Experiences of Constitutional Dialogue in Comparative Perspective' (2007) 21 Temple International & Comparative Law Journal 1; Mark Tushnet, 'Dialogic Judicial Review' (2009) 61 Arkansas Law Review 205.

285 Yap Po Jen, *Constitutional Dialogue in Common Law Asia* (Oxford University Press 2015) 80–86.

286 ibid, 88–89.

287 ibid, 101.

288 Rehan Abeyratne and Didon Misri, 'Separation of Powers and The Potential for Constitutional Dialogue in India' (2018) 5(2) Journal of International and Comparative Law 363, 371–376.

289 *Vishaka and others v State of Rajasthan and others* AIR 1997 SCC 3011.

290 Tom R Hickman, 'Constitutional dialogue, constitutional theories and the Human Rights Act 1998' (2005) Public Law 306.

291 Ridwanul Hoque, 'Constitutionalism and the Judiciary in Bangladesh' in Sunil Khilnani, Vikram Raghavan, and Arun K Thiruvengadam (ed.), *Comparative Constitutionalism in South Asia* (Oxford University Press 2012) 303, 307–308.

reactionary, and combative siblings shielded behind a watertight wall of separation. In this context, an HRA-styled democratic dialogic may appear untenable in Bangladesh. Still, there are areas of judicial activity that signal that a democratic dialogue could happen here. An early judicial precedent of the Bangladesh Supreme Court bears testimony to this.

In 1974, a Bangladeshi citizen, Mr *Kazi Mukhlesur Rahman*,[292] approached the Supreme Court to challenge a bilateral agreement between the Prime Minister of the newly independent Bangladesh and his Indian counterpart. The agreement was about ceding some enclaves of Bangladesh to India in exchange for some Indian ones. Mr Rahman argued that annexation or cessation of state territory is a privilege of Parliament only to be exercised through statutes.[293] The Court examined the breadth of the Prime Minister's executive power and Parliament's legislative power. It held that the bilateral agreement was unconstitutional and non-enforceable because any parliamentary statute did not support it.[294] The decision yielded what may be called the first-ever institutional dialogue between Bangladesh's judicial and legislative branches. A constitutional amendment followed the verdict, and the territories acquired and ceased through the agreement were declared as included and excluded territories as per the definitions provided in Article 2 of the Constitution.[295]

Though the *Kazi Mukhlesure Rahman* case remained an outlier in the Bangladesh Supreme Court's jurisprudence during the 1970s and 1980s, the Court started gaining momentum again in the mid-1990s. The development of PIL jurisprudence during the mid to late 1990s has opened up several avenues of institutional dialogue between the legislature and judiciary. In a series of cases involving the peoples' right to life and a healthy environment, separation of judiciary, the autonomy of local government bodies and the advisory jurisdiction of the Court, the Bangladesh Supreme Court engaged in overt and covert dialogue with the political branches.

292 *Kazi Mukhlesur Rahman v. Bangladesh* 26 DLR (SC) 44.

293 Constitution of Bangladesh (n 56) art 143(3) leaves the power to determine the boundaries of the landed territory, territorial waters and the continental shelf of Bangladesh with the Parliament.

294 *Kazi Mukhlesur Rahman* (n 292).

295 Constitution of Bangladesh (n 56) art 2 as amended by the Constitution (Third Amendment) Act of 1974.

5.1.1 Quasi-legislative Orders in the Right to Life and Healthy Environment Cases

In 1994, the Bangladesh Supreme Court formally endorsed the concept of PIL[296] and started environmental rights activism.[297] The Supreme Court's persistent push for environmental rights is believed to be responsible for its recent recognition in the Bangladesh Constitution.[298] The activism later expanded towards other unenforceable Fundamental Principles of State Policies[299] under the Court's right-to-life jurisprudence.[300] Exercise its "power to do complete justice",[301] the Supreme Court passed various prohibitive and mandatory orders upon the government to refrain from doing something or take appropriate legislative or administrative actions in certain areas.

5.1.2 Continuous Dialogue in the Separation of Judiciary Case

The *Separation of Judiciary case*[302] was the Court's most stressful, and successful, engagement with the government and Parliament. In 1998, District Judge Mr Masder Hossain and 441 subordinate judicial officers of Bangladesh sought the subordinate judiciary's separation from the executive as per Article 22 of the Constitution. Until then, the criminal courts in Bangladesh were controlled

---

296 *Dr Mohiuddin Farque* (FAP 20) (n 221); *National Board of Revenue v Abu Saeed Khan* 18 BLC (AD) 116.

297 *Dr Mohiuddin Farooque* (BELA) *v Bangladesh* 55 DLR (HCD) 69 (Environment Pollution Case); *Dr Mohiudin Farooquee v Bangladesh* 55 DLR (2003) (HCD) 613 (Two-Stroke Motor Vehicle Case).

298 Constitution of Bangladesh (n 56) art 18A (Protection and Improvement of Environment and Biodiversity) was inserted in the Constitution by the Constitution (Fifteenth Amendment) Act, 2011 (Act XIV of 2011).

299 Muhammad Ekramul Haque, 'Legal and Constitutional Status of the Fundamental Principles of State Policy as Embodied in the Constitution of Bangladesh' (2005) 16(1) Journal of the Faculty of Law 45; M Jashim Ali Chowdhury, 'Does inconsistency with Fundamental Principles of State Policy invalidate a Law?' (2009) 5 BRAC University Journal 71; Md. Reajul Hasan Shohag and ABM Asrafuzzaman, 'Enforcing Socio-Economic Rights Judicially: Experiments in Bangladesh, India and South Africa' (2012) 3 Northern University Journal of Law 87; M Waheduzzaman, 'Economic, Social and Cultural Rights under the Constitution: Critical Evaluation of Judicial Jurisprudence in Bangladesh' (2014) 14(1 & 2) Bangladesh Journal of Law 1.

300 *Ain O Shalish Kendra &Ors v Government of Bangladesh* 4 MLR (HCD) 358 (Slum Dwellers' case); *Professor Nurul Islam v. Govt. of Bangladesh & others* 52 DLR 413 (Gold Leaf's Voyage of Discovery Case); *Adv Zulhas Uddin Ahmed & Manzil Morshed* v. *Bangladesh* 15 MLR (HCD) 2010; *Chairman, National Board of Revenue v Advocate Julhas Uddin* (2010) 15 MLR (AD) 457 (VAT on Health Services Case).

301 Constitution of Bangladesh (n 56) art 104.

302 *Secretary, Ministry of Finance v Masdar Hossain* 52 DLR (AD) 82.

by the executive magistrates from the bureaucracy. Article 22 is placed in the Fundamental Principles of State Policy part of the Constitution and is, hence, judicially unenforceable.[303] Finding the direct enforcement of Article 22 problematic, the Court resorted to a structural approach to constitutional interpretation.[304] The Appellate Division meticulously examined various provisions of the Constitution and found that the overall structure of separation of power in the Bangladesh Constitution requires the state to separate its judicial and executive branches. The Appellate Division argued that the successive governments and parliaments were committing "constitutional deviation" from their obligation to ensure the independence and separation of the judiciary from the executive branch.[305] The subordinate judiciary could be separated through presidential rulemaking powers granted under Article 115 of the Constitution.[306] As the Court lacked the power to order the Parliament to pass necessary laws to fulfil the constitutional requirement of separation, it consciously avoided involving Parliament in this process. It rather argued that the President's rulemaking power in this regard was independent of Parliament's power to regulate the Court by laws.[307] The Court issued several directions to achieve the desired separation, including, among other things, the framing of Rules, creating a separate Judicial Service Commission and a separate Judicial Pay Commission, and maintaining the Supreme Court's financial independence from the executive.[308]

The initial eight weeks' time given by the Court was ignored. Later, three successive governments sought and were granted as many as twenty-two extensions over the next eight years. Then, an election-time caretaker government separated the subordinate judiciary on 1 November 2007. Subsequently, the Ninth Parliament (2009–2013) statutorily recognised the separation of the subordinate judiciary by making necessary laws. The *Masder Hossain* case reveals that structural orders[309] like this could open up scopes of back and forth between the executive and the judiciary. However, the "much-needed democratic dialogue"[310] between Parliament and the judiciary has remained absent since the Parliament of Bangladesh has failed to assert independence

303 Constitution of Bangladesh (n 56) art 8(2).
304 *Secretary, Ministry of Finance* (n 302) para 20, 28, 31.
305 Ridwanul Hoque (n 207) 410–411.
306 Constitution of Bangladesh (n 56) art 115.
307 *Secretary, Ministry of Finance* (n 302) para 32, 33.
308 ibid, para 49.
309 Chowdhury (n 222).
310 Ridwanul Hoque (n 207) 414.

and authority comparable to the UK, the House of Commons and its JCHR. Still, there have been occasions where the judiciary tried to stir up legislative response from the Parliament through something akin to Yap Po Jen's *Thin Democratic Dialogue*.[311]

5.1.3 "Thin Dialogic Review" in Local Government Cases

In *Sheikh Abdus Sabur* and *Kudrat Elahi Panir* cases, the Court was asked to judge the validity of certain legislative actions in the local government systems of Bangladesh. Instead of nullifying the parliamentary actions directly, the Court issued telling judgments that generated forceful public critique of the Parliament's actions. It ultimately prompted a delayed reaction from the Parliament.

For example, in *Sheikh Abdus Sabur v. Returning Officer*,[312] a law disqualifying the defaulters of bank loans from contesting in local government elections was challenged. Until then, candidates seeking election to Parliament had no such disqualification. Faced with discrimination and non-equality charges, Justice ATM Afzal decided to return the ball to the Parliament's Court. He held that "As long as the law enacted by it is within the bounds of the Constitution, it will be upheld by this Court, but if the law is otherwise open to criticism, it is for the Parliament itself to respond in the manner it thinks best".[313] By the end of the 1990s, the disqualification of bank loan default was attached to the parliamentary election.[314]

In *Kudrat-E-Elahi Panir and Others v. Bangladesh*,[315] a law abolishing the democratically elected local government body called *Upazila Parishad* and replacing it with bureaucrats was challenged. The Court found that democratic participation in local government, a Fundamental Principles of State Policy, was not judicially enforceable.[316] Still, the Court decided to send a strong signal of its disapproval of the action. Justice Mustafa Kamal wrote:

> [S]uppose the Parliament is struck with such madness. Is the High Court Division, in its writ jurisdiction, the only light at the end of the tunnel? What do public opinion, political parties, and elections do if Parliament goes berserk?[317]

---

311 Yap Po Jen (n 285).
312 *Sheikh Abdus Sabur v. Returning Officer* 41 DLR (AD) (1989) 30.
313 ibid, para 69 (Per ATM Afzal J).
314 ibid.
315 *Kudrat-E-Elahi Panir and Others v Bangladesh* 44 DLR (AD) 319.
316 ibid, para 22 (Per Shahabuddin Ahmed J).
317 ibid, para 86 (Per Mustafa Kamal J).

Instead of declaring the law invalid, the Court issued an open-ended order that gave the Parliament enough time to reckon with the consequences of its actions. The order read, "The government should replace the non-elected persons by designating the local government bodies as soon as possible – in any case, within a period not exceeding six months from the date"[318] of the judgement. The Parliament reintroduced the *Upazila Parishad* system around seven years later, in 1998. Suppose the Local government cases are considered thinly dialogic. However, the Supreme Court of Bangladesh has talked to the Parliament more directly in some of its Advisory Opinions.

5.1.4 Dialogue through the Advisory Jurisdiction Cases

Article 106 of the Constitution of Bangladesh provides a very influential tool for inter-branch dialogue. As per the provision, the President may send legal questions for an answer from the Appellate Division of the Supreme Court of Bangladesh on matters which are, in his opinion, "of such a nature and such public importance that it is expedient to obtain the opinion of the Supreme Court upon it."[319] The advisory jurisdiction of the Bangladesh Supreme Court has remained grossly underutilised.[320] During the fifty years of Bangladesh's existence, the jurisdiction was used only twice. In *Special Reference No. 1 of 1995*, the Supreme Court clarified the constitutional consequences of the resignation of 147 opposition Members of Parliament and helped the legislative branch avoid a constitutional vacuum. In *Special Reference No. 1 of 2009*, the political government and people's representatives in Parliament faced extreme pressure from the military to try Bangladesh Rifles (BDR) – currently the Border Guards Bangladesh (BGB) mutineers of 2009 – in martial law courts. The 2009 mutiny within Bangladesh's border force left around a hundred military officers killed, and the furious military force was vying for harsh and immediate justice under military tribunals.[321] The Supreme Court helped the government and the Parliament by upholding the legality of regular criminal courts instead of military tribunals. Accordingly, the Parliament passed the BDR Mutiny Act 2009, and the trial was conducted under the normal criminal court process.[322]

---

318 ibid, para 41.

319 Constitution of Bangladesh (n 56) art 106.

320 SM Masum Billah, 'Making the journey of constitutionalism smooth: Is 'Advisory Jurisdiction' a catalyst?' (2008) 19(1) Dhaka University Law Journal 131, 159–160.

321 Mehnaaz Momen, 'Bangladesh in 2009: the Peril Within' (2010) 50(1) *Asian Survey* 157.

322 *Special Reference No 1 of 2009* 15 BLC (AD) 1 para 15, 16.

While the Bangladesh Supreme Court's interaction with the legislative branch has featured what Swati Jhaveri calls the "combative"[323] trait of the Strong Form Judicial Review systems, the advisory jurisdiction of the Bangladesh Supreme Court shows that the framers of the Bangladesh Constitution expected a robust and ongoing dialogue to happen between the two organs.

6 Conclusion

Parliament and the judiciary's increasing level of interaction are apparent worldwide. Even in traditional systems of parliamentary sovereignty like the UK, the judiciary is now more frequently interacting with the legislative branch. Despite these constitutionally and conventionally articulated boundaries of mutual deference and comity between the two, the Parliament and Judiciary in Bangladesh have shown less respect for each other's boundaries. The parliamentarians have often disregarded the *sub judice* rule. The courts often ignored the exclusionary rule of interpretation and the international parliamentary proceedings doctrines. Bangladeshi courts are particularly resistant to parliamentary participation in the judicial accountability process. As it transpired from the *Sixteenth Amendment* and the *Speaker's Ruling* cases, the Court has also shown a clear disdain for any demand for judicial accountability. Also, the judicial review system of Bangladesh – particularly its fundamental rights review and constitutional amendment reviews – frequently places the judiciary in confrontation with the legislative and political branches, which often come out with combative and antagonistic responses. It appears that, despite working within a system of constitutional supremacy, the Bangladesh judiciary and Parliament assert conflicting claims of superiority over each other. Despite working within a parliamentary sovereignty system, the British Parliament and judiciary have shown a largely dialogic and conciliatory approach to their relationship. However, Bangladesh's main problem rests in the curtain of seclusion between the legislative and judicial branches and continued disinterest in deliberative engagement with each other. The country does not have a functionally independent and robust committee system that could support an ongoing institutional dialogue with the judiciary.[324] Also, the authoritarian and crudely partisan leaders of the executive branch decide

323 Swati Jhaveri, 'Interrogating Dialogic Theories of Judicial Review' (2019) 17(3) International Journal of Constitutional Law 811.

324 Nizam Ahmed (n 87) 128–129.

how the Parliament would react (not relate) to the judiciary. This chapter has considered whether a case could be made for the *Dialogic Model of Judicial Review* as a useful tool to repair this non-dialogic and antagonistic relationship between the Parliament and the judiciary. It is identified that there are at least four areas within Bangladesh's "strong form" judicial review system – PIL judgements in environmental rights and right-to-life cases, separation of judiciary, local government cases and the advisory jurisdiction cases – where the Supreme Court has shown a dialogic tendency. Understandably, appreciating this dialogic tendency on a larger scale should help better connecting the judicial and legislative branches.

CHAPTER 5

A Disengaged Electorate

1 Introduction

The political parties and their governments have electoral accountability to the people.[1] MPs have personal accountability to their constituents. As a constitutional organ, the Parliament also thrives on strong public trust in it.[2] Parties, governments, MPs and the Parliament's accountability to the people are both *ex-ante* and *ex-post*. They account to the people *ex-post* when they explain and justify their performances to the electorate on election day.[3] The *ex-ante* accountability, on the other hand, is continuous and operational. MPs need to continuously answer their constituents. Parliament needs to development strong public relations[4] and "invite society into its inner chambers"[5] by facilitating public participation in its activities. These sustain its social legitimacy. Social legitimacy bolsters the Parliament's strength and position *vis-à-vis* the executive and the judiciary. Fung and Wright call this a cycle of "empowered participatory governance".[6] If the people do not respect and trust the Parliament, it risks becoming a mere legitimiser – a "rubber stamp" – and loses the respect of and the ability to influence its co-ordinate constitutional organs such as the government and the judiciary.[7] Chapter 3 of this book has identified

---

1 O'Donell, GA 'Delegative Democracy' (1994) 5 (1) Journal of Democracy 55.

2 Steinar Askvik and Ishtiaq Jamil, 'The Institutional Trust Paradox in Bangladesh' (2013) 13(4) Public Organization Review 459.

3 Jonathan Fox, 'Civil society and political accountability: Propositions for discussion' (Conference on 'Institutions, Accountability and Democratic Governance in Latin America', The Helen Kellogg Institute for International Studies, University of Notre Dame, 8–9 May 2000) 1; Webster Siame Kameme, 'The Vertical and Horizontal Accountability in The Malawi Parliamentary Democracy' (Ph.D. thesis, University of Hull 2015); Craig T Borowiak, *Accountability and Democracy: the Pitfalls and Promise of Popular Control* (Oxford University Press 2011).

4 Mark Bennister and Phil Larkin, 'Accountability in Parliament' in Cristina Leston-Bandeira and Louise Thompson (eds.), *Exploring The Parliament* (Oxford 2018) 146–147; Robert Rogers and Rodhri Walters, *How Parliament Works* (London: Routledge, 2015) 79.

5 JM Ackerman, 'Co-governance for Accountability: Beyond 'Exit' and 'Voice'' (2004) 32(3) World Development 447, 448.

6 A Fung and E Wright. 'Deepening Democracy Innovations in Empowered Participatory Governance' (1998) 26(4) Politics and Society 15.

7 Vibeke Wang, 'Parliament in New Democracies: Tanzanian Perspectives; (2005) CMI Working Paper 2/2005, 6–7, accessed 19 October 2021.

 | DOI:10.1163/9789004720831_006

how Bangladesh's political parties bring the Parliament's accountability power over the executive branch to its knees. Chapter 4 has shown that a defiant judiciary's self-dealing tendencies have almost zeroed the Parliament's role in judicial accountability. This chapter would argue that the Parliament's declined institutional strength vis-à-vis the executive and judiciary is also attributable to its doubtful electoral legitimacy, the abysmal state of its public relations, and the meagre level of public participation in its processes.

Bangladeshi commentators have consistently questioned the country's electoral system and labelled it simply a tool of "legitimation"[8] and "preventive representation".[9] Election rigging, manipulation and voter suppression have been widespread. A failed electoral system feeds a constant legitimacy crisis for the Parliament. Next, the Bangladeshi MPs' constituency works aim to maintain an iron grip over their locality rather than addressing genuine constituency concerns. The MPs interfere in the elected local government bodies, turning them into largely subservient entities. At the institutional level, the Parliament's public relations strategies are archaic. There is a visible lack of commitment toward modernising its public relations practices. The scope of public participation in parliamentary processes is practically non-existent, and occasional exceptions to the trend usually come at the good grace of the party leaders rather than at the Parliament's initiative.

2 The Parliament's Electoral Accountability

The Parliament and its members' electoral accountability are the ultimate political controls that enable the people to reward or punish their overall performance.[10] It also marks the endorsement or rejection of policy proposals and priorities submitted by competing political parties for the next tenure of Parliament. However, an efficient discharge of this political accountability is dependent on the nature of the electoral system (whether the system elects an MP or a Prime Minister), its processes (whether there is fair competition and

8 Ahmed Shafiqul Huque and Muhammad A Hakim, 'Elections in Bangladesh: Tools of Legitimation' (1993) 19(4) Asian Affairs: an American Review 248.

9 M Moniruzzaman, 'Electoral Legitimacy, Preventive Representation, and Regularization of Authoritarian Democracy in Bangladesh' in Ryan Merlin Yonl (ed) *Elections: a Global Perspective* (Online: IntechOpen, 2019) 1–15.

10 Kaare Strøm, 'Delegation and Accountability in Parliamentary Democracies' (2000) 37(3) European Journal of Political Research 261.

a level playing field for the competing parties) and the fairness of its outcome (whether it yields a rightful winner).

2.1 *Nature of the Elections*

An electoral design determines how the electors choose between alternative focuses of their political judgment. Who do the People elect? – The Prime Minister? Or their Mercenaries? In Westminster's first-past-the-post system, electors are mostly forced to choose a potential ruling party and its Prime Ministerial candidate over the individual candidates for parliament membership.[11] It leads to what is called the Presidential tendency of the Parliamentary election.[12] Parliament members elected through this process are normally expected to work as partisan lobby fodder rather than conscientious legislators.

Electoral accountability within Westminster is significantly shaped by the degree of partisan cohesion. Several empirical studies of the UK's parliamentary elections show that except on one or two rare occasions of public disgust,[13] an MP candidate's volition and performance have a negligible impact on their electability.[14] MPs accused of corruption, impropriety, and scandals seldom receive electoral punishment,[15] and MPs maintaining a good track record

11 B Cain, J Ferejohn, and M Fiorina, 'The Constituency Service basis of the Personal Vote for US Representatives and British Members of Parliament' (1984) The American Political Science Review 110, 125; C Pattie and R Johnston, 'Party Knowledge and Candidate Knowledge: Constituency Campaigning and Voting and the 1997 British General Election' (2004) 23(4) Electoral Studies 795.

12 Nick Vivyana, Markus Wagner and Jessica Tarlov, 'Representative Misconduct, Voter Perceptions and Accountability: Evidence from the 2009 House of Commons Expenses Scandal' (2012) 31 (4) Electoral Studies 750, 762.

13 Andrew Eggers and Alexander Fischer, 'Electoral Accountability and the UK Parliamentary Expenses Scandal: Did Voters Punish Corrupt MPs?' *Political Science and Political Economy Working Paper 8/2011* (London: London School of Economics 2011), 32–33 (Only those MPs whose expenses claims received the most widespread media attention lost the election); David M Farrell, Ian McAllister and Donley T Studlar, 'Sex, Money and Politics: Sleaze and the Conservative Party in the 1997 Election' (1998) 8(1) British Elections and Parties Review 80, 87–88 (Neil Hamilton of Conservative party lose his seat in 1997 election as a direct fall out of cash-for-questions allegation).

14 P Norris, E Vallance and J Lovenduski, 'Do Candidates make a difference? Gender, Race, Ideology and Incumbency' (1992) 45(4) Parliamentary Affairs 496; P Dunleavy, S Weir and G Subrahmanyam, 'Public response and constitutional significance' (1995) 48(4) Parliamentary Affairs 606, 616; Farrell, McAllister and Studlar (n 13) 94.

15 J Curtice, S Fisher and R Ford, 'Appendix 2: an Analysis of the Results' in D Kavanagh and P Cowley (eds.), *The British General Election of 2010* (Palgrave Macmillan 2010); Eggers and Fischer (n 13), Vivyana, Wagner and Tarlov (n 12), 761.

also have a "very small or else very elusive" incumbency advantage.[16] This tendency to disregard a candidate's personal qualities results in reduced electoral accountability. Eggers and Fisher have called this a "general trade-off between individual electoral accountability and partisan competition."[17]

However, this is not to claim that individual performances of MPs do not matter in the UK. There are at least four reasons why the MPs need to maintain a strong constituency root throughout their parliamentary tenure in Westminster. First, Westminster's single-member constituency-based First-Past-The-Post (FPTP) system requires a direct geographical connection between the MPs and their constituencies, which is missing in closed-party list systems of Proportional Representation (PR).[18] Secondly, the British electorates show awareness of their MPs' constituency activities.[19] Thirdly, the democratic participation of the local party units in the candidate selection process makes it necessary for the MPs to maintain a constant and strong tie with party workers and supporters. Fourthly, due to the surge of professional, social, and business interest-based constituencies, the electors now pay attention to the individual MPs' voting records and speeches in Parliament.[20] MPs frequently distance themselves from their parties' unpopular policies.[21] Competing party campaigns highlight incumbent MPs' support or opposition to their party or government's unpopular policies.[22]

---

16 B Gaines, 'The Impersonal Vote? Constituency Service and Incumbency Advantage in British Elections, 1950–92' (1998) Legislative Studies Quarterly 167, 195.

17 Eggers and Fischer (n 13) 11.

18 Pippa Norris, 'The Twilight of Westminster? Electoral Reform and its Consequences' (2001) 49(5) Political Studies 877; Independent Commission on the Voting System (Jenkins Commission), *The Report of the Independent Commission on the Voting System* (London: The Stationery Office 1998).

19 D Cutts and N Shryane, 'Did Local Activism really matter? Liberal Democrat campaigning and the 2001 British General Election' (2006) 8(3) British Journal of Politics and International Relations 427; R Johnston and C Pattie, 'How Much Does a Vote Cost? Incumbency and the impact of Campaign Spending at English General Elections' (2008) 18(2) Journal of Elections, Public Opinion and Parties 129; CJ Kam, *Party Discipline and Parliamentary Politics* (Cambridge: Cambridge University Press 2009).

20 N Vivyan and M Wagner, 'Do Voters Reward Rebellion? The Electoral Accountability of MPs in Britain' (2012) 51(2) European Journal of Political Research 235, 255.

21 Flora Holmes, *Public Attitudes to Military Interventionism* (The British Foreign Policy Group 2020) 12 (In 2003 a staggering g number of 139 Labour MPs opposed the occupation of Iraq).

22 P Cowley and M Stuart, 'Being Policed? Or Just Pleasing Themselves? Electoral Rewards and Punishment for Legislative Behaviour in an Era of Localized Campaigning Effects: the Case of the UK in 2005' (Annual Conference of the EPOP Section of the Political Studies Association, Essex University, September 2005).

Like their British counterparts, the Bangladeshi electors prioritise the parties and the Prime Ministerial candidates over individual MPs. Of course, the Bangladeshi MPs maintain a strong constituency link. However, the nature of the engagement and the needs for this are fundamentally different from the Westminster. First, though they expect their MPs to be constituency-attached, the Bangladeshi electors are not guided by the motivation of accountability. Rather, it is the expectation of getting clientelist goods and benefits from their MPs that drives their demand. It makes the constituency works of Bangladeshi MPs fundamentally different from those of the UK. Secondly, the dynastic leaders' absolute control over the candidate selection process and suppression of local party units' say in the process ensure that MPs remain loyal to the party leaders, not their constituents.[23] Under such a system of electing some "partisan mercenaries",[24] the MPs' accountability to the electorate becomes practically unimportant.[25] Thirdly, given the electors' "cognitive lacking"[26] over their MPs' role orientation, the MPs remain mere development agents rather than legislators and scrutinisers. In that context, the Bangladeshi MPs are not expected to face questions about their votes and House speeches.

2.2 *Fairness of the Electoral Process*

Since Bangladesh's birth, the country's electoral institution, fairness, neutrality, and trustworthiness have been problematic. Except for a brief period (1996–2001) of election time Non-Party Caretaker Governments (NPCG),[27] parliamentary elections in Bangladesh have been constantly rigged, manipulated

23 Mohammad Mozahidul Islam, 'The Toxic Politics of Bangladesh: a Bipolar Competitive Neo-patrimonial State?' (2013) 21 (2) Asian Journal of Political Science 148, 149–51; Sabina Sharmin and AKM Jamal Uddin, 'Characteristics of Political Culture in Bangladesh: a Critical Analysis from the perspective of Political Development and Under development' (2013) 1 (1–2) Jagannath University Journal of Social Sciences 74, 77; Samiul Hasan, 'Corruption, Accountability and Political Parties in Bangladesh: Connections and Consequences', in T May and B Ray (eds.), *Democratic Ideals, Governance, and Corruption in South Asia* (Kolkata: Freedom Press 2006) 9–10.

24 M Rashiduzzaman, 'Political Unrest and Democracy in Bangladesh' (1997) 37(3) Asian Survey 254, 257.

25 HL Root, *Small Countries, Big Lessons: Governance and the Rise of East Asia* (Hong Kong: Oxford University Press 1996).

26 Muhammad Sayadur Rahman, 'Role of the Members of Parliament in the Local Government of Bangladesh: Views and Perceptions of Grassroots in the Case of Upazila Administration' (2013) 13 Public Organization Review 71.

27 Rashid Moten (n 33); M Moniruzzaman, 'Parliamentary Democracy in Bangladesh: an Evaluation of the Parliament during 1991–2006' (2009) 47(1) Commonwealth and Comparative Politics 100.

and corrupted.[28] Since the one-party monopolisation of Bangladesh in 2014, the Parliament's biggest legitimacy crisis currently concerns the extent to which it represents the people of Bangladesh.[29]

The Election Commission's power to ensure a level playing field for the competing parties suffered a setback in the very first election of 1973.[30] It was held under a partisan government, and there were credible allegations that the Commission was left at the mercy of the ruling party workers and the government in discharging its electoral responsibility.[31] The military rulers of 1975–1990 further corrupted the process and institution by subordinating the Election Commission to the government and rigging the election results in their favour. In none of those elections the military rulers or candidates belonging to their parties found it difficult to capture the polling stations, stuff the ballot boxes, and rig the electoral result.[32] After the fall of the military rulers, the four national elections held under the non-party caretaker governments during 1991–2009 were considered relatively fair and acceptable.[33] An intervening parliamentary election (the Sixth Parliament) held under a party government in 1996, however, restaged the electoral scenarios of the military era.[34] The NPCG was incorporated into the Constitution after an Awami League (AL)-led

28 Ali Riaz, 'Bangladesh's Failed Election' (2014) 25(2) Journal of Democracy 119, 129.

29 M Jashim Ali Chowdhury, 'Elections in 'Democratic' Bangladesh', in Mark Tushnet and Madhav Khosla (eds.), *Unstable Constitutionalism: Law and Politics in South Asia* 192–229 (Cambridge University Press 2015) 227–228; M Jashim Ali Chowdhury, 'Fifty Years of Electioneering in Bangladesh: the Collapse of a Constitutional Design' in M Rafiqul Islam and Muhammad Ekramul Haque (eds.) *The Constitutional Law of Bangladesh: Progression and Transformation at its 50th Anniversary* (Singapore: Springer Nature 2023) 173–193.

30 Abul Fazl Huq, 'Constitution Making in Bangladesh' (1973) 46(1) Pacific Affairs 59, 75.

31 Moudud Ahmed, *Bangladesh: Era of Sheikh Mujibur Rahman* (Dhaka: University Press Limited, 1983) 143–44.

32 Peter J Bertocci, 'Bangladesh in 1985: Resolute Against the Storms' (1986) 26(2) Asian Survey 229; Nizam Ahmed, 'Bangladesh,' in D Nohlen, F Grotz and C Hartmann (eds.), *Elections in Asia: a Data Handbook* (Oxford: Oxford University Press 2001) 528; Muahmmad A Hakim, *Bangladesh Politics: the Shahabuddin Interregnum* (Dhaka: University Press Limited, 1993) 27; Samina Ahmed, 'Politics in Bangladesh: the Paradox of Military Intervention' (1991) 9(1) Regional Studies 58.

33 Fakhruddin Ahmed, *The Caretakers: a Firsthand Account of the Interim Government of Bangladesh (1990–1991)* (Dhaka: University Press Limited 1998) 12–13; Zillur R Khan, 'Bangladesh's Experiments with Parliamentary Democracy' (1997) 37(6) Asian Survey 581; Nizam Ahmed, 'Non-Party Caretaker Governments And Parliamentary Elections In Bangladesh: Panacea Or Pandora's Box?' (2004) 11(1) South Asian Survey 49.

34 M Rashiduzzaman (n 24) 260.

violent political movement.[35] Ironically, in 2011, the caretaker government was abolished by the same AL, who staged months of violent street agitation demanding its introduction in 1996.[36] After that, the tenth (2014) and eleventh (2018) parliamentary elections held under the incumbent AL government saw the history of electoral corruption and wide-scale rigging repeated.[37] Another one-party election was held in January 2024, which the largest opposition party boycotted, and the ruling party permitted its own candidates to be challenged by rival independent candidates from their own party. That parliament being dissolved on 6 August 2024, the interim government formed by the protesting students faces a daunting task of addressing the electoral problems a fresh.

Though the Constitution of Bangladesh envisages an independent Election Commission,[38] successive political governments have captured the Commission by using its appointment power. The posts of the Chief Election Commissioner (CEC) and other commissioners are filled by the President as per the advice of the Prime Minister.[39] Until recently, there has been a recent practice of convening a Search Committee to find a CEC and other election commissioners.[40] However, the process was largely seen as a farce.[41] Appointments to the Commission continued to be shaped by the Prime Minister and the ruling parties' political convenience.[42]

In December 2022, the government reluctantly passed the Chief Election Commissioner and other Election Commissioners Appointment Act 2022[43]

---

35 Golam Hossain, 'Bangladesh in 1994: Democracy at Risk' (1995) 35(2) Asian Survey 171, 172; Nizam Ahmed, 'From Monopoly to Competition: Party Politics in the Bangladesh Parliament (1973–2001)' (2003) 76(1) Pacific Affairs 55, 59.

36 M Ehteshamul Bari, 'The Incorporation of the System of Non-Party Caretaker Government in the Constitution of Bangladesh in 1996 as a Means of Strengthening Democracy, Its Deletion in 2011 and the Lapse of Bangladesh into Tyranny Following the Non-Participatory General Election of 2014: a Critical Appraisal' (2018) 28(1) Transnational Law and Contemporary Problems 27.

37 Ali Riaz (n 28).

38 The Constitution of the Peoples' Republic of Bangladesh 1972, art 118 <http://bdlaws.minlaw.gov.bd/act-367.html>.

39 ibid, art 118 (1).

40 M Jashim Ali Chowdhury, 'The EC Search Committee: Towards a "consensual" constitutional convention?' *The Daily Star* (Dhaka, 7 February 2017).

41 Ashutosh Sarkar and Mohiuddin Alamgir, 'Law for EC Appointments: It's needed more than ever now', *The Daily Star* (Dhaka, 26 September 2021).

42 M Sakawat Hussain, *Electoral Reform in Bangladesh 1972–2008* (Dhaka: Palok Publishers 2012) 63.

43 The Chief Election Commissioner and other Election Commissioners Appointment Act, 2022 (Act No 1 of 2022) <http://bdlaws.minlaw.gov.bd/act-details-1397.html> accessed 28 February 2023.

at the behest of resounding demand across the political aisles.[44] The Act mandates the formation of a Search Committee to search and nominate ten names against the five Election Commissioners to be appointed.[45] A Judge of the Appellate Division now heads the Search Committee. It comprises five other members, including one High Court Division Judge, the Comptroller and Auditor General, the Chair of the Public Service Commission and two eminent citizens, including a woman.[46] The committee may consult the political parties and civil society representatives and invite the names of potential Election Commissioners.[47] There are, however, concerns about the openness and transparency of the committee's deliberation and decisions. Though the 2022 Act requires the committee to work in a "transparent and neutral way",[48] there are substantial doubts about its capability to ensure transparency.[49] Despite the demand from various quarters to publish its list of nominees submitted to the President, the 2022 Search Committee decided not to publish it. It instead published a list of 329 nominees proposed by various political parties and civil society members.[50] Most importantly, the constitutional obligation of the President to take and act upon the advice of the Prime Minister remains intact. The 2022 Act does not say anything about the binding force of the committee's recommendations.

Once constituted, the Commission must depend on the government bureaucracy, including the law enforcement agencies.[51] Understandably, Bangladesh's politicised bureaucracy stands as a 'formidable obstacle'[52] to transparency, the rule of law and accountable governance. The Constitution requires the President to staff the Commission as per its requirements.[53] However, the obligation to fulfil the requirements of the Commission does not indicate its strength. The Commission usually places numbers, for example, the returning

---

44 Partha Pratim Bhattacharjee and Mohiuddin Alamgir, 'EC Formation: Chance of a law slim', *The Daily Star* (Dhaka, 23 December 2021).

45 Appointment Act 2022 (n 43) sections 5, 6.

46 ibid, sec. 3.

47 ibid, sec. 4.

48 ibid, sec. 4(1).

49 Badiul Alam Majumder, 'Search Committee for EC: Transparency can counter confidence crisis', *The Daily Star* (Dhaka, 23 February 2022).

50 Staff Correspondent, 'With 322 names proposed for Election Commission, search committee is set to make final choices' *Bdnews24.com* (Dhaka, 15 February 2022).

51 Sakawat Hussain (n 42).

52 Quamrul Alam and Julian Teicher, 'The State of Governance in Bangladesh: the Capture of State Institutions' (2012) 35(4) South Asia: the Journal of South Asian Studies 858.

53 Constitution (n 38) art 120.

officers, polling officers and support staff, before the President. The President appoints them from within the executive bureaucracy.

The Constitution is silent about a separate Election Commission secretariat and requires the executive branch (the bureaucracy) to 'assist'[54] the Commission. In 2008, following a judicial order,[55] an Ordinance was issued separating the Commission Secretariat from the other government secretariats. It was made into law in 2009.[56] The 2009 Act provided that the Commission secretariat would not be under the administrative control or supervision of any ministry, department, or division of the government, and the overall control of the secretariat would remain with the Chief Election Commissioner.[57] This provision, however, has been respected mostly in the breach. The Election Commission secretaries and subordinate staff sent on deputation from other Ministries and departments are practically not expected to perform their responsibilities in ways that might draw the ire of their political bosses in the government.[58]

Understandably, political control of the election machinery is "the biggest problem" in Bangladesh,[59] and there is little faith among the public and the opposition parties in the Commission's capability to conduct a free and fair election under a party government. During the election, the party government in power makes it impossible for the Commission to command the administration. Therefore, the electoral legitimacy of the most of Bangladesh's previous Parliaments is sharply doubtful.

2.3 *Fairness of the Electoral Outcome*

Parliament's collective and institutional accountability is also related to the fairness of a country's electoral outcomes. The contemporary electoral reform agenda in the UK is focused on the problems of its First-Past-The-Post (FPTP) system. While the disproportionate distribution of parliamentary seats is also a concern in Bangladesh, its electoral process is struggling more with the fairness and credibility questions hanging over the system.

---

54 ibid, art. 126.

55 *Kazi Mamunur Rashid* v. *Government of Bangladesh* 28 BLD (2008) (HCD) 87 para 24 (per Mamnun Rahman J).

56 The Election Commission Secretariat Act 2009.

57 ibid, sec. 3(2), 5(1), 6(2) and 14.

58 M Jashim Ali Chowdhury, *An Introduction to the Constitutional Law of Bangladesh* (Chittagong: Book Zone, 4th Edition, 2016) 545–46.

59 Sakawat Hussain (n 42) 51.

The FPTP system usually favours the major political parties by helping them secure disproportionate seats against the percentile of popular votes they secure.[60] In the UK, the Liberal Democratic Party has been the traditional victim of this, though they have secured 72 seats against their 12.2 per cent votes on 4 July 2024 election. The Lib Dems have been long pressing for electoral reform[61] but failed to get political consensus due to the seat maximisation interest of the Labour and Conservative parties.[62] Bangladesh's FPTP system has yielded exceptionally disproportionate results too.[63] Though occasional calls for introducing a PR system have been made,[64] those are not grounded on

60 AT Russell, A Russell and E Fieldhouse, *Neither Left nor Right: the Liberal Democrats and the Electorate* (Manchester: Manchester University Press 2005) 6.

61 Thomas Carl Lundberg and Martin Steven, 'Framing Electoral Reform in the 2011 UK Alternative Vote Referendum Campaign' (2013) 48(1) Australian Journal of Political Science 15; John Curtice, 'Politicians, Voters and Democracy: the 2011 UK referendum on the Alternative Vote' (2013) 32(2) Electoral Studies 215; Matt Qvortrup, 'Voting on Electoral Reform: a Comparative Perspective on the Alternative Vote Referendum in the United Kingdom' (2012) 83(1) The Political Quarterly 108.

62 K Benoit, 'Models of Electoral System Change' (2004) 23 Electoral Studies 363.

63 A Rashid Moten, 'Parliamentary Elections in Bangladesh' (1981) 42(2) *The Indian Journal of Political Science* 58; Wikipedia, 'Elections in Bangladesh' <https://en.wikipedia.org/wiki/Elections_in_Bangladesh> accessed 30 July 2024 (In the first parliamentary election of Bangladesh in 1973, the wining party AL claimed 73.16 percent of the popular vote, which gave it 293 out of 300 seats. In the second parliamentary election of 1979, the wining party BNP got 207 out of 300 seats with 41.17 percent of total votes cast. The vote percentage and seat numbers for the wining party JP in the third parliament of 1986 was 42.34 percent and 153 out of 300 respectively. In the fourth parliamentary election of 1988, the winning party JP claimed 258 out of 300 seats against its 68.44 percent popular votes. In the fifth parliamentary election of 1991, the wining party BNP claimed 140 seats out of 300 against 30.81 percent of popular votes. The main opposition party AL in that election got 88 seats against 30.08 percent votes. The winner of seventh parliamentary election (1996) AL got 146 seats against 37.4 percent votes while the main opposition party BNP got 116 seats against 33.6 percent votes. Winner of the eighth parliamentary election of 2001, BNP secured 193 seats against 40.97 percent votes while the main opposition party AL secured only 62 seats against 40.13 percent votes. AL, the winner of the ninth parliamentary election in 2008 got 230 seats against 48.04 percent votes while the main opposition party BNP got only 30 seats against 32.50 percent popular votes. AL, the winner of the tenth, eleventh and twelfth parliamentary elections in 2014, 2018 and 2024 secured 234, 303 and 257 seats against 72.14, 74.96 and 74.63 per cent votes respectively. However, these elections being one-sided, the statistics do not potentially reflect the reality).

64 Harun ur Rashid, 'The case for proportional representation', *The Daily Star* (Dhaka, 6 November 2007); GM Quader, 'Proportional Representation Voting System: Bangladesh Perspective', *The Independent* (Dhaka, 1 February 2017); Mesbah Kamal, 'Proportional representation is of utmost importance', *The Daily New Age* (Dhaka, 29 November 2018); M Moniruzzaman, 'Electoral Legitimacy, Preventive Representation, and Regularization

a UK-styled demand for representational fairness for the smaller parties. Those calls are rather based on the fear of an abusive supermajority and total marginalisation of parliamentary opposition.[65] The super-majoritarian abuse[66] being a problem of political culture and party systems, the representative disparity does not appear to be the central issue with the Bangladesh Parliament's electoral accountability. As discussed earlier, its problem with elections is rather a more fundamental one – the fairness and credibility of the elections themselves.

3 The Parliament's Continuing Accountability

Once elected, Parliament's public relations practices work as significant trust-building and legitimising tools.[67] Public relations has both individual and collective aspects. While the constituency works are important for the MPs' re-election prospects, the people must also appreciate the Parliament's institutional worth. Unfortunately, people worldwide are losing faith in politics and its process, and the legislatures are receiving the brunt of the trend.[68] While the legislative process's complexities and technicalities might contribute to this,[69] a cost-benefit analysis is also involved.[70] Evidence shows that increased

of Authoritarian Democracy in Bangladesh' in Ryan Merlin Yonk (ed.), *Elections: a Global Perspective* (IntechOpen 2019).

65 Ahmed Shafiqul Huque and Muhammad A Hakim, 'Elections in Bangladesh: Tools of Legitimacy' (1993) 19(4) Asian Affairs 248.

66 Afroza Begum, 'Disrespecting Constitutional Safeguards for Fundamental Rights in Bangladesh: a Bird's Eye View from the Indian Context' (2007) 49(1) *Journal of the Indian Law Institute* 3, 3–4.

67 Philip Norton, 'The United Kingdom: Parliament Under Pressure' in Philip Norton (eds.), *Parliaments and Pressure Groups in Western Europe* (London: Routledge 1999) 19–42.

68 RJ Dalton, *Democratic Challenges, Democratic Choices: the Erosion of Political Support in Advanced Industrial Democracies* (Oxford: Oxford University Press 2004); G Stoker, *Why Politics Matters, Basingstoke* (Palgrave McMillan 2006); C Hay, *Why We Hate Politics* (Cambridge: Polity 2007).

69 Cristina Leston-Bandeira, 'The Pursuit of Legitimacy as a Key Driver for Public Engagement: the European Parliament Case' (2014) 67(2) Parliamentary Affairs 415, 419; R Hedlund, 'Organizational Attributes of Legislative Institutions: Structures, Rules, Norms, Resources', in Loewenberg, G, Patterson, S and Jewell, M (eds.), *Handbook of Legislative Research* (Cambridge, MA: Harvard University Press 1985) 321–391, 357.

70 Timothy Besley, Rohini Pande and Vijayendra Rao, *Political Selection and the Quality of Government: Evidence from South India* (London: London School of Economics, 2006) (Claiming that citizens' greater access to information about their representative lead to greater political accountability).

public circulation of information may not work the same way in corruption-prone societies as in relatively fairer societies.[71] In corruption-prone societies, the mere flow of information may not mobilise the people against the corrupt political elites.[72] In clientelist societies, the people may remain content with personal and local benefits and forego the demands for accountability, better legislation and executive oversight.[73] Next, too much negative information about politicians sometimes leads to mass detachment and withdrawal from the political process.[74] Increased access to education and information may create critical citizens who would abhor politics and its institutions.[75]

Despite these, the flow of parliamentary information helps raise public understanding of the institution. A better understanding, in its turn, feeds public trust,[76] association and participation[77] in the parliamentary process. Parliaments use various traditional and innovative public relations tools to reach their audience in public. At the individual level, the MPs have prioritised constituency work as an integral part of their parliamentary life.[78] Constituency works serve both the public relations goals of Parliament and the re-election prospects of its members.[79]

3.1 *Public Relations of the Parliament*

Parliaments continue using traditional and modern public relations tools to enhance public visibility. Despite some disadvantaged social groups'

71 Edmund Malesky, Paul Schuler and Anh Tran, 'The Adverse Effects of Sunshine: a Field Experiment on Legislative Transparency in an Authoritarian Assembly' (2012) 106(4) American Political Science Review 762.

72 Timothy Besley, Rohini Pande and Vijayendra Rao (n 70) (A study on voting in rural India has shown that a greater flow of information about corrupt candidates did not cause them to lose the elections).

73 S Lindberg, 'What Accountability Pressures Do MPs in Africa Face and How Do They Respond? Evidence from Ghana' (2010) 48(1) Journal of Modern African Studies 117.

74 M Bauhr and M Grimes, 'Indignation or Resignation: the Implications of Transparency for Societal Accountability' (2014) 27(2) Governance 291.

75 Pippa Norris, *Critical Citizens: Global Support for Democratic Governance* (Oxford 1999).

76 Philip Norton, 'Parliament and Citizens in the UK' (2012) 18(3–4) The Journal of Legislative Studies 403, 415.

77 Cristina Leston-Bandeira (n 69) 418.

78 Philip Norton (n 76) 405.

79 Philip Norton, *Parliament in British Politics* (McMillan International, Red Globe Press, 2013) 219–237, 229; Philip Norton, 'Conclusion: Developing the Links', in Philip Norton (ed.), *Parliament in Contemporary Western Europe Vol 3* (*Parliament and Citizens in Western Europe*) (Routledge, 2002) 178–192, 185; Philip Norton (n 76) 406–407.

accessibility barriers, the internet has opened up the Parliament remarkably.[80] It has rendered a space where citizens and their representatives can directly contact, bypassing the partisan channels and local agents.[81] Recent modernisation efforts within the UK Parliament have recognised public disengagement as a great threat to its representative morale. The UK House Modernisation Committee addressed the problem in 2004 and 2006.[82] It emphasised the importance of political interest building among the citizens, greater information sharing with people and increased public participation in the parliamentary process.[83] The UK Parliament started its first website in 1996. Since then, it has emerged as a very resourceful depository of information. After the creation of a separate Parliamentary ICT Service in 2006, the use of websites (institutional and individual), weblogs, and social media accounts (institutional and individual) has dramatically increased.[84] In the meantime, the Parliament has articulated an Outreach and Engagement Strategy.[85] The Speakers have shown strong interest in broadening and deepening the Parliament's public engagement. Bodies like the Speaker's Advisory Council on Public Engagement, the Commission on Digital Democracy, and the Commons Reference Group on Representation and Inclusion work on diversity and equal access to various parliamentary forums.[86]

Compared to that, the Bangladesh Parliament remains an open institution only on paper. Though the Parliament's Rules of Procedure (RoP) permit it to sit on camera occasionally, regular parliamentary sessions are public. There is scope for the people to observe the Parliament in session. People, however, do not have access to the committee meetings. Rule 201 of the RoP requires removing media and non-members from the committee rooms. Committees

---

80 Jeffrey Griffith and Cristina Leston-Bandeira, 'How Are Parliaments Using New Media to Engage with Citizens?' (2012) 18(3–4) The Journal of Legislative Studies 496; D Joshi and E Rosenfield, 'MP Transparency, Communication Links and Social Media: a Comparative Assessment of 184 Parliamentary Websites' (2013) 19(4) The Journal of Legislative Studies 526.

81 Cristina Leston-Bandeira, 'Towards a Trustee Model? Parliamentary Representation in the Internet Era: the Portuguese Case' (2012) 65 Parliamentary Affairs 425, 429.

82 Select Committee on the Modernisation of the House of Commons, *Connecting Parliament with the Public, First Report* (House of Commons Session 2003–4, HC 368).

83 Alexandra Kelso, 'Parliament and Political Disengagement: Neither Waving nor Drowning' (2007) 78(3) The Political Quarterly 364.

84 Nigel Jackson, 'Escaping from the Straitjacket: UK MPs and their e-newsletters' (2004) 56(6) Aslib Proceedings 335.

85 Cristina Leston-Bandeira, 'Why Symbolic Representation Frames Parliamentary Public Engagement' (2016) 18 The British Journal of Politics and International Relations 498.

86 Sarah Childs, *The Good Parliament* (Bristol: University of Bristol, 2016).

are given the power to call witness testimony from the public, civil society, or experts, though they have not shown much enthusiasm in utilising those powers.[87] Except occasionally, the committees have not shown any serious awareness of the public relations tools they have in disposition. Nor did the committee members and MPs show much inclination to value the alternative points of view and draw from there.

Parliamentary proceedings are recorded and printed verbatim, and there is a scope for obtaining copies of the printed parliamentary proceedings. Absent the digitalisation of those proceedings, as is done by the Hansard Society in the UK, public access to the physical copies of the proceedings is difficult. The parliamentary website (www.parliament.gov.bd) uploads each sitting day's order paper. However, the sessions are not broadcast on the website, nor are the recordings or written proceedings uploaded there. A United Nations Development Programme (UNDP) project named the "Strengthening Parliamentary Democracy (SPD) Project" attempted to digitalise the parliamentary proceedings.[88] The work did not proceed as expected and ultimately stopped once the funding for the project ended.

The parliamentary sessions are rather broadcast live on Parliament TV (*Sangsad* Bangladesh Television) since January 2011. Parliament TV is not live broadcast on its website. The Channel is terrestrial, so people with satellite connections on their TVs usually miss the program. Not being a favoured channel among the public, the satellite cable operators rarely relay the Channel. However, the official Facebook page of the Parliament sometimes live-streams the sessions as telecast on Parliament TV. The leaders and MPs of the ruling party share those on their respective social media handles.[89]

The Parliament building has a media centre. Apart from being a press conference venue for the parliamentary parties and officers, the centre has yet to contribute to the Parliament's public engagement process. The privately owned print and electronic media also show a conspicuous disinterest in covering parliamentary proceedings. Parliamentary sessions rarely make headlines except on the day of the budget speech. Newspapers rather focus on public rallies,

87 Nizam Ahmed, 'Parliament and Citizens in Asia: the Bangladesh Case' (2012) 18 (3–4) The Journal of Legislative Studies 463, 466.

88 ATM Obaidullah, Institutionalization of the Parliament in Bangladesh A Study of Donor Intervention for Reorganization and Development (Palgrave Macmillan, 2019); ATM Obaidullah, 'Bangladesh Parliament Secretariat: a Quest for Increasing Operational Efficiency' (2012) 57(2) Journal of the Asiatic Society of Bangladesh (Hum.) 223.

89 M Jashim Ali Chowdhury, 'How related is Parliament to the People', *The Daily Star* (Dhaka, 3 November 2020).

protests, and programs of the competing parties to get clues about the government policies and opposition manoeuvres. Like the media outlets, the law, social science, and public policy schools rarely show interest in the Parliament at work. Visits and lectures of the MPs and parliamentary staff to the universities are quite unknown. In a sense, this despairing state of public relations reflects the deep marginalisation of the Bangladesh Parliament in the nation's policy process and its non-contribution to legislative oversight and accountability. On the contrary, there is an apprehension that the increased audience of parliamentary sessions could risk further alienating the people because of the unruly behaviours, unparliamentary words, irrelevant speeches, lack of oversight zeal, and the MPs' submissiveness to their party leaders.[90]

3.2 *Constituency Works of the MPs*

In Westminster, there is a very little margin of personal votes for the MPs.[91] Still, some hard-working and constituency-rooted MPs do better than their party's poor show at the national level.[92] The growth of the public sector and the people's increased exposure to various governmental, non-governmental, autonomous and corporate bodies also make it important for the MPs to respond to the constituents' plea for help. Due to the "cognitive mobilisation"[93] of the citizens about the national priorities, the political parties have become unable to take the people's support for them for granted.[94] Moreover, in the democratic party systems, local party units play a very strong and decisive role in candidate selection and political recruitment. Therefore, the survival of the MPs' political career and their capability to mobilise full party force behind their candidature depends significantly on the level of their constituency attachments.[95]

However, certain matters determine the impact of the MPs' constituency works on the local government bodies. First, there is always a question of

90 Nizam Ahmed (n 87) 467.

91 Eggers and Fisher (n 13) 9–10 ("British voters seem to focus almost entirely on party labels to the exclusion of candidate characteristics that there is no sign of a large or growing incumbency advantage.")

92 David M Wood and Philip Norton, 'Do Candidates Matter? Constituency-specific Vote Changes for Incumbent MPs, 1983–1987' (1992) 40(2) Political Studies 227.

93 Michael Rush, *The Role of the Member of Parliament Since 1868: From Gentlemen to Players* (Oxford 2001) 204.

94 Philip Norton, 'The United Kingdom: Building the link between Constituent and MP' in Philip Norton (ed.), *Parliament in Contemporary Western Europe Vol 3* (*Parliament and Citizens in Western Europe*) (Routledge, 2002) 19–42, 20.

95 ibid, 34.

balancing.[96] MPs constantly struggle to adjust their time and priorities between the constituency and legislative works.[97] Secondly, the MPs deal with their constituency cases largely in a non-partisan approach, seeing themselves as MPs of the constituency rather than ones of their parties.[98] Correspondingly, the bureaucracy in the local government maintains the spirit of neutrality, tries to be fair to the MPs regardless of party affiliations, and generally, there is a good working relationship between MPs and local bureaucrats.[99] Thirdly, there might be a tendency of competitive credit claiming between an MP and the elected local councillors for development works implemented in the area.[100] Such competition could likely be tenser in councils controlled by councillors from an opposition party. In such cases, an MP could try to deal directly with local government officials and bypass the councillors.[101] If the council is dominated by the councillors from the MP's party, such friction is less likely. In such cases, the MPs may prefer to hold joint surgeries with local councillors to ensure that local problems go directly to local councillors, while s/he also gets some credits for being involved.[102]

Lord Philip Norton has offered a seven-point explanation of the MPs' constituency role. Lord Norton argues that the MPs work as safety valves, information providers, local dignitaries, advocates of professional causes and social interests, benefactors or welfare officers, powerful friends and promoters of constituency interest.[103] As a *safety valve* for their constituents, MPs represent their freedom of expression, opinion, and right to participate in governance. MPs act as a *source of authentic governmental, legislative and policy information* for their constituents. As *local dignitaries,* MPs conduct regular constituency surgeries, hear directly from their constituents and remain attached to their well and woes.[104] The bulk of the UK MPs' constituency works is believed to be expressed in the *local dignitary* mode. MPs do more constituency surgeries in

---

96 Philip Norton, 'Growth of the Constituency Role of the MPs' (1994) 47(4) Parliamentary Affairs 704, 719.

97 David Judge and Rebecca Partos, 'MPs and their Constituencies, Parties and MPs,' in Cristina Leston-Bandeira and Louise Thompson (eds.), *Exploring the Parliament* (Oxford 2018) 267.

98 Michael Rush (n 93) 219.

99 Vincent Buck and Bruce E Cain, 'British MPs in their Constituencies' (1990) 15(1) Legislative Studies Quarterly 127, 133.

100 ibid, 132–33.

101 ibid, 129–30.

102 ibid, 130–132.

103 Philip Norton (n 96) 706.

104 Michael Rush (n 93) 205.

constituencies having a tough electoral competition – "the greater one's electoral vulnerability, the greater his visibility".[105]

The MPs try to emerge as vocal *advocates of social, professional and interest-based causes*. In exceptional cases, they also work as benefactors or welfare officers for constituents looking for jobs, businesses, education, training and developments from the state.[106] In some cases, the constituents in need might also expect their MPs to intervene as *powerful friends* in their issues with public, private or local government bodies and help resolve those with the concerned authority. As a *promoter of their constituency* interests, MPs remain vigilant in the Palace of Westminster through private member bills,[107] questions, motions for debate and references to the Parliamentary Commissioner for Administration (the Ombudsman).[108] MPs also lobby the Ministers and the national bureaucracy through formal or informal channels on matters affecting their constituencies.[109] Considering Norton's framework, Bangladeshi MPs mostly play the *benefactor or welfare officers, powerful friends* and *active promoters of constituency interests.*

3.2.1 MPs as the Benefactors or Welfare Officers

While the benefactor role has declined in significance in the recent history of the UK,[110] trends in Bangladesh are the opposite. Bangladeshi MPs need to provide clientelist and reciprocal benefits to individuals, usually those who are needy or greedy or who might have claims or expectations of reciprocity in return for the contribution they make towards the MPs' election. A study by a Bangladeshi non-governmental organisation confirms that the constituents show a "cognitive lacking"[111] of the legislative and scrutiny functions of their MPs and look for their direct intervention in securing jobs (97.3%), public land allocations (12.1%), social safety benefits (19.7%) and even cash help for treatment and wedding (40.9%). The constituents also demand collective goods like roads, hospitals, schools, mosques, local electrification, poverty reduction

105 Philip Norton (n 94) 25–26.
106 Michael Rush (n 93) 210.
107 Oonagh Gay, 'MPs Campaigning for their Constituencies' in Cristina Leston-Bandeira and Louise Thompson (eds.), *Exploring the Parliament* (Oxford 2018) 275–276.
108 Philip Norton (n 94) 28.
109 Buck and Cain (n 99), 130.
110 Philip Norton (n 96), 706.
111 Muhammad Sayadur Rahman (n 26); Muhammad Sayadur Rahman, *Upazila Parishad* in Bangladesh: Roles and Functions of Elected Representatives and Bureaucrats' (2012) 11 Commonwealth Journal of Local Governance 100, 112.

projects, and industrial projects for the locality (43.9%).[112] The people complain that their MPs' constituency services, if any, are about corruption, unfairness, and partisanship in distributing projects and public goods, not their involvement in these activities.[113]

The MPs and their families vying for infallible loyalty from their constituents would need to earn and maintain their position through private charity, benevolence, and patronage. They also need adequate public funds to secure the individual and collective goods for the constituents. MPs are offered *ex officio* positions in various *ad hoc* and ongoing local development projects. The MPs also do not like the government social safety net programs distributed through the regular bureaucratic or local government channels. Some important pools of cash resources help the MPs build their benefactor image among the constituents. For example, the Ninth Parliament initiated the Important Rural Infrastructural Development Project (IRIDP). Under the scheme, the MPs were invited to bid for funding development projects (popularly known as the "MP Project"). They are also given yearly allowances of BDT 500,000/- (equivalent to GBP 5,000/- approximately) per year.[114] Also, every year, each MP is allocated a certain amount of food grain to implement different Food For Work (FFW) and Test Relief (TR) based development activities in their constituency.[115] The FFW and TR serve two purposes at the same time. It offers the constituency development seasonal jobs and cash benefits to the constituents. Being a direct cash-in-hand benefit to the people, MPs ensure that only they and their henchmen control who gets the jobs and where the development works are undertaken. The Bangladesh government also runs a Vulnerable Group Feeding (VGF) and Vulnerable Group Development (VGD) scheme, targeting the elderly and physically challenged people. Though distributed through the local government units, MPs ensure that the people of their choice are placed on the list of beneficiaries.[116]

---

112 Nizam Ahmed, 'Parliament and Poverty Reduction in Bangladesh: Role of the MP' (2018) 25 (1–2) South Asian Survey 163, 174.

113 Mohammad Tarikul Islam, 'Cooperation or Interference: Bangladesh MP's role in local government' (*South Asia@LSE Blog* 23 July 2019).

114 The Members of Parliament (Remuneration and Allowances) Order, 1973 (President's Order) (As amended up to 2016) Sec 6A <http://bdlaws.minlaw.gov.bd/act-455/section-10530.html> accessed 1 November 2023.

115 Barkat-e-Khuda, 'Social Safety Net Programmes in Bangladesh: a Review' (2011) 34(2) The Bangladesh Development Studies 87.

116 Rounaq Jahan and Amundsen, *The Parliament of Bangladesh: Representation and Accountability* (Centre for Policy Dialogue and Chr. Michelsen Institute, Dhaka and Bergen, 2012) 35–36.

The relationship of the MPs with local government bodies in their constituencies is one of domination and subordination.[117] They directly and disturbingly involve themselves in local government-level planning and their executions. Political parties, particularly the ruling parties, ensure their MPs are placed in influential positions within the local government, administrative and development bodies and agencies. MPs, their family members, and confides are assigned leadership positions in the management committees of the local schools, colleges, markets, hospitals, mosques, temples and charitable organisations. They use those positions and power to maintain their stronghold over local affairs and pour favour upon the constituents. Since the independence of Bangladesh, the MPs have been given the direct role of advisors in the local councils. Though they are the "advisors" in form, the discussion above has shown how the MPs directly dictate and interfere with local government bodies. They often undertake "mundane activities"[118] formally assigned to the elected local councillors. The elected Chairmen and Councilors of the local councils are standing powerless at the hands of the MPs.[119] The MPs have grown in influence and power to such an extent that they can dictate even those bodies to which they are not formally assigned any advisory role.

3.2.2 MPs as the Powerful Friends

Apart from being a "*benefactor*", the MPs must appear *powerful* enough to have a necessary connection, access and persuasion at the centre or upper echelon of the government, bureaucracy, and most importantly, the police administration. They need to prove to their constituents that they can outshine their opponents in competitively bringing projects and public goods. Since criminal justice and policing administration is corrupt and ruthlessly politicised,[120] the MPs must be powerful enough to shield their party men from arrest, criminal

---

117 N Ahmed, T Ahmed and M Faizullah, *Working of Upazila Parishad in Bangladesh: a study of twelve Upazilas* (Dhaka: United Nations Development Program, 2011).

118 PK Panday and MG Rabbani, 'Good governance at the grassroots: Evidence from union parishads in Bangladesh' (2011) 18(2) South Asian Survey 293.

119 Zillur Rahman Khan, 'Decentralized governance: Trials and Triumphs' In Raunaq Jahan (ed.), *Bangladesh Promise and Performance* (Dhaka: University Press Limited 2011); MS Rahman, 'Restructuring Local Government in Bangladesh: an Overview' (1997) 1(1) Public Administration Review 11; AE Sarker, 'Clientelism and Local Government in Bangladesh: a Study in Relations' (1997) 25(2) Asian Profile 151; Nizam Ahmed, 'Experiments in Local Government Reform in Bangladesh' (1988) 28(8) Asian Survey 813; Mohammad Sayadur Rahman, '*Upazila Parishad* in Bangladesh' (n 111) 107–109; Mohammad Sayadur Rahman, 'Role of the members of Parliament' (n 26) 79–80.

120 David Jackman, 'The Decline of Gangsters and Politicization of Violence in Urban Bangladesh' (2019) 50(5) Development and Change 1214.

trial, police investigation, and legal complexities.[121] In doing so, the MPs need to maintain their gang of musclemen, corrupt political allies, development contractors and miscreants who would dominate the locality and the local units of political parties. On the MPs' behalf, they largely intervene in the laypeople's domestic, property, land, and criminal disputes.[122] While such an abhorrent approach of dominance and control may appear unrealistic from an MP's re-election prospect, the elections in Bangladesh are manipulated in the ruling party's favour. Therefore, MPs belonging to the ruling party need enough control and muscle power in the locality to capture the polling stations and keep the opponents at bay. Challengers from the opposition parties also need their battalion of musclemen capable and brave enough to challenge the ruling party forces. A Bangladeshi anthropologist has identified this as the failure of representation in "a formal political sense" and a "shape-shifting towards an informal world where politics meet the culture".[123]

3.2.3 The Advocates of Constituency Interests

In the Parliament, the MPs' actual workplace, the Bangladeshi MPs play mostly the advocates of constituency interest. The MPs spend most of their parliamentary time popularising or pursuing the matters that concern their constituencies. Understandably, the constituency issues they raise on the floor are mainly the demands for collective goods like roads, culverts, schools, and electrification.[124]

Several arguments have been advanced to explain Bangladesh's total localisation of national MPs. Some argued that the Bangladeshi MPs' overemphasis on their constituency works is related to their re-election prospect. Arguably, the development of intense bipartisan competition between the Bangladesh Nationalist Party (BNP) and Awami League (AL) in the 1990s decreased the number of "safe seats" across the country.[125] MPs, therefore, needed an exceptionally strong and personal vote bank in their constituencies. The argument, however, appears internally contradictory. While some exceptionally popular and long-serving candidates might be able to overcome the partisan and prime

121 Zahir Ahmed, 'From Shape Shifting to Collusion in Violence: an Ethnography of Informal Relationships Between Bangladeshi Members of Parliament and Their Constituents' (2019) 42(1) Legal and Political Anthropology Review (PoLAR) 5, 11–13.

122 Mahfuzul H Chowdhury, 'Violence, politics and the state in Bangladesh' (2003) 3(2) Conflict, Security & Development 265.

123 Zahir Ahmed (n 121) 17.

124 Nizam Ahmed (n 112) 173.

125 Nizam Ahmed (n 87) 465–466.

ministerial tendencies of the national election, very few MPs could amaze such a significant personal vote bank. Most Bangladeshi MPs maintain a strong constituency profile to secure re-nomination from their respective parties.

Nizam Ahmed argues that the MPs' constituency works are conditioned by a mutuality of interests between MPs and their party high commands.[126] The central leadership in each party 'nominates' the candidates for parliamentary polls. Unlike the UK, where constituency units of the parties play a decisive role in candidate selection, local party units in Bangladesh often get their candidates imposed by the party leaders.[127] On the flip side of the matter, the localisation of the MPs downgrades the quality and quantity of their legislative and oversight works in the Parliament and allows the government a practical immunity from parliamentary scrutiny. In return, the government would compensate the MPs by allowing them vast control over the local government.[128] Dominating the local government office bearers, who enjoy their distinct claim of electoral legitimacy, through another set of elected representatives, *i.e.*, the MPs, is easier than trying to do it through the bureaucracy. Thus, localisation helps the government centralise its power and suppress the elected local government bodies.[129] The question of local government autonomy was litigated twice before the Supreme Court of Bangladesh, and the Court came out with contradictory arguments. In *Barrister Ziaur Rahman Khan v. Bangladesh*,[130] it was held that the MPs have overall and multi-faced responsibilities to look after the welfare of their constituencies, and their involvement in the development works in their constituencies is desirable. Next, in *Anwar Hossain Monju*,[131] the Court opined that the MP must not impair the work of separately elected local government bodies.

A second explanation for the localisation of Bangladeshi MPs is related to the political opposition. Bangladesh's political opposition is marked by distrust, conflict, and conspiracies. The ruling parties cannot rely only on the administration and police forces to tackle the destabilising tactics of the opposition. Rather, an alert and powerful MP at the constituency level ensures that hardline opposition or resistance does not rise from the bottom. It leaves the

126 Nizam Ahmed (n 112) 179.

127 Nizam Ahmed, 'In Search of Institutionalisation: Parliament in Bangladesh' (1998) 4(4) The Journal of Legislative Studies 34, 59–61.

128 Nizam Ahmed (n 112) 178.

129 Constitution of Bangladesh (n 38), art 59 and 60.

130 *Barrister Ziaur Rahman Khan v. Bangladesh* 20 BLD (HCD) 120.

131 *Anwar Hossain Monju v. Bangladesh* BLT (HCD) 86.

government and the police to focus on opposition activities in major cities and the Capital.[132]

A third explanation of the localising tendency is related to the MPs themselves. On the MPs' part, the incumbents must maintain a strong hold over their constituency and the local party units so that strong leadership contenders do not rise to prominence. They would cultivate factionalism within the party and establish an army of personally loyal workers to help maintain their "undisputed" leadership by suppressing any possible contender from the party's grassroots.[133] They would resist structural changes within the party and the grassroots.[134] At the same time, they would encourage their children or family members to take the baton in future. Therefore, the motivation for constituency entanglement remains to hold strong and try to reign as long as possible.

4 Parliament's Operational Accountability

The traditional concept of the Parliament's *ex-post* accountability, where the representatives work on behalf of the people and answer them at the end of every electoral cycle, is increasingly seen as insufficient to explain a parliament's relation to its society.[135] Therefore, side-by-side with information-sharing strategies, the scope of public participation is important at all stages of the parliamentary process.[136] Citizen access to the Parliament members and its legislative and scrutiny processes has democratic consequences.[137] It enforces the Parliament's continuing accountability outside the usual electoral cycle and legitimises parliamentary laws and public policies.[138] Public participation in the parliamentary process is another important indicator of democratic legitimacy. Public relations experts suggest that a well-trusted Parliament must travel beyond information sharing. Rather, the Parliament

132 Nizam Ahmed (n 112) 180.

133 Zahir Ahmed (n 121) 6–7; Nizam Ahmed (n 112) 169.

134 Nizam Ahmed (n 112) 166, 167.

135 Cristina Leston-Bandeira (n 69).

136 Dryzek, John S, *Deliberative Democracy and Beyond: Liberals, Critics, Contestations* (Oxford: Oxford University Press, 2000).

137 Geraint Parry, George Moyser, and Neil Day, *Political Participation and Democracy in Britain* (Cambridge University Press 1992).

138 Ruth Fox, 'Engagement and Participation: What the Public Want and How our Politicians Need to Respond' (2009) 62 Parliamentary Affairs 673; Nigel Jackson, 'Representation in the Blogosphere: MPs and Their New Constituents' (2008) 61(4) Parliamentary Affairs 642, 644.

must allow meaningful public participation in it.[139] As David Arter argues, an effective public relations strategy needs to emphasise the Parliament's visibility (through information sharing, transparency and openness of the proceedings), accessibility (through physical or virtual access to the persons and premises of the Parliament) and permeability equally (through legislative and policy inputs from outside).[140] Without access to it, people's cognitive awareness about Parliament could engender greater frustration over the institution.[141]

While the necessity of public participation in the parliamentary process is acknowledged, active participation is challenging. First, the people are showing reluctance toward traditional forms of political participation.[142] Election turnouts and party affiliations are declining, and so is the people's interest in political and policy debates.[143] Secondly, while people generally like to demand participation, they usually dislike engaging with substantial time and commitment. Formalistic participation might amplify rather than reduce traditional representation styles[144] unless the informed and committed participants are engaged.[145] While an informed participant might be disappointed to see their views not prevailing at the end, they will still likely accept the process if it gives them a fair chance of participation and hearing.[146] Thirdly, public participation is especially challenging in divided societies where there is a risk of the underrepresented and disadvantaged segments and minorities not being given adequate access and priority in the process.[147] Absent an inclusive environment, the excluded are more likely to choose agitation over participation.[148]

139 Ruth Fox (ibid).

140 David Arter, 'The Finnish Eduskunta: Still the Nordic 'Vatican'?' (2012) 18 (3–4) Journal of Legislative Studies 275, 276.

141 Thomas Saalfeld, 'Germany: From Dictatorship to Parliamentary Democracy' (1997) 50(3) Parliamentary Affairs 380.

142 Mathew Flinders and Alexandra Kelso, 'Mind the Gap: Political Analysis, Public Expectations and the Parliamentary Decline Thesis' (2011) 13 The British Journal of Politics and International Relations, 249; Meg Russell, and Philip Cowley, 'The Policy Power of the Westminster Parliament: the 'Parliamentary State' and the Empirical Evidence' (2016) 29 Governance, 121; L, Thompson, *Making British Law: Committees in action, Basingstoke* (Palgrave Macmillan 2015).

143 RJ Dalton (n 68).

144 Cristina Leston-Bandeira (n 69).

145 Ruth Fox (n 138) 683–84.

146 Christopher Carman, 'The Process is the Reality: Perceptions of Procedural Fairness and Participatory Democracy' (2010) 58(4) Political Studies 731.

147 Ian O'Flynn, *Deliberative Democracy and Divided Societies* (Edinburg University Press, 2000).

148 Paul Whiteley, 'State of Participation in Britain' (2003) 56(4) Parliamentary Affairs 610, 611–12.

Fourthly, due to the complexities of governance, the direct participation of people in a plebiscitary format, *i.e.*, referenda or opinion polls on every legislative proposal, appears less practicable even in well-established democracies.[149] In this scenario, influencing the policies rather than attempting to make the decision itself could prove more practical.[150]

4.1 *Avenues of Public Participation*

In an ideal situation, there should be the scope of public participation in the parliamentary process during the legislative agenda-setting, bill drafting, House deliberation and post-legislative scrutiny stages.[151] People may participate in the parliamentary agenda-setting process through political debates over the government white papers, public petitions to the Parliament, parliamentary studies and civil society reporting on particular issues as they arise. Engagement at the drafting stage may be achieved by inviting public input to legislative drafts. Participation at the deliberation stages could be achieved by sending bills to solicit public opinion through a referendum. During the post-legislative scrutiny stages, people may participate in the committees that follow up on the laws in action.

In the UK, the legislative programs of the government are published in White Papers. The scope of citizen, non-government organisations, pressure groups, or expert participation starts at this stage. Also, at the beginning of each Parliamentary session, the draft bills known as "Command Papers" are submitted for scrutiny by concerned departmental select, ad-hoc or joint committees. The committees may call for written and oral public submissions.[152] Such participation at the pre-legislative stage influences the laws at their formative stages by triggering more intense debate during the floor and committee stages of a bill. It also gives the government an early chance to reconsider its position before the resistance gets tougher.

Public participation in the parliamentary deliberation stage is relatively difficult but has recently increased in the UK. The 2013 Children and Families Bill tested an experimental public reading stage. The public was invited to comment on the bill's contents through a designated web forum. The experiment, however, failed to make substantial input to the subsequent floor and

149 David C Docherty and Stephen White, 'Parliamentary Democracy in Canada' (2004) 57(3) Parliamentary Affairs 613, 616–17.

150 Christopher Carman (n 146) 734.

151 ParlAmericas, *Citizen Participation in the Legislative Process* (Canada 2017).

152 Michel Rush, 'Making better Law: a Review of the Hansard Society Commission on the Legislative Process' (1993) 14 (2) Statute Law Review 75.

committee stage deliberations.[153] Bandeira and Thompson linked the failure with the non-recognition of the public reading stage as one of the formal stages of legislative procedure.[154]

The committee stage is so far considered the most engaging stage of law-making.[155] Members of the public are generally positive towards the select committees.[156] The committee stage participation gained momentum after the Expenses Scandal of 2009, which put the Parliament under intense pressure.[157] In the committee stage, the hearing of charities and campaign groups, businesses, trade associations, non-government organisations, professional associations, experts and individual citizens supply empirical insights into the committee report.[158] Such participation also allows the MPs to build policy expertise in particular areas.[159] In the Public Bill Committees, the MPs are often asked to sit on a bill over which they do not have enough expertise. Public participation there lends them valuable knowledge.[160] For the opposition members and the backbenchers, these inputs provide a balance against the government's monopoly of information and expertise.[161]

However, the selection and access of the participants is a crucial determiner of effective participation.[162] While the access should be as open as possible, including the relevant experts and stakeholders is important for maintaining

153 Cristina Leston-Bandeira and Louise Thompson, 'Truly Engaging Citizens with the Parliamentary Process? An Evaluation of Public Reading Stage in the House of Commons' (*The Twelfth Workshop of Parliamentary Scholars and Parliamentarians*, Wroxton College, 25–26 July 2015) 6–7.

154 Cristina Leston-Bandeira and Louise Thompson, 'Engaging the public with the scrutiny of legislation requires more than just asking for their views' (*LSE British Politics and Policy Blog*, 13 February 2018).

155 Ian Marsh, 'Democratic Discontents. Comment on: Flinders, M (2015) The Problem with Democracy' (2016) 69 Parliamentary Affairs 207; Ian Marsh, 'The Commons Select Committee System in the 2015–20 Parliament', The (2016) 87 Political Quarterly 96.

156 Hansard Society, *Tuned In or Tuned Off? Public Attitudes to Prime Minister's Questions* (London: Hansard Society, 2014).

157 Alexandra Kelso, 'Parliament on its Knees: MPs' Expenses and the Crisis of Transparency at Westminster' (2009) 80(3) The Political Quarterly 329.

158 Marc Geddes, 'Committee Hearings of the UK Parliament: Who gives Evidence and does this Matter?' (2018) 71 Parliamentary Affairs 283, 289–90.

159 ibid, 285.

160 Jessica Levy, 'Public Bill Committees: an Assessment Scrutiny Sought; Scrutiny Gained' (2010)63(3) Parliamentary Affairs 534.

161 Hannah White, *Select Committees under Scrutiny: the Impact of Parliamentary Committee Inquiries on Government* (London: Institute for Government 2015).

162 Marc Geddes (n 158) 289–90.

the quality of the inputs.[163] Again, exclusive and selective access could allow the elite and special interest groups to capture the process.[164] Therefore, a rightful balance is necessary. Online consultation has been touted as a desired balance.[165] Online consultation became a currency in the UK in 1998.[166] In 2015, a concept of the digital debate was introduced in pursuance of the Digital Democracy Commission's Report.[167] The idea was to initiate a digital debate on Twitter through a bespoke hashtag on a topic soon to be debated in the House or Westminster Hall.[168]

The internet has its problems, too. It has accessibility barriers.[169] There is also a feeling that the internet's utility in political awareness building[170] and influencing policy outcomes is limited.[171] Stephen Coleman's study on two online parliamentary consultations showed that deliberations in interactive spaces like weblogs, social media groups and pages have failed to influence the outcome and build trust between the people and their representatives as the participants doubted whether their views would ultimately count.[172] Lord Norton attributed the problem to the UK parliament's 'party dominant model' that prevents the MPs and their constituents from standing beyond the partisan line.[173] Though the MPs host websites, e-newsletters[174] and other public

---

163 ibid, 300–301; Stephen Coleman, *Technology: Enhancing Representative Democracy in UK?* (London: Hansard Society, 2002); Stephen Coleman and Josephine Spiller, 'Exploring New Media Effects on Representative Democracy' (2003) 9(3) The Journal of Legislative Studies 1; Stephen Coleman, John Taylor and Wim van de Donk (eds.), *Parliament in the Age of the Internet* (Oxford: Oxford University Press, 1999).

164 The House of Lords Select Committee on the Constitution, *The Legislative Process: the Passage of Bills Through Parliament* (24th Report of Session 2017–19 HL Paper 393, Witness Dr Thompson, pp. 34 para. 116).

165 Select Committee on the Constitution, *Parliament and the Legislative Process, Fourteenth Report* (House of Lords Session 2003–04, HL Paper 173-I, para. 213).

166 Select Committee on the Modernisation (n 82) 20–21.

167 Digital Democracy Commission, *Open Up! Report of the Speaker's Commission on Digital Democracy* (London 2015).

168 Cristina Leston-Bandeira and Alieen Waltker, 'Parliament and Public Engagement' in C Leston-Bandeira (ed.), *Parliaments and Citizens* (Abingdon: Routledge, 2013) 308, 313.

169 Wainer Lusoli, Stephen Ward and Rachel Gibson, '(Re)connecting Politics? Parliament, the Public and the Internet' (2006) 59(1) Parliamentary Affairs 24, 39–40.

170 Hansard Society, *Audit of Political Engagement* (London, 2010) 83.

171 Nigel Jackson (n 138), 651–52, 57–58.

172 Stephen Coleman 'Connecting Parliament to the Public via the Internet (2004) 7(1) Information, Communication & Society 1, 15.

173 Philip Norton, 'Four Models of Political Representation: British MPs and the Use of ICT' (2007) 13(3) The Journal of Legislative Studies 354, 356–357.

174 Nigel Jackson (n 84).

relations tools to bolster their image[175] and party standing among the constituents, Norton found that those did engender a trusteeship model of representation against the usual partisan delegate model (See: Chapter 3). Nor did those encourage a "tribune model" of representation where their constituents' views would guide their MPs.[176] Jackson's study of the regular e-newsletters published by the UK's five major political parties shows that the parties usually address their members and supporters rather than the non-partisan voters and people.[177] Therefore, unprecedented growth in public engagement in the UK has paradoxically accompanied their increased alienation from politics.

4.1.1 Public Participation in Bangladesh's Parliamentary Processes

In Bangladesh, public participation at the agenda-setting level is extremely low, though not absent. Much of the legislative agenda-setting is done by the Ministries. The civil society think tanks, media outlets, and the Law Commission may draft legislative proposals and initiate consultation thereon, but the governments attach little importance to those.[178]

Due to an exclusively cabinet-dominated legislative process in Bangladesh, the scope of the Parliament engaging the people in its legislative scrutiny role begins much later at the committee stage. However, there is a serious lack of transparency in committee proceedings. As per the RoP, committee sittings are compulsorily private unless specifically permitted.[179] The rules require "all *strangers* [persons other than a member of the Committee and officers of the Parliament Secretariat] to withdraw when Committee deliberates."[180] Also, the reports of the parliamentary committees are not easily accessible to the public. Deliberations, witnesses and dispositions before the committee and its reports are not publishable until they are on the table.[181] The committee may cause the whole or part of the evidence to be so laid. Nevertheless, the Speaker has the final authority to decide whether to make them public or hold them privately.[182]

---

175 Stephen Coleman, 'New mediation and direct representation: Reconceptualising Representation in the Digital Age' (2005) 7(2) New Media and Society 177; Pippa Norris, John Curtice, David Sanders, Margaret Scammell and Holli A Semetko, *On Message: Communicating the Campaign* (Sage Publications 1999).

176 Philip Norton (n 173) 361–365, 367.

177 Nigel Jackson, 'Party E-Newsletters in the UK' (2005) 1(4) Journal of E-Government 39, 58.

178 SM Masum Billah, 'Law Reform: 'Snail in coma'?', *The Daily Star* (Dhaka, 5 July 2016).

179 The Rules of Procedure (RoP) of Bangladesh *Jatya Sangsad* 1973, rule 199.

180 ibid, r 201.

181 ibid, r 210.

182 ibid, r 207(1–3).

Committees, however, can encourage citizen participation by inviting public submissions over the matters they discuss or inquire about,[183] though they rarely employ this.[184] Committees can also seek advice from experts. However, the ruling parties usually show hypersensitivity to civil society and non-government organisations. In 2014, a Minister called the civil society a "cancerous parasite".[185] Many MPs do not appreciate the civil society and non-government bodies much.[186] In a few exceptional cases where citizen input substantially informed the legislative policies, the government high-ups' *ex gratia* concession, rather than the committees' institutional capacity, made those possible.[187] Two recent examples could illustrate the trend – The All-Party Committee finalising the Constitution (Fifteenth Amendment) Proposal 2011 and the Standing Committee on Post, Telecommunication and Information Technology considering the Digital Security Bill 2018.

4.1.1.1 *The All-Party Committee on the Constitution (Fifteenth) Amendment 2011*

In 2011, the Appellate Division of the Supreme Court of Bangladesh declared the election time system of the caretaker government unconstitutional.[188] Before the judgment, the Awami League (AL) government, which came to power in 2009, started a constitution overhauling process. The Parliament constituted an All-Party Special Committee to discuss and finalise the reform proposal. The main opposition party – BNP – and its allies refused to join the committee, citing their lack of confidence in the government's motive. Hence, only the MPs from the ruling AL and its coalition partners constituted the "All-Party" Committee. Perhaps for the first time in the history of Bangladesh, a parliamentary committee heard more than one hundred experts, including several former Chief Justices, constitution experts, academics, intellectuals, and journalists. Of all the meetings held by the committee, the one about the reform of the caretaker government was considered the most important. While there were debates on alternative methods of choosing the caretaker government's

---

183 Taiabur Rahman, *Parliamentary Control and Government Accountability in South Asia, A comparative analysis of Bangladesh, India and Sri Lanka* (Routledge, 2008) 110–129.

184 ibid, 110.

185 Staff Correspondent, '14-party leaders bin civil society call for dialogue', *The Daily Star* (Dhaka, 9 February 2015).

186 Nizam Ahmed, 'Parliament, Public Engagement and Legislation in Bangladesh: a Case study of Domestic Violence Act of 2010' (2018) 24(4) The Journal of Legislative Studies 431.

187 ibid, 445; Muhammad Mustafizur Rahaman, 'Parliament and Good Governance: a Bangladeshi Perspective' (2008) 9(1) Japanese Journal of Political Science 39, 54–56.

188 *Abdul Mannan Khan v. Bangladesh* 64 DLR (AD) (2012) 107.

chief adviser, advisers, tenure and powers, all except one committee member favoured keeping the system intact at least for one next parliamentary election. Mr. Suranjit Sengupta, the Co-chairperson, briefed the media and said:

> [W]e all agree that, despite all the limitations of the present system [of the caretaker government], it should remain.[189]

However, the government seized upon the Appellate Division judgment, and the Prime Minister called for its abolition. The boycotting opposition party under BNP's leadership started airing serious grievances at this. Months later, the committee submitted its final report comprising tens of recommendations on various aspects of constitutional reform. However, it remained silent on the caretaker government, and the deliberations of the fourteenth meeting were not even mentioned in the report. Later, the Fifteenth Amendment to the Constitution abolished the caretaker government. BNP took straight to the street but to no avail. Since then, three controversial elections have been held under the AL government – first in January 2014, second in December 2018 and the last in January 2024.[190] Both the elections are marked by utterly exposed electoral frauds and won by AL in landslides.

4.1.1.2 *The Standing Committee on the Digital Security Bill 2018*

In Bangladesh, the Information and Communication Technology Act (ICT Act) 2006 and its section 57 were used as a powerful tool for the oppression and harassment of political opponents, critics, and rights activists.[191] In 2015, the Digital Security Act (DSA) was proposed to replace the ICT Act and address the concerns over section 57 of the Act. However, the Digital Security Bill 2018, as presented to the Parliament, contained many new content restrictions and other measures that could be used to limit freedom of expression.[192] It was particularly worrying for the electronic and print media that a newly proposed section 32 of the Act gave the government the power to prosecute anybody entering any government, semi-government or autonomous institution's

---

189 This statement is quoted from Adeeba Aziz Khan, 'The Politics of Constitutional Amendments in Bangladesh: the Case of the Non-political Caretaker Government' (2015) 3 International Review of Law 11–13.

190 Ole Solvang, *Democracy in the crossfire: opposition violence and government abuses in the 2014 pre-and post-election period in Bangladesh* (Human Rights Watch 2014).

191 Tuhin Shubhra Adhikary, The Trap of Section 57, *The Daily Star* (Dhaka, 7 July 2017).

192 Center for Law and Democracy, *Bangladesh: Analysis of the Draft Digital Security Bill* (May 2018) <https://www.law-democracy.org/live/wp-content/uploads/2018/05/Bangladesh.Digital-Security-Analysis.18-05.final_.pdf> accessed 30 July 2024.

building and recording anything there. The law defined the action as "espionage", and the person responsible could be imprisoned for up to 14 years and fined up to BDT 200,000/- (equivalent to GBP 2000/- approximately). Section 32 alarmed the journalists and media organisations so much that a movement named "*Ami Guptachar*" (I am the Spy) started nationwide.[193] The Editors' Council, comprising the editors of all the electric and print media outlets, condemned the bill, urged the government not to finalise it in a hurry, and invited the editors to consultation.[194] The parliamentary committee – the Standing Committee on Post, Telecommunication and Information Technology – and several influential government Ministers sat with the editors several times and assured them their views would be considered. However, the parliamentary committee's report did not accommodate those views.[195] On 18 September 2018, the Act was passed almost in the same format as the government tabled it. It is believed that the government high-up was utterly dismissive of the journalists and citizen voices, and hence all the Ministerial and committee stage consultations went in total vain.[196]

4.2 *Petitioning the Parliament*

Petitioning the Parliament is considered a key participation tool for the public. Petitions could work as the citizen's "safety valve"[197] against the executive's abuse of power by "fire alarming"[198] the Parliament's oversight machinery. Like other participation tools, it can reinforce Parliament-Citizen relations by "deepening the participatory democracy".[199] Public petitions also have an "agenda-setting potential"[200] for parliamentary works.

---

193 Pantha Rahman Reza, 'According to the Digital Security Law, 'I am a Spy': Bangladeshi Journalists Defend Their Right to Investigate' (Original writing in Bangla, translated to English by Rezwan, The Global Voices Advox, 7 February 2018).

194 Dhaka Tribune Desk, 'Government should consult all stakeholders on Digital Security Act', *The Dhaka Tribune* (Dhaka, 5 May 2018).

195 Sabrina Hasan, 'Journey from Digital Security Bill, 2018 to Digital Security Act, 2018: Reviewing Past Concern on Proposed Law Regarding Cybercrimes and Outcome in Effect – Analysis', *The EuroAisa Review* (1 October 2021).

196 Julhas Alam, 'Journalists slam pending Bangladesh digital security law. Experts call for review of Digital Security Act' *The Dhaka Tribune* (Dhaka, 30 September 2018).

197 M Asher, C Leston-Bandeira and V Spaiser, 'Assessing the effectiveness of e-petitions through Twitter conversations' (*PSA annual conference*, Glasgow, April 2017).

198 T Saalfeld and R Dobmeier, 'The Bundestag and German Citizens: More Communication, Growing Distance' in C Leston-Bandeira (ed.), *Parliaments and Citizens* (Abingdon: Routledge, 2013) 50–69.

199 Vernon Bogdanor, *The New British Constitution* (Oxford: Hart Publishing, 2009) 140.

200 C Bochel, 'Different Dimensions of Voice and Influence in the Scottish Parliament and the National Assembly for Wales' (2012) 46(2) Social Policy and Administration 142; Tobias

The public can petition the paper in paper and online. Paper petitions can only be presented to the House by an MP through a formal or informal presentation. An MP can formally present a petition in person at the end of each sitting day and before the adjournment debate. S/he may also informally present it by putting the petition into the petition bag behind the Speaker's chair. Once presented, the petition is printed in Hansard and sent to the government. It would usually get a response within two months of its presentation, which is printed in Hansard.

However, unless the system's universal accessibility and effectiveness[201] are ensured, it might become a "parliamentary black hole".[202] Scraping the sponsorship requirement and introducing electronic petitions was driven by a motivation to ensure accessibility of the petition system for all and secure the government responses more urgently.[203] To that end, the E-petition system, first introduced by the Scottish Parliament (2000) and followed up by the German (2005) and British (2006) parliaments,[204] stands as an important innovation. The UK Modernisation Select Committee's Report of May 2004, titled *Connecting Parliament with the Public,* emphasised the need for an e-petition system.[205] The 2008 Report of the Procedure Committee took the matter again.[206] The first Petitions Committee was established on 20 July 2015, and a public petitions site (https://petition.parliament.uk) was opened the next day.[207]

Currently, at least six people are needed to sponsor an e-petition. It is then published on the Petitions Site for public signature. Once a petition receives 10000 signatures, it gets a right to be replied to by the government and would potentially be debated in Parliament. The Petitions Committee considers those and decides the appropriate course of action. It may send a petition to the

---

Escher and Ulrich Riehm, 'Petitioning the German Bundestag: Political Equality and the Role of the Internet' (2017) 70(1) Parliamentary Affairs 132.

201 Richard Hough, 'Do Legislative Petitions Systems Enhance the Relationship between Parliament and Citizen?' (2012) 18 (3–4) The Journal of Legislative Studies 479, 483.

202 ibid, 480.

203 Sonia A Palmieri, 'Petition Effectiveness: Improving Citizens' Direct Access to Parliament' (2008) 23(1) Australasian Parliamentary Review 121.

204 Ralf Lindner and Ulrich Riehm, 'Broadening Participation Through E-Petitions? An Empirical Study of Petitions to the German Parliament' (2011) 3(1) Policy & Internet 1.

205 Select Committee on Modernisation (n 82) para 99–100.

206 Lucinda Maer, 'Proposals for an e-petitions system for the House of Commons' (*House of Commons Research Briefing* SN/PC/4725, Library of the House of Commons, 2010).

207 Thomas Erskine May, 'A brief history of petitioning Parliament' in *Treatise on the Law, Privileges, Proceedings, and Usage of Parliament* Part III, Chapter 24, Paragraph 24.2 (25th Edition Online 2019).

government or another parliamentary committee or debate it in Westminster Hall. If a petition is considered important for debate in the House, the matter is forwarded to the Backbench Business Committee. Petitions have frequently contributed to awareness-raising causes.[208] Since its inception in the UK, 574 e-petitions have been responded to by the government, and around 106 e-petitions have been discussed in Parliament.[209] However, apart from generating awareness and opinion pressure, concrete outcomes of the petitions are likely to take years.[210]

4.2.1 Public Petition System of Bangladesh Parliament

Bangladesh Parliament has a paper-based public petition system. A Petition Committee, usually headed by the Speaker, deals with petitions on "any bill or matter of importance under its consideration or any other matter of public importance".[211] A Member of Parliament must countersign the paper-based petition.

Unfortunately, the current system does not deliver the actual benefits it was intended to supply. MPs show little or no interest in the system. The public is also rarely aware of the opportunity. So, it is grossly underutilised.[212] The Petition Committee also has taken a lacklustre approach to the matters referred. It rarely sits in a meeting. Surprisingly, the past petition committees have referred petitions to the Ministers rather than the House. There is no follow-up process or time limit for responding to or acting on the petitions. Out of 248 petitions submitted to Parliament between 1991 to July 2010, only three were accepted, while all others were rejected, withdrawn or lapsed.[213] Also, the petitions submitted so far primarily concerned the petitioners' issues rather than legislative policy and public concerns.

Bangladesh does any have an e-petition system. While countries like New Zealand have used petitioning the Ombudsman as an alternative to petitioning

---

208 Scott Wright, 'E-petitions' in Stephen Coleman, and Deen Freelon (eds.), *Handbook of Digital Politics* (Edward Elgar Publishing, 2015) 136–150; Cristina Leston-Bandeira, 'The Role of Parliamentary Petitions in the 21st Century: Reflections Drawing from the 2015 House of Commons e-Petitions System' *The e-Parliamentary Scholars and Parliamentarians Workshop* (Wroxton, July 2017) 20–21.

209 Petitions: the UK Government and Parliament <https://petition.parliament.uk> accessed 17 July 2024.

210 Cristina Leston-Bandeira, 'What is the Point of Petitions in British Politics?' (*LSE British Politics and Policy Blog* 7 February 2017).

211 Rules of Procedure (n 179) r. 100.

212 Nizam Ahmed (n 87) 468–69.

213 Nizam Ahmed (n 87).

the Parliament,[214] Bangladeshi citizens do not have that route either. Though the Bangladesh Constitution requires the establishment of the office of the Ombudsman, it has been kept abeyance by refusing to activate a law passed according to the Constitution decades ago.[215]

5 Conclusion

People's disengagement with Parliament is unhelpful for the institution. It causes a decline in support for it, and its marginalisation in the public gaze directly impacts its institutional strength. In the wake of the print, electronic and social media revolution, people would likely see those as the primary channels of democratic accountability. If Parliament and other accountability institutions are relegated to a secondary or even tertiary status, the enforcement of democratic accountability could become farcical, inefficient, and dependent on the political mode of the society. It is, therefore, extremely important that Parliament remains constantly attached to and vertically accountable to its electorate. The study of Bangladesh Parliament's vertical accountability to the people attempted in this chapter shows that its electoral and continuing accountabilities are dismal. There are three reasons behind this.

The nature and process of parliamentary elections in Bangladesh are deeply problematic. Overly partisan election manipulation has made the MPs' electoral accountability near non-existent. On the other hand, the politicisation, manipulation and criminalisation of the electoral institutions and processes have resulted in opposition-less parliaments and parliaments without electoral legitimacy. Therefore, the periodic election as a tool of vertical accountability is dysfunctional in Bangladesh.

Next, the Bangladesh Parliament has largely remained a "closed" institution, unconcerned about its relationship gap with the people. The MPs' connection with their constituents through the constituency works is also based on a clientelist relation of patron and beneficiaries. Constituency works have not been able to ensure the MPs' vertical accountability to the people. Rather, it has invaded and paralysed the elected local government bodies in the periphery.

While the UK parliament has gained significant traction towards public participation through lobbying, think-tank and advocacy group engagement

---

214 Larry B Hill, 'Parliamentary Petitions, The Ombudsman and Political Change in New Zealand' (1974) 22(3) Political Studies 337.

215 Naimuddin Ahmed, 'The Ombudsman in Bangladesh' (2004) 8(1–2) Bangladesh Journal of Law 1.

and transparent campaign financing,[216] the Bangladesh parliament lacks any broad-based participatory or deliberative approach. Appealing directly to the people and engaging them more within the parliamentary process could have brought greater legitimacy and strength. However, the Bangladesh Parliament continues to neglect public participation in its operational process.

---

216 Karen Syma Czapanskiy and Rashida Manjoo, 'The Right of Public Participation in The Law-Making Process and the Role of Legislature in the Promotion of this Right (2008) 19 Duke Journal of Comparative & International *L*aw 1; Renee Scott, 'An Analysis of Public Participation in the South African legislative sector' (*Master of Public Administration Thesis*, Stellenbosch University 2009) 28–39.

CHAPTER 6

The Problems of Reform

1 Introduction

Parliamentary researchers in Bangladesh decry the lack of political commitment to institutionalise the legislative branch. A study by Obaidullah blamed the "lack of political will" for the failure of some donor-initiated reform initiatives in the 2000s.[1] Nizam Ahmed identified the "ambiguous consensus" among the political parties to resist progressive changes as the primary reason for the minimal or no success of various post-1990 reform initiatives. Ahmed also blamed structural constraints like lack of backbench autonomy within the Parliament.[2] This chapter travels beyond the "commitment/will" argument and attempts a deeper appraisal of the timing of various reform proposals, the political contexts surrounding those, the political actors' attitude to those and the institutional structure and procedure within which those were processed, materialised or resisted.

Reforms usually happen through relatively slow-moving institutional and social processes when a political system keeps growing through trial and error. Occasionally, reforms may come through deliberate consideration of the legislature's operational necessities and the country's constitutional objectives. Political scandals or national shocks prompt quicker reforms.[3] Also, the political parties staying out of power for a long time usually have major reform proposals on their agenda.[4] In the end, institutional factors, such as the operational rules and conventions of the institution and the power relations between various stakeholders shape the outcome. Therefore, a mere evolutionary reading of political history, ignoring these influential institutional factors, may not adequately explain why and how various reform initiatives were conceived, advanced, succeeded or failed.

---

1 ATM Obaidullah, *Institutionalization of the Parliament in Bangladesh A Study of Donor Intervention for Reorganization and Development* (Palgrave Macmillan, 2019).

2 Nizam Ahmed, 'Reforming the Parliament in Bangladesh: Structural Constraints and Political Dilemmas' (1998) 36(1) Commonwealth and Comparative Politics 68.

3 For example, the UK's expenses scandal in 2009 led to a significant overhauling of the British Parliament's financial auditing and processes.

4 For example, the constitutional reform sponsored by Tony Blair's New Labour Government coming to power in 1997 after eighteen years of Conservative rule brought far-reaching changes in the UK's constitutional system in 1998, 1999 and 2005.

 | DOI:10.1163/9789004720831_007

History is a particularly inadequate explainer of Bangladesh's parliamentary reform. While the British Constitution evolved gradually over the years, decades and even centuries rather than through sudden breaks or violent political changes,[5] Bangladesh's major political changes came through the breakdown of existing constitutional orders or military coups. There are at least six identifiable phases of revolutionary breakaways in Bangladesh – the adoption of the parliamentary system in 1972, the demise of the system in 1975, the military regimes of 1975–1990, the revival of the parliamentary system in 1991, the indirect military intervention of 2007 and the August 2024 extra-constitutional interim government led by the student protesters. In 1972, the parliamentary system was adopted after a bloody war of independence against Pakistan. It was scrapped in 1975 by the ruling party, who used its brute majority in Parliament to radically change the Constitution. They called it a "second revolution".[6] The military regimes of 1975–1990 came to power through a series of bloody coups and counter-coups. The democratic revival of 1991 resulted from a violent political movement against the military regime, which was forced to hand over power to an extra-constitutional 'caretaker' government hurriedly formed to facilitate the transition. An amendment later constitutionalised that government. After the electoral turmoil of 2006, a military-backed caretaker government came to power in 2007 and ruled the country until early 2009. Unlike the 1991 caretaker government, it was never constitutionalised by any subsequent amendment.[7] Lastly, as this manuscript is being finalised, Bangladesh has found another revolutionary extra-constitutional interim government that promises to reform almost everything of the country. Pending those uncharted vague and ambitious reforms, the prospect of a new election and democratic revival seems distant. Beyond these revolutionary breakaways, Bangladesh underwent three other phases of partisan governments: the brief period of party government 1972–1975, intense bipartisan competition during the 1990s and 2000s, and the era of single-party authoritarianism during 2009–2024.

Part 2 of this chapter will argue that various progressive reforms touted at Bangladesh's critical revolutionary moments were sharply in contrast with the revolutionaries' internal lack of motivation. Various reforms attempted by the military regimes of the 1970s and 80s were mostly power-perpetuating rather than democratic institution-building. The political pact of the early

5 Anthony King, *The British Constitution* (Oxford: Oxford University Press 2009) 1–14.

6 M Jashim Ali Chowdhury, *An Introduction to the Constitutional Law of Bangladesh* (Chittagong: Book Zone, 4th Edition, 2016) 633–36.

7 ibid, 649.

1990s democratic revolutionaries soon fell apart due to the party leaders' power-perpetuation aptitudes. The reform packages touted by the 2006–2007 indirect military regimes aimed to vilify and discredit the major political parties and their leaders and consolidate the military establishment's grip over the power. There are signs that the interim govnerment established after the August 2024 protest is heading towards a similar direction.[8] Bangladesh's post-revolutionary regimes almost invariably failed peoples' trust or abused their powers, perpetuating the *status quo*.

The next part will consider certain notable reforms attempted or negotiated during the 1970s, 1990s, 2000s and 2010s, such as those touching upon the election commission, election time caretaker government, parliamentary committees, and parliamentary bureaucracy. It appears that those added to the chaos and weakened, rather than strengthened, the Parliament. The post-independence leadership of the early 1970s lacked a "democratic instrumental vision"[9] of state-building. Hence, the country's electoral institutions emerged weak. One of the major reforms of the 1990s, the Caretaker Government, was bargained hurriedly and in bad faith. Hence, it did not achieve what a principled "constitutional bargain"[10] should ideally achieve. They failed because they did not align with the regimes' longer-term power-perpetuating interests. A few other trivial reforms of the 1990s, 2000s and 2010s, such as those around the parliamentary committee system and the election commission, came as benevolent concessions from the leadership as long as those did not disturb their personal grip over the power.

Given the context, the last part of this chapter tries to take a holistic institutional sense of Bangladesh's major, minor, cosmetic, or failed political reforms. It considers some of Bangladesh's notable reform windows and initiatives in light of Philip Norton's "formalist and attitudinal"[11] and Alexandra Kelso's "contextual and institutional"[12] theories. It appears that Norton and Kelso's theories

---

8 M Jashim Ali Chowdhury, 'The Agenda and Dilemmas of Constitutional Reform in Bangladesh', *ConstitutionNet, International IDEA*, 18 November 2024, <https://constitutionnet.org/news/voices/agenda-and-dilemmas-constitutional-reform-bangladesh> accessed 18 November 2024.

9 Johan P Olsen, *Governing through Institution Building: Institutional Theory and Recent European Experiments in Democratic Organisation* (Oxford: OUP, 2010).

10 Roger D Congleton, *Perfecting Parliament Constitutional Reform, Liberalism and the Rise of Western Democracy* (Cambridge 2011).

11 P Norton, *The Commons in Perspective* (Oxford: Martin Robertson, 1981); P Norton, 'The Norton View', in D Judge (ed.), *The Politics of Parliamentary Reform* (London: Heinemann, 1983); Philip Norton, 'Reforming Parliament in the United Kingdom: the Report of the Commission to Strengthen Parliament' (2000) 6(3) *The Journal of Legislative Studies* 1.

12 Alexandra Kelso, *Parliamentary Reform at Westminster* (Manchester University Press 2013).

persuasively explain, in a complementary way, how the time, the political leadership, their agenda and the Parliament's institutional structure and procedures contribute to Bangladesh's abysmal state of parliamentary reform. The chapter concludes by arguing that, like its other institutional problems identified throughout Chapters 3–5, Bangladesh's problems of parliamentary reform are related to its political parties.

2 The Failed "Revolutions"

Reforms may come in revolutionary or evolutionary processes.[13] The revolutionary processes see institutions emerging suddenly, by armed revolution, constitutional breakdown, deliberative constitutional convention, legislative assemblies, or any combination of those.[14] On the other hand, evolutionary reforms happen incrementally and over a prolonged period. Unlike Britain, Bangladesh seems to be a more suitable case study for revolutionary reforms. Bangladesh has witnessed a series of violent and often bloody breakaways from the past. The country was born through a bloody war for independence in 1971. Then, the reversal of the parliamentary system and introduction of a Soviet-style one-party political system in 1975 was followed by the murder of *Bangabandhu* Sheikh Mujibur Rahman – the founder of the country[15] and the emergence of a dictatorial, military, and presidential form of government for the next fifteen years. By the time the parliamentary system was revived in 1991, Bangladesh had gone through a series of coups, counter-coups, the murder of a military ruler and a mass political upsurge against another in 1990.[16] The chaos of the 2007 parliamentary election invited another military intervention in politics.[17] The latest round of extra-constitutional "interim" government (August 2024) came apparently as the response to an electoral system broken since 2014.

Revolutionary moments tend to lose track due to illiberal and power-entrenching tendencies of politics. There could be two explanations for this. First, the new regimes usually seek to avoid anarchy and stabilise the situation

13 Congleton (n 10).

14 ibid, 590.

15 Lawrence Lifschultz and Kai Bird, 'Bangladesh: Anatomy of a Coup' (1979) 14(49) *Economic and Political Weekly* 1999.

16 Mushtaq H Khan, 'The Political Settlement and its Evolution in Bangladesh' 75 <https://core.ac.uk/download/pdf/2794329.pdf> accessed 30 July 2024.

17 ibid.

as quickly as possible.[18] Therefore, the changes are either cosmetic or minimal and do not drastically dislodge the unseated system. Secondly, the new regimes do not usually pursue a committed liberal agenda that would require them to give up their grip on power.[19] Therefore, the post-revolutionary leaders, though very vocal about the need for progressive changes, do little to unsettle the *status quo*. They would prefer an incremental reform strategy that keeps "open the door to a material entrenchment of the *status quo*, and, consequentially, to an entrenched conservatism".[20] The momentum for progressive changes gets dislodged in the process, and a more repressive regime emerges soon. Bangladesh's 1975–90 and 2007–8 military regimes vividly exemplify the process.

2.1 *The Military Rulers of 1975–1990*

Bangladesh's Second (1979–1982), Third (1986–1988) and Fourth (1988–1990) Parliaments were dominated by the political parties hurriedly assembled by the military usurpers. While the two usurpers assumed the presidency with their so-called motivation to "revive the multiparty democracy"[21] and "the alleviation of political corruption",[22] the changes attempted by them soon ended in the entrenchment of their dictatorial presidencies, perpetuation of corruption, and the emergence of servile parliaments working under various formal and informal limitations. While the military rulers and their political enablers claimed those parliaments as "Independent and Sovereign", their inability to make the government answerable, the President's absolute authority to dissolve those and consistent bypassing of those through presidential Ordinances earned those the badges of "rubber stamp" parliaments.[23] Those so-called reforms were largely cosmetic and aimed at political point-scoring for the regimes rather than empowering the institution of Parliament. For example, the Second Parliament (1979–1981) started appointing Committee Chairs from the MPs who were not Ministers. However, the change appeared to be driven by the military dictator's need to patronise those leaders of his

18 Congleton (n 10) 597.

19 ibid, 598.

20 Hanna Lerner, *Making Constitutions in Deeply Divided Societies* (Cambridge University Press 2011) 210.

21 Mushtaq H Khan, 'Bangladesh: Partitions, Nationalisms and Legacies for State-Building' (School of Oriental and African Studies, 2010) 71–73.

22 Md Ataur Rahman, 'Bangladesh in 1982: Beginnings of the Second Decade' (1983) 23(2) Asian Survey 149, 150–151.

23 Azizul Haque, 'Bangladesh 1979: Cry for a Sovereign Parliament' (1980) 20(2) Asian Survey 217, 221–2.

party who could not be included in the cabinet.[24] Since the empowerment of the Parliamentary Committee System was not the primary motivation behind the reform, it did not get ripe into any binding norm for the future. Committees remained dependent on the sweet will of the ruler of the time.

The next Parliament, the Third Parliament (1986–1988), elected to legitimise the second military ruler, constituted a few general standing committees but did not establish any ministerial or departmental standing committee. The Public Accounts Committee of that Parliament produced only three reports. The Fourth Parliament (1988–90), elected under the same military ruler, was notorious for hosting unknown political parties collectively called the Combined Opposition Party. This coalition of unknown political parties hurriedly coalesced together before the controversial parliamentary election of 1988, which the leading political parties boycotted. The collation was mockingly termed as "Domesticated Opposition".[25] Though the Fourth Parliament established a detailed range of parliamentary committees – for the first time in the history of Bangladesh – all the committees together produced only five reports.[26]

2.2 *The Military-Backed Government of 2007–2008*

As briefly discussed in Chapter 5, Bangladesh's parliamentary era of the 1990s failed to create a political consensus about the periodic and orderly transfer of power. The actions of the competing political parties throughout the 1990s and onwards suggest that they never gave up the desire for a perpetual grasp on power and the total elimination of political opponents at any cost. The non-party caretaker government's relative success in holding three parliamentary elections between 1996 and 2001 collapsed in 2006 when the BNP attempted to install a partisan President as the head of the non-partisan caretaker government.[27] The resulting political violence and crisis caused a two-year emergency caretaker government (2007–2008) openly backed by the military. The military-backed government took over the power, vowing to restore democracy,

24 Nizam Ahmed, *The Parliament of Bangladesh* (Ashgate 2002 Routledge reprint 2018) 133.

25 Syedur Rahman, 'Bangladesh in 1988: Precarious Institution Building Amid Crisis Management' (1989) 29(2) *Asian Survey* 216, 217.

26 Salahuddin Aminuzzaman, 'Institutional Processes and Practices of Administrative Accountability: the Role of Jatiyo Sangsad of Bangladesh' (1993) 10(2) South Asian Studies 44, 58.

27 Nizam Ahmed, 'Party Politics under a non-party Caretaker Government in Bangladesh: the Fakhruddin Interregnum (2007–09)' (2010) 48(1) Commonwealth and Comparative Politics 23.

political accountability and electoral fair play.[28] However, it soon became apparent that the military leadership would follow its predecessors' footsteps and prolong their hold over the power under the guise of public interest.[29] They tried to forcefully change the leadership of the two main political parties by implementing a so-called "*minus two*" formula,[30] coercing some of their senior leaders into intra-party rebellions[31] and harassing the mid-level workers and leaders under a controversial anti-corruption drive.[32] In the meantime, the army chief tried to launch a new political party, keeping some prominent civil society faces to the front.[33] The overall legacy of the caretaker government appeared retrogressive, and the institutional changes, *e.g.*, the reorganisation of the Election Commission, were temporal. By the time, the military-backed caretaker government was obliged to schedule the Ninth Parliament election in December 2008, the grip of the two parochial leaders over the two major political parties – AL and BNP – became even stronger, and the landscape for the illiberal bipartisanship of the 1990s appeared intact.

3 The "Constitutional Bargain"-ers without "Democratic Instrumental Vision"

The revolutionary impulse aside, evolutionary reforms may come through what Roger D Congleton calls a "constitutional bargain"[34] between various stakeholders. "Constitutional Bargain" is a theory of incentive-driven "intermediate" reforms, which are the bargained outcomes between the short-term and immediate interests of beneficiaries of the existing institutional setup and the longer-range demands of the reform advocates.[35] In the bargaining process, rules are likely to be changed only when the elites' position in authority

28 Baladas Ghoshal, 'The Anatomy of Military Interventions in Asia: the Case of Bangladesh' (2009) 65(1) India Quarterly 67.

29 ibid, 69–70.

30 The Economist, 'The minus-two solution' (6 September 2007).

31 Kazi SM Khasrul Alam Quddusi, 'Criminalisation, Militarization and Democratic Restoration in Bangladesh' (2009) 13(4) *World Affairs: the Journal of International Issues* 136, 138.

32 Ali Riaz, 'The "Anti-Corruption Drive" in Bangladesh: Where is it Going?' (*Georgetown Journal of International Affairs Blog*, 16 December 2019).

33 Sufi Faruq, 'The political aspirations of Dr Yunus' *The Opinion Pages: bdnews24.com* (Dhaka, 14 July 2018).

34 Congleton (n 10), 600.

35 ibid.

remains comparatively stable. The existing rules usually remain tilted towards the interests of those who can change them. If the tilt is to be shaken, there must be some constitutional gains for the current power elites. Hence, reforms will be bargained over and (occasionally) adopted,[36] where the immediate interest of continuity for the presently powerful elites is protected, and the long-term interest of the reformists is moderated in incremental phases. It allows reforms to be voluntarily adopted by the negotiating parties, but the adopted reforms are almost always intermediate rather than radical or drastic. However, those intermediate reforms could yield progressive outcomes only if the negotiating parties are driven by what Olsen calls a 'Democratic Instrumental Vision' – of institutional reforms, their purposes, sustainability, and impact.[37] Olsen's democratic–instrumental framework emphasises purposeful and institutional goal-oriented political intervention in democratic institutions.[38] It is the presence and absence of this 'democratic instrumental vision' that differentiates the 'well-entrenched, stable polities' from the 'unsettled, emerging and transitory'[39] ones.

In Bangladesh, the ruling parties and the actors working for reform frequently changed the rules and institutions in ways that best served their power-retaining purposes, not the delicate institutional balance contemplated in the Constitution of 1972.[40] Various reforms and restructuring done around Bangladesh's Election Commission, Caretaker Government, and the Parliament show that those have been deinstitutionalised by the short-sighted and selfish reform formulas sponsored and steered by the political parties and their coteries. The absence of the people and wider stakeholders' voice in the "constitutional bargain" processes and the reformers' lack of "democratic instrumental vision" led to the disastrous failure of those democratic institutions.

3.1 *A Crippled Election Commission*

As noted earlier, Bangladesh's electoral system has been a constant controversy since the country's birth in 1971. Despite the Constitution's remarkable

36 ibid, 592.

37 Olsen (n 9) 6.

38 RE Goodin, *The Theory of Institutional Design* (Cambridge: Cambridge University Press, 1996).

39 ibid 7.

40 Ridwanul Hoque, 'The Politics of Unconstitutional Amendments in Bangladesh' in Rehan Abeyratne and Ngoc Son Bui (eds.), *The Law and Politics of Unconstitutional Constitutional Amendments in Asia* (London: Routledge, 2021) 210–28.

attention to the functional independence of the Election Commission,[41] the Commission needs to depend on the government bureaucracy, including the law enforcement agencies.[42] Bangladesh's politicised bureaucracy is a 'formidable obstacle'[43] to transparency, the rule of law and accountable governance. The Constitution requires the President to staff the Commission as per its requirements.[44] However, the 'requirement of the Commission' does not indicate its strength. The Commission usually places some numbers, for example, the returning officers, polling officers and support staff, before the President. The Constitution is silent about a separate Election Commission secretariat and requires the executive branch (the bureaucracy) to "assist"[45] the Commission. In 1984, Ershad brought the secretariat under the direct supervision of the President's office. After the 1990 democratic revival, it continued to be attached to the Prime Minister's office. The Commission's principal officer – the Secretary – was appointed on deputation from the Prime Minister's office. Thus, the Election Commissioners led an organisation they could not command. Later, in 2008, following a judicial order,[46] an Ordinance was issued separating the Commission Secretariat from the Prime Minister's office. It was made into law in 2009.[47] However, as discussed in Chapter 5, the 2009 law has failed to ensure meaningful insulation of the commission secretariat from the government's control. Similarly, a 2022 law for the appointment of the Chief Election Commissioner and other Commissioners has left the Prime Minister's say in the appointment process intact.

As Muzaffar and Schedler argue, an efficient election administration requires balancing 'three conflicting imperatives' – administrative efficiency, political neutrality, and public accountability of the bureaucracy.[48] In Bangladesh, the ruling or opposition parties rarely discuss civil service reform, the Public Service Commission (PSC)'s independence[49] and a depoliticised

---

41 The Constitution of the Peoples' Republic of Bangladesh 1972, art 118 <http://bdlaws.minlaw.gov.bd/act-367.html> accessed 30 July 2024.

42 Sakhawat Hussain, *Electoral Reform in Bangladesh 1972–2008* (Dhaka: Palok Publishers, 2012) 63.

43 Quamrul Alam and Julian Teicher, 'The State of Governance in Bangladesh: the Capture of State Institutions' (2012) 35(4) *South Asia: the Journal of South Asian Studies* 858.

44 Constitution (n 41) art 120.

45 ibid art 126.

46 *Kazi Mamunur Rashid* v. *Government of Bangladesh* 28 BLD (2008) (HCD) 87 para 24 (per Mamnun Rahman J).

47 The Election Commission Secretariat Act 2009.

48 Shaheen Mozaffar and Andreas Schedler, 'The Comparative Study of Electoral Governance: Introduction' (2002) 223(1) *International Political Science Review* 5, 8.

49 Constitution (n 41) art 137.

and professional bureaucracy. Political parties in power and opposition would rather showcase some cosmetic reforms such as the election commission secretariat laws or the election commissioners' appointment laws. Another notable strategy of the political parties was creating parallel institutions, such as the caretaker government that will neutralise the politicised bureaucracy briefly and then leave it as it is for the next party government. The cycle of innovation, mishandling, and destruction of the institution of caretaker government constitutes another textbook example of the lack of a "Democratic Instrumental Vision" in democratic consolidation and institution building.

3.2 *A Stillborn and Failed Caretaker Government*

The concept of a Caretaker Government was aired in 1994 as an oven-ready solution to the country's lifelong problems with electioneering. The proponents of the model looked back to the extra-constitutional transitional government of 1991 and blatantly emphasised that the judges of the Supreme Court could fix the nation's electoral problem.[50] In 1994, an election-time caretaker government led by a retired Chief Justice of the Supreme Court was considered the best solution to Bangladesh's electoral problems. This view apparently disregarded Bangladesh's troubling past of controversial connivance of higher court judges with various extra-constitutional and martial law regimes.[51] Later, the judges' brokerage of the caretaker government caused rampant politicisation of the judiciary, scandalisation of the judges and compromise of judicial independence.[52]

Importantly, while passing the Thirteenth Amendment, the ruling party BNP – forced to introduce it – framed the system as a reluctant concession and tried, in every possible way, to weaken the Chief Adviser of the caretaker government *vis-à-vis* a partisan President elected by their political parties.[53] It created a system of dual government that contained a looming threat of destabilising the election-time government.[54] Days before the Seventh

50 Md Zakir Hossain and M Jashim Ali Chowdhury, 'The Caretaker Government: a Constitutional Evaluation and Search for Alternatives' (In Bangla) (2014) 19 The Chittagong University Journal of Law 228, 243–44.

51 Justice Mustafa Kamal, *Bangladesh Constitution Trends and Issues* (Dhaka: The University of Dhaka 1994).

52 M Jashim Ali Chowdhury, 'Elections in 'Democratic' Bangladesh, in Mark Tushnet and Madhav Khosla (eds.), *Unstable Constitutionalism: Law and Politics in South Asia* (Cambridge: Cambridge University Press 2015) 220–24.

53 Hossain and Chowdhury (n 50) 236.

54 Habib Zafarullah and Muhammad Yeahia Akhter, 'Non-Political Caretaker Administrations and Democratic Elections in Bangladesh: an Assessment' (2003) *Government and Opposition* 345, 362–63.

Parliamentary Election in 1996, BNP-appointed President Abdur Rahman Biswas exercised his military powers dubiously, which almost invited a military coup and caused the fall of Justice Habibur Rahman's caretaker government.[55] Operationally, the Chief Advisers of the 1996 and 2001 caretaker governments found their constitutional mandate unclear and had often been forced to perform various balancing acts in the face of competing demands of the political parties. As Akter and Zafarullah put it, their role has always been managing by compromising.[56] The system, therefore, marked a 'hotchpotch' that violated 'the entire scheme of the Constitution'.[57]

From a democratic instrumental view, Bhuiyan's evaluation of the Thirteenth Amendment reveals that the system was introduced neither through an expert-driven process nor through public participation, careful study of the nation's political history or deliberative bargain between the political parties.[58] The BNP MPs elected in the sixth Parliament were not the people's representatives in the true sense of the term. The opposition parties staging street agitation demanding its introduction did not demand any participation in drafting the Bill, nor were they interested in wasting time negotiating its texts. They were interested in the BNP government resigning and making way for them.[59]

Assuming the power the very next time, in 2001, the BNP-Jamat coalition government amended the Constitution to ensure that a judge favourable to them led the next caretaker government of 2006.[60] Failing the plot, BNP-appointed President Iaj Uddin Ahmed staged a constitutional coup and usurped the leadership of the October 2006 caretaker government.[61] It invited another round of military intervention in politics. A so-called 'military-backed

55 Hossain and Chowdhury (n 50) 237.

56 Zafarullah and Akhter (n 54) 365.

57 *Abdul Mannan Khan v. Bangladesh* 64 DLR (AD) (2012) 107, 428 (per SK Sinha J); Full text available in <http://ago.portal.gov.bd/sites/default/files/files/ago.portal.gov.bd/page/7f393557_475c_4317_b42a_5a850868beae/Constitutional%2013th%20Amendment%20Case.pdf> (accessed on 30 July 2024). Page numbers referred here correspond to the full text available in the above web address.

58 Md Shahjahan Hafez Bhuiyan, 'The Caretaker Government in Bangladesh: an Appraisal of its Formation' (2003) 40 Politics Administration and Change 33, 46–47.

59 Md Morshedul Islam, '1996's Non-party Caretaker Government Movement and the Role of Opposition in Bangladesh: a Politico-legal Analysis' (2016) 3(6) Global Journal of Political Science and Administration 20.

60 Nizam Ahmed, 'Party Politics under a Non-party Caretaker Government in Bangladesh: the Fakhruddin Interregnum (2007–09)' (2010) 48(1) Commonwealth and Comparative Politics 23.

61 M Shah Alam, 'Article 58C and assumption of office of the Chief Adviser by the President' *The Daily Star* (Dhaka, 11 November 2006).

caretaker government' continued for two years (2007–2008)[62] and conducted the Ninth (2008) Parliamentary Election.[63] While the BNP may be accused of tampering with the system in nakedly visible ways, the AL and BNP calculatedly politicised the judicial appointment process in their bids to get favourable Chief Justices leading the caretaker governments over the years.[64] As we will see later in this Chapter, the system was controversially abolished in 2011. Thus, the caretaker government's 'unusual legal structure' was created and abolished as a mere élite preference rather than deliberative and participatory decision-making.[65]

Besides their farcical experiments with the Election Commission and election-time Caretaker Government, the regimes mostly ignored the demands for institutionalisation of the Parliament. Parliament as an institution was either ignored or suppressed. Even some proposals for relatively regular administrative reforms were thwarted for self-serving rationales.

3.3 *Reluctance in Capacity Building*

By the time the mass upsurge of 1990 came, the underlying power distribution had shifted substantially toward competitive clientelism within the major political parties.[66] The post-1990 parliamentary life and reforms were thwarted by a deeply divided society and illiberal bipartisanship that emerged through fifteen years of militarisation and radical politics. The three post-revolutionary parliaments of Bangladesh (1991–2006) failed to get the institutional strength and maturity expected of a standard Westminster Parliament. The political parties orchestrating the mass upsurge of the 1990s were less committed to long-term progressive reform than they initially pretended to be. Governments deliberately bypassed the parliaments, and the opposition parties regularly discarded the House. Parliamentary businesses were devoted more to partisan bickering than legislation and scrutiny.[67]

The Fifth Parliament (1991–1995) was dominated by the BNP – a political force ideologically faithful to the pre-1990 military rulers' presidential

62 Quddusi (n 31) 138.

63 Nizam Ahmed, 'Critical Elections and Democratic Consolidation: the 2008 Parliamentary Election in Bangladesh' (2011) 19(2) *Contemporary South Asia* 137.

64 *Abdul Mannan Khan* (n 57) 313 (per Khairul Hoque CJ).

65 Sonia Zaman Khan, *The Politics and Law of Democratic Transition: Caretaker Government in Bangladesh* (London: Routledge, 2017) 2.

66 Enayet Ullah Patwary, 'Democratisation and Intra-party Democracy: Bangladesh Experience' (2022) 16(4) *Society and Change* 67.

67 M Moniruzzaman, 'Parliamentary Democracy in Bangladesh: an Evaluation of the Parliament during 1991–2006 (2009) 47(1) Commonwealth and Comparative Politics 100.

tendencies. This Parliament showed an unfortunate trend of excessive executive law-making and bypassing of the Parliament. On the other hand, the Seventh Parliament (1996–2001) was led by AL – a political force loyal to the 1972 scheme of the parliamentary system. It reduced executive law-making through presidential Ordinances and allowed the committee system some foothold. However, like its predecessors, this Parliament was also hit by the party backbenchers' tune-deaf loyalty to their party leaders and the opposition's distaste for institutionalising the opposition.

During the tenure of the Eighth Parliament (1996–2001), the donor agencies and international development partners took an active interest in parliamentary capacity building. In 1997, the UNDP, Denmark, DFID, and the Netherlands joined a parliamentary reform project called "The Strengthening Parliamentary Democracy (SPD)".[68] The SPD achieved certain reorganisation in the Parliament Secretariat and made progress in the digitalisation of Parliament, its knowledge and resources.[69] It also helped the Parliament set up a visiting cell to encourage the public to visit the Parliament.[70] However, the donors' interest in meaningful reform in the parliamentary procedure, committee strength and opposition rights faced reluctant responses from the ruling parties.[71] Failing to change the *modus operendi* of Bangladesh's parliamentary politics, mere logistic and technical renovations did not attract donors for long.[72] At one point, the DFID withdrew its support to the project,[73] decrying the "highly adversarial relationship between the government and the opposition"[74] that could not be repaired through development aid.

The Eighth Parliament (2001–2006) continued with no backbench autonomy, boycotting, and agitating opposition. In the waning days of its life, the ruling party introduced a highly controversial and partisan amendment to the Constitution, again without any meaningful participation from the

---

68 Muhammad Mustafizur Rahaman, 'The Limits of Foreign Aid in Strengthening Bangladesh's Parliament: Analysis of the U.N.'s Strengthening Parliamentary Democracy Project' (2010) 50(3) Asian Survey 474, 488, 494.

69 Abul Hasnat Monjurul Kabir, 'Does Parliamentary Development Assistance Matter? An Examination of the Aid Effectiveness in Parliamentary Oversight' (Ph.D. Thesis: University of Hull 2014) 160–170.

70 ATM Obaidullah, 'Standing Committees on Ministries in the Bangladesh Parliament: the Need for Reorganisation' (2011) 18(2) South Asian Survey 317, 333–335.

71 David E Guinn, and Jeffrey D Straussman, 'Implementing Legislative Strengthening Programmes: Who is in Control?' (2019) 37(5) Development Policy Review 621, 634.

72 Nizam Ahmed, *Aiding the Parliament of Bangladesh: Experience and Prospect* (University Press Limited: Dhaka 2012).

73 Mustafizur Rahaman (n 68) 487.

74 Abul Hasnat Monjurul Kabir (n 69) 162.

backbench or the opposition. The Fourteenth Amendment of 2004 controversially increased the retirement age of the Supreme Court, keeping in the eyes a particular Chief Justice of the Supreme Court who would be heading the next election-time caretaker government but for this amendment.[75] The agitating opposition took violence to the street and caused another military intervention in politics in 2007.

Interestingly, a minor but institutionally important reform – removing the Ministers from the leadership of the parliamentary standing committees – happened during the Seventh Parliament (1996–2001). However, its outcome was largely symbolic and impact the minimal. Until the Seventh Parliament (1996–2001), there was a ludicrous rule of appointing the Ministers as Chair of the parliamentary Committee on their Ministries.[76] That rule was changed in 1997, but it came as an *ex-gratia* concession from the then Prime Minister rather than being drawn through institutional deliberation and negotiation.[77] Still, the Minister concerned was given an *ex officio* membership in the committee. Ministers and cabinet members being the senior leaders of the parties, a committee chair chosen from the backbench would feel the hegemony of the Ministers sitting as right in their committees.[78] There has been a proposal to scrap the Minister's *ex officio* membership. Not heeding that demand, governments since the 9th Parliament (2009–2013) appointed some ex-Ministers as standing committee chairs.[79] While this practice could help expertise development and reduce the ministerial influence in committee works,[80] the appointment still depends on the Prime Minister's good grace – the ultimate party leader – who would select or deselect whatever ex-Ministers s/he likes. Also, missing the cross-party and non-partisan modes in committee businesses and lacking meaningful intra-party assertiveness, a symbolic transfer of committee leadership from the Ministers to ordinary party members would not yield meaningful change in Parliament's accountability power. Additionally, despite repeated calls for appointing chairs of Public Accounts, Public Undertaking and Estimate Committees from the opposition parties,[81] it was not heeded

75 M Shah Alam, 'Article 58C and assumption of office of the Chief Adviser by the President' *The Daily Star* (Dhaka, 11 November 2006).

76 The Rules of Procedure (RoP) of Bangladesh *Jatya Sangsad* 1973, rule. 247(2).

77 Nizam Ahmed (n 2) 73–74.

78 Nizam Ahmed (n 24) 156.

79 KM Mahiuddin, 'The Parliamentary Committee System in Bangladesh An Analysis of its Functioning' (Ph.D. Thesis, Ruprecht-Karls-Universität Heidelberg 2009) 135.

80 M Jashim Ali Chowdhury, '11th Parliament: Rays of hope for the Committee System' *The Daily Star Law and Our Rights* (Dhaka, 05 March 2019).

81 ATM Obaidullah (n 1) 107–138.

until the Eleventh Parliament (2019–2023). In the Eleventh Parliament, a law-maker from the main opposition party, JP, has been appointed the Chair of the PAC. The change again came as an *ex-gratia* gesture from the ruling party, who would not commit to following it in future as a matter of convention.[82]

4 Parliamentary Reform: the Role of Time, Attitude and Institutions

The timing of reform, the attitude of the reformers and the institutions within which the reform proposals are made and processed matter. Two notable parliamentary scholars of the UK, Philip Norton and Alexandra Kelso, offer two important institutional theories that relatively successfully capture why reforms happen at a particular time and fail at another time. Philip Norton's "Attitudinal and Formalist" (political will and opportunity-driven) and Alexandra Kelso's "Contextual and Institutional" (institutional rules and norms-driven) understandings of reform complementarily capture the time, people and institution within a single theoretical framework.

4.1 *Norton's Attitudinal and Formalist Theory*

Philip Norton's Attitudinal and Formalist theory underscores the importance of the MPs' individual and collective attitudes toward reform proposals. MPs have formidable power to vote against their government;[83] if they are willing to use it, the executive-legislature relations in Westminster can be transformed drastically.[84] Norton also lays down the formal process through which reform could be accomplished. Reform will be forthcoming when there is "a window of opportunity" for the reform, *e.g.*, the beginning of a new parliament with a new government or some fortuitous circumstances (like the Expenses Scandal 2009) that brew the climate for reform. Once the "window of opportunity" is open, all the reformers need is "a coherent reform agenda" behind which the members can unite, and the leadership can commit a "political will" to execute it.[85]

Norton's trigonometry of the window, agenda and political will explains the failure of the UK's Alternative Voting referendum in 2011, for example. While the Conservative-Liberal Democrat coalition agreement for the referendum could have opened a "window of opportunity", there was an apparent lack of a

82 M Jashim Ali Chowdhury (n 80).
83 Norton, *Commons in Perspective* (n 11) 234.
84 P Norton, 'The Norton View' (n 11) 54, 61.
85 Norton, 'Reforming Parliament in the United Kingdom' (n 11) 13.

"coherent reform agenda" and a gross institutional rational choice reflected in "political will".[86] Absent the support of the coalition's dominant partner – the Conservative Party,[87] the procedural "window of opportunity" that opened for the Liberal Democrats was a mere chance to bring their case directly to the people. A public pressure-driven "coherent reform agenda" was missing then. Such an agenda is also unlikely to emerge until the current majoritarian system ends in a systematic failure of just representation and yields a grossly wrong winner in the election.[88] The Conservative Party had no reason to believe an alternative voting system would better serve its immediate or intermediate power interests.[89] Absent a coherent reform agenda, the leadership and political will behind the alternative voting system was weak, hence the reform's defeat.

In contrast, the proposal for total democratisation of the UK's House of Lords seems to be missing all of Norton's formal requirements – the "window of opportunity", a "coherent reform agenda", and the "political will" on the part of the leadership. The closest window of opportunity that came so far was before the 2010 general election. There appeared to be an apparent consensus reached during the twilight of the Labour Government in early 2010. The Labour Party tacitly agreed that the House of Lords should indeed be predominantly or wholly elected by that time.[90] The election, however, went in the Conservatives' favour. Since then, the consensus has faded, and the coherence of the reform agenda has dislodged. The House of Commons, in general, has

---

86 John Curtice, 'Politicians, voters and democracy: the 2011 UK referendum on the Alternative Vote' (2013) 32(2) Electoral Studies 215.

87 John Curtice, 'The Death of a Miserable Little Compromise: the Alternative Vote Referendum' (2011) 2(2) Political Insight 14.

88 Matthew Soberg Shugart, 'Inherent and Contingent Factors in Reform Initiation in Plurality Systems', in Blais (ed.), *To Keep or to Change First Past the Post? The Politics of Electoral Reform* (Oxford University Press 2008) 7–60; Alan Siaroff, 'Spurious Majorities, Electoral Systems and Electoral System Change' (2003) 41(2) Commonwealth and Comparative Politics 143.

89 Adrian Blau, 'Electoral Reform in the UK: a Veto-Player Analysis', in André Blais (ed.), *To Keep or to Change First Past the Post? The Politics of Electoral Reform* (Oxford University Press 2008) 61–89, 73–75; Adrian Blau, 'Majoritarianism under Pressure: the Electoral and Party Systems', in Robert Hazell (ed.), *Constitutional Futures* (Palgrave Macmillan 2008) 233–48; Alan Renwick, 'How Likely is Proportional Representation in the House of Commons? Lessons from International Experience' (2009) 44(4) Government and Opposition 366; Patrick Dunleavy and Helen Margetts, 'From Majoritarian to Pluralist Democracy? Electoral Reform in Britain since 1997' (2001) 13(3) Journal of Theoretical Politics 295.

90 Peter Dorey and Alexandra Kelso, *House of Lords Reform Since 1911 Must the Lords Go?* (Palgrave McMillan 2011) 222.

shown a hesitation with a fully elected House of Lords that may claim an equal level of democratic legitimacy.[91] Even if a cross-party consensus does emerge in some distant future favouring an elected second Chamber, the key questions remain about how the House of Lords would be elected – the majoritarian first-past-the-post vs the proportional representation. Now that the "electoral question" has become the key point of conflict among the main parties,[92] the question of "coherent reform agenda" and "political will" do not arise. In case of some fortuitous event in the future, the call for an elected House of Lords might get substantial traction, and another window of opportunity open. Then, the reform agenda and necessary political will should come rather quickly.

4.2 *Kelso's Contextual and Institutional Theory*

Alexandra Kelso's contextual and institutional account of reform endorses Norton's formal account but questions his attitudinal plank. She argues that the institutional values and norms may constitute formidable challenges for a "political will" for reform to emerge.[93] So, a mere attitudinal account will not sufficiently answer the reform questions. The institutional contexts – structures, norms, and processes to be considered. Philip Norton's attitudinal view fails to recognise the contexts around a reform initiative.

Within the Westminster-type parliamentary system, parliamentary sovereignty is being drained into executive dominance of the legislative process. The ministerial responsibility convention is utilised to undermine the accountability and scrutiny of government. Partisanship operates to whip and discipline the individual MPs. In the presence of these norms and values to the advantage of the government and party elites, it appears difficult to have sufficient "political will" behind the empowerment of Parliament and sufficient scope for the MPs to form and display their autonomous will powers. Philip Norton's window of opportunity, coherent reform agenda and political will for reform depend on how the country's political mode, intra-party tension, and leaders' control over their backbenchers play out in a given time. Therefore, Kelso acknowledges the role of political and institutional context that affects the reform.[94] She considers the norms and values such as parliamentary sovereignty, ministerial responsibility, executive dominance and strong party government – as the most important institutional contexts within which strategies

91 ibid, 218–221.

92 ibid, 224.

93 Kelso, *Parliamentary Reform at Westminster* (n 12) 5.

94 ibid, 6.

for institutional change must operate.[95] The contextual approach also values the institution's historical development to understand why reform does not always proceed as expected. From an institutional point of view, Kelso would ask three questions: "Why reform? Why now? Why have certain parliamentary reforms had differing degrees of success?"[96] Mathew Flinders' study of the UK Parliament's Modernisation Committee works during 2001–5 may provide a good case study for Kelso's contextual and institutional account.

The Modernisation Committee was established as soon as the "window of opportunity" was opened in May 1997, when the Labour government won the general election with an unprecedented majority comprising 418 seats out of 651 seats in the House of Commons. The first reform package of the Modernisation Committee (1997–2001) was based on a Labour-Liberal Joint Consultative Constitutional Reform Committee report prepared by J Robin Cook and Robert MacLennan. Its reform packages regarding the programming of legislative proposals and better engagement of the committees in legislative scrutiny received Cabinet endorsement. However, the government soon changed its mind, and by 2000, it became apparent that most of the Modernisation Committee proposals remained unimplemented by the government.[97] The second Modernisation Committee was constituted in June 2001. This time, the coherent reform agenda for modernisation, the second requirement of Norton, was provided by the works of the Newton Commission, working on behalf of the Hansard Society[98] and the Norton Commission, working on behalf of the Conservative party.[99] Finally, the appointment of Robin Cook as Leader of the House fulfilled the third requirement – the political will. Robin Cook was a senior, pro-reform leader and an astute parliamentary operator. Despite all these, the 2001–2005 window of opportunity yielded largely minor and "incremental-bound reforms"[100] that could not drastically empower the legislature vis-a-vis the executive. It is where Kelso's account of institutionalism – the institutional context – comes into play. Westminster's institutional context of executive dominance over the legislature was poised

95 ibid, 9–14.

96 ibid, 4.

97 Andrew Kennon, *The Commons: Reform or Modernisation* (The Constitution Unit, School of Public Policy, University College London 2000) 5–7.

98 Report of the Hansard Society Commission (Newton Commission) on Parliamentary Scrutiny, *The Challenge for Parliament: Making Government Accountable* (Hansard Society 2011).

99 Norton, 'Reforming Parliament' (n 11).

100 Matthew Flinders, 'Analysing Reform: the House of Commons 2001–5' (2007) 55 Political Studies 174, 176–179.

to resist proposals that might threaten the central aspects of its dominance, *e.g.,* the powers of the whips concerning appointments and electoral reforms. On the other hand, mild concessions that would not radically disturb the *status quo* but vent some of the frustrations of the backbench members, e.g., the Prime Minister's appearance before the Liaison Committee and payments for the select committee chairs, could be introduced.[101] Therefore, Kelso's contextual account of reform seems to better account for the Parliament's internal contexts that shape the success and failures of reform proposals.

Back to Bangladesh, Norton and Kelso's institutional approaches seem to make sense of most of Bangladesh's milestone political reforms mentioned at the beginning of this Chapter. Subsequent sections of this part will discuss some progressive and retrogressive milestones, such as the Introduction of the Parliamentary System in 1972, its Abolition in 1975, its Revival in 1991, and the Abolition of the Caretaker Government in 2011.

4.3 *Adoption of the Parliamentary System in 1972*

The military authoritarianism of undivided Pakistan and the *Bangalee* peoples' struggle against it caused the emergence of Bangladesh through a blood bath in 1971. The adoption of the Westminster parliamentary system in the Constitution of 1972 was informed by the failure of the Pakistani state to realise the parliamentary system in its letter and spirit. The Constituent Assembly of the newly independent Bangladesh was called into session on 10 April 1972. A 34-member Constitution Drafting Committee was set up among the Constituent Assembly members. The committee comprised five ministers of the government, with one of them as the Chairman of the Committee. All the committee members belonged to the ruling AL, except one lone opposition member from the National Awami Party (NAP). NAP, however, was an ideological ally of the then-ruling party. The Constitution came into force on 16 December 1972, the first liberation anniversary of Bangladesh.

It appears that Norton's first requirement of reform – the window of opportunity – was there in the newly independent Bangladesh. A historical political event – the Liberation War of 1971 – created a mass impasse for discarding the Pakistani era presidential authoritarianism. Norton's second requirement – a coherent reform agenda – was also drawn well before Pakistan's last parliamentary election in 1970.[102] The four structural pillars of the Bangladesh Constitution (secularism, socialism, democracy, meaning parliamentary

101 ibid, 196.

102 M Waheeduzzaman Manik, 'The historic six-point movement and its impact on the struggle for independence', *The Daily Star* (Dhaka, 7 June 2008).

democracy and nationalism) took shape in the Bangladeshi political parties' decades-long struggle against Pakistani political elites' religion-based politics of division, communal hatred, authoritarianism and capitalism. Norton's third requirement of political will was reflected in the conduct of Bangladesh's revolutionary government. Within months of the end of the liberation war with Pakistan, the first President of the country, *Bangabandhu* Sheikh Mujibur Rahman, abdicated his immense authoritarian wartime authority[103] and assumed the position of Prime Minister under a new provisional constitution which was designed in the Westminster Parliamentary format[104] and which worked as a blueprint for the Constitution Drafting Committee in 1972.

Considering Kelso's contextual point of view, there were understandable reasons that adopting the 1972 Constitution was relatively smooth. During the Constitution-making process, no significant opposition parties or groups would have questioned the four foundational pillars – including the Parliamentary Democracy. Bangladesh's pro-China leftist parties, who were not very enthusiastic about the liberation war and who had no representation in the Constituent Assembly, always questioned the legality of the formation of a Constituent Assembly based on a pre-war elected held in 1970 and promised to adopt a new constitution when they got a chance. The ruling party – AL's newly emerged political rival, the *Jatyo Sanajtantrik Dal* (JSD), criticised the monopolising tendency of AL and the lack of enough socialist guarantees in the Constitution. None of the operative political groups seriously questioned the four structural pillars. Later, when the political landscape changed, the military rulers of the mid-1970s favoured a presidential form of government over the parliamentary system and posed an existential challenge to the three other foundational pillars – namely, socialism, nationalism and secularism.[105] Ironically, the same context of one party and one person's monopoly over the

103 The Proclamation of Independence adopted on 10 April 1971, devised a Presidential form of government vesting in the President all the executive and legislative powers of the Republic, supreme command of the Armed Forces, power to appoint the Prime Minister and Cabinet, summon and adjourn the Constituent Assembly, levy taxes and authorize expenditures and "do all other things that may be necessary to give the people of Bangladesh an orderly and just Government."

104 On the 11th of January 1972, the President promulgated the Provisional Constitution of Bangladesh Order adopting a Westminster style government and making them bound by the Prime Minister's advice.

105 M Jashim Ali Chowdhury, 'Making and Unmaking the Constitution of Bangladesh', in Ngoc Bui Son and Mara Malagodi (eds.), *Asian Comparative Constitutional Law Volume 1: Constitution Making*, 363–382 (Hart Publishing: London 2023) 369.

constitutional agenda-setting explains how the Parliamentary System could be scrapped within three years after its adoption.

4.4 *Abolition of the Parliamentary System and Failure of the One-Party System in 1975*

As adopted in 1972, the Constitution was hailed as the most progressive Constitution of its time.[106] The initial years under the new Constitution, however, remained chaotic. By 1975, the country fell into emergency proclamation, a ruthless struggle for power, violent political opposition, a deteriorated law and order situation and the practical death of the parliamentary system.[107] Now the question is, why did the system immediately reverse in 1975? Alexandra Kelso's contextual and institutional understanding perhaps offers a convincing answer. The institutional context surrounding the constitution-making of 1972, the legal context within which the newly adopted Constitution started working and the political-cultural contexts within which the political leadership and the MPs operated would explain why this was the case.

First, while the 1972 window of opportunity was created and the reform agenda was crystallised through a mass and well-mobilised armed liberation war, the political will of a chosen few – especially that of *Bangabandhu* Sheikh Mujibur Rahman – controlled the formation, deliberation, and decisions of the 1972 Constituent Assembly. The personalising tendency of the power was apparent in almost every step – minor or major – of the post-war state-building process.[108] In 1972, the wartime Constituent Assembly was turned into the legislative branch. The legislature, however, was given the sole mandate of framing the Constitution within the shortest possible time.[109] The President was exercising the legislative power of the Republic advised by the Prime Minister. By the time the Constitution came into force in December 1972, the bulk of Bangladesh's civil, administrative, and public laws were built upon by the executive branch at the sole discretion of one leader – *Bangabandhu* Sheikh

106 Abul Fazl Huq, 'Constitution-Making in Bangladesh' (1973) 46(1) Pacific Affairs 59; Ridwanul Hoque, 'The Founding and Making of Bangladesh's Constitution', in Kevin YL Tan and Ridwanul Hoque (eds.), *Constitutional Foundings in South Asia* (Hart Publishing 2021) 91–119.

107 Moudud Ahmed, Bangladesh: Era of Sheikh Mujibur Rahman (Dhaka: University Press Ltd, 1983).

108 Firoj Ahmed, 'The Constitution of Bangladesh: Colonial Legacies'(Bangla) (*Rashtrochinta Blog*, 9 June 2020).

109 Chowdhury (n 6) 56.

Mujibur Rahman.[110] Therefore, the start of the "Westminster" Parliament of Bangladesh was a very low-key one. Throughout the later history of Bangladesh, parliaments would remain secondary in the legislation and policy process and almost always abdicate in favour of the Executive branch.

Secondly, as discussed in Chapter 3, the new Constitution of 1972 incorporated the floor-crossing bar or anti-defection clause – Article 70. This clause would later take Westminster's system of partisan whipping to a literal extreme level unheard of in other Westminster traditions. One commentator labelled it a "Damocles' sword"[111] over parliamentary backbenchers, leading to the Prime Minister's dictatorship under the Westminster parliamentary system's cloak. Therefore, the parliamentary committee system and backbench autonomy expected of a standard Westminster Parliament would not work in post-independence Bangladesh.

Thirdly, one of the most important requirements of the Westminster model – conservative-liberal bipartisanship was conspicuously missing in Bangladesh in 1972. The conservative political forces of undivided Pakistan coalesced around the Muslim League (ML) and Jamaat Islami (JI), both of whom actively opposed the liberation of Bangladesh and hence lost their right to do politics in the newly independent Bangladesh. In the first election following the Constitution, Awami League (AL), the party spearheading the 1971 liberation war, gained an absolute majority with only 6 MPs elected from the opposition.[112] The political vacuum created suddenly could not be filled up by the leftist political parties and other minority groups who had an insignificant mass base in the Bangladeshi political landscape.[113] The radical leftists attempted a counter-revolutionary challenge to the ruling party, AL, and created a dismal state of law and order situation across the country. The ruling party soon replied by creating paramilitary forces who resorted to extra-judicial killings and excessive human rights violations. The post-war absolutist grip of the ruling party over the power and its monopolising tendency conveyed an early warning that the Westminster Parliamentary System would face an uphill challenge in Bangladesh.

110 Justice Mustafa Kamal, *Bangladesh Constitution: Trends and Issues* (University of Dhaka, 1994) 6.

111 Justice Badrul Haider Chowdhury, Former Chief Justice of Bangladesh quoted in AKM Shamsul Huda, *Constitution of Bangladesh, Vol 2* (Rita Court, Chittagong, Bangladesh, 1997) 560.

112 Rounaq Jahan, 'Bangladesh in 1973: Management of Factional Politics' (1974) 14(2) Asian Survey 125.

113 Dina M Siddiqi, 'Secular Quests, National Others: Revisiting Bangladesh's Constituent Assembly Debates' (2018) 49(2) Asian Affairs 238, 245–246.

Fourthly, though AL emerged as a democratic and mass-based political party in its twenty-four-year-long political mobilisation against Pakistani authoritarianism, due to the lack of internal democracy and the strong presence of factionalism within it, the party could not be resolved through intra-party democratic competition. By 1975, the AL became Mujib's party by all accounts and standards. Missing the backbench autonomy required for the accountability of the government and absent any scope of a leadership challenge within the party, conspiracies and sabotage became the inevitable danger for the ruling elites. In January 1975, Prime Minister *Bangabandhu* Sheikh Mujibur Rahman disbanded the AL and switched the parliamentary system into a "French-styled presidential one"[114] in his capacity. The Fourth Amendment of 1975 introduced an all-party-combined-in-one system.[115] The Westminster Parliamentary was discarded within three years of its adoption, and a soviet style socialist party system was installed. Parliament and the judiciary were made subservient to the presidency.[116]

Seen through Norton's window, agenda and will triangle, in 1975, there was a window of opportunity (emergency and economic crisis), a clear reform agenda (the structure and ideals of a one-party system) and political will in the ruling party to abolish the caretaker government. Accordingly, the 1975 second revolution was done swiftly. However, the institutional contexts mattered, and the one-party system faced a stiff uphill challenge. It was reasonably believed that *Bangabandhu* attempted the "revolutionary change" without mobilising enough consensus and intra-party consultation. The Fourth Amendment of 1975 was passed in Parliament without any backbench input or participation and literally within minutes of tabling it on the floor. The major opposition party – JSD – vehemently opposed the move. Having little representation in Parliament, the pro-JSD actors within the military started mobilising. The disgruntled section of AL also conspired with the pro-JSD and pro-Pakistani elements in the military.[117] They seized the opportunity of *Bangabandhu*'s

114 Zillur R Khan, 'Bangladesh's Experiments with Parliamentary Democracy' (1997) 37(6) Asian Survey 575, 580; Syed Badrul Ahsan, 'Lifting the long silence on Baksal' *Dhaka Tribune* (Dhaka, 29 January 2020).

115 Md Morshedul Islam, 'The Politics behind the Passage of Fourth Amendment to the Constitution of the People's Republic of Bangladesh and Its Provisions: a Modest Analysis' (2014) 4(9) Public Policy and Administration Research 55.

116 Shakhawat Liton, 'Fourth Amendment: It 'impairs freedom of lower judiciary'' *The Daily Star* (Dhaka, 2 August 2017).

117 Abdul Mannan, 'The Conspiracy behind the Assassination of Bangabandhu' *The Daily Star* (Dhaka, 15 August 2016).

deteriorating public appeal.[118] He was brutally killed along with almost all of his family members on 15 August 1975. The One-Party System of 1975 died prematurely within months of its introduction. The pro-JSD elements within the military were soon eliminated, and the pro-Pakistani elements took power. Bangladesh took a turn towards the Pakistani-styled military presidential dictatorship.

These the historical, political and institutional contexts within which Bangladesh's 1972 Westminster system worked show that Kelso's contextual and institutional account of reform sufficiently explains why Bangladesh's Parliamentary System, as introduced in 1972, was so short-lived and how the institutional and cultural contexts shape formulation, implementation and success or failure of reform.

4.5 *Revival of the Parliamentary System in 1991*

After a decade-long political mobilisation against the post-1975 military dictators, Bangladesh restored the 1972 scheme of the Parliamentary System in 1991.[119] At the end of the 1990 mass upsurge against the military regime, there was a window of opportunity for change.[120] A coherent reform agenda was shaped by the end of 1990. During the mass mobilisation of the 1980s, political parties have already developed a national consensus on the parliamentary form of government. *Bangabandhu*'s party AL was revived in the 1980s, spearheaded the anti-regime movement and contested the fifth parliamentary election (1991) on an electoral promise of reviving the parliamentary system. The majority of the MPs of the fifth Parliament belonging to both AL and BNP favoured the parliamentary system. Even before that 1990 joint manifesto of the three political alliances staging street mobilisation against the military regime agreed that rubber stamp parliaments working under the military's presidential regime would be replaced with a Westminster parliament having institutional power to hold the government accountable.[121] The matter of

---

118 Emajuddin Ahmed, 'The Military and Democracy in Bangladesh', in RJ May, Viberto Selochan (eds.), *The Military and Democracy in Asia and the Pacific* (ANU Press 2004) 105–115; Amin Al Zaman, 'Party Factionalism in Bangladesh: a Case Study of the Awami League (1971–97)' (Ph.D. Thesis, Aligarh Muslim University 2004) 131–148.

119 Md. Masum Sikdar and Md. Mehedi Hasan Shohag, 'Democracy and Authoritarianism: Understanding Three Decades of Bangladesh Politics' (2016) 6(24) Research on Humanities and Social Sciences 6, 15.

120 Craig Baxter, 'Bangladesh a Parliamentary Democracy, if They Can Keep It' (1992) 91(563) Current History 132.

121 Talukder Maniruzzaman, 'The Fall of the Military Dictator: 1991 Elections and the Prospect of Civilian Rule in Bangladesh' (1992) 65(2) Pacific Affairs 203, 223.

political will was clumsy. The BNP Chairperson, Begum Khaleda Zia, elected the Prime Minister in the fifth parliamentary election, would continue with the presidential format. However, she could not resist the political momentum created for the system by the end of 1990.[122] The Twelfth Amendment to the Constitution of Bangladesh restored the 1972 constitutional formula of the Westminster parliamentary system.[123]

If considered through Kelso's contextual and institutional lens, it appears that there were other contextual reasons why Prime Minister Begum Khaleda Zia's personal preference for the presidential system had to give way to her backbench members' wishes. During the initial days of her reign over BNP, Khaleda Zia could not emerge as omnipotent a party leader as her husband, Major Ziaur Rahman, was. Relatively new in politics, Begum Zia had to consider the views of other senior leaders of the party. Moreover, her majority in the Fifth Parliament (1991–1996) was slim. Khaleda Zia's government was hinging on Jamat-i-Islami (JI)'s support, which favoured the parliamentary system. Her presidential nominee, Abdur Rahman Biswas, faced an uphill battle to win the presidential election, with as many as 46 party members refraining from voting. The opposition party AL was so far the strongest official opposition party in the parliamentary history of Bangladesh. AL and other opposition parties combined created immense pressure upon the government to restore the Parliamentary System. The joint manifesto of the three political alliances in the late 1990s was also not quite distant a memory. The result of the 1991 parliamentary election showed a very close contest between BNP and AL in terms of the percentage of each party's total votes. Given both parties' nearly equal popular support base, victory was guaranteed for the BNP in the presidential election. All combined, the people had a consensus over the parliamentary system.

A strong opposition party willing to assert its rightful participatory rights, AL presented its own draft bill. The government party BNP presented its own Bill, too. BNP's draft was heavily criticised; hence, the Parliament formed a special parliamentary committee comprising 8 ruling party members and 7 opposition party members. The committee's compromise draft was later placed for parliamentary approval. As per the constitutional requirement, the Twelfth Amendment had to be submitted to a referendum, which passed with an overwhelming majority.[124]

---

122 Nizam Ahmed, 'From Monopoly to Competition: Party Politics in the Bangladesh Parliament (1973–2001)' (2003) 76(1) Pacific Affairs 55.

123 Craig Baxter, 'Bangladesh in 1991: a Parliamentary System' (1992) 32(2) Asian Survey 162.

124 Muhammad A Hakim and Ahmed Shafiqul Huque, 'Governmental Change and Constitutional Amendments in Bangladesh' (1995) 2(2) South Asian Survey 255, 268–269.

4.6 *Abolition of the Caretaker Government in 2011*

However, the second life of Bangladesh's Westminster Parliamentary System soon fell into another round of illiberal, bipartisan and competitive authoritarianism.[125] Conflict over the electoral processes, strong personal rivalry between the party leaders and the emergence of personal and dynastic control over the parties lead to a chaotic phase of political violence and instability. At the end of the illiberal bipartisan phase (1994–2008), the government of AL that came to power in 2009 had a clear "window of opportunity" to institutionalise the Parliament. It had a landslide parliamentary majority, which gave it the power to amend the Constitution, work on the loopholes of the electoral system and institutionalise the democratic institutions. Coming to power with a much-celebrated political manifesto named the "Vision 2020",[126] the government is strongly committed to economic recovery, infrastructure, export and agricultural revolution. The new government showed decisive commitment to overcome the state's decade-long dilemma in trialling the persons and political parties accused of a crime against humanity and genocide during Bangladesh's liberation war in 1971.[127] The government, however, lacked the "political will" and "coherent agenda" for political reforms related to democratic governance, institution building, the rule of law, freedom of speech and political opposition.[128] The most decisive blow to the competitive bipartisanship and parliamentary democracy came in 2011.

Later, in 2011, the Appellate Division of the Supreme Court of Bangladesh controversially[129] declared the election time system of the caretaker government unconstitutional.[130] The Court declared it unconstitutional but still supported holding at least two next parliamentary elections under the system

---

125 Shafi Md Mostofa and DB Subedi, 'Rise of Competitive Authoritarianism in Bangladesh' (2021) 14(3) Politics and Religion 431.

126 Anupam Mazumdar and Husam Helmi Alharahsheh, 'Digital Bangladesh – Vision 2021: What is the Digital Bangladesh Concept?' (2020) 2(1) South Asian Research Journal of Engineering and Technology 6.

127 Suzannah Linton, 'Completing the Circle: Accountability for the Crimes of the 1971 Bangladesh War of Liberation' (2010) 21 Criminal Law Forum 191.

128 Ali Riaz, 'Legislature as a Tool of the Hybrid Regime: Bangladesh Experience,' (2019) 52(2) Political Science & Politics 275–276.

129 Mohammad Omar Faruque, 'Integrity Crisis of the Electoral System in Bangladesh: the 13th Amendment Judgment and Beyond' *Workshop on Constitutional Resilience in South Asia* (University of Melbourne, Australia, 5–7 December 2019); Ridwanul Hoque, 'Constitutionalism and the Judiciary in Bangladesh' in Sunil Khilnani, Vikram Raghavan and Arun K Thiruvengadam (eds.), *Comparative Constitutionalism in South Asia* (New Delhi: OUP 2013) 317.

130 *Abdul Mannan Khan v. Bangladesh* 64 DLR (AD) (2012) 107.

slightly modified in terms of its composition.[131] The government was quick to cease upon the opportunity. Ignoring the Appellate Division's recommendation to arrange two more elections under the caretaker government system, the top government leadership supported its abolition. The opposition parties under BNP's leadership started airing serious grievances at this. Months before the Supreme Court judgement, an All-Party Parliamentary Committee was finalising proposals for the upcoming Fifteenth Amendment to restore the original Constitution's dislodged principles. It consulted hundreds of constitutional experts, Supreme Court judges, civil society leaders, journalists, and people from different walks of life.[132] As of March 2011, the committee was convinced that the caretaker government was still necessary but needed reform.[133] On 10 May 2021, the Appellate Division of the Supreme Court passed the judgment. Parliamentary Committee followed up on the matter within the next two weeks and, on 29 May 2011, concluded that the system should be retained subject to some modifications. However, the committee was called to a "meeting" with Prime Minister Sheikh Hasina the next day. The Prime Minister had already switched her position after the 10 May decision of the Supreme Court, and now she stood for the total abolition of the caretaker government. After the meeting, the committee decided to take a position of silence on the issue.[134] Months later, the Fifteenth Amendment of 2011 abolished the caretaker government, despite a visible necessity of the system's continuance for a short term at least.[135] The amendment was passed. BNP took straight to the street but to no avail. Since then, three controversial elections have been held under the AL government – one in January 2014, the second in December 2018 and the latest in January 2024.[136] Both the elections were marked by utterly exposed electoral frauds and won by AL in landslides, and Bangladesh turned essentially into

131 Nizam Ahmed, 'Abolition or Reform? Non-party Caretaker System and Government Succession in Bangladesh' (2011) 100 (414) Round Table: the Commonwealth Journal of International Affairs 303.

132 Adeeba Aziz Khan, 'The Politics of Constitutional Amendments in Bangladesh: the Case of the Non-political Caretaker Government' (2015) 3 International Review of Law 11–13.

133 Nizam Ahmed, 'Party Politics under a non-party Caretaker Government in Bangladesh: the Fakhruddin Interregnum (2007–09)' (2010) 48(1) Commonwealth and Comparative Politics 23.

134 Maimul Ahsan Khan, 'Constitutional Disaster and 'Legal' Impunity: Constitutional Amendments in Perspective', *Asian Human Rights Commission* <http://www.humanrights.asia/resources/journals-magazines/article2/special-report-inexistent-rule-of-law-in-bangladesh/04-2/> accessed 30 July 2024.

135 Khan (n 65) 198.

136 Ole Solvang, *Democracy in the crossfire: Opposition Violence and Government Abuses in the 2014 pre-and post-election period in Bangladesh* (Human Rights Watch 2014).

a system of one-party authoritarianism. The government's unilateral move to scrap the caretaker government system later resulted in total paralysation of the parliamentary system and opposition-less one-party Parliament.

Seen through Kelso's Contextual and Institutional lens, the abolition of Bangladesh's caretaker government system constitutes a clear example of how the political contexts, intra-party power distribution and institutional weaknesses of the Parliament contribute to the retrogressive changes in the system. First, the change was guided by Prime Minister Sheikh Hasina's sole discretion and personal behest, whose grip over her Party (AL) and the Parliament was absolute in all possible senses. Therefore, the suppression of the Constitution Reform Committee epitomises the institutional weaknesses of the political parties and their falling hostages to the whims of the persons in the lead.[137]

Secondly, the main opposition party, BNP and its allies have been boycotting the Parliament since January 2011. It also refused to nominate any of its members to the Fifteen Member Special Committee. In doing this, the BNP lost all possible scopes of registering their protest in the institutional channel. It took it to the street but with significantly low strength that might be required to force the government to reconsider its position. Several amendment proposals to the Fifteenth Amendment Bill tabled by leftist political allies of the ruling party were comfortably rejected by voting in the House. The ruling party's historical disregard for the opposition parties and the extra-parliamentary mode of parliamentary opposition has again facilitated an illiberal reform in Bangladesh.

Thirdly, the government presented the Constitution (Fifteenth Amendment) Bill on 25 June 2011. It was passed on the same day without further scrutiny and any significant debate on the matter. Knowing the Prime Minister's choice, no single backbench MP from the ruling party criticised the Bill or its position. The amendment was passed within minutes without any substantial discussion on the floor.[138] Done in a way much similar to the Fourth Amendment of 1975, it completes a cycle of constitutional evolution in Bangladesh and reconfirms the frustrating absence of intra-party democracy within the Bangladeshi political parties.

137 M Ehteshamul Bari, 'The Incorporation of the System of Non-Party Caretaker Government in the Constitution of Bangladesh in 1996 as a Means of Strengthening Democracy, Its Deletion in 2011 and the Lapse of Bangladesh into Tyranny Following the Non-Participatory General Election of 2014: a Critical Appraisal' (2018) 28(1) Transnational Law and Contemporary Problems 27.

138 Khan (n 134).

5 Conclusion

This Chapter tried to make sense of the parliamentary reforms attempted in Bangladesh and consider how the political culture, attitude, institutional structures, and processes determined their fate. While the "lack of political will" in addressing the procedural and technical flaws of Parliament appears to be an apparent cause of no-reform or retrogressive reform,[139] a deeper appreciation of Bangladesh's reform politics shows that the political actors, their attitude, the culture of distrust, hatred and monopolisation, and the institutional landscape of parliamentary politics determine the outcome of the initiatives.

Political institutions owe their existence to a process of deliberative institution-building realised through public deliberation and informed choice. Absent the scope of adequate deliberation and public participation, democratic instrumentalism is almost certain to be missing. The participatory, inclusive and deliberative democratic process also forms the bedrock of Congleton's "Constitutional Bargain Model", Olsen's "Democratic Instrumental Vision", Norton's "Window-Agenda-Will Triangle", and Kelso's "Institutional Context Thesis". These four theories considered in this Chapter form part of the institutional design literature broadly influenced by the institutional logic of "rational choice".[140]

Rational choice institutionalists argue that institutional changes happen only when the individuals in charge of the institutions find a reform proposal convenient to their best rational interests. While individuals might be motivated by their internal rationality, they should be able to find a collective rational choice for the institution they comprise.[141] Although there are questions as to whether all the individual preferences could be informed ones, whether the choices would be predominantly 'rational', whether the individuals' rational choices could always be identifiable with the institutions' best interests,[142]

139 Editorial, 'Decline of Parliamentary Governance: Indian Scenario,' (2017) 3(2) Rostrum's Law Review 1.

140 M Zey, 'Rational Choice and Organization Theory' in Neil J Smelser and Paul B Baltes (eds.), *International Encyclopedia of the Social & Behavioral Sciences* 12751–12755 (Elsevier, 2001).

141 Mark P Petracca, The Rational Choice Approach to Politics: a Challenge to Democratic Theory (1991) 53(2) The Review of Politics 289, 314–15; J Mansbridge, 'Self-interest in the Explanation of Political Life' (1990) 18(1) Political Theory 132.

142 Mark Tushnet, 'Authoritarian Constitutionalism' (2015) 100 Cornell Law Review 391, 440 (Tushnet argues, in relation to Singapore, that even some autocrats might have "steady desires of national glory or economic development" which might be separate from their personal interest in prolongation of power).

whether all individual rationalities will ultimately merge into a common collective institutional rationality;[143] the rational choice logic continues to be a strong foundation of institutional reform theories. Particularly on the possibility of amalgamation of individual rationalities into one common institutional rationality, Petracca argues that the processes of democratic deliberation could help to refine "individual self-interest" "for the discovery and creation of the collective public good."[144] Unsurprisingly, the institutional designers or constitutional bargainers in power and those out of power may not always have clear, consistent, and stable goals. In such cases, the outcome would depend on the scope of participatory influence of other public and societal institutions and interest groups in the process.

Democratic deliberation, therefore, requires a participatory citizen body and a system of governmental accountability to the people's representatives. Reforms bargained between the non-representative miniscule political or intellectual elites run every risk of abruptly ignoring long-term institutional goals. This Chapter's evaluation of Bangladesh's various parliamentary reform initiatives through the institutional context-based theories, such as those of Congleton, Olsen, Norton and Kelso, suggests that the mighty regimes of the dynastic, patriarchal and clientelist party system, the absolute authority of the Prime Ministers and party leaders over their respective parties and the resultant lack of participatory political processes are standing on the way to the Parliament's institutionalisation in Bangladesh. Bangladesh's 'informal rules of politics',[145] for example, clientelism and patrimonialism,[146] personal charisma,[147] and privatisation of public interests,[148] often substitute the formal structures and processes.[149] Therefore, institutional designers in power and opposition do not prioritise institutional goals over their self-serving and

---

143 Francis Fukuyama, *Identity: the Demand for Dignity and the Politics of Resentment* (Farrar, Straus and Giroux, 2018) (Fukuyama argues that apart from individual self-interest, people are likely to care about human dignity and values also).

144 Petracca (n 140) 317–319.

145 Eric Wold, 'Kinship, Friendship and Patron-Client Relations in Complex Societies', in Eric Wolf (ed.), *Pathways of Power* (California: University of California Press 2001) 167.

146 S Aminul Islam, 'The Predicament of Democratic Consolidation in Bangladesh' (2006) 3(2) *Bangladesh e-Journal of Sociology* 4.

147 Goran Hyden, *African Politics in Comparative Perspective* (Cambridge: Cambridge University Press, 2006) 94–116; Michael Bratton, 'Formal Versus Informal Institutions in Africa' (2007) 18 *Journal of Democracy* 97.

148 Mushtaq Khan, 'Markets, States and Democracy: Patron-Client Networks and the case for Democracy in Developing Countries' (2005) 12(5) *Democratization* 704, 714.

149 Hans Joachim Lauth, 'Informal Institutions and Democracy,' (2000) 7 *Democratization* 21, 25.

short-term political goals.[150] Absent a fair and free process of political competition and the participatory influence of other public and societal institutions and interests, reform proposals, including the vague and broad reform agenda that are being aired by Bangladesh's newly formed "interim" government, are mostly impulse driven, short-sighted, hurriedly framed, or purposefully destructive.[151]

As Muzaffar and Seidher put it, the difference between authoritarian and democratic actors lies in their attitude towards uncertainty. While the former seeks to reduce the uncertainty of outcomes, the latter works to reduce the uncertainty of institutions.[152] For the five decades of Bangladesh's existence, political parties worked to reduce the uncertainty of their retaining power. Therefore, the country has failed to establish any political consensus about the periodic and orderly power transfer. Different make-shift solutions and proposals inspired by temporal impulses have been suggested. In contrast, the conversation on the political party system, intra-party democracy, professional civil service, independent Election Commission or other integrity institutions, and most importantly, an institutionalised parliamentary system has been consciously avoided.

---

150 Steven Levitsky and Gretchen Helmke, 'Informal Institutions and Comparative Politics: a Research Agenda' (Working Paper 307, Kellogg Institute for International Studies, September 2003) 5.

151 M Jashim Ali Chowdhury, 'Fifty Years of Electioneering in Bangladesh: the collapse of constitutional design', in M Rafiqul Islam and Muhammad Ekramul Haque (eds.) *The Constitutional Law of Bangladesh: Progression and Transformation at its 50th Anniversary* (Springer Nature: Singapore, 2023) 173–193.

152 Mozaffar and Schedler (n 47) 11.

CHAPTER 7

The "Eastminster Deviations" and Ways Ahead

1 Introduction

Bangladesh's original constitutional scheme of 1972 was purportedly a Westminster parliamentary system. The choice was influenced, among others, by postcolonial political elites' over-appreciation of the British parliamentary system as the most adaptable institution for Commonwealth countries. In the case of the newly independent Bangladesh, a desire to reverse the decades-long suppression by Pakistani authoritarian presidentialism also provided strong motivation. However, fifty years into its constitutional beginning, Bangladesh had undergone different cycles of constitutional changes involving one-party presidentialism, military dictatorships, unelected non-political caretaker governments, illiberal bipartisanships, and, again, the latest ongoing round of one-party monopoly. Curiously, the vicious cycle of constitutional dismemberment and restoration, realised through several constitutional amendments, shows that the 1972 scheme of the parliamentary system has a remarkable level of perseverance. Except for three brief intervals from 1975–1979, 1982–1984 and 2007–2008, Bangladesh parliament endured as a constitutional institution, albeit subject to the limitations imposed by various presidential, military, extra-constitutional and authoritarian party governments. Though the country is now being ruled another extra-constitutional "interim" government (August 2024) who talks about reforming the country from its root, there seems to no outright rejection of the idea of parliamentary system. This book attempted to evaluate the institutional value that the Parliament of Bangladesh (*Jatiya Sangsad*) has carried within this paradox of constitutional design and its political mishandling.

Chapters 3–5 considered the Parliament's constitutional position, role and contribution within a quadrangular accountability framework involving the legislature, executive, judiciary and people. Chapter 6 considered the problems that prevent progressive reform and institutionalisation of parliament. It transpired throughout the discussions that three of Kumarasingham's five "Eastminster Deviations", identified in Chapter 1, determine the parliament's operational logic. The three identified Eastminster deviations are – the 'selective dictatorship' over the country's governance, an undemocratic and dynastic party system and the absence of an ideologically grounded liberal-conservative bipartisanship.

 | DOI:10.1163/9789004720831_008

2 Three "Eastminster" Deviations

Typical of a Westminster parliament, the Parliament of Bangladesh is dominated by the executive branch, *i.e.,* the Cabinet. However, the ascendancy of the executive here is accompanied by a near abdication of meaningful debate and scrutiny on the floor and committee stages, which is not a Westminster-like norm by any means. The "Selective Dictatorship" – absolute dominance of one or a chosen few from certain families or coteries over the political parties, government, and administrative hierarchies has created absolute command, not the Westminster's typical "whipping", over the parliament members.[1] In selective dictatorships, the rule of political selection – the people's access to the political parties, leadership and power – is determined to the advantage of the chosen or fortunate few.[2] It effectively cuts down the Westminster system's vertical chain of delegation that flows from the people to the political parties through the Cabinet to the Prime Minister.

Secondly, Bangladesh has utterly failed the core Westminster norms of liberal-conservative competitiveness within a two-party setup and institutionalised opposition. Bangladesh's parliamentary system is un-forgivingly harsh to the opposition.[3] Though the power has been alternated between the country's two major political parties – AL and BNP – several times since the independence, principled liberal-conservative competition has suffered a setback thanks to the historical distrust between the two parties and animosity between their leaders.[4] The Speakers of successive parliaments remained staunchly loyal to their parties and showed reluctance to assert their discretion beyond their party dictates. It has resulted in an endemic disincentive for the opposition parties to air their opposition through parliamentary channels.[5] As Ahmed observed:

1 Nizam Ahmed, 'Parliament-Executive Relations in Bangladesh' (1997) 3(4) The Journal of Legislative Studies 70, 85–88.

2 Sadiat Mannan Md Harun-Or-Rashid Jens Stanislawski Niaz Ahmed Khan, 'Realpolitik: Democratic, Embeddedness within Major Political Parties in Bangladesh', *BRAC Institute of Governance Studies, Working Paper No 25* (BRAC University Dhaka, 2015) 27–28.

3 Mohammad Mohabbat Khan and Syed Anwar Husain, 'Process of Democratization in Bangladesh' (1996) 5(3) Contemporary South Asia 319, 331.

4 Elora Shehabuddin, 'Bangladesh in 1999: Desperately Seeking a Responsible Opposition' (2000) 40(1) Asian Survey 181, 185.

5 Rounaq Jahan and Amundsen, *The Parliament of Bangladesh: Representation and Accountability* (Centre for Policy Dialogue and Chr. Michelsen Institute, Dhaka and Bergen, 2012) 54.

> Unlike other democratic systems, where the opposition is at least listened to, if not always consulted, the government in Bangladesh generally looked upon the opposition with suspicion.[6]

On the flip side, the opposition also remained unforgivingly extra-parliamentary. Opposition parties in Bangladesh have historically preferred the streets over the House.[7] The trend started with the country's independence in 1971 and continued throughout the later decades. Even the revival of parliamentary democracy at the beginning of the 1990s through a historic mass-upsurge against military authoritarianism could not mark an exception to the trend.[8] Violence on the street and reckless use of force as a demonstration tool has faded the prospect of a workable Westminster Parliamentary System.[9]

Historically, there have been four types of parliamentary opposition in Bangladesh – no opposition,[10] marginal opposition,[11] strong but disruptive and boycotting opposition,[12] and domesticated

---

6 Nizam Ahmed (n 1) 90.

7 M Jashim Ali Chowdhury, 'In Search of Parliamentary Opposition in Bangladesh' *IACL-AIDC Blog* (University of Melbourne, 21 January 2021).

8 Shehabuddin (n 4).

9 Nizam Ahmed, 'From Monopoly to Competition: Party Politics in the Bangladesh Parliament (1973–2001)' (2003) 76(1) Pacific Affairs 55; M Moniruzzaman, 'Parliamentary Democracy in Bangladesh: an Evaluation of the Parliament during 1991 – 2006' (2009) 47(1) Commonwealth and Comparative Politics 100.

10 Nizam Ahmed, *The Bangladesh Parliament A Data Handbook* (Institute of Government Studies (IGS), BRAC University, Dhaka, 2013) 31–32 (Bangladesh's First (1972–1975) and Sixth (March-April 1996) parliaments had no opposition in a practical sense. In the First Parliament, only 7 opposition and independent members (out of 300) were elected. In the Sixth Parliament, only 11 (out of 300) opposition and independent members were elected).

11 ibid (in Bangladesh's Second, Eighth and Ninth parliaments, the majority of the ruling parties were absolute. The *Second (1979–1981) Parliament* of Bangladesh was constituted through an election conducted by servile Election Commission saw the President's party sweeping it and a small number of opposition party candidates got elected. The Second Parliament had a total of 93 (out of 300) opposition and independent members elected. The *Eighth Parliament (2001–2006)*, though elected through an election organised under a non-party caretaker government, saw only 90 (out of 300) opposition and independent members elected. The *Ninth Parliament (2009–2013)*, another one elected under a caretaker government, had only 43 (out of 300) opposition and independent elected).

12 Ahmed (n 1); Nizam Ahmed, 'Parliamentary Opposition in Bangladesh: a Study of its Role in the Fifth Parliament' (1997) 3(2) Party Politics 147 (The Third, Fifth and Seventh Parliaments saw very strong ratio of opposition presence. The ruling party in those parliaments however refused to allow the opposition their rightful participation in parliamentary process. The opposition parties also showed seriously disruptive tendencies and rather preferred to boycott the parliament and resort to street agitation and violence. The

opposition[13] and co-opted opposition.[14] The opposition's minimal power to influence and contribute to the parliamentary process encouraged them to base their activities on street agitation and other extra-parliamentary avenues. To take an example, absenteeism in the seventh (1996–2001), eighth (2001–2005) and ninth (2009–2013) parliaments were 43 per cent, 60 per cent and 75 per cent, respectively.[15] While opposition participation in the Tenth

---

Third Parliament (1984–1986) had a total of 147 (out of 300) opposition and independent members elected. The military ruler of the time dissolved it within two years of its election, finding the margin of his parliamentary majority slim and uncomfortable. Excluding the government party and its coalition partners, the *Fifth Parliament (1991–1995)* had 142 (out of 300) elected opposition and independent members. Three years into its tenure, the opposition parties resigned from the Parliament and staged one of the most violent political agitations in the history of Bangladesh demanding the introduction of a caretaker government. Excluding the ruling party and its collation partner, the *Seventh Parliament (1996–2001)* had the 122 opposition and independent members elected. The opposition party, however, boycotted the Parliament consistently and preferred street agitation).

13 The Fourth, Tenth and Eleventh Parliaments saw the presence of what is called "domesticated opposition" who happened to the political allies of the ruling party but participated the election to fill up the vacuum created by the main opposition parties boycotting the parliamentary election. In the Fourth (1998–1990) Parliament a so-called Combined Opposition Party coalesced hurriedly at the behest of the President, participated the election boycotted by the mainstream opposition parties, got elected in some seats and then played the dummy opposition's role in the Parliament. In the Tenth Parliament (2014–2018) the ruling party's coalition partner Jatya Party (JP) contested the election boycotted by all other major political parties, got elected in some seats left uncontested by the ruling party and they even took ministerial positions within the cabinet. JP continues to play a similar role in the Eleventh Parliament (2019–2024), though there are around 6 members elected from the main opposition party – BNP in an election widely believed to be rigged in the ruling party's favour.

14 In the Twelfth Parliament (January-August 2024), 62 independent candidates got elected by beating candidates from the majority party Awami League and other political parties. Interestingly, 58 of them were members of the Awami League who contested elections against candidates nominated by the AL high command. Due to the absence of BNP and allied parties, AL wanted the election to be competitive and, hence, did not discipline its rebel candidates. As a result, the 62 independent candidates emerged as the biggest block of the non-ruling party MPs. This time, the Jatya Party (JP) got only 11 seats. Per the Parliament's Rules of Procedure, the Independents could form a block and claimed the status of the main opposition. However, the AL high command instructed its independent MPs not to do so. With its 11 seats, JP was recognised as the main opposition party. The problem with this scenario was that JP constantly risked losing its main opposition status. If the situation required it, AL might not have hesitated to create an opposition block out of its independent MPs and out seat the JP from the opposition bench. This co-opted opposition brand appeared even more damaging than the domesticated version Bangladesh saw earlier.

15 Jahan and Amundsen (n 5).

(2014–2018) and Eleventh Parliaments (2019–2024) is strikingly good, it fails to qualify as a positive development for a peculiar reason. With the BNP boycotting the 2014 election, the Jatya Party (JP)'s role as the official opposition in the Tenth Parliament was merely ceremonial. This time, the opposition unusually took ministerial positions and cooperated, rather than critiqued, the government. The JP did not take any ministerial position in the eleventh parliament. However, their leaders and members maintained strong ties with the ruling party. The trend of domesticated opposition has taken a new twist in the newly formed Twelfth Parliament (2024-present), where the independent MPs constitute the largest non-ruling party block. However, almost all of the independents are members of the ruling party who got elected on non-partisan tickets, and the ruling party has allowed JP, with its mere 11 seats, to be the main opposition.

Thirdly, the absence of democracy within the political parties and the rise of competitive dynasties have effectively shut down the MPs on the floor and the committees.[16] Though routinely asked and answered, the parliamentary questions disappointingly fail to touch upon key accountability issues of the government and bureaucracy.[17] Government backbenchers take a strict party line on the House and committees alike. Successive parliaments, therefore, invariably failed to criticise the governmental policies and actions, let alone make them accountable.[18] Lack of intra-party democracy and accumulation of absolute and unquestionable authority in person, family or political dynasty's favour prevents leadership selection from the bottom.

3 Parliament's Failure to Hold the Executive Accountable

As mentioned in Chapter 3, the Bangladesh Parliament's capacity to enforce even a foundational Westminster convention – the Ministerial Responsibility is doubtful. The Parliament is reduced to a mere legitimizer's position in the legislation and national policy process. It has been materialized by clogging

16 Ahmed Shafiqul Huque, 'Accountability and Governance: Strengthening Extra-bureaucratic Mechanisms in Bangladesh' (2011) 60(1) International Journal of Productivity and Performance Management 59, 68.

17 Salahuddin Aminuzzaman, 'Institutional Processes and Practices of Administrative Accountability: Role of Jatya Sangsad in Bangladesh' (1993) 10(2) South Asian Studies 44, 55.

18 Muhammad Mustafizur Rahman, 'Parliament and Good Governance: a Bangladeshi Perspective' (2008) 9(1) Japanese Journal of Political Science 39, 47–48.

the parliament's control over its agenda and cartelizing the parliamentary committees.

3.1 *Ministerial (Non)Responsibility*

Bangladesh's party leadership is purely selective and non-democratic. Parties thrive and run based on personal allegiance and hereditary family lines.[19] In such a system, the scope of grassroots party members being nominated as party candidates in the parliamentary election through democratic processes is almost non-existent. As per articles 55(3) and 57(2) of the Constitution of Bangladesh, if the Prime Ministers cease to retain the support of a majority of the members of parliament, they shall either resign their office. As a rule of collective ministerial responsibility, a Prime Minister's fall would mean the Cabinet's fall.[20] Though partisan cohesion and whipping are likely to prevent the fall of a government through a motion of no confidence in Westminster, the Prime Ministers in the UK frequently face a leadership challenge from the party backbenchers. However, no prime minister in Bangladesh has ever faced a no-confidence motion in the parliament, nor did they face a leadership challenge from within their parties. For Individual Ministerial Responsibility, Article 58(2) of the constitution has made a Minister answerable to the Prime Minister. Article 58 empowers the prime minister to ask for a minister's resignation, failing which the president would be advised to terminate such minister. While members of parliament may ask questions, call attention, seek explanation, or criticize a minister in a highly exceptional case, they cannot enforce his resignation unless the Prime Minister so intends.

3.2 *A Mere Legitimizer*

The Bangladesh parliament's general capability to deliberate and influence the legislation has been minimal. In the parliamentary system, there must be an acknowledgement of the opposition's right to exist and their right to contribute to the parliamentary business. Strict partisan control over the legislative process has minimized the parliament's ability to legislate. Until the mid-1990s, governments frequently legislated through presidential ordinances. After the demise of military rule in 1990, around one-third of laws passed by the Fifth Parliament (1991–1996) were the approval of presidential ordinances issued

---

19 Md Enayet Ullah Patwary, 'Democratization and Intra-Party Democracy: Bangladesh Experience' (2022) 16(4) Society and Change 67.

20 The Constitution of the People's Republic of Bangladesh, art. 58(4) <http://bdlaws.minlaw.gov.bd/act-367.html> accessed 13 October 2023.

earlier.[21] Most of them, including most other regular parliamentary bills, did not go through committee scrutiny either.[22] The number of ordinances has decreased since the Seventh Parliament (1996–2001). However, the parliament's legislative power did not increase. Transparency International Bangladesh (TIB)'s study of the incumbent parliament's legislative activities in 2019 shows that it spent an average of 32 minutes passing each bill laid on the table. The time included time for formal presentment, MPs' discussion, the minister's speech and voting.[23] One of the latest examples of the trend has been the Chief Election Commissioner and other Election Commissioners' Appointment Act, 2022.[24] The Act established a Search Committee to appoint the Chief Election Commission Commissioner and other Election Commissioners.[25] While the government defiantly resisted a call to pass such a law until December 2021,[26] it suddenly changed its mind in early January 2022. In late January 2022, the bill was passed with lightning speed and without adequate deliberation.[27]

Unlike the UK, there are no "Usual Channels" and "Pairing System"[3] in Bangladesh that could yield a more vigilant role for the parliamentary opposition in the legislative process. Also, the procedural tool for countering opposition obstructionism is very crude. While the ruling party in the UK would choose from one of the Closure Motion, Guillotine Motion and Programming Motions, the Bangladesh Parliament allows the government to invoke a closure motion straight, halt the debate and put the question to voting and there.[28] Apart from the government motion of closure, the Speaker is authorised to note the "sense of the House" to limit the "discussion on any stage of the Bill" and immediately put the question to vote.[29] Also, much to the comfort of the ruling party, consistently partisan Speakers tend to ignore opposition amendments

21 Md Abdul Halim, *Constitution, Constitutional Law and Politics: Bangladesh Perspective* (2nd Ed, Dhaka: Md Yusuf Ali Khan 2003) 261–164; M Habibur Rahman, 'Our Experience with Constitutionalism' (1998) 2(2) Bangladesh Journal of Law 115, 126.

22 Nizam Ahmed, 'In Search of Institutionalisation: Parliament in Bangladesh' (1998) 4(4) The Journal of Legislative Studies 34, 55.

23 Transparency International Bangladesh, 'Parliament Watch, Eleventh Parliament (1st to 5th Sessions; January-December 2019)' (TIB, Dhaka, September 2020) 17.

24 The Chief Election Commissioner and other Election Commissioners Appointment Act, 2022 (Act No 1 of 2022).

25 ibid sec. 5, 6.

26 Partha Pratim Bhattacharjee and Mohiuddin Alamgir, 'EC Formation: Chance of a law slim', *The Daily Star* (Dhaka: 23 December 2021).

27 Staff Correspondence, 'EC formation bill placed in JS amid opposition' *The New Age* (Dhaka: New Age, 23 January 2022).

28 The Rules of Procedure (RoP) of Bangladesh *Jatya Sangsad* 1973, rule. 290(2).

29 ibid r 291.

in general.[30] While Standing Order 14 of the UK House of Commons allows 20 opposition days and thirty-five backbench days for debates on the floor, Bangladesh Parliament is content with weekly dates assigned to consider private member bills.

3.3 *Controlled Deliberation*

On a general appraisal, the legislative procedure in Bangladesh is controlled by the discretion of the executive. However, the executive's control is marked by an unprecedented scale of abdication of debate in the House and the committees. The constitution contains an anti-defection clause, Article 70, which bars the members from voting against their parties on the floor of parliament. Article 70's purpose and impact have been widely debated. The framers of the constitution justified it as a protection against amoral defections by the MPs and the consequent fall of governments.[31] Though it is popularly identified as the sole troublemaker in Bangladesh's parliamentary politics, the article does not appear to be the only reason for the lack of backbench assertiveness.[32] Apart from a voting restriction, it does not bar the MPs from debating their government's policies on the House floor and scrutinising the government in the committees. Though the controversial article 70 does not attack the committee proceedings, backbenchers have habitually and invariably taken strict party lines. The overall trend in the executive-legislature relation is, therefore, a dominant-dormant one.[33]

3.4 *Cartelized Committees*

The ascendancy of the executive branch has also led to a near abdication of meaningful scrutiny in parliamentary committees. In Bangladesh, parliamentary committees play only a marginal role in ensuring accountability and legislative quality.[34] Bangladesh's parliamentary standing committee system suffers structural (institutional and procedural), political and behavioural

---

30 Nizam Ahmed, 'Development and Working of Parliaments in South Asia' (2001) 9(1) Asian Journal of Political Science 18, 29.

31 Sabbir Ahmed, 'Article 70 of the Constitution of Bangladesh: Implications for the Process of Democratisation' (2010) 31 (1) BIISS Journal 1, 3–7.

32 Hasanuzzaman, 'To amend Article 70 or not', *The New Age* (Dhaka, 22 April 2011).

33 MM Khan, *Dominant Executive and Dormant Legislature: Executive-Legislature Relations in Bangladesh* (India: South Asian Publishers Pvt Ltd, 2006).

34 Quamrul Alam and Julian Teicher, 'The State of Governance in Bangladesh: the Capture of State Institutions' (2012) 35(4) South Asia: Journal of South Asian Studies 858, 876–880.

(attitudinal) setbacks.[35] Party influence over the committee agenda and hard-lined party stances of the members on key issues hamper the committees' autonomous functioning. Partisan control over the appointment of members and chairs of the committees jeopardises the committees' assertiveness and retards their expertise. Committees have been structurally weakened by factors like Ministers' presence in the Committee as *ex officio* members, nominal logistic support for the committees and the negative attitude of the bureaucracy towards the committees. Political governments usually try to bypass or control committees scrutinising bills or ministries.[36] The development of a committee system *vis-a-vis* the bureaucracy has also been asymmetrical.[37] There is not much political will to change the status quo either.[38] Governments have consistently maintained a "step-mother or step-brother" attitude towards the committees.[39] Therefore, the committee system continues to suffer structural (institutional and procedural), political and behavioural (attitudinal) dilemmas.[40]

On the political level, party influence over the committee agenda and hard-lined party stances of the members on key issues hampers the autonomous functioning of the committees. On a behavioural analysis, the political clog over the conscience and autonomy of the party MPs and their inexperience have contributed substantially to the below-the-bench performance of the committees. Partisan control over appointing committee members and chairs has jeopardised assertiveness and expertise development in many ways. Committee works offer almost no career prospects for the members.[41] The scope of deliberation on committee reports and dissenting opinions in the House is very limited in Bangladesh. The minority members in the committees

35 Nizam Ahmed, 'Reforming the Parliament in Bangladesh: Structural Constraints and Political Dilemmas' (1998) 36(1) Commonwealth and Comparative Politics 68, 71; Nizam Ahmed, 'Parliamentary Committees and Parliamentary Government in Bangladesh' (2001) 10(1) Contemporary South Asia 11, 31–33.

36 Ahmed (n 1) 77–78, Nizam, 'Reforming the Parliament (n 35).

37 ATM Obaidullah, 'Standing Committees on Ministries in the Bangladesh Parliament: the Need for Reorganisation' (2011) 18(2) South Asian Survey 317, 322.

38 Muhammad Mustafizur Rahaman, 'The Limits of Foreign Aid in Strengthening Bangladesh's Parliament: Analysis of the U.N.'s Strengthening Parliamentary Democracy Project' (2010) 50(3) Asian Survey 474, 483–94.

39 Muhammad Mustafizur Rahman, 'Parliament and Good Governance: a Bangladeshi Perspective' (2008) 9(1) Japanese Journal of Political Science 39.

40 Nizam Ahmed, 'Parliamentary Committees' (n 35).

41 Navid Saifullah, 'Effectiveness of the Parliamentary Standing Committees in Bangladesh' (Masters in Governance and Development Thesis: BRAC University Dhaka 2006).

are usually not allowed to prepare and submit their report except to record a "note of dissent," which is appended to the committee report.[42]

In short, centralization of the party and government authorities in persons rather than the institutions (selective dictatorship), lack of space for the opposition (crude majoritarianism) and lack of intra-party democracy (pure delegate model of representation) have extremely crippled the parliament's power to enforce the Ministerial Responsibility, scrutinize the government through the debate, question and committee work.

4 Antagonistic Relation with the Judiciary

As discussed in Chapter 4, Bangladesh's parliament and judiciary's respect and commitment to the rules and norms of mutual deference and inter-branch comity are not based on constitutionally articulated and conventionally acknowledged principles. The parliament and its members disrespected the judiciary when it appeared politically convenient. On the other hand, the Supreme Court has perceived its role in safeguarding the country's constitutional supremacy expansively and showed an inclination to intrude into the parliament's internal proceedings. The court has been extraordinarily resistant to the parliament playing any role in the judicial accountability process. Though the approach has been criticized as "self-serving", the judiciary seems apprehensive of the dominant political parties' control over the legislative branch.[43]

Secondly, Bangladesh's judicial review system is intrusive and antagonistic towards the other co-equal branches of the government. The philosophy of judicial review seems to be informed by an understanding that the legislative and executive branches are not in an ideal position to respect the democratic rights of the people, and the judiciary, being the sole guardian of the country's constitutional supremacy, must step up as the most trustworthy organisation of the state. The judiciary is particularly dismissive of the parliament and its

42 RoP (n 28) r 208.

43 In the Sixteenth Amendment case – *Advocate Asaduzzaman Siddiqui v Bangladesh* (2016) 10 ALR (AD) 03 – for example, the Supreme Court judges considered the article 70 as an ominous threat to the parliament's autonomy (M Jashim Ali Chowdhury and Nirmal Kumar Saha, '*Advocate Asaduzzaman Siddiqui v. Bangladesh*: Bangladesh's Dilemma with Judges' Impeachment' (2017) 3(3) Comparative Constitutional and Administrative Law Quarterly 7, 16).

members. Therefore, the system rarely, if there is any, yields inter-institutional conversation between the constitutional organs.

The Bangladesh Judiciary is travelling beyond the constitutional scheme of separation of power and making inroads into the parliament's authorities under the garb of its judicial review power. The higher courts in the Indian subcontinent, including the Bangladesh Supreme Court, interfere with the parliament and Speaker's authorities. Consequently, a weakened parliament is losing its institutional prestige and reputation at the hands of the other two organs of the government, namely the executive and judiciary.[44]

In the *Sixteenth Amendment Case*,[45] the High Court Division declared the parliamentary removal of the Supreme Court judges unconstitutional,[46] and the Appellate Division agreed.[47] However, the reasoning offered by the High Court Division in invalidating the amendment highlighted the parliament's reduced institutional prestige and depicted a very negative picture of the legislature. The High Court Division apprehended that the MPs, if given the power to remove the Supreme Court judges, might try to bring the judges into a parliamentary discussion on retaliatory motives and character assassinate them.[48] One of the *amicus curies* in the case, Dr Kamal Hossain, expressed concern that the parliamentary removal process may be influenced by "political clout and pressure."[49] The apprehensions emphasised by the Court include, among others, the following facts: "Around 70 per cent of the Members of Parliament are businessmen, who are unmindful of their legislative responsibilities",[50] "quality of their legislative performance is of the low standard",[51] "a lot of them have criminal records",[52] and "they are severely restrained by article

44 Ashutosh Kumar, 'Why is Parliament in State of Decline?' in Ajay K Mehra (ed.), *The Indian Parliament and Democratic Transition* (India: Routledge 2017) 65, 75.

45 *Advocate Asaduzzaman Siddiqui v Bangladesh* 2012 CLC (HCD) 41 (full text of the judgment is available at: <http://www.supremecourt.gov.bd/resources/documents/783957_WP9989of2014_Final.pdf> accessed 17 November 2023; The page reference put in the footnotes correspond to the page numbers of the full text found in the above link).

46 ibid.

47 *Bangladesh v Advocate Asaduzzaman Siddiqui* (2016) 10 ALR (AD) 03 (Full text of the Appellate Division judgment is available at: <http://www.supremecourt.gov.bd/resources/documents/1082040_C.A.6of2017_Final_3.8.2017.pdf> accessed 30 July 2024; Pages referred to in subsequent footnotes correspond to the page numbers of the full text Appellate Division judgment in the above link).

48 ibid 126, 132 (Justice Moyeenul Islam Chowdhury).

49 ibid 123 (Justice Moyeenul Islam Chowdhury).

50 ibid 45.

51 ibid 146 (Justice Moyeenul Islam Chowdhury).

52 ibid 50 (Barrister Ajmalul Hossain QC).

70 of the Constitution and partisan directives".[53] Like the High Court Division judgment, the Appellate Division judgment was based on a negative perception of the parliament's institutional virtuosity. The Appellate Division posed a question mark over the calibre of the parliamentarians[54] and observed:

> There is no chance of resting the matter in the safe hands of purely institutional virtuosity. The working of democratic institutions, like all other institutions, depends on the activities of human agents in utilising opportunities for reasonable realisation.[55]

Like their colleagues in the High Court Division, the judges of the Appellate Division were convinced that parliamentary involvement in judges' removal would threaten the judiciary's independence and, hence, must be rejected. Some of the comments and observations made in the Appellate Division's judgement read like this: In the absence of a free and fair election, the parliament may lack wise politicians and, therefore, may not be mature enough to handle the removal of the Supreme Court judges.[56] The criminalisation of parliament and politics is a serious concern.[57] The power is, therefore, not safe in the hands of "power monsters".[58] Parliamentarians moved for the amendment in a "knee-jerk reaction" to some earlier tussles between the executive and the judiciary.[59] Parliamentarians are extremely interested in legislating on judges' removal while failing to legislate on their appointment first.[60] Before assuming power, parliamentarians should have thought about "whether they can deal with such responsibility".[61] The power would be used as an instrument to penalise or intimidate judges.[62] A judge may be removed for a decision on an important or sensitive issue.[63] Judges may face a dilemma in handling cases against parliamentarians.[64] "The parliament is unable to transact its

53 ibid 39 (Dr Kamal Hossain) 124 (Justice Moyeenul Islam Chowdhury).
54 *Bangladesh v. Asaduzzaman Siddiqui* (n 47), 223 (Per Chief Justice Surendra Kumar Sinha).
55 ibid 229.
56 ibid 205.
57 ibid 192.
58 ibid 228.
59 ibid 601.
60 ibid 782.
61 ibid 223.
62 ibid 328.
63 ibid 473, 549.
64 ibid 199.

basic functions, but [it ironically] wants to wise-pull one of the most successful organs of the state, that is, the Supreme Court of Bangladesh".[65] The women members in the reserved seats are not elected and, hence not suitable to sit over the impeachment of judges.[66] Even the elected representatives will not exercise their judgement-free from party dominance due to the infamous article 70.[67] As regards article 70, the Court held:

> We find no infirmity in the views taken by the High Court Division on the construction of article 70; and that given article 70, the members of parliament must toe the party line in case of removal of any Judges of the Supreme Court. Consequently, the Judges will be left at the mercy of the party high command. We find nothing wrong in taking the above view.[68]

While the Chapter 4 has shown with greater precision how the judiciary's disregard for the representative branch of the Republic is motivated by its self-aggrandised perception of superiority over the other organs and sole guardianship of the country's constitution, the judges' observations pointed out above shows that Bangladesh Parliament's trust, accountability and electoral legitimacy deficit and total subjugation to the illiberal partisanship and dictatorial prime ministers constituted the focal point of the Supreme Court's arguments.

5 Detachment from the People

Parliament's vertical accountability to the people is a three-track process – first, parliament accounts to the people through regular elections; second, the parliament and its members continually account to their electorates by their public relations; and thirdly, the citizens contribute to the parliamentary processes. Chapter 5 has shown Bangladesh's gross anomaly in this three-track process. First, the ruthless partisan competition for perpetual power has hijacked the electoral institutions and processes. Parliamentary elections have become controversial, except, on a few occasions, parliaments elected through this electoral process lacked representational legitimacy and remained distant from the electorate. Secondly, the MPs' excessive entanglement in the local governments, claiming to be peoples' benefactors, friends and advocates, has

65 ibid 219.

66 ibid 214.

67 ibid 270–282.

68 ibid 281–82 (Per Chief Justice Surendra Kumar Sinha).

caused a serious setback in the local government bodies. It has also reduced the quality of MPs' legislative, and scrutiny works. Thirdly, the citizens' near-complete detachment from, and severely restricted access to, the institutional processes of parliament have substantially eroded its representative legitimacy.

5.1 *Crisis of Electoral Legitimacy*

The parliament's electoral legitimacy has been generally doubtful, and its democratic legitimacy and vertical accountability to the people are questionable.[69] Concerns surrounding a free, fair and credible parliamentary election continue to hurt Bangladesh's democracy.[70] Instead of several relatively fair and free voting in the 1990s that oversaw the alteration of powers between bipartisan regimes, Bangladesh failed to achieve any significant democratic consolidation. The rigged electoral system facilitates non-accountable behaviour from the political parties and their members in Bangladesh. Parliamentary elections have produced opposition-less and even practically unelected parliaments.[71] The clique of intellectual and political elites posited at the helm of public power through a farcical electoral process diffused the Westminster system's chain of the democratic delegation from electors to the ruling parties.[72] The post-2010 scenario is even worse. As discussed in Chapter 5, the utterly exposed and degraded electoral process is now reduced to a total farce and peoples' right to franchise a mere paper entitlement. With the current and immediate past parliaments' electoral legitimacy being in doubt, the Bangladesh Parliament's vertical accountability to the people remains seriously undermined.

The crisis of electoral legitimacy is closely related to what Maniruzzaman calls the elections of "preventive representation".[73] It is a system that operates 'to renew the legitimacy – and ascertain the longevity – of the ruling parties or regimes' and, simultaneously, to prevent the opponents or peoples' desired representatives from coming to power.[74] Preventive representation is a necessary

---

69 Ali Riaz, 'Bangladesh's Failed Election' (2014) 25(2) Journal of Democracy 119.

70 Nizam Ahmed, 'Critical Elections and Democratic Consolidation: the 2008 Parliamentary Elections in Bangladesh' (2011) 19(2) Contemporary South Asia 137, 149.

71 Tahmina Rahman, 'Party System Institutionalization and Pernicious Polarization in Bangladesh' (2019) 681(1) The Annals of the American Academy of Political and Social Science 173.

72 Robert Blackburn, 'The Future of UK Constitutional Law', in Xenophon Contiades and Alkmene Fotiadou (eds.), *The Routledge Handbook of Comparative Constitutional Change* (London: Routledge 2020) 374.

73 M Moniruzzaman, 'Electoral Legitimacy, Preventive Representation, and Regularization of Authoritarian Democracy in Bangladesh' in Ryan Merlin Yonl (ed) *Elections: a Global Perspective* (Online: IntechOpen, 2019) 1–15.

74 ibid 5.

outcome of perpetuation tendencies. The Eastminster's personalised political parties endorse a crude version of majoritarianism that craves for elimination, rather than toleration, of political competition. While an institutionalised liberal-conservative bipartisan competition is considered a vital requirement for parliamentary democracy,[75] conditions supportive of such an environment are largely absent in the 'Eastminster'. Therefore, the crude majoritarianism and illiberal bipartisanship that operate in an 'Eastminster' are unprincipled, conspiracy-laden and antagonistic.[76] Losing the power being a too costly bet to take, competing political parties, therefore, would find comfort in the 'preventive representation' system.

5.2 *The Localised MPs*

MPs in Westminster must constantly be in touch with their constituents, hear the local voices and attend to the local causes. The re-election bids of the MPs are particularly dependent on the local units of parties and their support base. While the MPs' constituency role as people's representatives constitutes an important part of their overall job description, balancing their law-making, oversight and representation roles remains important.

Excessive entanglement of the members of parliament in local government affairs has been a constant problem in Bangladesh. An interesting dichotomy is that while the parliament remains detached from the people, its members stand excessively constituency-focused. MPs rather remained unmindful of their legislative and scrutiny works. Paradoxically, this total localisation of the MPs has not been able to ensure the parliament's vertical accountability to the people either. The Constitution of Bangladesh has a declared policy of encouraging the widest possible extent of democratic self-governance at all levels of governance.[77] Article 59 of the Constitution requires that the people directly elect the local government bodies. The parliament is constitutionally required to maintain and respect the autonomy of the local government bodies.[78] However, as is shown in Chapter 5, Bangladesh's clientelist party system works to the sheer disadvantage of local government autonomy. MPs in the top rank of the local party units dominate and interfere in the due administration of local government bodies. The relationship between the elected Chairs and members of the local councils remains one of subordination, collision and, in

75 Peter Trubowitz and Nicole Mellow, '"Going Bipartisan": Politics by Other Means' (2005) 120(3) Political Science Quarterly 433, 434.

76 M Jashim Ali Chowdhury 'In Search of Parliamentary Opposition' (n 7).

77 Constitution (n 20) art 9.

78 ibid art 60.

exceptional cases, conflict.[79] The elected officials of local government bodies are unlikely to survive a conflict with their local MPs. The excessive engagement of the MPs in the local government has resulted in misgovernance at the local level and painfully low standards of legislative and scrutiny work in the parliament. It appears that the localisation is mutually beneficial to the parties and their MPs.[80] The government can secure a practical immunity from parliamentary scrutiny by diverting the MPs' attention from their legislative and oversight functions. It compensates the MPs by allowing them wide control over local affairs.[81] The localised MPs help the government ensure the opposition parties do not mobilise from the rural areas.[82] They also ensure that they maintain a strong personal grip over their local party units and ensure that future leadership challenges do not arise from the local parties' internal sources. The case of Bangladesh, however, is different. The institutional weaknesses and capacity deficit of parliament here in the face of the parties' highly dictatorial and top-bottom structure are so pervasive that the MPs are cornered to the constituencies rather than the House of Parliament. Also, the Clientelist party structures require the MPs to have strong control over the local party units to suppress the emergence of future leaders through the democratic process from the root. The constituents also show "cognitive lacking"[83] in the desired level of their MPs' constituency involvement. People usually emphasise that their MPs pay more attention to local issues than national policy discourses.[84] Additionally, the pressure upon the MPs may arise from the local party units.

5.3 *A Detached Citizenry*

Once elected, the Parliament of Bangladesh shows utter negligence of its public relations and trust-building responsibilities. It has been generally dismissive of public participation in its internal businesses. Therefore, the scope of parliamentary agenda-setting through opinion pressure, advocacy groups' lobbying, public participation in the committees and petitioning the parliament is very

---

79 N Ahmed, T Ahmed and M Faizullah, *Working of Upazila Parishad in Bangladesh: a study of twelve Upazilas* (UNDP Dhaka 2011).

80 Nizam Ahmed, 'Parliament and Poverty Reduction in Bangladesh: Role of the MP' (2018) 25 (1–2) South Asian Survey 163, 179.

81 ibid 178.

82 ibid 180.

83 Muhammad Sayadur Rahman, 'Role of the Members of Parliament in the Local Government of Bangladesh: Views and Perceptions of Grassroots in the Case of Upazila Administration' (2013) 13 Public Organization Review 71.

84 Philip Norton, 'The Growth of the constituency role of the MP' (1994) 47(4) Parliamentary Affairs 705.

limited. The Rules of Procedure (RoP) of the Bangladesh Parliament allow it to meet mostly in public and occasionally in secret. The public can witness the house proceedings as visitors, not committee sittings.[85] Committees may invite public submissions or public hearings on any issue under consideration. Committees can also seek expert opinions. Unfortunately, most committees do not use or seem aware of this power. Parliamentary deliberations and proceedings are published and supplied to the MPs. Interested citizens may get copies but with lots of hurdles. Radio and television broadcasts through dedicated parliamentary channels are also in place. The problem, however, is in the non-interest of the people and academia in the parliamentary debates and proceedings due to the low-quality deliberations and misdemeanours shown by the politicians.[86] Public relations affairs of the parliament are vastly neglected. There have been occasional attempts to popularise parliamentary issues by a guided tour of parliament or parliamentary outreach programs at the district level. All these produced less than expected.

Though there is a provision for citizen petitions to the parliament, the system remains odd with the one at Westminster. Unlike the UK, the Bangladesh Parliament will not allow e-petition. Nor is there any obligation upon the government to answer the petitions. The RoP provides no follow-up process or time limit for responding or acting on the submitted petitions. No petition has even been debated in the House. The agenda-setting potential of the petition system is, therefore, missing.[87] The Petition Committee also has taken a sluggish attitude to the petition process.[88] The Committee's sitting is irregular. Committees have referred the petitions to the concerned ministers rather than the House. The public has been unmindful of the opportunity and remains grossly underutilized. A direct result of this parliament-people disconnect marginalizes the parliament in national policy making, governance and agenda setting.

85 RoP (n 28) r 201.

86 Nizam Ahmed, *The Parliament of Bangladesh* (Ashgate 2002 Routledge reprint 2018).

87 Ross Cotton, 'Political Participation and E-Petitioning: an Analysis of the Policy-Making Impact of the Scottish Parliament's E-Petition System' (2012) 6(1) University of Central Florida Undergraduate Research Journal 33.

88 Nizam Ahmed, 'Parliament and Citizens in Asia: the Bangladesh Case' (2012) 18(3–4) The Journal of Legislative Studies 463, 468.

6 Roadblocks to Parliamentary Reform

Reform and institutionalisation of Parliament continue to face an uphill challenge in Bangladesh. Chapter 6 of this book tried to unearth the underlying reasons behind minimal, cosmetic, and often no reforms in Bangladesh's parliamentary system. It studied at length the various reform experiments with Bangladesh's parliamentary system during the periods of the military (1975–1990 and 2007–2008), bipartisan competitive (1991–2006), and one-party (1972–1975 and 2009–2024) authoritarianism. It transpires that almost all of the windows of parliamentary reform in Bangladesh's history resulted in retrogressive changes or continuance of illiberal policies of a previous era. Now, the country's newly established extra-constitutional "interim" government (August 2024) declaredly aims to drastically reform the system. However, the initial signs, such as forcing the entire bench of the Appellate Division of the Supreme Court to resign and openly suppressing the country's biggest political party – AL, seem to raise doubt about its ultimate destiny too.[89]

The Chapter 6 evaluated the problems of Bangladesh's parliamentary reform through an institutional-theoretical lens that takes into account the time, political contexts, institutional structures and procedures surrounding the reform proposals. It appears that the three "Estaminster Deviations" have a role here too. Bangladesh's personalised, patriarchal, dynastic and clientelist party system places the Prime Minister or the leader of the party or the persons in authority, the "selective dictators", above the institutional processes. Therefore, the success or failure of reforms depends on the whims of the chosen few, in exclusion of the opposition, party backbenches, and all other stakeholders. The most glaring example is the reforms of the parliamentary committee system. The limited consolidation of the parliamentary committee system over the years also came either under international donner pressures[90] or as a mere good will concession from the party leadership rather than through any deliberative reform process.[91] Currently, there is a proposition that the Deputy Speaker be elected from the opposition parties which seems

---

89 M Jashim Ali Chowdhury, 'The Agenda and Dilemmas of Constitutional Reform in Bangladesh', *ConstitutionNet, International IDEA*, 18 November 2024, <https://constitutionnet.org/news/voices/agenda-and-dilemmas-constitutional-reform-bangladesh> accessed 18 November 2024.

90 ATM Obaidullah, *Institutionalization of the Parliament in Bangladesh A Study of Donor Intervention for Reorganization and Development* (London: Palgrave Macmillan, 2019).

91 M Jashim Ali Chowdhury, 'Working and Impact of Parliamentary Committees in the UK and Bangladesh: a Theoretical Analysis' (2021) 32(2) Dhaka University Law Journal 175, 194.

to completely depend on the will of the leader of the current ruling party. The demand has been rejected so far.

While one of the major political reforms of the country in 1992 – the restoration of parliamentary democracy – was realised through intense backbench pressure of the ruling party leadership, it stands as a very striking contrast to all other significantly retrogressive reforms, such as the one-party system and the scrapping of the caretaker government, where the intra-party or backbench voices did not stand a chance. Hoque's study shows that Bangladesh's first four constitutional amendments (1973–1975) were conceived and drafted at the sole discretion of the party in power.[92] Those were later tabled and passed in parliament with almost no deliberation. The most controversial one – the fourth amendment – altered the constitution drastically. Still, it was passed through less than 30 minutes of parliamentary deliberation.[93] The fifth to tenth amendments (1979–1990) were passed by three "rubber stamp parliaments"[94] working to "achieve constitutional changes desired by the military rulers".[95] The eleventh and twelfth amendments (1992) were largely based on a political consensus outside the parliament. The eleventh amendment legitimized a Chief Justice-led government which conducted the 1991 parliamentary election. The twelfth amendment restored the parliamentary system. The thirteenth amendment (1996) included the election-time caretaker government system in the constitution. Again, its basic principle was agreed upon through "mere élite preferences rather than deliberative and participatory decision making".[96] With the key principles decided outside the parliament, its texts lacked input from the government backbench or parliamentary committees.[97] The fourteenth (2001), fifteenth (2011), and sixteenth (2016) amendments represent what Hoque calls examples of "abusive constitutional amendments".[98] All these again confirm that the institutionalisation of the parliamentary system in Bangladesh remains a daunting task facing the undemocratic and non-accountable party system.

---

92 Ridwanul Hoque, 'Deconstructing Public Participation and Deliberation in Constitutional Amendment in Bangladesh' 2021 21(2) Australian Journal of Asian Law 7, 11–13.

93 ibid.

94 Azizul Haque, 'Bangladesh 1979: Cry for a Sovereign Parliament' (1980) 20(2) Asian Survey 217, 221–222.

95 Hoque (n 92) 15.

96 Sonia Zaman Khan, *The Politics and Law of Democratic Transition: Caretaker Government in Bangladesh* (London: Routledge, 2017) 2.

97 Md Shahjahan Hafez Bhuiyan, 'The Caretaker Government in Bangladesh: an Appraisal of its Formation' (2003) 40 Politics Administration and Change 33, 46–47.

98 Hoque (n 92) 17–18.

7 The "Perseverance Despite"

Fifty years into its constitutional beginning, the institutional value that the Parliament of Bangladesh (*Jatiya Sangsad*) carries within the body politic is extremely marginal. However, while the assertiveness of the Bangladesh Parliament continues to fall hostage to the whims of the country's illiberal and undemocratic party system, the institution's half-a-century-long endurance is not a matter to be taken lightly. The people's faith in the institution's inner resilience must not be lost. The decline of democratic norms and institutions is a global phenomenon.[99] So is the counter force of resilience that helps democracies withstand and sustain retrogression pressures. The Bangladesh Parliament's resilience should resonate from the people's preference for the parliamentary system over all other deviant versions that different regimes have tested. The people rejected each of those and consistently reaffirmed their faith in the parliamentary system as the most preferable method of governance.[100] Bangladesh has experienced various syntheses of party rule, martial law, and presidential and parliamentary forms of government. Military involvement in politics through Zia (1976–1981), Ershad (1982–1990) and Moin Uddin Ahmed (2007–2008) have been discredited and rejected. Mujib's one-party experiment became extremely unpopular and failed. Begum Zia's attempt to continue presidential government in 1991 was resisted.[101] Experiments with the Supreme Court-led caretaker governments also failed. The current "interim" government, though replicates structures and modes of the caretaker governments, presents an unclear picture about its future ambitions. Going through all these rollercoaster rides of constitutional experiments, the people of Bangladesh seem to settle firmly on their belief in the parliamentary system.[102]

---

99 Nancy Bermeo, 'On Democratic Backsliding' (2016) 27(5) Journal of Democracy 5.

100 M Jashim Ali Chowdhury, 'Is the 1972 Scheme of Parliamentary System Dead?' *The Daily Star* (Dhaka, 19 March 2019).

101 The Twelfth Amendment to the Constitution in 1991 marked the revival of the parliamentary system as devised in the original constitution of Bangladesh. A product of the political commitment of the three different alliances staging a mass movement against the military rule of HM Ershad in 1990, the Political Declaration of 1990 promised demilitarization of politics and shunning down of presidential system introduced since 1975. Begum Khaleda Zia's government coming to power in 1991 being a part of the Political Declaration was reluctantly held to bring the Twelfth Amendment with a cross-party support (Muhammad A Hakim, *Bangladesh politics: the Shahabuddin interregnum*, The University Press Limited, Dhaka, 1993).

102 Nizam Ahmed, 'In Search of Institutionalisation: Parliament in Bangladesh', in Philip Norton and Nizam Ahmed (eds.), *Parliaments in Asia*, London: Frank Cass (1999) 40.

In fifty years of struggle with the parliamentary system, Bangladesh has come to a position where civilian rule is preferred over military intervention, parliamentary form is preferred over the presidential system, and almost all post-1990 parliaments fulfilled their tenure. It is a resilience of 'perseverance despite',[103] if not of the persistence and durability,[104] which are rather advanced manifestations of democratic resilience.

Parliament has witnessed occasional resilience from the backbench, too. In a rare show of parliamentary assertiveness, the ruling party backbench of the Fifth Parliament joined the opposition to force the government to rethink its policy decisions at least twice.[105] On the first occasion, many ruling party MPs refrained from voting for the government's controversial presidential candidate. The government's pick barely escaped a defeat at the hand of the opposition candidate.[106] On the second occasion, the prime minister was forced to respect her electoral promise to restore the Parliamentary system and pass the Constitution (Twelfth) Amendment Act of 1991.[107] Bangladesh has also introduced innovative procedural devices like the prime minister's question time with limited success.

The parliamentary committee system has consolidated to some extent, thanks mainly to the increased pressure from international donor agencies and development partners[108] and sometimes to the benevolent concession of the prime minister.[109] Until the fifth parliament (1991–1996), the ministerial standing committees were confined to scrutinising bills concerning a relevant ministry. After a 1992 amendment in the parliament's Rules of Procedure (RoP), ministerial standing committees got scrutiny power over the administration and policies of the ministries.[110] Parliamentary committees now broadly shadow the ministries and departments of the government.[111] Until the ninth

---

103 Peter Burnell and Peter Calvert, 'The Resilience of Democracy: an Introduction' (1999) 6(1) Democratisation, 1, 7.

104 ibid, 3–4.

105 Ahmed, 'Parliamentary Opposition' (n 12).

106 Nizam Ahmed, *The Parliament of Bangladesh* (Ashgate 2002 Routledge reprint 2018) 233.

107 Nizam Ahmed, 'Parliamentary Politics in Bangladesh' (1994) 32(3) *The Journal of Commonwealth and Comparative Politics* 364, 375; Zillur R Khan, 'Bangladesh in 1992: Dilemmas of Democratisation' (1993) 33(2) *Asian Survey* 150.

108 ATM Obaidullah, *Institutionalization of the Parliament in Bangladesh A Study of Donor Intervention for Reorganization and Development* (London: Palgrave Macmillan, 2019).

109 Chowdhury (n 91), 194.

110 The Constitution (n 20) art 76(2)(c); Rules of Procedure (n 28) r 246–48.

111 Ahmed, 'Parliamentary Committees2' (n 34); Taiabur Rahman, *Parliamentary Control and Government Accountability in South Asia: a comparative analysis of Bangladesh, India and Sri Lanka* (London: Routledge 2008).

parliament, the committees were not formed until the lapse of a significant portion of its tenure.[112] However, the ninth (2009–2013), tenth (2014–2018) and eleventh (2019–2024) parliaments constituted the committees within the first session.[113] A revision of RoP in June 1997 also ensured that ministers would not chair the committee on their ministry. Ministers now remain in the committees as *ex officio* members. The tenth and eleventh parliaments have appointed senior party leaders and former ministers as the chairs of parliamentary committees. If continued, the practice would benefit the committee system by drawing from the chairs' expertise and political superiority over the ministers.[114] Until the ninth parliament, the ruling parties used to claim the most committee chairs.[115] Since the ninth parliament, chairs are distributed among the parties pro-rata.[116] Though there were repeated calls for appointing the chairs of Public Accounts, Public Undertaking and Estimate Committees from the opposition parties, the Eleventh Parliament (2019–2024) appointed an opposition member as the chair of the Public Accounts Committee (PAC).

8 The Ways Ahead

Bangladesh's parliament survived the test of time and showed resilience despite all its political pitfalls and cultural drawbacks. At the current juncture, there appear to be several ways forward.

8.1 *Incremental and Intermediate Reforms*

The Bangladesh parliament's weaknesses stem from the weaknesses of its party system.[117] There is a clear lack of genuine political will to redress the procedural and substantive problems of parliament. In this scenario, drastic and pervasive institutional overhauling will most likely be resisted. Demands for

112 Jalal Firoj, 'Forty Years of Bangladesh Parliament: Trends, Achievements and Challenges' (2013) 58(1) Journal of the Asiatic Society of Bangladesh (Humanities) 83; Alam and Teicher (n 34); Ahmed (n 35) 68–69.

113 M Jashim Ali Chowdhury, '11th Parliament: Rays of hope for the Committee System' *The Daily Star Law and Our Rights* (Dhaka, 05 March 2019).

114 ibid.

115 KM Mahiuddin, 'The Parliamentary Committee System in Bangladesh An Analysis of its Functioning' (Ph.D. Thesis, Ruprecht-Karls-Universität Heidelberg 2009) 104–106.

116 Ahmed (n 1).

117 Paul G Thomas, 'Parliament and Legislatures: Central to Canadian Democracy?' in John C Courtney and David E Smith (eds.), *The Oxford Handbook of Canadian Politics* (Oxford 2010) 157.

intermediate and minor reforms are more likely to succeed if they do not drastically shake the political elites' immediate hold over the powers.[118] Hence, as an incremental empowerment strategy, civil society and international development partners may press for incremental changes in several areas of the parliament's operational rules.

First, under the current state of affairs, it appears most convenient for the Parliament to return to the people and look for its democratic legitimation. Some incrementally bound attempts towards that direction could enhance parliament's public relations activities, reinforce its representational claim against the executive and judicial branches and relieve some of the frustrations over its failure in law-making and accountability areas.[119] Scopes of greater public access to the parliamentary businesses and committees could gradually challenge the elite domination[120] over the institution and pave the way to its greater democratisation. In one of the recent publications on Bangladesh parliament, Abdullah Al Faruque duly emphasised the importance of changes in Rule 246 of the Parliament's rules of procedure to facilitate people's better engagement with the parliamentary committees.[121] Bruce Ackerman famously argued that the 'democracy branches'[122] outside the three traditional branches of the state – such as the election commission, national audit bodies, universities, media and civil societies – are powerful reservoirs of resilience for the constitutional system. They can offer significant public resistance to misappropriating legislative, executive and judicial powers and thereby emerge a powerful aide of the parliament. In this sense, the future of parliament in Bangladesh hinges on robust and institutionalized interaction of the parliament with these

118 In contexts more or less similar to Bangladesh, the Indian scholars advocate incrementalism as the most sensible approach where parliamentarians "wilfully miss the opportunities to strengthen the Parliament through non-participation in parliamentary sittings and debates, question hours, budget-related discussions." For India, "[t]he call is not to change the whole institution in one go. It is also in no sense viable. The idea is to bring changes, even incremental, that can help the Parliament to recover from present condition and faith of people is restored in Parliament." (Afroz Alam, 'Decline of Parliamentary Governance: Indian Scenario' (2015) 3(2) Rostrum Law Review).

119 Paul G Thomas (n 117) 160.

120 Ersin Kalaycioglu, 'Why Legislatures Persist In Developing Countries: the Case of Turkey' (1980) 5(1) Legislative Studies Quarterly 123, 123–4.

121 Dr Abdullah Al Faruque, 'Role of Parliament in Ensuring Democratic Accountability in Bangladesh: Setting the Agenda for a Strengthened Parliamentary System' in M Rafiqul Islam and Muhammad Ekramul Haque (eds.) The Constitutional Law of Bangladesh: Progression and Transformation at its 50th Anniversary (Springer Nature: Singapore, 2023) 121–137.

122 Bruce Ackerman, 'The New Separation of Powers' (2000) 113 (3) Harvard Law Review, 633.

fourth-branch organizations. Continuous engagement with the citizens, civil society and other "fourth branch" organisations should build its independent public support base. Parliament's own public support base should gradually challenge the dynastic political parties' exclusive claim to democratic representation and pave the way for the Parliament's institutional assertiveness. Reliance on 'democracy branches' is particularly important for Bangladesh, where the parties, persons and dynasties are less likely to concede to a drastic structural realignment of the system unless forced by an exceptional amount of democratic and opinion pressure.

Second, priority should be given to limiting the pervasive impact of Article 70, the anti-defection clause and press the government to amend it suitably, at least to make it incapable in legislative voting, while keeping the clause operative for no-confidence motion and budget approval. Parliament's most distinctive weak point is in the powerlessness of its backbench, whose lips are tied to their party hierarchy. As discussed earlier, the purpose of Article 70 was to prevent the MPs from switching their parties and causing the fall of governments through horse-trading. As per the Constitution, no-confidence motion and budget legislation are the only areas where failure to secure majority support causes the government's fall.[123] There are strong benefits in allowing the MPs freedom of voice in all other cases where the government's existence is not threatened.

Thirdly, much of Bangladesh's existing parliamentary literature mentions the Speaker's neutrality as one of the key problems of the parliamentary process. Studies and research around the powers, functions, discretion and influence of the office of the Speaker and modes of its execution, with a special focus on the historical precedents set by the past office bearers, could substantially inform Bangladesh's future parliamentary reform agenda. While the current partisan selection process of the Speakers is unlikely to change soon, the demand for electing a Deputy Speaker from the Opposition party is gaining momentum. An additional demand to be pressed could be around the speaker's denouncing their partisan allegiance and trying to establish a convention that the speakers are elected unopposed. If the profile of the office of the Speaker could be enhanced, especially by reducing the Prime Minister's influence in the Business Advisory Committee and pressing for separating the

123 The Constitution (n 20). Article 57(2) requires the Prime Minister to resign if a motion of no-confidence is passed in the parliament and then article 92(3) permits the government to spend money from the public accounts a maximum of 90 days whether the parliament does not approve the budget. Beyond that point, the government is unable to move forward the country's finances without parliamentary approval.

House leadership from the government leadership, the Prime Minister could provide some starting point for the quality of the Speakers' works.

8.2 *A Democratic Dialogue between the Parliament and Judiciary*

The Bangladesh parliament's relationship with the judiciary has been studied scarcely.[124] Chapter 4 of this thesis has revealed a visible and almost watertight separation between the legislative and judicial branches. Bangladesh's judicial review system has been excessively intrusive, and the Parliaments' reactions to various judicial pronouncements have been largely antagonistic. The judges do not answer the parliamentary committees, nor are they called there. While Chapter 4 tried to argue for the adoption of a "Democratic Dialogue" approach in Bangladesh's judicial review system, there is no significant research, particularly by the legal academics of Bangladesh, as to why the legislative and judicial branches of Bangladesh could not interact each other more directly and through institutional channels. The concept of "Democratic Dialogue" is grossly unstudied in Bangladesh, and this book could, at best, be considered a modest beginning in this area. There are grey areas around the proposed "dialogue" and its impact on the overall body politic. Apart from the institutional arrangements of the "dialogue", there are questions about the parliament's role in the judicial accountability processes. The higher judiciary of Bangladesh continues to communicate with the parliament, if it ever does, through an authoritarian executive branch that dooms the legislature's capacity to respond efficiently.[125] Chapter 4 argued that the parliament's increased interaction with the judiciary, especially through its committee hearings and judicial participation in pre- and post-legislative stages, could empower it to achieve constitutional counter-balancing of judicial powers through formal and informal channels. A recent study by Alison Young shows that "Democratic Dialogue" can happen both in the Commonwealth model (unwritten constitution, no judicial review and political constitutionalism approach) and the Strong constitutional enforcement of rights protection model.[126] Alison argues that such dialogue may serve an important purpose

---

124 One of the most recent studies has been that of Nizam Ahmed (*Parliaments in South Asia: India, Pakistan and Bangladesh*, Routledge 2020). Though Professor Ahmed treats the relation from a historical perspective, pure constitutional perspective from any legal academic is largely missing in Bangladesh.

125 Nizam Ahmed, *Parliaments in South Asia: India, Pakistan and Bangladesh* (Routledge 2020) 128–129.

126 Alison L Young, 'Inter-institutional Interactions', chapter in *Democratic Dialogue and the Constitution* (Oxford: Oxford University Press 2017) 117–146, 118.

of "constitutional collaboration" between institutions which might not be formally well designed for "constitutional counter-balancing" (*i.e.*, strong adherence to separation of power and checks and balances).[127] Such collaboration works through mutual self-reasoning and reflection on the other's reasoning. As suggested earlier, the "democratic dialogue" project, if seriously pursued and further researched, could provide an alternative channel of "cooperative and educative collaboration"[128] between Bangladesh's two marginalized constitutional branches – the legislature and the judiciary – and help them draw strength from each other.

8.3 *Waiting for a Realignment of the Political Landscape*

The final way forward is perhaps to hold on to the system and wait for new political alignment to emerge organically from within the society. The best shot at hope is perhaps waiting for AL-BNP and JI rivalry to cool down a bit. As is seen throughout this book, the recurrent challenge for Bangladesh's parliamentary system is the waning of one of the two arch-rivals and the rise of one-party monopoly whenever each of these parties ascend to power. While the danger of party authoritarianism is constant, an optimist' may view the waning of the extremely confrontational political discourse as a chance too. Such could help reduce the temperature of political confrontation and emerge new political alignment and forces from within the parties. In this regard, it might be useful to consider America's 1820 "Era of Good Feelings" when the highly combative ideological competition between the Jeffersonian Republicans and Hamiltonian Federalists waned after an absolute dominance of the Republicans was established. By that time, the Americans started identifying themselves more as Americans than Republicans or Federalists.[129] Later, the Democratic and Republican parties emerged from within the Jeffersonian Republicans, and America started walking towards its trademark liberal-conservative bipartisanship. Could there be a similar political evolution in Bangladesh after the fall of Sheikh Hasina's fifteen years long monopoly? While it is difficult to predict now, Bangladesh's newly formed "interim" government (August 2024), with its overt BNP-JI leaning, shows little hope that such political alignment will emerge soon. Still, if Bangladesh's parliamentary system continues to survive the country's recurring military or extra-constitutional interventions, politics should surely take its turn.

---

127 ibid, 140.

128 ibid, 125.

129 M Jashim Ali Chowdhury, *Comparative Constitutional Law: Issues, Debates and Stories from the US, UK and Indian Jurisdictions* (Bengal Press 2022) 29–32.

9 Conclusion

In 1972, Bangladesh started with an idolized Westminster System. It soon faced reality and turned back to a one-party presidential system through the Fourth Amendment, 1975. That system was replaced within months by a military dictatorship after August 1975. It later gave way to an authoritarian presidential system with a controlled legislature established through the Fifth Amendment of 1979. The process was re-rolled during 1982–1986. The country completed its "full constitutional cycle"[130] in 1991 when the Fifth Parliament (1991–1995) restored the parliamentary system as devised in the original Constitution of 1972. The next sixteen years of the revived parliamentary system (1991–2006) marked highly illiberal politics of confrontation and a selective dictatorship of two prominent party leaders. The military dictatorship re-appeared again for a brief period of two years (2007–2008), only to give way to a single-party authoritarianism (2009–2024) and a fresh round of constitutional breakdown (August 2024). Still, the signs of resilience are there. This book suggests that the parliament has a future, and that future is attached to the sustenance of the "democracy branches" and the people. As Lipset noted, democratic institutions survive on the force of a politically engaged citizenry.[131]

130 Syed Istiaq Ahmed, 'Constitution and Democracy in Bangladesh since 1972', 44 DLR Journal 52.

131 Seymour Martin Lipset, *Political Man: the Social Bases of Politics* (New York: Doubleday 1963) 72.

Bibliography

Books

Ahmed, Fakhruddin, *The Caretakers: a First-hand Account of the Interim Government of Bangladesh (1990–1991)* (Dhaka: University Press Limited 1998).

Ahmed, Kawser (ed), *Proceedings of Bangladesh Constituent Assembly: Debates relating to the Constitution Making Volume 1* (Bangla) (Dhaka: Pencil Publication 2021).

Ahmed, Nizam, *Aiding the Parliament of Bangladesh: Experience and Prospect* (University Press Limited: Dhaka 2012).

Ahmed, Nizam, *Limits of Parliamentary Control: Public Spending in Bangladesh* (University Press Limited: Dhaka 2006).

Ahmed, Nizam, *Non-party Caretaker Government in Bangladesh: Experience and Prospect* (University Press Limited: Dhaka 2004).

Ahmed, Nizam, *Parliament and Public Spending in Bangladesh: Limits of Control* (Bangladesh Institute of Parliamentary Studies: Dhaka, 2000).

Ahmed, Nizam, *Parliaments in South Asia India, Pakistan and Bangladesh* (Routledge 2020).

Ahmed, Nizam, *The Bangladesh Parliament A Data Handbook* (Institute of Government Studies (IGS), BRAC University, Dhaka, 2013).

Ahmed, Nizam, *The Parliament of Bangladesh* (Ashgate 2002 Routledge Reprint 2018).

Bangladesh Parliament, *Summary of the Proceedings of the Tenth Session of the (Fifth) Parliament* (Dhaka: Parliament Secretariat 1993).

Birch, AH, *Representation* (London: Macmillan 1972).

Blackburn, Robert, Kennon, Andrew and Wheeler-Booth, Michael (eds.), *Griffith and Ryle on Parliament: Functions, Practice and Procedures* (Sweet and Maxwell 2003).

Bogdanor, Vernon, *The New British Constitution* (Oxford: Hart Publishing, 2009).

Chalcraft, John and Noorani, Yaseen (eds.), *Counter-Hegemony in the Colony and Postcolony* (London: Palgrave Macmillan 2007).

Chandrachud, Chintan, *Balanced Constitutionalism: Courts and Legislatures in India and the United Kingdom* (Oxford University Press 2017).

Chatterjee, Partha, *Nationalist Thought and the Colonial World: a Derivative Discourse?* (London: Zed, 1986).

Chatterjee, Partha, *The Nation and Its Fragments: Colonial and Postcolonial Histories* (Duke University Press 2018).

Childs, Sarah, *The Good Parliament* (Bristol: University of Bristol, 2016).

Chowdhury, M Jashim Ali, *An Introduction to the Constitutional Law of Bangladesh* (Book Zone, Chittagong, Bangladesh, 3rd Edition 2020).

Chowdhury, M Jashim Ali, *Comparative Constitutional Law: Issues, Debates and Stories from the US, UK and Indian Jurisdictions* (Bengal Press 2022).

Coleman, Stephen, Taylor, John and Donk, Wim van de (eds.), *Parliament in the Age of the Internet* (Oxford: Oxford University Press, 1999).

Congleton, Roger D, *Perfecting Parliament Constitutional Reform, Liberalism and the Rise of Western Democracy* (Cambridge 2011).

Dalton, RJ, *Democratic Challenges, Democratic Choices: the Erosion of Political Support in Advanced Industrial Democracies* (Oxford: Oxford University Press 2004).

Dorey, Peter and Kelso, Alexandra, *House of Lords Reform Since 1911 Must the Lords Go?* (Palgrave McMillan 2011).

Drewry, Gavin (ed), *The New Select Committees: a Study of the 1979 Reforms* (Clarendon Press 1985).

Dryzek, John S, *Deliberative Democracy and Beyond: Liberals, Critics, Contestations* (Oxford: Oxford University Press 2000).

Flinders, Matthew, *The Politics of Accountability in the Modern State* (Ashgate 2001, Routledge Revival 2019).

Fukuyama, Francis, *Identity: the Demand for Dignity and the Politics of Resentment* (Farrar, Straus and Giroux, 2018).

Go, Julian, *Postcolonial Thought and Social Theory* (Oxford: 2016).

Goldsworthy, Jeffrey, *Parliamentary Sovereignty Contemporary Debates* (Cambridge, 2010).

Goldsworthy, Jeffrey, *The Sovereignty of Parliament: History and Philosophy* (Oxford, 1999).

Gramsci, Antonio, *Selections from the Prison Notebooks* (New York: International Publishers 1971).

Gramsci, Antonio, *The Gramsci Reader: Selected Writings 1916–1935* (New York: NYU Press 2000).

Guha, Ranajit, *Dominance Without Hegemony: History and Power in Colonial India* (Cambridge, MA: Harvard University Press, 1998).

Hakim, Muhammad A, *Bangladesh Politics: the Shahabuddin Interregnum* (Dhaka: University Press Limited, 1993).

Halim, Abdul, *Constitution, Constitutional Law and Politics: Bangladesh Perspective* (2nd Ed, Dhaka: Md. Yusuf Ali Khan 2003).

Hossain, Kamal, *Bangladesh: Quest for Freedom and Justice* (Karachi: Oxford University Press 2013).

Huda, AKM Shamsul, *Constitution of Bangladesh, Vol 2* (Rita Court, Chittagong, Bangladesh, 1997).

Hussain, M Sakawat, *Electoral Reform in Bangladesh 1972–2008* (Dhaka: Palok Publishers 2012).

Jalal, Ayesha, *Democracy and authoritarianism in South Asia: a Comparative and Historical Perspective* (Cambridge University Press 1995).

Jen, Yap Po, *Constitutional Dialogue in Common Law Asia* (Oxford University Press 2015).

Jenning, M Kent and E Man, Thomas, *Elections at Home and Abroad Essays in Honour of Warren Miller* (Michigan University Press 1994).

Jogerst, Michael A, *Reform in the House of Commons: the Select Committee System* (University Press of Kentucky 1993).

Kam, CJ, *Party Discipline and Parliamentary Politics* (Cambridge University Press 2009).

Kaul, MN, *Parliamentary Institutions and Procedures* (New Delhi: National Publishing House 1979).

Kavanagh, Aileen, *Constitutional Review under the UK Human Rights Act* (Cambridge 2009).

Kelso, Alexandra, *Parliamentary Reform at Westminster* (Manchester University Press 2013).

Khan, MM, *Dominant Executive and Dormant Legislature: Executive-Legislature Relations in Bangladesh* (India: South Asian Publishers Pvt Ltd, 2006).

Khan, Sonia Zaman, *The Politics and Law of Democratic Transition: Caretaker Government in Bangladesh* (London: Routledge, 2017).

Krehbiel, Keith, *Information and Legislative Organization* (University of Michigan Press 1991).

Kumarasingham, Harshan (ed.), *Viceregalism: the Crown as Head of State in Political Crises in the Postwar Commonwealth* (Palgrave McMillan 2020).

Kumarasingham, Harshan (ed.), *A Political Legacy of the British Empire: Power and the Parliamentary System in Postcolonial India and Sri Lanka* (I.B. Tauris: London, 2013).

Lijphart, Arend, *Patterns of Democracy* (Yale University Press 2012).

Loewenberg, G and Patterson, SC *Comparing Legislatures* (University Press of America 1997).

Mackintosh, JP, *The British Cabinet* (Stevens and Sons Ltd: London 1977).

Mackintosh, JP, *The Government and Politics of Britain* (London: Hutchinson 1970).

Marleau, R and Montpetit, C (eds.), *House of Commons Procedure and Practice* (House of Commons: Ottawa 2000).

Martin, Lanny W and Vanberg, Georg, *Parliaments and Coalitions: the Role of Legislative Institutions in Multiparty Governance* (Oxford University Press 2011).

May and Thomas Erskine, *Treatise on the Law, Privileges, Proceedings, and Usage of Parliament* (25th Edition Online 2019).

Mezey, Michael L, *Comparative Legislatures* (Duke University Press 1979).

Norton, Philip (ed.), *Legislatures* (Oxford: Oxford University Press 1992).

Norton, Philip, *Parliament in British Politics* (2nd Edition, Palgrave 2013).

Norton, Philip, *The 1922 Committee: Power Behind the Scenes* (Manchester University Press 2023).

Norton, Philip, *The Commons in Perspective* (Oxford: Martin Robertson, 1981).

Norton, Philip, *Governing Britain, Parliament, Ministers and Our Ambiguous Constitution* (Manchester University Press 2020).

Obaidullah, ATM *Institutionalization of the Parliament in Bangladesh A Study of Donor Intervention for Reorganization and Development* (Palgrave Macmillan, 2019).

Parry, Geraint, Moyser, George and Day, Neil, *Political Participation and Democracy in Britain* (Cambridge University Press 1992).

Pitkin, H, *The Concept of Representation* (University of California Press 1967).

Prosch, Sevn Oliver and Slapin, Jonathan B, *The Politics of Parliamentary Debate: Parties, Rebels and Representation* (Cambridge University Press 2015).

Rahman, Tabibur, *Parliamentary Control and Government Accountability in South Asia, A comparative analysis of Bangladesh, India and Sri Lanka* (Routledge, 2008).

Rashid, M Humaiyun (ed.) *Rulings of the Speaker* (Dhaka: Institute of Parliament Studies 2000).

Rhodes, RAW Wanna, John and Weller, Patrick (eds.), *Comparing the Westminster* (Oxford 2011).

Riaz, Ali, *Bangladesh: a Political History since Independence* (London: I.B. Tauris, 2016).

Richardson, JJ and Jordan, AG, *Governing Under Pressure: the Policy Process in a Post-Parliamentary Democracy* (Martin Robertson 1979).

Rogers, Robert and Walters, Rodhri, *How Parliament Works* (London: Routledge, 2015).

Rush, Michael, *The Role of the Member of Parliament Since 1868: From Gentlemen to Players* (Oxford 2001).

Russell, Meg and Gover, Daniel, *Legislation at Westminster: Parliamentary Actors and Influence in the Making of British Law* (Oxford University Press 2017).

Said, Edward W, *Orientalism* (Pantheon Books 1978).

Shahabuddin, Mohammad, *Minorities and the Making of Postcolonial States in International Law* (Cambridge: Cambridge University Press, 2021).

Shepsle, Kenneth A, *The Giant Jigsaw Puzzle: Democratic Committee Assignments in the Modern House* (University of Chicago Press 1978).

Srivastava, Neelam and Bhattacharya, Baidik (eds.), *The Postcolonial Gramsci* (London: Routledge 2013).

Thompson, L, *Making British Law: Committees in Action, Basingstoke* (Palgrave Macmillan 2015).

Tushnet, Mark, *Weak Courts, Strong Rights* (Princeton University Press 2008).

Young, Alison L, *Democratic Dialogue and the Constitution* (Oxford University Press 2017).

Book Chapters

Ahamed, Emajuddin, 'The Military and Democracy in Bangladesh', in May, RJ Selochan, Viberto (eds.), *The Military and Democracy in Asia and the Pacific* 105–115 (ANU Press 2004).

Ahmed, Nizam, 'Bangladesh,' in Nohlen, D, Grotz, F and Hartmann, C (eds.), *Elections in Asia: a Data Handbook* (Oxford: Oxford University Press 2001).

Ahmed, Nizam, 'In Search of Institutionalisation: Parliament in Bangladesh', in Philip Norton and Nizam Ahmed (eds.), *Parliaments in Asia*, London: Frank Cass (1999).

Ahmed, Nizam, 'Including the Excluded: Government Backbenchers and Opposition in the Parliamentary Process in Bangladesh' in Ahmed, Nizam (ed.), *Inclusive Governance in South Asia: Parliament, Judiciary and Civil Service* 39–60 (Palgrave McMillan 2018).

Ahmed, Nizam and Hasan, Sadik, 'Alangkar or Ahangkar? Reserved-Seat Women Members in the Bangladesh Parliament' in Ahmed, Nizam (ed.) *Women in Governing Institutions in South Asia, Parliament, Civil Service and Local Government,* 17–39 (Springer 2018).

Ahmed, Samina, 'The Westminster Model and Pakistan: a Continuing Mirage', in Patapan, Haig, Wanna, John and Weller, Patrick (eds.), *Westminster Legacies: Democracy and Responsible Government in Asia -and the Pacific,* 36–62 (University of New South Wales Press 2005).

Andeweg, Rudy B, 'Parties in Parliament: the Blurring of Opposition' in Müller, WC and Narud, HM (eds.), *Party Governance and Party Democracy* 99–114 (Springer, 2013).

Bandeira, Cristina Leston and Waltker, Alieen, 'Parliament and Public Engagement' in Bandeira, C Leston (ed.), *Parliaments and Citizens* (Abingdon: Routledge, 2013).

Bennister, Mark and Larkin, Phil, 'Accountability in Parliament' in Bandeira, Cristina Leston and Thompson, Louise (eds.), *Exploring the Parliament*, 143–151 (Oxford 2018).

Blackburn, Robert, 'The Future of UK Constitutional Law', in Contiades, Xenophon and Fotiadou, Alkmene (eds.), *The Routledge Handbook of Comparative Constitutional Change* 369–387 (1st Edition, Routledge 2020).

Blackburn, Robert, 'The Nature and Importance of Parliamentary Procedure' in Blackburn, Robert, Carminati, Arianna and Spadacini, Lorenzo (eds.), *Parliament as the Cornerstone of Democracy: Studies on the UK and Italian Parliaments in commemoration of Magna Carta's 800th Anniversary* (Kings College London, University of Brescia and Magna Carta 800th Anniversary Commemoration Committee 2018).

Blackburn, Robert, 'The Politics of Parliamentary Procedure at Westminster Revisited' in TBC (ed.), TBC: Volume of Essays in Honour of Emeritus Professor Kostas Mavrias (Sakkoulas 2020).

Blau, Adrian, 'Electoral Reform in the UK: a Veto-Player Analysis', in Blais, André (ed.), *To Keep or to Change First Past the Post? The Politics of Electoral Reform* 61–89 (Oxford University Press 2008).

Blackburn, Robert, 'Majoritarianism under Pressure: the Electoral and Party Systems', in Hazell, Robert (ed.), *Constitutional Futures* 233–248 (Palgrave Macmillan 2008).

Caygill, Thomas and Griffiths, Anne Marie, 'Parliament and Petitions', in Bandeira, Cristina Leston and Thompson, Louise (eds.), *Exploring the Parliament*, 322–331(Oxford 2018).

Chowdhury, M Jashim Ali, 'Bangladesh's Inconsistency with the Prospective Invalidation', in Yap, Po Jen (ed.), *Constitutional Remedies in Asia* 33–46 (London: Routledge 2019).

Chowdhury, M Jashim Ali, 'Elections in 'Democratic' Bangladesh', in Tushnet, Mark and Khosla, Madhav (eds.), *Unstable Constitutionalism: Law and Politics in South Asia* 192–229 (Cambridge University Press 2015).

Chowdhury, M Jashim Ali, 'Fifty Years of Electioneering in Bangladesh: the collapse of constitutional design', in M Rafiqul Islam and Muhammad Ekramul Haque (eds.) *The Constitutional Law of Bangladesh: Progression and Transformation at its 50th Anniversary* 173–193 (Springer Nature: Singapore, 2023).

Chowdhury, M Jashim Ali, 'Making and Unmaking the Constitution in Bangladesh', in Ngoc Bui Son and Mara Malagodi (eds.), *Asian Comparative Constitutional Law Volume 1: Constitution Making* 363–382 (London: Hart Publishing, 2023).

Chowdhury, M Jashim Ali, 'Parliament of Bangladesh: Constitutional Position and Contributions' in Ridwanul Hoque and Rokeya Chowdhury (eds.), *A History of the Constitution of Bangladesh: the Founding, Development, and Way Ahead* 145–160 (London: Routledge, 2023).

Chowdhury, M Jashim Ali, 'The Parliament (Jatiya Sangsad) of Bangladesh', in Yap, PJ, & Abeyratne, R, (eds.), *Routledge Handbook of Asian Parliaments* 103–124 (London: Routledge, 2023).

Cowley, Philip, 'The Coalition and Parliament' in Seldon, A, and Finn, M (eds.), *The Coalition Effect 2010–2015*, 136–156 (Cambridge University Press 2015).

Evans, D Hugh, 'Bangladesh: an Unsteady Democracy' in Shastri, A, and Wilson, AJ (eds.), *The Postcolonial States of South Asia*, 69–87 (New York: Palgrave Macmillan 2001).

Faruque, Abdullah Al, 'Role of Parliament in Ensuring Democratic Accountability in Bangladesh: Setting the Agenda for a Strengthened Parliamentary System' in Islam, M Rafiqul and Haque, Muhammad Ekramul (eds.) *The Constitutional Law of Bangladesh: Progression and Transformation at its 50th Anniversary*, 121–137 (Singapore: Springer Nature 2023).

Franklin, Mark and Norton, Philip, 'Questions and Members', in Franklin and Norton (eds.), *Parliamentary Questions*, 104–122 (Oxford: Clarendon Press 1993).

Gay, Oonagh, 'MPs Campaigning for their Constituencies' in Bandeira, Cristina Leston and Thompson, Louise (eds.), *Exploring the Parliament*, 274–284 (Oxford 2018).

Grote, Rainer, 'Westminster Democracy in an Islamic Context: Pakistan, Bangladesh, Malaysia', in Rainer Grote and Tilmann J Röder (eds.) *Constitutionalism in Islamic Countries: Between Upheaval and Continuity* (Oxford: Oxford University Press 2012).

Haig, Patapan and Wanna, John, 'The Westminster legacy: Conclusion' in Haig, Patapan, Wanna, John and Weller, Patrick (eds.), *Westminster Legacies: Democracy and Responsible Government in Asia and the Pacific*, 242–255 (University of New South Wales Press 2005).

Hallerberg, M, 'Electoral Laws, Government, and Parliament' in Doring, H, and Hallerberg, M, (eds.) *Patterns of Parliamentary Behaviour*, 11–33 (Aldershot Ashgate 2004).

Hallerberg, M, 'The Role of Parliamentary Committees in the Budgetary Process within Europe' in Strauch, RR Hagen, J, Von (eds.) *Institutions, Politics and Fiscal Policy* 87–106 (Kluwer 2000).

Hasan, Samiul, 'Corruption, Accountability and Political Parties in Bangladesh: Connections and Consequences', in May, T, and Ray, B, (eds.), *Democratic Ideals, Governance, and Corruption in South Asia* (Kolkata: Freedom Press 2006).

Hedlund, R, 'Organizational Attributes of Legislative Institutions: Structures, Rules, Norms, Resources', in Loewenberg, G, Patterson, S, and Jewell, M, (eds.), *Handbook of Legislative Research* 321–391 (Cambridge, MA: Harvard University Press 1985).

Hoque, Ridwanul, 'Constitutionalism and the Judiciary in Bangladesh' in Khilnani, Sunil, Raghavan, Vikram and Thiruvengadam, Arun K, (ed), *Comparative Constitutionalism in South Asia* (Oxford University Press 2012).

Hoque, Ridwanul, 'The Founding and Making of Bangladesh's Constitution', in Tan, Kevin YL and Hoque, Ridwanul (eds.), *Constitutional Foundlings in South Asia*, 91–119 (Hart Publishing 2021).

Hussain, Md Lokman, 'Constituting Limits and Accountability of the Executive Power in Bangladesh', in R, Hoque and R, Chowdhury (eds.) *A History of The Constitution of Bangladesh: the Founding, Development, and Way Ahead*, 129–144 (London: Routledge 2023).

Judge, David and Partos, Rebecca, 'MPs and their constituencies, Parties and MPs' in Bandeira, Cristina Leston and Thompson, Louise (eds.), *Exploring Parliament* 267–279 (Oxford University Press 2018).

Khator, Renu, 'The Political Party System of India: From One-Party Dominance to No-Party Dominance', in Rimanelli, M, (eds.), *Comparative Democratization and Peaceful Change in Single-Party-Dominant Countries* 339–361 (Palgrave Macmillan, New York 1999).

King, Anthony, 'Britain's Traditional Constitution' in *The British Constitution* 39–62 (Oxford University Press 2009).

King, Anthony, 'Modes of Executive-Legislative Relations: Great Britain, France and West Germany' in Norton, Philip (ed.), *Legislatures* 186–207 (Oxford University Press 1990).

Kumar, Ashutosh, 'Why is Parliament in the State of Decline?' in Mehra, Ajay K. (ed.), *The Indian Parliament and Democratic Transition*, 61–82 (India: Routledge 2017).

Kumarasingham, Harshan, 'Eastminster – Decolonisation and State-Building in British Asia' in Kumarasingham, Harshan (ed.), *Constitution-Making in Asia – Decolonisation and State-Building in the Aftermath of the British Empire* 1–35 (Routledge: London 2016).

Lavarch, M, 'Fighting the Friends from Finance' in Stacy, H, Lavarch, M, (ed.), *Beyond the Adversarial System* (The Federation Press, Sydney, 1999).

Macintosh, John P, 'Introduction: Attitude to the Representative Role of Parliament' in *People and Parliament* 1–10 (Saxon House 1979).

Mattson, Ingvar and Strom, Kaare, 'Parliamentary Committees' in Dohring, Herbert (ed), *Parliament and Majority Rule in West Europe* 249–307 (University of Mannheim 1995).

Mezey, Michael L, 'Parliament in the New Europe', in Hayward, J, and Page, E, (eds.), *Governing the New Europe* (Polity Press 1995).

Moniruzzaman, M, 'Electoral Legitimacy, Preventive Representation, and Regularization of Authoritarian Democracy in Bangladesh' in Yonk, Ryan Merlin (ed.), *Elections: a Global Perspective* (IntechOpen 2019).

Norton, Philip, 'Conclusion: Developing the Links', in Norton, Philip (ed.), *Parliament in Contemporary Western Europe Vol 3* (*Parliament and Citizens in Western Europe*) 178–192 (Routledge, 2002).

Norton, Philip, 'Introduction: Parliament since 1960', in Franklin, Mark and Norton, Philip (eds.), *Parliamentary Questions* (Oxford, 1993).

Norton, Philip, 'Introduction: the Institution of Parliaments', in Norton, Philip (ed.), *Parliaments and Governments in Western Europe* 1–15 (London: Frank Cass 1998).

Norton, Philip, 'Old Institution, New Institutionalism? Parliament and Government in the UK' in Norton, Philip (ed.), *Parliaments in Contemporary Western Europe* 16–43 (Routledge 1998).

Norton, Philip, 'The Norton View', in Judge, D. (ed.), *The Politics of Parliamentary Reform* 54–70 (London: Heinemann, 1983).

Norton, Philip, 'The United Kingdom: Building the link between Constituent and MP' in Norton, Philip (ed.), *Parliament in Contemporary Western Europe Vol 3* (*Parliament and Citizens in Western Europe*) 19–42 (Routledge, 2002).

Norton, Philip, 'The United Kingdom: Parliament Under Pressure' in Norton, Philip (eds.), *Parliaments and Pressure Groups in Western Europe* 19–42 (London: Routledge 1999).

Norton, Philip and Ahmed, Nizam, 'Legislatures in Asia: Exploring Diversity' in Norton, Philip and Ahmed, Nizam (eds.), *Parliaments in Asia* (Frank Cass 1999).

Polsby, Nelson W, 'Legislatures' in Norton, P, (ed.), *Legislatures*, 130–148 (Oxford: Oxford University Press 1990).

Prakash, Gyan, 'Anxious Constitution-Making' in Prakash, Gyan, Laffan, Michael and Menon, Nikhil (eds.), *The Postcolonial Moment in South and Southeast Asia*, 141–162 (Bloomsbury Academic 2018).

Rhodes, RAW and Weller, Patrick, 'Westminster Transplanted and Westminster Implanted: Exploring Political Change' in Patapan, Haig, Wanna, John and Weller, Patrick (eds.), *Westminster Legacies: Democracy and Responsible Government in Asia and the Pacific* 1–12 (University of New South Wales Press 2005).

Rush, Michael, 'Parliamentary Scrutiny' in Pyper, Robert and Robins, Lynton (eds.), *Governing the UK in the 1990s*, 108–30 (St Martin's Press 1995).

Saalfeld, T and Dobmeier, R, 'The Bundestag and German Citizens: More Communication, Growing Distance' in Bandeira, C Leston (ed.), *Parliaments and Citizens* 50–69 (Abingdon: Routledge, 2013).

Shephard, Mark and Caird, Jack Simson, 'The Role of Backbench MPs', in Bandeira, Cristina Leston and Thompson, Louise (eds.), *Exploring Parliament* 187–195 (Oxford University Press 2018).

Smyth, Liam Laurence, McKee, Glenn, Korris, Matt, 'The Legislative Cycle', in Bandeira, Cristina Leston, Thompson, Louise (eds.), *Exploring Parliament* 67–79 (Oxford University Press 2018).

Stuart, Mark, 'Whips and Rebels' in Bandeira, Cristina Leston and Thompson, Louise (eds.), *Exploring Parliament* 67–79 (Oxford University Press 2018).

Sueur, A Le, 'Parliamentary Accountability and the Judicial System' in Bamforth, N, and Leyland, P, (eds.) *Accountability in the Contemporary Constitution* 200–230 (Oxford, OUP 2013).

Tan, Kevin YL and Hoque, Ridwanul, 'South Asian Constitutional Foundings: Beyond History' in Tan, Kevin YL and Hoque, Ridwanul (eds.), *Constitutional Foundings in South Asia* (Oxford: Hart Publishing, 2021).

Thomas, Paul G, 'Parliament and Legislatures: Central to Canadian Democracy?' in Courtney, John C, and Smith, David E, (eds.), *The Oxford Handbook of Canadian Politics* (Oxford 2010).

Thomassen, J, 'Empirical Research into Political Representation: Failing Democracy or Failing Models?' in Jennings, MK and Mann, T, (eds.), *Elections at Home and Abroad: Essays in honour of Warren E Miller*, 237–264 (Michigan: University of Michigan Press 1994).

Thomassen, J and Schmitt, H, 'Political Representation and Legitimacy in the European Union' in Schmitt, H, and Thomassen, J, (eds.), *Political Representation and Legitimacy in the European Union* 3–24 (Oxford: Oxford University Press 1999).

Tushnet, Mark, 'Judicial Accountability in Comparative Perspective' in Bamforth, Nicholas and Leyland, Peter (eds.), *Accountability in the Contemporary Constitution* 57–74 (Oxford: Oxford University Press 2013).

Stern, Robert W, 'India's Westminster System' in Patapan, Haig, Wanna, John and Weller, Patrick (eds.), *Westminster Legacies: Democracy and Responsible Government in Asia and the Pacific*, 13–35 (University of New South Wales Press 2005).

Walkland, SA, 'Government Legislation in the House of Commons' in Walkland, SA, (ed), *The House of Commons in the Twentieth Century: Essays by Members of the Study of Parliament Group* (Oxford: Clarendon Press, 1979).

Welikala, Asanga, 'The Eastminster Viceroy and the Republican Monarch: the Sri Lankan Head of State and the 2018 Constitutional Crisis in Historical Context' in Kumarasingham, H (ed.), *Viceregalism: the Crown as Head of State in Political Crises in the Postwar Commonwealth* 231–252 (Palgrave Macmillan, 2020).

Weller, Patrick and Sharma, Bishnu, 'Transplanting Westminster to Nepal: the stuff of dreams dashed', in Patapan, Haig, Wanna, John and Weller, Patrick (eds.), *Westminster Legacies: Democracy and Responsible Government in Asia -and the Pacific* 63–80 (University of New South Wales Press 2005).

Wiberg, M, 'Parliamentary Questionings: Control by Communication?' in Doring, H, (ed.), *Parliaments and Majority Rule in Western Europe*, 179–222 (St. Martin Press 1995).

Winetrobe, Barry K, 'The Autonomy of Parliament', in Oliver, Dawn and Drewry, Gavin (eds.), *The Law and Parliament* 14–32 (Butterworths 1998).

Wright, Scott, 'E-petitions' in Coleman, Stephen and Freelon, Deen (eds.), *Handbook of Digital Politics* 136–150 (Edward Elgar Publishing, 2015).

Journal Articles

Ahmed, Nizam, 'Abolition or Reform? Non-party Caretaker System and Government Succession in Bangladesh' (2011) 100 (414) Round Table: the Commonwealth Journal of International Affairs 303.

Ahmed, Nizam, 'Critical Elections and Democratic Consolidation: the 2008 Parliamentary Elections in Bangladesh' (2011) 19(2) Contemporary South Asia 137.

Ahmed, Nizam, 'Development and Working of Parliaments in South Asia' (2001) 9(1) Asian Journal of Political Science 18.

Ahmed, Nizam, 'Experiments in Local Government Reform in Bangladesh' (1988) 28(8) Asian Survey 813.

Ahmed, Nizam, 'From Marginal to Minimal Legislature: Development of Parliament in Bangladesh (1991–2018)' (2018) South Asia Journal 120.

Ahmed, Nizam, 'From Monopoly to Competition: Party Politics in the Bangladesh Parliament (1973–2001)' (2003) 76(1) Pacific Affairs 55.

Ahmed, Nizam, 'In Search of Institutionalization: Parliament in Bangladesh' (1998) 4(4) The Journal of Legislative Studies 34.

Ahmed, Nizam, 'Non-Party Caretaker Governments and Parliamentary Elections in Bangladesh: Panacea or Pandora's Box?' (2004) 11(1) South Asian Survey 49.

Ahmed, Nizam, 'Parliament and Citizens in Asia: the Bangladesh Case' (2012) 18(3–4) The Journal of Legislative Studies 463.

Ahmed, Nizam, 'Parliament and Democratic Consolidation in Bangladesh' (2011) 26(2) Australasian Parliamentary Review 53.

Ahmed, Nizam, 'Parliament and Poverty Reduction in Bangladesh: Role of the MP' (2018) 25(1–2) South Asian Survey 163.

Ahmed, Nizam, 'Parliament, Public Engagement and Legislation in Bangladesh: a Case Study of Domestic Violence Act of 2010' (2018) 24(4) The Journal of Legislative Studies 431.

Ahmed, Nizam, 'Parliamentary Committees and Parliamentary Government in Bangladesh' (2001) 10(1) Contemporary South Asia 11.

Ahmed, Nizam, 'Parliamentary Opposition in Bangladesh: a Study of its Role in the Fifth Parliament' (1997) 3(2) Party Politics 147.

Ahmed, Nizam, 'Parliamentary Politics in Bangladesh' (1994) 32(3) Journal of Commonwealth and Comparative Politics 364.

Ahmed, Nizam, 'Parliament-Executive Relations in Bangladesh' (1997) 3(4) The Journal of Legislative Studies 70.

Ahmed, Nizam, 'Party Politics under a non-party Caretaker Government in Bangladesh: the Fakhruddin Interregnum (2007–09)' (2010) 48(1) Commonwealth and Comparative Politics 23.

Ahmed, Nizam, 'Reforming the Parliament in Bangladesh: Structural Constraints and Political Dilemmas' (1998) 36(1) Commonwealth and Comparative Politics 68.

Ahmed, Nizam and Ahmad, SZ, 'The Parliamentary Elections in Bangladesh, October 2001' (2003) 3(22) Electoral Studies 503.

Ahmed, Nizam and Ahmed, Aftab, 'The Quest for Accountability: Parliament and Public Administration in Bangladesh' (1996) 18 Asian Journal of Public Administration 70.

Ahmed, Nizam and Hasan, Sadik, 'Does Public Engagement Matter? Parliament, Public Engagement and the Budget Process in Bangladesh' (2019) 34(1) Australasian Parliamentary Review 28.

Ahmed, Nizam and Khan, Shahnaz, 'The Development of Parliamentary Oversight in Bangladesh: a Research Note' (1995) 20(4) Legislative Studies Quarterly 573.

Ahmed, Sabbir, 'Article 70 of the Constitution of Bangladesh: Implications for the Process of Democratisation' (2010) 31(1) BIISS Journal 1.

Ahmed, Samina, 'Politics in Bangladesh: the Paradox of Military Intervention' (1991) 9(1) Regional Studies 58.

Ahmed, Syed Imtiaz, 'Civilian Supremacy in Democracies with 'Fault Lines': the Role of the Parliamentary Standing Committee on Defence in Bangladesh' (2006) 13(2) Democratization 283.

Ahmed, Syed Istiaq, Constitution and Democracy in Bangladesh since 1972, 44 DLR Journal 52.

Ahmed, Zahir, 'From Shape Shifting to Collusion in Violence: an Ethnography of Informal Relationships Between Bangladeshi Members of Parliament and their Constituents' (2019) 42(1) Legal and Political Anthropology Review 5.

Alam, Afroz, 'Decline of Parliamentary Governance: Indian Scenario' (2015) 3(2) Rostrum Law Review 1.

Alam, Quamrul and Teicher, Julian, 'The State of Governance in Bangladesh: the Capture of State Institutions' (2012) 35(4) South Asia: Journal of South Asian Studies 858.

Alderman, RK, 'The Leader of the Opposition and Prime Minister's Question Time' (1992) 45(1) Parliamentary Affairs 66.

Allan, TRS, 'Constitutional Dialogue and The Justification of Judicial Review' (2003) 23(4) Oxford Journal of Legal Studies 563.

Aminuzzaman, Salahuddin, 'Institutional Processes and Practices of Administrative Accountability: Role of *Jatya Sangsad* in Bangladesh' (1993) 10(2) South Asian Studies 44.

Amundsen, Inge, 'Democratic Dynasties? Internal Party Democracy in Bangladesh' (2016) 22(1) Party Politics 49.

Askvik, Steinar and Jamil, Ishtiaq, 'The Institutional Trust Paradox in Bangladesh' (2013) 13(4) Public Organization Review 459.

Bailer, Stefanie, 'People's Voice or Information Pool? The Role of, and Reasons for, Parliamentary Questions in the Swiss Parliament' (2011) 17(3) The Journal of Legislative Studies 302.

Ball, Stuart, 'The 1922 Committee: the Formative Years, 1922–45' (1990) 9(1) Parliamentary History 129.

Bandeira, Cristina Leston, 'The Pursuit of Legitimacy as a Key Driver for Public Engagement: the European Parliament Case' (2014) 67(2) Parliamentary Affairs 415.

Bandeira, Cristina Leston, 'Towards a Trustee Model? Parliamentary Representation in the Internet Era: the Portuguese Case' (2012) 65 (2) Parliamentary Affairs 425.

Bandeira, Cristina Leston, 'Why Symbolic Representation Frames Parliamentary Public Engagement' (2016) 18 The British Journal of Politics and International Relations 498.

Bari, M Ehteshamul, 'The Incorporation of the System of Non-Party Caretaker Government in the Constitution of Bangladesh in 1996 as a Means of Strengthening Democracy, Its Deletion in 2011 and the Lapse of Bangladesh into Tyranny Following the Non-Participatory General Election of 2014: a Critical Appraisal' (2018) 28(1) Transnational Law and Contemporary Problems 27.

Barroso, LR, 'Counter majoritarian, Representative, and Enlightened: the Roles of Constitutional Courts in Democracies' (2019) 67(1) The American Journal of Comparative Law 109.

Bates, Thomas R, 'Gramsci and the Theory of Hegemony,' (1975) 36(2) Journal of the History of Ideas 351.

Baxter, Craig, 'Bangladesh a Parliamentary Democracy, if They Can Keep It' (1992) 91(563) Current History 132.

Baxter, Craig, 'Bangladesh in 1991: a Parliamentary System' (1992) 32(2) Asian Survey 162.

Baxter, Craig, 'Bangladesh: Can Democracy Survive?' (1996) 95(600) Current History 182.

Beatson, Sir Jack, 'The New Model Judiciary and the Other Two Branches of the State' (2015) 20(2) Judicial Review 63.

Beattie, Alan, 'Why the case for Parliamentary reform in Britain is so weak' (1998) 4(2) The Journal of Legislative Studies 1.

Beaulac, Stephane, 'Parliamentary Debates in Statutory Interpretation: a Question of Admissibility or of Weight?' (1998) 43(3) McGill Law Journal 288.

Begum, Afroza, 'Disrespecting Constitutional Safeguards for Fundamental Rights in Bangladesh: a Bird's Eye View from the Indian Context' (2007) 49(1) Journal of the Indian Law Institute 3.

Begum, Afroza, 'Politics in Bangladesh Need for a Reconceptualization of the Politico-Legal Approach to Mitigate Women's Disadvantaged Positions in the Parliament' (2009) 44(2) Journal of Asian and African Studies 171.

Bellamy, Richard, 'Political Constitutionalism and the Human Rights Act 1998' (2011) 9(1) International Journal of Constitutional Law 86.

Bennister, Mark and Heffernan, Richard, 'Cameron as Prime Minister: the Intra-Executive Politics of Britain's Coalition Government' (2012) 65 Parliamentary Affairs 778.

Bercow, John, 'Prime Minister's Questions in the United Kingdom' (2012) Canadian Parliamentary Review 9.

Bernauer, Julian and Vatter, Adrian, 'Can't get no satisfaction with the Westminster Model? Winners, Losers and the Effects of Consensual and Direct Democratic Institutions on Satisfaction with Democracy' (2012) 51(4) European Journal of Political Research 435.

Bertocci, Peter J, 'Bangladesh in 1985: Resolute Against the Storms' (1986) 26(2) Asian Survey 229.

Bhuiyan, Md Shahjahan Hafez, 'The Caretaker Government in Bangladesh: an Appraisal of its Formation' (2003) 40 Politics, Administration and Change 33.

Billah, SM Masum, 'Making the journey of constitutionalism smooth: Is 'Advisory Jurisdiction' a catalyst?' (2008) 19(1) Dhaka University Law Journal 131.

Blackburn, Robert, 'The Politics of Parliamentary Procedure at Westminster' (2017) The Journal of International and Comparative Law 279.

Blondel, Jean, 'Party Systems and Patterns of Government in Western Democracies' (1968) 1(2) Canadian Journal of Political Science 180.

Bochel, C, 'Different Dimensions of Voice and Influence in the Scottish Parliament and the National Assembly for Wales' (2012) 46(2) Social Policy and Administration 142.

Brazier, Rodney, 'The Constitutional Role of the Opposition' (1989) 40 Northern Ireland Legal Quarterly 131.

Buck, Vincent and Cain, Bruce E, 'British MPs in their Constituencies' (1990) 15(1) Legislative Studies Quarterly 127.

Burbank, Stephen B, 'Judicial Independence, Judicial Accountability, and Interbranch Relations' (2006–2007) 95 The Georgetown Law Journal 909.

Cain, J, Ferejohn B, and M, Fiorina, 'The Constituency Service basis of the Personal Vote for US Representatives and British Members of Parliament' (1984) The American Political Science Review 110.

Campbell, Enid, 'Expulsion of Members of Parliament' (1971) 21(1) University of Toronto Law Journal 15.

Carrington, Paul D, 'Judicial Independence and Democratic Accountability in Highest State Courts' (1998) 61(3) Law and Contemporary Problems: Judicial Independence and Accountability 79.

Chowdhury, M Jashim Ali, 'Basic Structure Tendencies of the UK Parliament Prorogation Judgement' (2020) 3(2) SCLS Law Review 88.

Chowdhury, M Jashim Ali, 'Claiming a 'Fundamental Right to Basic Necessities of Life': Problems and Prospects of Adjudication in Bangladesh' (2011–12) 5 Indian Journal of Constitutional Law 184.

Chowdhury, M Jashim Ali, 'Does inconsistency with Fundamental Principles of State Policy invalidate a Law?' (2009) 5 BRAC University Journal 71.

Chowdhury, M Jashim Ali, 'Judicial Review of "Internal Parliamentary Proceedings": the Dialogic and Non-Dialogic Approaches' (2021) 6(1) Comparative Constitutional Law and Administrative Law Journal 28.

Chowdhury, M Jashim Ali, 'The Antagonistic Style of Judicial Review in Bangladesh: a Good Candidate for the Dialogic Model?' (2021) 15 Journal of Parliamentary and Political Law, 549.

Chowdhury, M Jashim Ali, 'Working and Impact of Parliamentary Committees in the UK and Bangladesh: a Theoretical Analysis' (2021) 32(2) Dhaka University Law Journal 175.

Chowdhury, M Jashim Ali and Mamun, Md Abdullah Al, 'The Comptroller and Auditor General of Bangladesh: Arguments for "Substantial Independence"' (2016) 21 The Chittagong University Journal of Law 159.

Chowdhury, M Jashim Ali and Rafid, Raihan Rahman, 'Parliaments during the Pandemic: a "Dual State" Explanation of Bangladesh Parliament (Jatya Sangsad)' (2020) 18(1–2) Bangladesh Journal of Law 25.

Chowdhury, M Jashim Ali and Saha, Nirmal Kumar, '*Advocate Asaduzzaman Siddiqui v. Bangladesh*: Judiciary's Dilemma with Impeachment' (2017) 3(3) Constitutional and Administrative Law Quarterly 7.

Chowdhury, M Jashim Ali and Saha, Nirmal Kumar, 'Amendment Power in Bangladesh: Arguments for the Revival of Constitutional Referendum' (2020) 9 Indian Journal of Constitutional Law 38.

Chowdhury, Mahfuzul H, 'Dynamics of Political Parties in Bangladesh' (1995) 2 South Asian Survey 63.

Chowdhury, Mahfuzul H, 'Violence, Politics and the State in Bangladesh' (2003) 3(2) Conflict, Security & Development 265.

Chowdhury, Md Yasin Khan, 'Removal of Judges Under 16th Amendment of Bangladesh Constitution: a Euphemism to Curb on Judiciary' (2015) 3 DIU Journal of Humanities and Social Science 89.

Chowdhury, Rokeya, 'The Doctrine of Basic Structure in Bangladesh: From 'Calfpath' to Matryoshka Dolls' (2014) 14 Bangladesh Journal of Law 43.

Cole, Michael, 'Accountability and quasi-government: the role of Parliamentary Questions' (1999) 5(1) The Journal of Legislative Studies 77.

Coleman, Stephen, 'Connecting Parliament to the Public via the Internet (2004) 7(1) Information, Communication and Society 1.

Coleman, Stephen, 'New mediation and direct representation: Reconceptualising Representation in the Digital Age' (2005) 7(2) New Media and Society 177.

Cotton, Ross, 'Political Participation and E-Petitioning: an Analysis of the Policy-Making Impact of the Scottish Parliament's E-Petition System' (2012) 6(1) University of Central Florida Undergraduate Research Journal 33.

Cowley, Philip and Norton, Philip, 'Rebels and Rebellions: Conservative MPs in the 1992 Parliament' (2002) 1(1) British Journal of Politics & International Relations 84.

Cowley, Philip and Stuart, Mark, 'In the Brown stuff? Labour Backbench Dissent Under Gordon Brown, 2007–10' (2014) 28(1) Contemporary British History 1.

Crines, Andrew Scott, Jeffery, David and Heppell, Timothy, 'The British Labour Party and leadership election mandate(s) of Jeremy Corbyn: patterns of opinion and opposition within the parliamentary Labour Party' (2018) 28(3) Journal of Elections, Public Opinion and Parties 361.

Curtice, John, 'Politicians, voters and democracy: the 2011 UK Referendum on the Alternative Vote' (2013) 32(2) Electoral Studies 215.

Curtice, John, 'The Death of a Miserable Little Compromise: the Alternative Vote Referendum' (2011) 2(2) Political Insight 14.

Cutts, D, and Shryane, N, 'Did Local Activism really matter? Liberal Democrat campaigning and the 2001 British General Election' (2006) 8(3) British Journal of Politics and International Relations 427.

Czapanskiy, Karen Syma and Manjoo, Rashida, 'The Right of Public Participation in The Law-Making Process and the Role of Legislature in the Promotion of this Right (2008) 19 *Duke* Journal of Comparative & International Law 1.

Davis, FF 'Parliamentary Supremacy and the Re-Invigoration of Institutional Dialogue in the UK' (2012) 67 Parliamentary Affairs 137.

Docherty, David C and White, Stephen, 'Parliamentary Democracy in Canada' (2004) 57(3) Parliamentary Affairs 613.

Dowding, Keith and Kang, Won-Taek, 'Ministerial Resignations 1945–1997' (1998) 76 Public Administration 411.

Dunleavy, P, and Jones, G, 'Leaders, Politics and Institutional Change: the Decline of Prime Ministerial Accountability to the House of Commons, 1868–1990' (1993) 23(3) British Journal of Political Science 267.

Dunleavy, Patrick and Margetts, Helen, 'From Majoritarian to Pluralist Democracy? Electoral Reform in Britain since 1997' (2001) 13(3) Journal of Theoretical Politics 295.

Editorial, 'Decline of Parliamentary Governance: Indian Scenario,' (2017) 3(2) Rostrum's Law Review 1.

Elgie, Robert and Stapleton, John, 'Testing the Decline of Parliament Thesis: Ireland, 1923–2002' (2006) 54 Political Studies 465.

Escher, Tobias and Riehm, Ulrich, 'Petitioning the German Bundestag: Political Equality and the Role of the Internet' (2017) 70(1) Parliamentary Affairs 132.

Eulau, Heinz, Wahlke, John C, Buchanan, William and Ferguson, Leroy C, 'The Role of the Representative: Some Empirical Observations on the Theory of Edmund Burke' (1959) 53(3) The American Political Science Review 742.

Feldman, Shelley, 'Bangladesh in 2014: Illusive Democracy' (2015) 55(1) Asian Survey 67.

Ferdous, Jannatul, 'Representation of Women in Parliament of Bangladesh: Is it Hopeful?' (2019) 6(2) Journal of Governance and Public Policy 110.

Firoj, Jalal, 'Forty Years of Bangladesh Parliament: Trends, Achievements and Challenges' (2013) 58(1) Journal of the Asiatic Society of Bangladesh (Humanities) 83.

Fish, M Steven, 'Stronger Legislature, Stronger Democracies' (2006) 17(1) Journal of Democracy 5.

Flinders, M, 'Mechanisms of judicial accountability in British central government' (2001) 54(1) Parliamentary Affairs 54.

Flinders, M, 'Analysing Reform: the House of Commons 2001–5' (2007) 55 Political Studies 174.

Flinders, M, 'Shifting the Balance? Parliament, the Executive and the British Constitution' (2002) 50(1) Political Studies 23.

Flinders, Mathew and Kelso, Alexandra, 'Mind the Gap: Political Analysis, Public Expectations and the Parliamentary Decline Thesis' (2011) 13 The British Journal of Politics and International Relations 249.

Foster, David H, 'Going 'Where Angels Fear to Tread': How Effective was the Backbench Business Committee in the 2010–2012 Parliamentary Session?' (2015) 68(1) Parliamentary Affairs 116.

Fox, Ruth, 'Engagement and Participation: What the Public Want and How our Politicians Need to Respond' (2009) 62 Parliamentary Affairs 673.

Fraser, Catherine A, 'Constitutional Dialogues between Courts and Legislatures: Can We Talk?' (2005) 14(3) Forum Constitutionnel 7.

Fung, A, and Wright, E, 'Deepening Democracy Innovations in Empowered Participatory Governance' (1998) 26(4) Politics and Society 15.

Gaines, B, 'The Impersonal Vote? Constituency Service and Incumbency Advantage in British Elections, 1950–92' (1998) Legislative Studies Quarterly 167.

Geddes, Marc, 'Committee Hearings of the UK Parliament: Who gives Evidence and does this Matter?' (2018) 71 Parliamentary Affairs 283.

Ghoshal, Baladas, 'The Anatomy of Military Interventions in Asia: the Case of Bangladesh' (2009) 65(1) India Quarterly 67.

Gilligan, Thomas and Krehbiel, Keith, 'Asymmetric Information and Legislative Rules with a Heterogeneous Committee' (1989) 33 American Journal of Political Science 459.

Gilligan, Thomas and Krehbiel, Keith, 'Collective Decision-Making and Standing Committees: an Informational Rationale for Restrictive Amendment Procedures' (1987) 3 Journal of Law, Economics and Organization 287.

Gilligan, Thomas and Krehbiel, Keith, 'Organization of Informative Committees by a Rational Legislature' (1990) 34 American Journal of Political Science 531.

Go, Julian, 'Modelling the State: Postcolonial Constitutions in Asia and Africa, Southeast Asian Studies' (2002) 39(4) Southeast Asian Studies 558.

Griffith, Jeffrey and Bandeira, Cristina Leston, 'How Are Parliaments Using New Media to Engage with Citizens?' (2012) 18(3–4) The Journal of Legislative Studies 496.

Guinn, David E, and Straussman, Jeffrey D, 'Implementing Legislative Strengthening Programmes: Who is in Control?' (2019) 37(5) Development Policy Review 621.

Hakim, Muhammad A, 'Bangladesh: the Beginning of the end of Militarised Politics?' (1998) 7(3) Contemporary South Asia 283.

Haque, Azizul, 'Bangladesh in 1979: Cry for a Sovereign Parliament' (1980) 20(2) Asian Survey 217.

Harding, Andrew, 'The 'Westminster Model' Constitution Overseas: Transplantation, Adaptation and Development in Commonwealth States' (2004) 4 Oxford University Commonwealth Law Journal 143.

Harper, David, 'Parliament and Judiciary: Judicial Independence and nature of the relationship between parliament and the judiciary' (2015) 30(2) Australasian Parliamentary Review 8.

Hazell, RJD and O'Brien, PC 'Meaningful Dialogue: Judicial Engagement with Parliamentary Committees at Westminster' (2016) Public Law 54.

Helms, Ludger, 'Studying Parliamentary, Opposition in Old and New Democracies: Issues and Perspectives' (2008) 14(1–2) The Journal of Legislative Studies 6.

Herman, Valentine and Lodge, Juliet, 'The European Parliament and the "Decline of Legislatures" Thesis' (1978) 13(1) Politics 10.

Hickman, Tom R, 'Constitutional Dialogue, Constitutional Theories and the Human Rights Act 1998' (2005) Public Law 306.

Hiebert, Janet L, 'Interpreting a Bill of Rights: the Importance of Legislative Rights Review' (2005) 35 British Journal of Political Science 235.

Hiebert, Janet L, 'Interpreting A Bill of Rights: the Importance of Legislative Rights Review' (2005) 35(2) British Journal of Political Science 235.

Hiebert, Janet L, 'Parliament and the Human Rights Act: Can the JCHR help facilitate a Culture of Rights?' (2006) 4(1) International Journal of Constitutional Law 1.

Hill, Larry B, 'Parliamentary Petitions, the Ombudsman and Political Change in New Zealand' (1974) 22(3) Political Studies 337.

Hockin, Thomas A, 'The Roles of the Loyal Opposition in Britain's House of Commons: Three Historical Paradigms' (1971) 25(1) Parliamentary Affairs 50.

Hogg, Peter W Thornton, Allison A Bushell and Wright, Wade K, 'Charter Dialogue Revisited: Or "Much Ado About Metaphors"' (2007) 45(1) Osgoode Hall Law Journal 1.

Hogg, Peter and Bushell, Allison, 'The Charter Dialogue Between Courts and Legislatures (Or perhaps The Charter of Rights isn't such a bad thing after all)' (1997) 35 Osgoode Hall Law Journal 75.

Hoque, Ridwanul, 'Can the Court Invalidate an Original Provision of the Constitution?' (2016) 2 University of Asia Pacific Journal of Law and Policy 13.

Hoque, Ridwanul, 'Deconstructing Public Participation and Deliberation in Constitutional Amendment in Bangladesh' 2021 21(2) Australian Journal of Asian Law 7.

Hoque, Ridwanul, 'Taking justice seriously: judicial public interest and constitutional activism in Bangladesh' (2006) 15(4) Contemporary South Asia 399.

Hoque, Ridwanul, 'The Recent Emergency and the Politics of the Judiciary in Bangladesh' (2009) 2(2) NUJS Law Review 183.

Hossain, Golam, 'Bangladesh in 1994: Democracy at Risk' (1995) 35(2) Asian Survey 171.

Hossain, Golam, 'Bangladesh in 1995: Politics of Intransigence' (1996) 36(2) Asian Survey 196.

Hossain, Md Zakir and Chowdhury, M Jashim Ali, 'The Caretaker Government: a Constitutional Evaluation and Search for Alternatives' (In Bangla) (2014) 19 The Chittagong University Journal of Law 228.

Hough, Richard, 'Do Legislative Petitions Systems Enhance the Relationship between Parliament and Citizen?' (2012) 18 (3–4) The Journal of Legislative Studies 479.

Huq, Abul Fazl, 'Constitution-Making in Bangladesh' (1973) 46(1) Pacific Affairs 59.

Huq, MM 'Call Attention Motions and Accountability of Public Corporations in the Bangladesh First Parliament' (1991) 12(1) Dhaka University Studies Part-C 101.

Huque, Ahmed Shafiqul, 'Accountability and Governance: strengthening Extra-bureaucratic Mechanisms in Bangladesh' (2011) 60(1) International Journal of Productivity and Performance Management 59.

Huque, Ahmed Shafiqul and Hakim, Muhammad A, 'Elections in Bangladesh: Tools of Legitimacy' (1993) 19(4) Asian Affairs 248.

Huque, Ahmed Shafiqul, 'The Impact of Colonialism: Thoughts on politics and governance in Bangladesh' (1997) 28(1) Asian Affairs 15.

Ijaz, Saroop, 'Judicial Appointments in Pakistan: Coming Full Circle' (2014) 1 LUMS Law Journal 86.

Islam, Md Morshedul, '1996's Non-party Caretaker Government Movement and the Role of Opposition in Bangladesh: a Politico-Legal Analysis' (2016) 3(6) Global Journal of Political Science and Administration 20.

Islam, Md Morshedul, 'The Politics behind the Passage of Fourth Amendment to the Constitution of the People's Republic of Bangladesh and its Provisions: a Modest Analysis' (2014) 4(9) Public Policy and Administration Research 55.

Islam, Md Nazrul, 'Non-Party Caretaker Government in Bangladesh (1991–2001): Dilemma for Democracy?' (2013) 3(8) Developing Country Studies 116.

Islam, Mohammad Mozahidul, 'The Toxic Politics of Bangladesh: a Bipolar Competitive Neo patrimonial State?' (2013) 21(2) Asian Journal of Political Science 148.

Islam, S Aminul, 'The Predicament of Democratic Consolidation in Bangladesh,' (2006) 3(2) Bangladesh e-Journal of Sociology 4.

Jackman, David, 'The Decline of Gangsters and Politicization of Violence in Urban Bangladesh' (2019) 50(5) Development and Change 1214.

Jackson, Nigel, 'Escaping from the Straitjacket: UK MPs and their e-newsletters' (2004) 56(6) Aslib Proceedings 335.

Jackson, Nigel, 'Party E-Newsletters in the UK' (2005) 1(4) Journal of E-Government 39.

Jackson, Nigel, 'Representation in the Blogosphere: MPs and Their New Constituents' (2008) 61(4) Parliamentary Affairs 642.

Jahan, Rounaq, 'Bangladesh in 1973: Management of Factional Politics' (1974) 14(2) Asian Survey 125.

Jahan, Rounaq, 'Bangladesh in 2002: Imperilled Democracy' (2003) 43(1) Asian Survey 222.

Jahan, Rounaq, 'Members of Parliament in Bangladesh' (1976) 1(3) Legislative Studies Quarterly 355.

Jahan, Rounaq, 'The Parliament of Bangladesh: Representation and Accountability' (2015) 21(2) The Journal of Legislative Studies 250.

Jain, DC 'Judicial Review of Parliamentary Privileges: Functional Relationship of Courts and Legislatures in India' (1967) 9(2) Journal of the Indian Law Institute 205.

Jogerst, Michael A, 'Backbenchers and Select Committees in the British House of Commons: Can Parliament offer useful roles for the frustrated?' (1991) 20 European Journal of Political Research 21.

Johnson, N, 'Parliamentary Questions and the Conduct of Administration' (1961) Public Administration 131.

Johnston, R, and Pattie, C, 'How Much Does a Vote Cost? Incumbency and the impact of Campaign Spending at English General Elections' (2008) 18(2) Journal of Elections, Public Opinion and Parties 129.

Joseph, Philip A, 'Parliament, the Courts, and the Collaborative Enterprise' (2004) 15 King's College Law Journal 321.

Joseph, Philip A, 'Parliamentary Privilege Developments in New Zealand: the Good, the Bad and the Ugly' (2015) 30(2) Australasian Parliamentary Review 115.

Joshi, D, and Rosenfield, E, 'MP Transparency, Communication Links and Social Media: a Comparative Assessment of 184 Parliamentary Websites' (2013) 19(4) The Journal of Legislative Studies 526.

Jowell, Jeffrey, 'Parliamentary Sovereignty under the New Constitutional Hypothesis' (2006) Public Law 562.

Judge, David, 'Backbench Specialisation- A Study in Parliamentary Questions' (1973) 27(4) Parliamentary Affairs 171.

Judge, David, 'Representation in Westminster in the 1990s: the Ghost of Edmund Burke' (1999) 5 The Journal of Legislative Studies 12.

Judge, David, Public Petitions and the House of Commons (1978) 31(4) Parliamentary Affairs 391.

Kaiser, Shahidulla, 'Culture of Parliament Boycott and the Future of Parliamentary Democracy in Bangladesh' (2015) 19(2) Himalayan and Central Asian Studies 44.

Kalaycioglu, Ersin, 'Why Legislatures Persist in Developing Countries: the Case of Turkey' (1980) 5(1) Legislative Studies Quarterly 123.

Kavanagh, Aileen, 'What's so weak about "Weak-Form Review"? The case of The UK Human Rights Act 1998' (2015) 13(4) International Journal of Constitutional Law 1008.

Keith, Russell, 'Judicial Intervention in Parliamentary Proceedings: the Implications of Egan v Willis' (2000) 28(3) Federal Law Review 549.

Kellermann, Michael, 'Electoral Vulnerability, Constituency Focus, and Parliamentary Questions in the House of Commons' (2016) 18(1) The British Journal of Politics and International Relations 90.

Kellermann, Michael, 'Sponsoring Early Day Motions in the British House of Commons as a Response to Electoral Vulnerability' (2013) 1(2) Political Science Research and Methods 263.

Kelso, Alexandra, 'Parliament and Political Disengagement: Neither Waving nor Drowning' (2007) 78(3) The Political Quarterly 364.

Kelso, Alexandra, 'Parliament on its Knees: MPs' Expenses and the Crisis of Transparency at Westminster' (2009) 80(3) The Political Quarterly 329.

Kelso, Alexandra, 'Political Leadership in Parliament: the Role of Select Committee Chairs in the UK House of Commons' (2016) 4(2) Politics and Governance 115.

Khan, Adeeba Aziz, 'Power, Patronage, and the Candidate-nomination Process: Observations from Bangladesh' (2020) 54(1) Modern Asian Studies 314.

Khan, Adeeba Aziz, 'The Politics of Constitutional Amendments in Bangladesh: the Case of the Non-political Caretaker Government' (2015) 3 International Review of Law 11.

Khan, Mohammad Mohabbat, 'Legislature in Bangladesh: Past Experience and Present Concerns' (1994) 55(4) The Indian Journal of Political Science 371.

Khan, Mohammad Mohabbat and Husain, Syed Anwar, 'Process of Democratization in Bangladesh' (1996) 5(3) Contemporary South Asia 319.

Khan, Mohammad Mohabbat and Islam, Md Shahriar, 'Democracy and Good Governance in Bangladesh: Are they Compatible?' (2014) 5(1) Millennial Asia 23.

Khan, Zillur Rahman, 'Bangladesh in 1992: Dilemmas of Democratization' (1993) 33(2) Asian Survey 150.

Khan, Zillur Rahman, 'Bangladesh's Experiments with Parliamentary Democracy' (1997) 37(6) Asian Survey 575.

Kim, DH and Loewenberg, G, 'The Role of Parliamentary Committees in Coalition Governments: Keeping tabs on Coalition partners in the German Bundestag' (2005) 38 Comparative Political Studies 1104.

Kochanek, Stanley A, 'Bangladesh in 1996: the 25th Year of Independence' (1997) 37(2) Asian Survey 136.

Kochanek, Stanley A, 'Governance, Patronage Politics, and Democratic Transition in Bangladesh' (2000) 40(3) Asian Survey 530.

Kubala, Marek, 'Select Committees in the House of Commons and the Media' (2011) 64(4) Parliamentary Affairs 694.

Kumarasingham, Harshan, 'Written Differently: a Survey of Commonwealth Constitutional History in the Age of Decolonisation' (2018) 46(5) The Journal of Imperial and Commonwealth History 874.

Lazardeux, S, 'The French National Assembly's Oversight of the Executive: Changing Role, Partisanship and Intra-Majority Conflict' (2009) 32(2) West European Politics 287.

Leonardi, Robert, Nanetti, Raffaella and Pasquino, Gianfranco, 'Institutionalization of Parliament and Parliamentarization of Parties in Italy' (1978) 3(1) Legislative Studies Quarterly 161.

Levy, Jessica, 'Public Bill Committees: an Assessment Scrutiny Sought; Scrutiny Gained' (2010) 63(3) Parliamentary Affairs 534.

Li-ann, Thio, 'The Right to Political Participation in Singapore: Tailor-Making a Westminster-modelled Constitution to Fit the Imperatives of Asian Democracy' (2002) 6 Singapore Journal of International and Comparative Law 181.

Lifschultz, Lawrence and Bird, Kai, 'Bangladesh: Anatomy of a Coup' (1979) 14(49) Economic and Political Weekly 1999.

Lijphart, Arend, 'Consociational Democracy' (1969) 21(2) World Politics 207.

Lijphart, Arend, 'Democratic Political Systems: Types, Cases, Causes, and Consequences' (1989) 1(1) Journal of Theoretical Politics 33.

Lindberg, S, 'What Accountability Pressures Do MPs in Africa Face and How Do They Respond? Evidence from Ghana' (2010) 48(1) Journal of Modern African Studies 117.

Lindner, Ralf and Riehm, Ulrich, 'Broadening Participation Through E-Petitions? An Empirical Study of Petitions to the German Parliament' (2011) 3(1) Policy & Internet 1.

Lipson, Leslie, 'The Two-Party System in British Politics' (1953) 47(2) The American Political Science Review 337.

Liu, Margaret L, 'Ministerial Responsibility and Constitutional Law' (2002) 7(2) Coventry Law Journal 25.

Loewenberg, Gerhard, 'The Influence of Parliamentary Behaviour on Regime Stability: Some Conceptual Clarifications' (1971) 3(2) Comparative Politics 177.

Lundberg, Thomas Carl and Steven, Martin, 'Framing Electoral Reform in the 2011 UK Alternative Vote Referendum Campaign' (2013) 48(1) Australian Journal of Political Science 15.

Lusoli, Wainer, Ward, Stephen and Gibson, Rachel, '(Re)connecting Politics? Parliament, the Public and the Internet' (2006) 59(1) Parliamentary Affairs 24.

Malagodi, Mara, 'Ivor Jennings's Constitutional Legacy beyond the Occidental-Oriental Divide' (2015) 42(1) Journal of Law and Society 102.

Malesky, Edmund, Schuler, Paul and Tran, Anh, 'The Adverse Effects of Sunshine: a Field Experiment on Legislative Transparency in an Authoritarian Assembly' (2012) 106(4) American Political Science Review 762.

Maniruzzaman, Talukder, 'The Fall of the Military Dictator: 1991 Elections and the Prospect of Civilian Rule in Bangladesh' (1992) 65(2) Pacific Affairs 203.

Mansbridge, J, 'Self-interest in the Explanation of Political Life' (1990) 18(1) Political Theory 132.

Marsh, Ian, 'Democratic Discontents. Comment on: Flinders, M, (2015) The Problem with Democracy' (2016) 69 Parliamentary Affairs 207.

Marsh, Ian, 'The Commons Select Committee System in the 2015–20 Parliament', The (2016) 87 Political Quarterly 96.

Martin and Whitaker, Richard, 'Beyond Committees: Parliamentary Oversight of Coalition Government in Britain' (2019) 42(7) West European Politics 1464.

Martin, Lanny W, and Vanberg, Georg, 'Coalition Government, Legislative Institutions, and Public Policy in Parliamentary Democracies' (2020) 64(2) American Journal of Political Science 325.

Martin, Lanny W, and Vanberg, Georg, 'Coalition Policymaking and Legislative Review' (2005) 99(1) American Political Science Review 93.

Martin, Lanny W, and Vanberg, Georg, 'Policing the Bargain: Coalition Government and Parliamentary Scrutiny' (2004) 48 American Journal of Political Science 13.

Martin, Shane, 'Parliamentary Questions, the Behaviour of Legislators, and the Function of Legislatures: an Introduction' (2011) 17(3) The Journal of Legislative Studies 259.

Martin, Shane and Mickler, Tim A, 'Committee Assignments: Theories, Causes and Consequences' (2019) 72(1) Parliamentary Affairs 77.

Martin, Wayne, 'Parliament and the Courts: a Contemporary Assessment of the Ethic of Mutual Respect' (2015) 30(2) Australasian Parliamentary Review 80.

Mickler, Tim A, 'Committee autonomy in Parliamentary Systems – coalition logic or congressional rationales?' (2017) 23(3) The Journal of Legislative Studies 367.

Miller, Laura, 'E-Petitions at Westminster: the Way Forward for Democracy?' (2009) 62(1) Parliamentary Affairs 162.

Mitchell, P, 'Voters and their Representatives: Electoral Institutions and delegation in parliamentary democracies' (2000) 37(3) European Journal of Political Research 335.

Momen, Mehnaaz, 'Bangladesh in 2009: the Peril Within' (2010) 50(1) Asian Survey 157.

Moniruzzaman, M, 'Parliamentary Democracy in Bangladesh: an Evaluation of the Parliament during 1991–2006' (2009) 47(1) Commonwealth and Comparative Politics 100.

Moniruzzaman, M, 'Parliamentary Democracy in Bangladesh: an Evaluation of the Parliament during 1991–2006' (2009) 47(1) Commonwealth and Comparative Politics 100.

Moten, A Rashid, 'Parliamentary Elections in Bangladesh' (1981) 42(2) The Indian Journal of Political Science 58.

Muller, Wolfgang C, 'Political Parties in Parliamentary Democracies: Making Delegation and Accountability Work' (2000) 37 European Journal of Political Research 309.

Murphy, Gavin, 'How Legislation is drafted and enacted in Bangladesh' (2006) 27(3) Statute Law Review 133.

Norris, Pippa, 'The Twilight of Westminster? Electoral Reform and its Consequences' (2001) 49(5) Political Studies 877.

Norris, Pippa, Vallance, E, and Lovenduski, J, 'Do Candidates make a difference? Gender, Race, Ideology and Incumbency' (1992) 45(4) Parliamentary Affairs 496.

Norton, Philip, 'A Democratic Dialogue? Parliament and Human Rights in the United Kingdom' (2013) 21 Asia Pacific Law Review 141.

Norton, Philip, 'A Democratic Dialogue? Parliament and Human Rights in the United Kingdom' (2013) 21(2) Asia Pacific Law Review 141.

Norton, Philip, 'Four Models of Political Representation: British MPs and the Use of ICT' (2007) 13(3) The Journal of Legislative Studies 354.

Norton, Philip, 'Growth of the Constituency Role of the MPs' (1994) 47(4) Parliamentary Affairs 704.

Norton, Philip, 'Making Sense of Opposition' (2008) 14 (1–2) The Journal of Legislative Studies 236.

Norton, Philip, 'Parliament and Citizens in the United Kingdom' (2012) 18 (3–4) The Journal of Legislative Studies 403.

Norton, Philip, 'Parliament in the United Kingdom: Balancing Effectiveness and Consent?' (1990) 13(3) West European Politics 10.

Norton, Philip, 'Parliaments: a Framework for Analysis' (1990) 13(3) West European Politics 1.

Norton, Philip, 'Playing by the Rules: the Constraining Hand of Parliamentary Procedure' (2001) 7(3) Journal of Legislative Studies 13.

Norton, Philip, 'Power behind the Scenes: the Importance of Informal Space in Legislatures' (2019) 72 Parliamentary Affairs 245.

Norton, Philip, 'Reforming Parliament in the United Kingdom: the Report of the Commission to Strengthen Parliament' (2000) 6(3) The Journal of Legislative Studies 1.

Norton, Philip, 'The Growth of the Constituency Role of the MP' (1994) 4(1) Parliamentary Affairs 705.

Obaidullah, ATM, 'Bangladesh Parliament Secretariat: a Quest for Increasing Operational Efficiency' (2012) 57(2) Journal of the Asiatic Society of Bangladesh (Humanities) 223.

Obaidullah, ATM, 'Standing Committees on Ministries in the Bangladesh Parliament: the Need for Reorganization' (2011) 18(2) South Asian Survey 317.

Okpaluba, Chuks, 'Can a Court review the internal affairs and processes of the Legislature? Contemporary developments in Southern Africa' (2015) 48(2) Comparative and International Law Journal of Southern Africa 183.

Palmieri, Sonia A, 'Petition Effectiveness: Improving Citizens' Direct Access to Parliament' (2008) 23(1) Australasian Parliamentary Review 121.

Panday, PK and Rabbani, MG 'Good governance at the grassroots: Evidence from Union Parishads in Bangladesh' (2011) 18(2) South Asian Survey 293.

Panday, Pranab Kumar, 'Representation without Participation: Quotas for Women in Bangladesh' (2008) 29(4) International Political Science Review 489.

Pattie, C, and Johnston, R, 'Party Knowledge and Candidate Knowledge: Constituency Campaigning and Voting and the 1997 British General Election' (2004) 23(4) Electoral Studies 795.

Patwary, Md Enayet Ullah, 'Democratization and Intra-Party Democracy: Bangladesh Experience' (2022) 16(4) Society and Change 67.

Paun, Akash, 'After the Age of Majority? Multi-party Governance and the Westminster Model' (2011) 49(4) Commonwealth and Comparative Politics 440.

Polidano, Charles, 'The Bureaucrat Who Fell under a Bus: Ministerial Responsibility, Executive Agencies and the Derek Lewis affair in Britain' (1999) 12(2) Governance 201.

Qvortrup, Matt, 'Voting on Electoral Reform: a Comparative Perspective on the Alternative Vote Referendum in the United Kingdom' (2012) 83(1) The Political Quarterly 108.

Rahaman, Muhammad Mustafizur, 'Origins and Pitfalls of Confrontational Politics in Bangladesh' (2007) 14(1) South Asian Survey 101.

Rahaman, Muhammad Mustafizur, 'Parliament and Good Governance: a Bangladeshi Perspective' (2008) 9(1) Japanese Journal of Political Science 29.

Rahaman, Muhammad Mustafizur, 'The Limits of Foreign Aid in Strengthening Bangladesh's Parliament: Analysis of the U.N.'s Strengthening Parliamentary Democracy Project' (2010) 50(3) Asian Survey 474.

Rahman, M Habibur, 'Our Experience with Constitutionalism' (1998) 2(2) Bangladesh Journal of Law 115.

Rahman, Md Ataur, 'Bangladesh in 1982: Beginnings of the Second Decade' (1983) 23(2) Asian Survey 149.

Rahman, Muhammad Sayadur, 'Restructuring Local Government in Bangladesh: an Overview' (1997) 1(1) Public Administration Review 11.

Rahman, Muhammad Sayadur, 'Role of the Members of Parliament in the Local Government of Bangladesh: Views and Perceptions of Grassroots in the Case of *Upazila* Administration' (2013) 13 Public Organization Review 71.

Rahman, Muhammad Sayadur, *Upazila Parishad* in Bangladesh: Roles and Functions of Elected Representatives and Bureaucrats' (2012) 11 Commonwealth Journal of Local Governance 100.

Rahman, Syed, 'Bangladesh in 1989: Internationalization of Political and Economic Issues' (1990) 30(2) Asian Survey 150.

Rahman, Syedur, 'Bangladesh in 1988: Precarious Institution Building Amid Crisis Management' (1989) 29(2) Asian Survey 216.

Rahman, Tahmina, 'Party System Institutionalization and Pernicious Polarization in Bangladesh' (2019) 681(1) The Annals of the American Academy of Political and Social Science 173.

Rahman, Ziaur, 'Democracy: Freedom of Speech and Floor-crossing Interface' (2010) 1 The Northern University Journal of Law 24.

Rashiduzzaman, M, 'Political Unrest and Democracy in Bangladesh' (1997) 7(3) Asian Survey 254.

Renwick, Alan, 'How Likely is Proportional Representation in the House of Commons? Lessons from International Experience' (2009) 44(4) Government and Opposition 366.

Riaz, Ali, 'Bangladesh in 2005: Standing at a Crossroads' (2006) 46(1) Asian Survey 107.

Riaz, Ali, 'Bangladesh's Failed Election' (2014) 25(2) Journal of Democracy 119.

Riaz, Ali, 'Legislature as a Tool of the Hybrid Regime: Bangladesh Experience,' (2019) 52(2) Political Science and Politics 275.

Rix, Kathryn, 'Whatever Passed in Parliament Ought to be Communicated to the Public': Reporting the Proceedings of the Reformed Commons, 1833–50' '2014) 33(3) Parliamentary History 453.

Rockman, Bert A, 'Legislative-Executive Relations and Legislative Oversight' (1984) 9(3) Legislative Studies Quarterly 387.

Rohde, D, and Shepsle, Kenneth A, 'Democratic Committee Assignments in the House of Representatives: Strategic Aspects of a Social Choice Process,' (1973) 67 American Political Science Review 889.

Rozenberg, Oliver, Chopin, Oliver and Hoeffler, Catherine, et al., 'Not Only a Battleground: Parliamentary Oral Questions Concerning Defence Policies in Four Western Democracies' (2011) 17(3) The Journal of Legislative Studies 340.

Rush, Michael, 'Making better Law: a Review of the Hansard Society Commission on the Legislative Process' (1993) 14 (2) Statute Law Review 75.

Russell, Meg and Cowley, Philip, 'The Policy Power of the Westminster Parliament: the 'Parliamentary State' and the Empirical Evidence' (2016) 29 Governance 121.

Ryan, Frances H, 'Can Question Period be Reformed?' (2009) Canadian Parliamentary Review 18.

Saalfeld, Thomas, 'Germany: From Dictatorship to Parliamentary Democracy' (1997) 50(3) Parliamentary Affairs 380.

Saleh, Md Abu, 'Law Making Process in Bangladesh Parliament' (2013) 1(6) Jahangirnagar Journal of Administrative Studies 143.

Sarker, AE, 'Clientelism and Local Government in Bangladesh: a study in Relations' (1997) 25(2) Asian Profile 151.

Shafi, Md Mostofa and Subedi, DB 'Rise of Competitive Authoritarianism in Bangladesh' (2020) Politics and Religion 1.

Shakil, Md Rajib Hasnat and Marzia, Kaniz, 'Problems of Party Funding and Expenditure Political Parties and Good Governance: Bangladesh Perspective' (2013) 8(5) IOSR Journal of Humanities and Social Science (IOSR-JHSS) 37.

Sharmin, Sabina and Uddin, AKM Jamal, 'Characteristics of Political Culture in Bangladesh: a Critical Analysis from the perspective of Political Development and Under development' (2013) 1(1–2) Jagannath University Journal of Social Sciences 74.

Shehabuddin, Elora, 'Bangladesh in 1998: Democracy on the Ground' (1999) 39(1) Asian Survey 148.

Shehabuddin, Elora, 'Bangladesh in 1999: Desperately Seeking a Responsible Opposition' (2000) 40(1) Asian Survey 181.

Shepsle, Kenneth A, and Weingast, BR, 'Political Preferences for the Pork Barrel: a Generalization' (1981) 25 American Journal of Political Science 96.

Siaroff, Alan, 'Spurious Majorities, Electoral Systems and Electoral System Change' (2003) 41(2) Commonwealth and Comparative Politics 143.

Siddiqi, Dina M, 'Secular Quests, National Others: Revisiting Bangladesh's Constituent Assembly Debates' (2018) 49(2) Asian Affairs 238.

Sikdar, Md Masum and Shohag, Md Mehedi Hasan, 'Democracy and Authoritarianism: Understanding Three Decades of Bangladesh Politics' (2016) 6(24) Research on Humanities and Social Sciences 6.

Snyder, Ann E, 'Britain and the European Economic Community: the Decline of Parliamentary Sovereignty in the International Legal Arena' (1991) 18 Ohio Northern University Law Review 131.

Strøm, Kaare, 'Delegation and Accountability in Parliamentary Democracies' (2000) 37(3) European Journal of Political Research 261.

Strøm, Kaare, Wolfgang C Muller and Daniel Markham Smith, 'Parliamentary Control of Coalition Governments' (2010) 13 Annual Review of Political Science 517.

Sultana, Mahbuba, 'Reserved Seats and Women's Representation in Bangladesh Parliament: Gaps between Expectations and Reality' (2018) 3(1) Premier Critical Perspective 41.

Talukder, M Jafar Ullah and Chowdhury, M Jashim Ali, 'Determining the Province of Judicial Review: a Re-evaluation of 'Basic Structure of the Constitution of Bangladesh' (2009) 2(2) Metropolitan University Journal 161.

Thomas, GT, 'United Kingdom: the Prime Minister and Parliament' (2004) 10 (2–3) The Journal of Legislative Studies 4.

Thompson, L, 'Debunking the Myths of Bill Committees in the British House of Commons' (2016) 36(1) Politics 36.

Thompson, L, 'More of the Same or a Period of Change? The Impact of Bill Committees in the Twenty-First Century House of Commons' (2013) 66 Parliamentary Affairs 459.

Trench, Alan, 'Wales and the Westminster Model' (2010) 63(1) Parliamentary Affairs 117.

Trubowitz, Peter and Mellow, Nicole, '"Going Bipartisan": Politics by Other Means' (2005) 120(3) Political Science Quarterly 433.

Turner, Ian, 'Judicial Review, Irrationality, and the Limits of Intervention by the Courts' (2010) 21(2) King's Law Journal 311.

Tushnet, Mark, 'Authoritarian Constitutionalism' (2015) 100 Cornell Law Review 391.

Tushnet, Mark, 'Dialogic Judicial Review' (2009) 61 Arkansas Law Review 205.

Tushnet, Mark, 'New Forms of Judicial Review and the Persistence of Rights- and Democracy-based Worries' (2003) 38 Wake Forest Law Review 813.

Vaughn, Robert G, 'A Comparative Analysis of the Influence of Legislative History on Judicial Decision-Making and Legislation' (1996) 7(1) Indiana International and Comparative Law Review 1.

Vivyan, Nick and Wagner, Markus, 'Do Voters Reward Rebellion? The Electoral Accountability of MPs in Britain' (2012) 51(2) European Journal of Political Research 235.

Vivyan, Nick, Wagner, Markus and Tarlov, Jessica, 'Representative Misconduct, Voter Perceptions and Accountability: Evidence from the 2009 House of Commons Expenses Scandal' (2012) 31 (4) Electoral Studies 750.

Waheduzzaman, M, 'Economic, Social and Cultural Rights under the Constitution: Critical Evaluation of Judicial Jurisprudence in Bangladesh' (2014) 14(1 & 2) Bangladesh Journal of Law 1.

Webber, Gregoire, 'Loyal Opposition and the Political Constitution' (2017) 37(2) Oxford Journal of Legal Studies 357.

Weill, Rivka, 'Reconciling Parliamentary Sovereignty and Judicial Review: On the Theoretical and Historical Origins of the Israeli Legislative Override Power' (2011) 39 Hastings Constitutional Law Quarterly 457.

Whiteley, Paul, 'State of Participation in Britain' (2003) 56(4) Parliamentary Affairs 610.

Wolf, Siegfried O, 'Civil-Military Relations and Democracy in Bangladesh' (2013) Spotlight South Asia Special Issue 1.

Wood, David M and Norton, Philip, 'Do Candidates Matter? Constituency-specific Vote Changes for Incumbent MPs, 1983–1987' (1992) 40(2) Political Studies 227.

Woodhouse, Diana, 'Ministerial Responsibility in the 1990s: When do ministers resign?' (1993) 46(3) Parliamentary Affairs 277.

Woodhouse, Diana, 'Ministerial Responsibility: Something Old, Something New' (1997) 2 Public Law 262.

Zubek, Radoslaw, 'Coalition Government and Committee Power' (2015) 38(5) West European Politics 1020.

Parliamentary Studies/Reports

Independent Commission on the Voting System (Jenkins Commission), *The Report of the Independent Commission on the Voting System* (London: The Stationery Office 1998).

Joint Committee on Parliamentary Privilege, Session 1998–1999, *Parliamentary Privilege* (HL 43-I / HC 214-I).

Library of Congress, '*Bangladesh: Special Parliamentary Committee on Constitution Formed to Review All Past Amendments*' <https://www.loc.gov/item/global-legal-monitor/2010-08-13/bangladesh-special-parliamentary-committee-on-constitution-formed-to-review-all-past-amendments/>.

Mannan, Sadiat, Rashid, Md Harun-Or, Stanislawski, Jens and Khan, Niaz Ahmed, 'Realpolitik: Democratic Embeddedness within Major Political Parties in Bangladesh' Working Paper Series No 25 (BRAC Institute of Governance and Development, BRAC University 2015).

Prison Security: Learmont Report <https://api.parliament.uk/historic-hansard/lords/1995/oct/16/prison-security-learmont-report>.

Report of the Hansard Society Commission (Newton Commission) on Parliamentary Scrutiny, *The Challenge for Parliament: Making Government Accountable* (Hansard Society 2011).

Second Report from Public Service Committee, *Ministerial Accountability and Responsibility*, H. C. 313-I, 1995–96.

Select Committee on the Constitution, *Parliament and the Legislative Process, Fourteenth Report* (House of Lords Session 2003–04, HL Paper 173-I, para. 213).

Select Committee on the Modernisation of the House of Commons, *Connecting Parliament with the Public, First Report* (House of Commons Session 2003–4, HC 368).

The House of Lords Select Committee on the Constitution, *The Legislative Process: The Passage of Bills Through Parliament* (24th Report of Session 2017–19 HL Paper 393).

The Ninth Report of Session 2006–07, *The Meaning of Public Authority under the Human Rights Act* (HL Paper 77/HC 410).

The Seventh Report of Session 2003–04, *The Meaning of Public Authority under the Human Rights Act* (HL Paper 39/HC 382).

The UK House of Lords Constitution Committee, 'Sixth Report, Chapter 3: Parliament and Judiciary' (House of Lords, 11 July 2007).

Transparency International Bangladesh, 'Parliament Watch, Eleventh Parliament (1st to 5th Sessions; January-December 2019)' (TIB, Dhaka, September 2020).

Thesis/Dissertations

Cotton, Ross, 'Political Participation and E-Petitioning: an Analysis of the Policy-Making Impact of the Scottish Parliament's E-Petition System', *Honours in Major Thesis* (University of Central Florida 2011).

Kabir, Abul Hasnat Monjurul, 'Does Parliamentary Development Assistance Matter? An Examination of the Aid Effectiveness in Parliamentary Oversight' (Ph.D. Thesis: University of Hull 2014).

Khan, Adeeba Aziz, 'Electoral Institutions in Bangladesh: a Study of Conflicts between the Formal and the Informal' (Ph.D. Thesis: SOAS, London 2015).

Mahiuddin, KM 'The Parliamentary Committee System in Bangladesh: an Analysis of its Functioning' (Ph.D. Thesis, Ruprecht-Karls-Universität Heidelberg 2009).

Rahman, Md. Saidur, 'Institutionalization of Democracy in the Political Parties in Bangladesh: Does Culture Matter?' (LL.M. Dissertation, North South University, Dhaka 2010).

Saifullah, Navid, 'Effectiveness of the Parliamentary Standing Committees in Bangladesh' (Masters in Governance and Development Thesis: BRAC University Dhaka 2006).

Scott, Renee, 'An Analysis of Public Participation in the South African Legislative Sector' (*Master of Public Administration Thesis*, Stellenbosch University 2009).

Webster, Siame Kameme, 'The Vertical and Horizontal Accountability in The Malawi Parliamentary Democracy' (Ph.D. thesis, University of Hull 2015).

Zaman, Amin Al, 'Party Factionalism in Bangladesh: a Case Study of the Awami League (1971–97)' (Ph.D. Thesis, Aligarh Muslim University 2004).

Index